The
Science Teacher's
BOOK OF LISTS

The Science Teacher's BOOK OF LISTS

Frances Bartlett Barhydt, M.A.

Paul W. Morgan, Ph.D.

PRENTICE HALL

Library of Congress Cataloging-in-Publication Data

Barhydt, Frances Bartlett.
    The science teacher's book of lists / Frances Bartlett Barhydt,
Paul Morgan.
        p.   cm.
    Includes bibliographical references (p.   ).
    ISBN 0-13-793381-9
    1. Science—Study and teaching (Elementary)—Handbooks, manuals,
etc.   2. Science—Study and teaching (Secondary)—Handbooks,
manuals, etc.   I. Morgan, Paul W.   II. Title.
LB1585.B286   1993   92-26920
507'.1'2—dc20   CIP

Printed in the United States of America

10   9   8   7   6

ISBN 0-13-793381-9

Special thanks to Dover Publications for
permitting us to use illustrations from
their Dover Clip Art series.

PRENTICE HALL
Paramus, NJ 07652

On the World Wide Web at http://www.phdirect.com

DEDICATION

This book is dedicated to a number of people who have enriched our lives:

The creative individuals who recognized the need and value of establishing federal funding for summer and in-service science institutes and follow-up support for elementary and secondary teachers of science; my parents, James and Frances Bartlett, who nurtured a love of discovery and who never said little girls don't play with mud, worms, plants, hammer, and nails or take radios and clocks apart; my husband, James, who tolerates a collection of shells, rocks, bones, field guides, and science books, which mushroom about our house, and never once thought my place was solely in our kitchen; and my son, Matthew, who encouraged me to complete the metamorphosis from full-time teacher and part-time writer to full-time writer and science education consultant.

—F. B.

The memory of Elsie Bridges Morgan for unfailing support in my career and for participation and companionship in our many ventures into the world of nature.

—P. M.

The young people who will come to know the joys and wonders of the sciences and the natural world, including our grandchildren: Elizabeth Marie Hollenbeck, Anne Harding, William Clay Harding, Peter Harding, Kristin Kuhl, and Timothy Kuhl.

—F. B. and P.M.

ACKNOWLEDGMENTS

Family members, friends, and colleagues have made this book possible through their contributions. We are grateful to:

STEVE AMOS, author and Director of Development of the Fairbanks Museum, St. Johnsbury, Vermont, for answering questions about the rain forests.

JAMES BARHYDT, media consultant and writer who kept our home intact for the two years necessary to write this book and who edited every list.

ESTELLE BURTON, educator, shepherd, and friend who read our manuscript and made many valuable recommendations.

NANCY CLARK, M.S., R.D., who granted us permission to use charts and information from *Sports Medicine*.

D. ROBERT COULSON, chemist, Du Pont Company, and friend, who reviewed the chemistry section.

WILLIAM DRYDEN for information on legal exposure and residue limits of toxic substances.

BALLARD EBBETT, associate professor of geology who devised a geological time scale, recommended valuable resources, answered questions about geological time and checked examples of life events and occurrences during different epochs.

MICHELE EISENSTEIN, microbiologist, lab coordinator, and science instructor, who lent valuable resources and reviewed the life science sections.

JEFF FAIR, author of *The Great American Bear*, for answering questions about bears and hibernation.

PAUL E. FITZGERALD, Chief Communication Services Staff, U. S. Department of Justice, Drug Enforcement Administration, for permission to use the chart, "Controlled Substances—Uses & Effects."

PAT GRAHAM, Director of the Dissection Hotline, who sent us copies of her alternatives to dissection, granted us permission to use them, and answered a variety of questions.

PATRICIA HAZLEHURST, librarian, Cobleigh Public Library, who located many references.

SANDRA HUTCHISON, editor, who suggested this exciting project and was available throughout the years of investigation and writing.

KATHY McGOWN, children's librarian, Cobleigh Public Library, who located many references.

DESMOND MORRIS, zoologist and author, who granted us permission to print his Animal Bill of Rights.

JOHN PELLERIN, assistant professor of chemistry and secondary education, Lyndon State College, who lent us chemistry education references.

GARET NELSON, librarian, Lyndon State College Library, who helped with the search for women scientists.

HARVEY RETTEW for information on trees and wood products.

BARRY RICHWIEN, assistant professor of meteorology, who gave us charts and posters, helped us with terms used in meteorology, and edited the meteorology section.

PHILLIP F. SCHEWE, science writer, American Institute of Physics, who provided an explanation of the Chaos Theory and granted permission to use "Chaos: A Glossary," edited by Schewe and Gollub.

LAURAL STANLEY, librarian, Lyndon State College Library, who helped with the search for women scientists.

DALE STEEN, nutritionist, for contributing information about foods and nutrition.

ELIZABETH AVERY WIER, science educator and friend, who lent us copies of childrens' science books that she wrote and granted us permission to use the information.

METIN YERSEL, associate professor of physics, Lyndon State College, who reviewed our physics terms.

SPECIAL ACKNOWLEDGMENT TO:

JOANNE NOYES, artist, who provided the science diagrams for this book.

ABOUT THE AUTHORS

FRANCES BARTLETT BARHYDT has an M.A. in teaching. Her more than thirty years of teaching includes experience at the elementary, junior high, and university levels. She is currently a part-time faculty member of Lyndon State College and is Director of the Vermont Energy Education Program. She is co-author with Dr. Elizabeth A. Wier of a number of teacher resource manuals, including *BUZ: A Hands-on Energy Education Program*. She is the author of *Science Discovery Activities Kit*, published by The Center for Applied Research in Education in 1989. Among her many teaching honors are the Order of the First State awarded in 1984 by the Governor of Delaware for excellence in science education; recognition in 1984 and 1985 by the National Science Teachers Association for excellence in science education for the state of Delaware; and election in 1990 to "Who's Who in American Education." Mrs. Barhydt continues to serve as a science fair judge and works as an elementary science education consultant.

PAUL MORGAN has a Ph.D. in organic chemistry and is a retired Senior Research Fellow of the DuPont Company, where he did research on new materials for synthetic fibers. He was associated with the origin and development of Nomex® and Kevlar® aramid fibers and has forty U.S. patents and numerous foreign patents. He has written several articles on his research which have appeared in professional journals, including the *Journal of Chemistry Education*. He has a wide range of interests in the natural sciences such as geology, mineralogy, botany, wild edible plants, forestry, and ornithology. Other interests include gardening, woodworking, photography, hiking, camping, and wilderness survival. He has taught many of these subjects and chemistry to Boy Scouts and in lectures and demonstrations for elementary and high school students. Dr. Morgan has been a frequent science fair judge.

He has received numerous awards for his professional work, including DuPont's Lavoisier Medal in 1991 for Technical Achievement. He is a Life Fellow of the Franklin Institute, was elected to the National Academy of Engineering, and appears in "Who's Who in America" and "Who's Who in the World." He is the discoverer of the widely used desk-top experiment for making a nylon, the "Nylon Rope Trick."

When Dr. Morgan agreed to speak to Mrs. Barhydt's fourth-grade science classes in 1982, about physical and chemical changes and new inventions in chemistry, neither realized this was the beginning of a new science education adventure for both.

ABOUT THIS RESOURCE

For science teachers in grades K–12, here is an all-in-one resource of over 290 basic and advanced lists you can photocopy for student use or keep on hand as a comprehensive reference tool in planning lessons and activities.

The Science Teacher's Book of Lists is a "user-friendly" resource for busy classroom teachers—a ready fund of ideas and information for discussions, lessons, investigations, concept maps and science fair projects, with the convenience of ready-to-photocopy lists of scientific terms, generalizations, theories, laws, formulas, symbols, abbreviations, notations, conversion charts, and more.

For ease of use, these lists have been organized into twelve main sections:

Section 1, PLANT SCIENCE, provides thirty-three basic to advanced lists, including "What Plants Need to Grow and Reproduce," "Examples of Endangered Plants," "Carnivorous Plants," and "Immigrant Plants."

Section 2, ANIMAL SCIENCE, offers forty lists ranging from "Introduction to the Five Kingdoms" to "Animals With Misleading Common Names," "Stages of Complete Metamorphosis," "Animals That Migrate," and "Alternatives to Animal Dissection."

Section 3, HUMAN HEALTH AND NUTRITION, includes forty-eight up-to-date lists on topics including human body systems, reproduction, dietary guidelines, diseases, substance abuse and more, in lists such as "Developmental Stages in Human Beings," "A Translator's Guide to Food Labels," "Some Birth Control Methods and Rate of Failure," and "AIDS Vocabulary."

Section 4, CHEMISTRY, offers twenty-two lists ranging from terms, elements, and other basic information to reproducible, step-by-step hand-outs for "Determining the Mole of a Compound" and "Balancing Equations," as well as lists such as "Composition of Substances About the Household" and "Giant Molecules."

Section 5, PHYSICS, provides twenty-three lists including "Simple Machines," "Do's and Don'ts for Electrical Safety," "Subatomic Particle Terminology," "Some Laws of Physics," and "Chaos Theory."

Section 6, EARTH SCIENCE, includes thirty-two lists, with "Some Interesting Facts about Rocks and Minerals," a basic and an advanced list for Mohs' scale of mineral hardness, "Crystal Growing," "Size of an Earthquake," and "Classification, Pronunciation, and Length of Selected Dinosaura Genera."

Section 7, METEOROLOGY, offers sixteen lists, including "Types of Precipitation," "Watches, Warnings and Advisories for Non-Routine Weather," "Clouds," "Sky Cover Symbols," and "Poetic Weather Predictions."

Section 8, AVIATION AND SPACE SCIENCE, provides twenty lists for this high-interest category, including selected events in the history of various modes of flight (from balloons to the space shuttle), as well as lists having to do with stellar bodies, such as "Planetary Time: Rotation and Revolution," "Many Moons," and "The Constellations."

Section 9, MEASUREMENTS AND NUMBERS, covers the metric system, various measurement systems and conversions, and a variety of related topics in twenty-three lists that include "Useful Formulas," "How Much Would You Weigh on Other Planets?" "Some Interesting Numbers," and "Symbols and Signs Frequently Used in Science and Math."

Section 10, SELECTED SCIENTISTS AND THEIR CONTRIBUTIONS, gathers together in one place information about various award winners, discoveries, and inventions, with eleven lists such as "English Words of Science and Technology Derived from People's Names" and "Some Noted Women Scientists."

Section 11, SCIENCE AND SCIENCE EDUCATION RESOURCES, offers six lists that include information about professional and science organizations, environmental groups, and sources for scientific equipment and supplies.

Section 12, POTPOURRI, provides a variety of twenty-one lists that defy classification, including "Some Fields of Science and Medicine," "Science Process Skills and Definitions," "Ideas for Science Projects," "Some Firsts and Technological Superlatives," "Superstitions," and "Notable Quotables."

More than just a collection of dry scientific data, *The Science Teacher's Book of Lists* offers many ready-to-use lists that intrigue or amuse. It offers exciting possibilities for introducing new topics, filling in the odd moment, or providing a change of pace in the classroom. Lists like "Birds That Don't Fly," "Monsters, Dragons, and Other Animals Stranger than Fiction," and "Weather Sayings" offer motivation as well as education.

Space limitations restricted the length of many of our lists and the number and breadth of topics we could cover. To further investigate one of the lists in this book, we suggest you turn to "Recommended References" in Section 12, which includes those resources we found most helpful.

A NOTE ABOUT SPELLING, CAPITALIZATION, AND THE SEARCH FOR TRUTH

You may find that some of the spelling and capitalization in this resource varies from what you have seen elsewhere. As we discovered in our research, these variations and others are quite common and may explain the persistence of Latin as a scientific standard across the world. Spelling was especially variable in names that had been translated into English from another language. We regret that we were unable to include accents and other marks our American equipment could not handle.

When writing the common name of an animal species, we stay in lower case unless a proper noun is included (thus: gray squirrel, African elephant). However, since ornithologists capitalize all bird names (Peregrine Falcon, Blue Jay), we have adopted that style for bird's names throughout the book.

In the process of researching these lists, we fairly often encountered conflicting facts and interpretations. Science is a never-ending search for truth and knowledge about our world, and science information is constantly being updated and reinterpreted. We have made use of the most recent data available to us and hope to update it in future editions.

We hope you will use and enjoy this research. If you wish to comment on it, feel free to write to us in care of the publisher (Professional Publishing Division, Education Group, Prentice Hall Building, Englewood Cliffs, New Jersey 07632).

Fran Barhydt
Paul Morgan

On May 28, 1992, Paul Morgan died due to heart failure. He will be remembered by many for his outstanding contributions to polymer chemistry, especially for his contributions to the development of two life-protecting aramid fibers: Kevlar® used in bullet-proof clothing and Nomex® used in protective clothing worn by race car drivers and fire fighters. But I fondly remember working with this humble and humorous man in his kitchen to develop science demonstrations and hands-on experiences for children.

Fran Barhydt

TABLE OF CONTENTS

SECTION 3   HUMAN HEALTH AND NUTRITION ...105

SECTION 4   CHEMISTRY 175

SECTION 5   PHYSICS 217

SECTION 6   EARTH SCIENCE 265

SECTION 7   METEOROLOGY 309

SECTION 8   AVIATION AND SPACE SCIENCE 335

SECTION 9   MEASUREMENTS AND NUMBERS 367

SECTION 10   SCIENTISTS AND THEIR CONTRIBUTIONS 397

PLANTS

LIST 1–1. INTRODUCTION TO GROUPING PLANTS

The plant kingdom is composed of organisms that are capable of photosynthesis, that is, the process by which plants use light energy to convert water and carbon dioxide into food energy and release oxygen into the biosphere. There are thousands of plants. They range in size from small duckweeds to giant sequoias. For the purposes of identification and study, scientists group plants into one of four major groups.

Major Plant Groups

- Mosses and other bryophytes (nonvascular)
- Ferns and fern allies (vascular, seedless)
- Gymnosperms or cone-bearing (vascular, form naked seeds)
- Angiosperms or flowering (vascular, form seeds enclosed within the fruit)

LIST 1–2. PROPERTIES OF PLANTS

- Plants are made up of cells.
- Plant cells have cell walls made of cellulose.
- Plants make their own food by the process of photosynthesis.
- Most plants cannot move on their own.
- Plants have multicellular reproductive organs.
- Plants pass through distinct developmental stages.
- Within the plant kingdom, plants are grouped into two groups: bryophytes (nonvascular plants) and tracheophytes (vascular plants).

Mosses are examples of nonvascular plants; maple trees, pine trees, fruit trees, berry bushes, daisies, and daffodils are examples of vascular plants.

LIST 1–3. WHAT PLANTS NEED TO GROW AND REPRODUCE

1. Light
2. Water
3. Carbon dioxide
4. Oxygen
5. Minerals
6. A temperature range suited to its species
7. Space

LIST 1–4. VASCULAR AND NONVASCULAR PLANTS

The plant kingdom can be divided into two major groups based on possession of a vascular system to transport water, minerals, and food. Not having a vascular system restricts the potential growth of a plant. The larger plants have vascular systems.

Members of the Plant Kingdom

VASCULAR	NONVASCULAR
(Possessing xylem for water and mineral conduction, phloem for food conduction)	(Possessing no xylem or phloem)
Psilophyta (whisk ferns)	Bryophyta (bryophytes)
Pterophyta (ferns)	Mosses
Sphenophyta (horsetails)	Liverworts
Lycophyta (club mosses)	Hornworts
Coniferophyta (conifers)	
Cycadophyta (cycads)	
Ginkgophyta (ginkgo)	
Gnetophyta (gnetophytes)	
Angiospermophyta (flowering plants)	

Flowering plant

The Science Teacher's Book of Lists, © 1993 by Prentice Hall

LIST 1–5. CLASSIFICATION OF PLANTS

The plant kingdom can be divided into two groups, vascular and nonvascular. The nonvascular group includes bryophytes, mosses, liverworts, and hornworts. The vascular group can be classified into two groups: those with seeds and those without seeds. The seedless group includes ferns, whisk ferns, horsetails, and club mosses. The seed group is divided into angiosperms and gymnosperms. Angiosperms include flowering plants, which can be further divided into dicots and monocots. Gymnosperms include conifers, cycads, ginkgo, and gnetophytes.

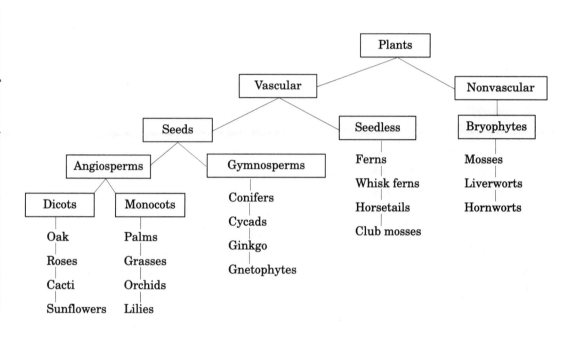

LIST 1–6. PLANT TERMINOLOGY

alternate leaves—not opposite each other at the nodes

angiosperms—flowering plants that produce seeds

anther—part of the stamen (male reproductive structure) that produces pollen

auxin plant—plant growth and development hormone

biennial—a plant that takes two years to complete its life cycle

binary fission—equal division of a cell or organism; usually a form of asexual reproduction

binomial nomenclature—system of naming organisms by their genus and species names

biosphere—the zone of air, land, and water at Earth's surface that is occupied by living organisms

bud—an undeveloped shoot that can develop into a plant part

calyx—collective term for the sepals, outer circle of floral leaves

cellulose—the material that composes the cell walls of plants

chlorophyll—light-trapping green pigments found in plants

chloroplast—the chlorophyll-bearing intercellular part of a plant where photosynthesis takes place

compound leaf—a leaf that is divided into separate smaller leaflets

cone—a reproductive structure in gymnosperms

conifers—gymnosperms with needle-like leaves

cotyledon—the seed leaf of the plant embryo, usually contains food

deciduous—plants that lose their leaves at the end of their growing season

dicotyledon—(dicot) flowering plant with two seed leaves

drupe—fleshy fruit with a nut or stone

filament—stalk of the stamen

fruit—a mature, ripened ovary, in angiosperms

gamete—a cell that functions in sexual reproduction

gametophyte—the gamete-producing stage in the life cycle of a plant

grain—simple, dry fruit in which the fruit wall is fused to the seed coat (examples: corn and wheat)

herbs—fleshy, nonwoody plants

irregular flower—not symmetrical

legume—simple dry fruit that splits open along two seams to release its seeds

lignin—the chief noncarbohydrate constituent of wood; together with cellulose is responsible for the woody nature of plant stems and roots

The Science Teacher's Book of Lists, © 1993 by Prentice Hall

(Continued)

LIST 1–6. (Continued)

The Science Teacher's Book of Lists, © 1993 by Prentice Hall

metagenesis—events in certain organisms of sexual (gametophyte) and asexual (sporophyte) reproduction

monocotyledon—(monocot) flowering plants that have one cotyledon (seed leaf) in the seed

node—area on a plant stem where the leaf attaches

ovaries—develop into fruits after seeds are fertilized; see *ovule*

ovule—plant part that develops into seeds after fertilization

perennial—a plant whose life cycle repeats year after year

petals—white or colored cluster of modified leaves that form part of the flower

petiole—part of the leaf that attaches to the stem

phloem—vascular tissue that transports sap in plants

photosynthesis—the chemical production of organic material from carbon dioxide and water using light energy; carried out by plants, algae, and some bacteria

pistil—female organ of a flower made up of ovary at the base, style, a slender stalk, and stigma at the tip

pollen—the male gametophyte of seed plants, capable of fertilization

pollination—in seed plants, the transfer of pollen from the male to the female part

pome—fleshy fruit having seeds but no pit, such as apples and pears

radicle—embryonic root of a seed plant

receptacle—end of a flower stalk where the floral parts are attached

rhizome—horizontal underground stem that gives rise to above-ground leaves

root cap—protective covering of cells over root tip

root hair—an extension of the outer cell in roots; increases the absorptive capacity of roots

seed—a plant reproductive body composed of an embryonic plant and food supply

sepals—outermost parts of a flower that protect it when the flower is a bud

spore—a reproductive cell that develops into an offspring in plants

sporophyll—leaf-like structure that bears spores

sporophyte—the spore-producing phase in plants that reproduce by metagenesis

stamen—male part of flowers that produces pollen; made up of a slender stalk with a knoblike anther at the end, bearing the pollen

stigma—the tip of the pistil where the pollen lands prior to fertilization

(Continued)

LIST 1–6. (Continued)

style—stalklike part of the pistil between the stigma and the ovary

tap root—a root system that has one main root with smaller root branches

tendril—a leaf or stem that is modified for holding or attaching (example: pea plants)

tropism—a growth response in plants caused by outside stimulus, such as *phototropism* (plants growing towards light) or *geotropism* (roots growing downward)

tubers—thick, underground stems that store food (example: potato)

vessel element—water-conducting cell in plant xylem

xylem—vascular tissue that transports water and dissolved minerals in vascular plants

Flower with stamen

LIST 1–7. EXAMPLES OF GYMNOSPERMS: NONFLOWERING PLANTS

Gymnosperms do not have flowers. They produce naked seeds, usually on the scale of a cone. Many are evergreen, having needle-like or scale-like foliage. There are nearly 700 species, including family members of pines, firs, yews, and cycads.

Examples of Gymnosperms

Pacific yew
Torreya
Zamia
Sago palm
Sugar pine
Eastern white pine
Western white pine
Whitebark pine
Limber pine
Foxtail pine
Pinyon pine
Jack pine
Red pine
Lodgepole pine
Shortleaf pine
Slash pine
Bishop pine
Sand pine
Virginia pine
Spruce pine
Table-mountain pine
Ponderosa pine

Lebanon cedar
Black spruce
Red spruce
Douglas fir
Big Cone Douglas fir
Balsam fir
Fraser fir
Grand fir
Pacific silver pine
White fir
Bristlecone pine
Giant sequoia
Redwood
Incense cedar
Northern white cedar
Ginkgo
Podocarps
Monkey puzzle
Norfolk Island pine
Tamarack
Western larch
Subalpine larch

Jeffrey pine
Knobcone pine
Coulter pine
Digger pine
Apache pine
Pitch pine
Loblolly pine
Longleaf pine

Chilean
incense cedar

The Science Teacher's Book of Lists, © 1993 by Prentice Hall

LIST 1–8. EXAMPLES OF ANGIOSPERMS: FLOWERING PLANTS

Angiosperms are the flowering plants. They are divided into two classes: monocots (having one seed leaf), and dicots (having two or more seed leaves). Monocots include members of the grass, palm, lily, pineapple, banana, and orchid families. Dicots include members of the oak, willow, ash, maple, hickory, birch, elm, and other families.

Examples of Monocots:

Florida silver palm
Cabbage palmetto
Saw palmetto
Paurotis
California Washingtonia
Florida Royal palm
Coconut palm
Date palm
Madagascar palm
Joshua tree
Soaptree yucca
Aloe yucca
Fragrant water lily
White trout lily
White trillium
Painted trillium
Tiger lily
Daylily
Wood lily
Yellow fringed orchis
Showy orchis
Snowy orchis
Small white lady's slipper
Showy lady's slipper
Moccasin flower
Spring tresses
Rose pogonia
Calopogon
Calypso fairy-slipper

Examples of Dicots:

Sugar maple
Silver maple
Florida maple
Sycamore maple
Red Maple
Striped maple
Mountain maple
White ash
Green ash
Pumpkin ash
Slippery elm
American elm
Live oak
Scarlet oak
Bur oak
Black willow
White oak
Pacific willow
Pussy willow
Weeping willow
White willow
Basket willow
Bitternut hickory
Pecan
Swamp hickory
Paper birch
Yellow birch
Sweet birch
Gray birch

The Science Teacher's Book of Lists, © 1993 by Prentice Hall

The Science Teacher's Book of Lists, © 1993 by Prentice Hall

LIST 1–9. NORTH AMERICAN TREES: PROPERTIES AND USES

COMMON NAME	LATIN NAME	DENSITY[a] G/CM³	GENERAL[b] PROPERTIES	USES[c]
Ash, black	Fraxinus nigra	0.526	C,H,J	F,U
Ash, white	Fraxinus americana	0.638	A,B,D,F	F,H,K,Q,R,U,Y,Z
Aspen, large toothed	Populus grandidentata	0.412	C,E,I	K,L,V
Basswood	Tilia americana	0.398	C,F,I	H,K,L,T
Beech, American	Fagus americana also Fagus grandifolia	0.655	A,B,I	E,H,X,Z
Birch, black/sweet	Betula lenta	0.762	A,B,D,I	E,K,T,X
Birch, paper/white	Betula papyrifera	0.600	B,D,I	S,T,V,X
Birch, yellow	Betula alleghaniensis/lutea	0.668	A,D,I	H,I,U,Z
Cedar, eastern red	Juniperus virginiana	0.492	I,K,N,M	F,H,I,L
Cedar, northern white	Thuja occidentalis	0.315	B,C,E,L,M	A,D,K,O,S,Y
Cedar, western red	Thuja plicata	0.344	C,F,K,N,M	C,D,F,N,P
Cherry, black	Prunus serotina	0.534	B,D,F,I,N	F,H
Corkwood	Leitneria floridana	0.207[d]	C,I	Z
Cottonwood, eastern	Populus deltoides	0.433	C,F	H,K,L,V
Cypress, bald	Taxodium distichum	0.482	F,H,K,L	C,N,Q,Y
Dogwood, flowering	Cornus florida	0.796	A,B,D	R,Y,Z
Elm, American	Ulmus americana	0.554	A,B,D,H	H,R,Q,Y
Fir, balsam	Abies balsamea	0.414	C,I,M	K,V
Fir, Douglas	Pseudotsuga menziesii	0.512	C,F,G	A,M
Gum, black/sour	Nyssa sylvatica	0.552	A,C,D,F	H,K,Q,T,U,Z
Gum, tupelo	Nyssa aquatica	0.524	H,K,L	H,K,L,Q,U,Y,Z
Hemlock, eastern	Tsuga canadensis	0.431	B,E,F	A,K,V
Hemlock, western	Tsuga heterophylla	0.432	F	A,V
Hickory, shagbark	Carya ovata	0.837	A,D,F,I	R,Z

(Continued)

LIST 1–9. (Continued)

COMMON NAME	LATIN NAME	DENSITY[a] G/CM³	GENERAL[b] PROPERTIES	USES[c]
Ironwood, black (Leadwood)	*Krugiodendron ferreum*	1.3[e]	A,B,E,I,N	T,Z
Locust, black/yellow	*Robinia pseudoacacia*	0.708	A,D,L	O,Q
Magnolia, cucumber	*Magnolia acuminata*	0.516	C,E,F,K	C,F,H,T,Y
Maple, red	*Acer rubrum*	0.546	C,E,I	H,K,V,Y
Maple, sugar	*Acer saccharum*	0.676	A,F,I	E,F,H,I,J,S,T,Y
Oak, live	*Quercus virginiana*	0.977	A,B,D	N,Y
Oak, northern red	*Quercus rubra*	0.657	A,B,D,I	E,H,L,Q,X
Oak, white	*Quercus alba*	0.710	A,B,D,I	E,H,N,O,Q,X
Pine, eastern white	*Pinus strobus*	0.373	C,F,G,I,M	A,B,F,G,H,I,Y
Pine, loblolly	*Pinus taeda*	0.593	C,E,F	A,V
Pine, longleaf	*Pinus palustris*	0.638	F,G	A,E,N,W
Pine, ponderosa	*Pinus ponderosa*	0.420	C,F	A,Q
Pine, red	*Pinus resinosa*	0.507	B,F,I	A,K,P,V,Y
Pine, western white	*Pinus monticola*	0.450	C,F	A
Poplar, yellow/tulip	*Liriodendron tulipifera*	0.427	C,D,E,F,I	C,F,H,J,T,Z
Redwood	*Sequoia sempervirens*	0.436	C,F,G,J,K,N	C,D,H
Sassafras	*Sassafras albidum*	0.473	C,E,L	H,O
Spruce, Engelmann	*Picea engelmannii*	0.350	F	A
Spruce, red/yellow	*Picea rubens*	0.413	C,F	J,K,V
Spruce, white	*Picea glauca*	0.431	C,F	A,V
Spruce, Sitka	*Picea sitchensis*	0.370	F,I	A,Z
Sycamore, American	*Platanus occidentalis*	0.539	A,B,D,H	C,F,H,J,K,Y
Tamarack/Am.larch	*Larix laricina*	0.558	B,D,L	I,O,P,N
Walnut, black	*Juglans nigra*	0.562	B,D,F,L,N	F,H,I

The Science Teacher's Book of Lists, © 1993 by Prentice Hall

LIST 1– 9. (Continued)

Notes

[a]Values for kiln-dried samples. To convert g/cm^3 to lb./cu. ft. multiply by 62.43.

[b]Codes for properties

A: heavy (dense)
B: hard
C: soft
D: tough
E: brittle

F: tall
G: straight grained
H: coarse grained
I: fine grained
J: splits easily

K: stable to weather
L: stable to soil
M: resinous
N: deeply colored

[c]Codes for uses:

A: construction lumber
B: log homes
C: siding
D: shingles
E: flooring
F: panels; interiors
G: millwork
H: furniture
I: cabinet making

J: musical instruments
K: crates and/or boxes
L: cooperage
M: plywood
N: boats
O: posts
P: poles
Q: railroad ties

R: tool handles
S: spools
T: woodenware
U: baskets
V: pulpwood
W: turpentine and rosin
X: firewood
Y: ornamental
Z: specialty items

[d]The density of balsa wood is 0.12 to 0.20 g/cm^3.

[e]Sinks in water; heaviest wood of the United States (Florida).

LIST 1–10. TYPES OF HABITAT WITH EXAMPLES OF PLANT LIFE

Bog Plants

balsam fir
birch
bladderwort
butterwort
blueberry
bog rosemary
cotton grass
common
   winterberry
dwarf raspberry
eastern hemlock

fringed orchid
lady's slipper
large cranberry
laurel
marsh marigold
pitcher plant
poison sumac
red maple
sundew
tamarack

Lake and Pond Plants

arrowhead
black grass
blue flag
bulrush
bur reed
cattail
duckweed
fragrant water
   lily
pondweed
quillwort

rush
silverweed
stonewort
sweetflag
water celery
water hyacinth
water milfoil
water plantain
water smartweed
yellow water
   buttercup

Mangrove Swamp Plants

black mangrove
button mangrove
cabbage palmetto
cattail
glasswort
gumbo-limbo
inkwood
paradise tree
red mangrove
milkbark

saw grass
sea grape
sweetbay
West Indies
   mahogany
white mangrove
willow bustic
wingleaf
   soapberry

River and Stream Plants

arrowhead
arrowwood
black ash
burweed
cardinal flower
duckweed
forget-me-not
horsetail
Indian cucumber
   root

Indian poke
jewelweed
marsh marigold
pondweed
riverweed
rush
watercress
water hyacinth
wild rice
yellow pond lily

(Continued)

The Science Teacher's Book of Lists, © 1993 by Prentice Hall

LIST 1–10. (Continued)

Sandy Beach and Dune Plants

American beach grass
Australian pine
bayberry
beach heather
beach pea
beach plum
cherry
dusty miller
evergreen bearberry
golden aster
hibiscus
holly
Japanese honeysuckle

maples
oaks
oleander (poisonous)
poison ivy
prickly pear cactus
reindeer moss
sassafras
seaside goldenrod
sundew
reindeer moss
wild indigo

Salt Marsh Plants

American holly
black grass
black needlerush
common winterberry
glasswort
inkberry
marsh elder
marsh thistle
poison ivy
reed

salt marsh aster
salt marsh pink
sea lavender
seaside gerardia
seaside goldenrod
spike grass
slough grass
switch grass
widgeon grass
wood sage

Transition Forest Plants

alternate-leaf dogwood
American beech
black cherry
downy Solomon's seal
downy yellow violet
eastern hemlock
eastern white pine
elderberry
maple
mountain laurel

northern red oak
partridgeberry
prickly gooseberry
rattlesnake fern
shining club moss
stiff club moss
white ash
white baneberry
yellow birch

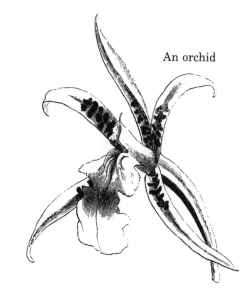

An orchid

LIST 1–11. FRUITS AND VEGETABLES

According to the American Home Economics Association, fruits and vegetables can be classified as follows:

Fruits

Berries

blackberry
blueberry
boysenberry
cranberry
currant
gooseberry
grape
raspberry
strawberry

Citrus

grapefruit
kumquat
lemon
lime
orange
tangerine
tangelo

Drupes or Stonefruits

apricot
cherry
nectarine
peach
plum
prune

Vegetables

Bulbs

garlic
onion
shallot

Flowers and Fruits

artichoke
broccoli
cauliflower
corn
cucumber
eggplant
okra
pepper
pumpkin
squash
tomato

Stems and Leaves

asparagus
brussels sprout
cabbage
celery
Chinese cabbage
lettuce
rhubarb
spinach

(Continued)

The Science Teacher's Book of Lists, © 1993 by Prentice Hall

LIST 1–11. (Continued)

Pomes

apple

pear

Roots

beet

carrot

parsnip

radish

rutabaga

turnip

Legumes

lima bean

lentil

pea

soybean

LIST 1–12. ABOUT EDIBLE WILD PLANTS AND SOME EXAMPLES

Getting Started

There are hundreds of wild plants that have some edible parts. Some are common and, because they are found in cultivated gardens and crops, are thought of as undesirable weeds. Examples are dandelion, plantain, sorrel, purslane, and winter cress. As in the home garden, wild plants are in the best condition for use at different seasons. Most greens are ready in spring and early summer. Fruits mature from summer to fall. Some roots and tubers can be found both in spring and late summer or early fall.

The Latin names of the plants have not been given in the lists and some may go by other common names. Be sure you can recognize a plant before gathering it for food. The way to learn is by a careful study of books and field guides and/or with the guidance of an expert familiar with the plants. Start with some abundant, easy-to-identify plants.

Plants should not be gathered when they are scarce or in danger of extinction. Also, there are laws of trespass that forbid taking plants. Gathering plants is prohibited in most parks and on many public lands. Know your own countryside; get permission when necessary.

One Last Concern: Today in urban and suburban areas vegetation may have been treated with herbicides and pesticides; streams and swamps may be polluted; roadsides may have been contaminated with lead from vehicle exhausts. These are concerns but should not lead to unreasonable fears. The best place to start is your own or a friend's lawn and garden, assuming it has not been treated with herbicides and/or pesticides.

Examples of Edible Wild Plants

Fruits

barberry	ground cherry	persimmon
beach plum	hawthorne	prickly pear cactus
blackberry	Juneberry (serviceberry)	raspberry
black crowberry	manzanita	rum cherry
blueberry	may apple	strawberry
bunchberry	mountain ash	viburnum
cabbage palm	mulberry	wild grape
chokecherry	partridge berry	wineberry
elderberry	pawpaw	yucca

(Continued)

The Science Teacher's Book of Lists, © 1993 by Prentice Hall

LIST 1–12. (Continued)

Nuts

beech	chestnut oak	hickory
black walnut	hazelnut	white oak

Seed and Seed Pods

black mustard	knotweed	piñon pine
common sunflower	lamb's-quarter	purslane
honey locust	maple	wild rice

Greens

amaranth	dwarf mallow	shepherd's purse
burdock	lamb's-quarter	sow thistle
chickweed	marsh marigold	stinging nettle
chicory	miner's lettuce	watercress
curled dock	sego (mariposa) lily	winter cress
dandelion	sheep sorrel	violet (blue and others)

Shoots, Stems, and Flower Buds

asparagus	fiddlehead fern	prickly pear cactus
bracken	great bulrush	purslane
burdock	knotweed (Japanese)	winter cress (buds)
daylily (shoots and buds)		

Roots and Tubers

Arrowhead (duck potato)	great bullrush	wild garlic
breadroot (Indian potato)	greenbrier	wild ginger
cattail	jerusalem artichoke	wild onion (allium)
burdock	Queen Anne's lace	yampa (squawroot)

Beverages and Flavors

bergamot	pennyroyal	violet (blue)
black birch	peppermint	wild garlic
black spruce	rose hips	wild ginger
catnip	rose petals	wild onion (allium)
chicory (root)	sassafras	wood sorrel
Kentucky coffee tree	spearmint	
lemon balm	spice bush	
maple (sap)	sumac (red fruit)	

LIST 1–13. RECIPES FOR WILD PLANT FOODS

Some plants are edible uncooked. For example, most fruit is edible. Other plants are toxic when raw and must be cooked.

Cooking wild plants is a little different from cooking cultivated plants. Cook the plant until it has the degree of tenderness desired. Some greens and other plant parts require cooking in one or more changes of water to reduce a bitter or otherwise undesirable taste. Several recipes follow.

Red Mulberry Jelly: Wash one quart of ripe red mulberries and remove stems. Place in a deep sauce pan with a little water, bring to a boil, and simmer 15 minutes. Crush fruit with a potato masher and strain through cheese cloth. Measure juice and add one cup of sugar for each cup of juice. Mix and bring to boil. Add $1\frac{1}{2}$ ounces of liquid pectin, mix, and boil for one minute. Skim and pour into hot, sterile glasses. Seal if to be stored without refrigeration.

Violet Greens: Gather a quantity of the leaves of blue violet or those of a related violet of the *Viola* group. Remove any stems, wash and cut with scissors or knife to prevent matting while cooking. Cook in lightly salted water to just cover until tender (5 to 10 minutes). Violet leaves are quite bland and the taste may be improved by adding some other greens such as dandelion, winter cress, or garlic mustard. These greens by themselves usually require one or more changes of water to reduce the strong flavor.

Pokeweed: In late spring gather shoots and young leaves that are about 10 inches or less in height. Wash and cut up as needed. Cover well with lightly salted water and cook for 10 minutes. Discard this water, barely cover with fresh water, add a little salt, butter, margarine, or bacon drippings, and simmer for 30 minutes. Resembles asparagus. *Caution:* Older plants and berries are poisonous.

Cattail and Daylily Sprouts: Pull cattail shoots up to about 2 feet high, peel off any tough outer leaves, and use the tender, light-colored core. Similarly, daylily shoots may be pulled or cut at the root line and peeled. These shoot cores are edible raw and can be used in salads. Or, they may be cut up, boiled in water for a few minutes, and served seasoned with butter, pepper, and salt.

Daylily Tubers: Dig a clump of daylilies at any time of year. Break off only the firm, small tubers and replant the clump. Trim the tubers and boil in lightly salted water for a few minutes. Serve as a vegetable or potato substitute. These tubers are edible raw. You may wish to remove the skins at some times of the year.

Jerusalem Artichoke Tubers: This plant is a member of the sunflower family and bears 3-inch to 4-inch yellow flowers. The small tubers are available in early spring or late summer and fall. The tubers occur in two colors, dull red and pale brown. The tubers are edible raw and can be used in a salad. Cook in boiling water as for potatoes but keep the time quite short (5 to 10 minutes).

(Continued)

LIST 1–13. (Continued)

Sumac Drink: All of the sumacs bearing red flower stalks are non-poisonous. They contain malic acid, which is also found in apples. Gather the red flower clusters, cover with water, and stir vigorously for 10 minutes or allow to soak for 30 minutes or so with occasional stirring. Be sure to strain the liquid through two or three layers of cheesecloth to remove the plant hairs and stalks. Sweeten to taste, cool, and drink. Tastes a bit like pink lemonade.

LIST 1–14. DYES FROM PLANTS

Plants have been used as a source of dyes from ancient times. They were used by the American Indians and in American households until the end of the 19th century. Synthetic dyestuffs, discovered by William Perkin in 1856, gradually took over as the preferred coloring materials. However, the natural dyes have continued in use as a practice of early crafts.

Many plants can be used as coloring materials on wool and cotton, but not all produce colors of equal wash and light resistance. The natural dyes often require added dyeing assistants such as mordants, salts or acids. Some of these agents are listed below under dyeing recipes.

PLANT	LATIN NAME	PART USED	COLOR[a]
alder	*Alnus incana*	inner bark	brown
maple, Norway	*Acer platanoides*	inner bark	rose-tan
white birch	*Betula papyrifera*	inner bark	yellow-tan
red-osier dogwood	*Cornus stolonifera*	inner bark	light red[b]
butternut	*Juglans cinerea*	bark, root, nuts	brown
black walnut	*Juglans nigra*	hulls or bark	dark olive/brown
		leaves (fresh)	black
red oak	*Quercus rubra*	bark or acorns	black or brown
hemlock	*Tsuga canadensis*	inner bark	reddish brown
osage orange	*Maclura pomifera*	wood or root	yellow-tan
chokecherry	*Prunus virginiana*	fruit and roots	purplish red
sumac	*Rhus glabra*	inner bark and pulp of stalk	yellow
		berries	yellow-tan
bloodroot (puccoon)	*Sanguinaria canadensis*	root bark	yellowish red
barberry	*Berberis vulgaris*	root	yellow
pokeberry	*Phytolacea discaudea*	berries	crimson and yellow
elderberry	*Sambucus canadensis*	berries	blue
grape	*Vitis species*	fruit	blue/violet
blueberry	*Vaccinium species*	fruit	blue*
cranberry	*Vaccinium macrocarpon*	fruit	light red
sunflower	*Helianthus annuus*	flowers	gold
dahlia	*Dahlia species*	flowers	orange
onion, yellow	*Allium cepa*	skin	burnt orange
ragweed	*Ambrosia artemisiifolia*	leaves	green
black tea	*Camellia sinensis*	leaves	brown/rose-tan
coffee	*Coffea arabica*	ground beans	yellow-tan
prickly pear	*Cactus opuntia*	fruit	rose

[a]The colors given are for wool with alum mordant except those with an asterisk. Other mordants may give different shades. There is some variation in colors reported by different writers. In general, shades are lighter on cotton. Different shades and colors can be obtained by mixing dyestuffs.
[b]Used with an equal quantity of alder root bark.

LIST 1–15. DYEING PROCEDURES

The colors obtained will vary with the source of dyestuff, the procedure, the concentration of the dye and the amount of fabric or yarn, and the length of time in the bath. Since there is so much variation, all material to be used in a craft project should be dyed in one batch.

Wool should be stirred gently and squeezed free of liquid, not wrung, to prevent shrinkage. Wool yarn or fabric may have oils or a finish, so a gentle washing in mild soap solution is recommended before dyeing.

The plant materials to be extracted for a dye bath should be placed in a cheesecloth bag or filtered from the bath before use. As a precaution, aprons and gloves should be worn to avoid staining clothing and hands. Dye solutions should be stored only with refrigeration as they may ferment.

The procedures have been written for 4 ounces of fiber but can be changed to larger or smaller quantities by proportion.

Dyeing With Mordants (To Fix the Colors)

Commonly used mordants are alum (potassium aluminum sulfate), potassium dichromate, ferrous sulfate, and tannins.

To prepare an alum mordant on wool, dissolve 1 ounce of potassium alum and $\frac{1}{4}$ ounce of cream of tartar in 1 gallon of water. Wet 4 ounces of wool in water, squeeze out excess water, and immerse in mordant bath. Gradually heat the bath to boiling, turning the material gently. Heat for one hour replacing any water that is evaporated. Stand overnight, and the next day squeeze out excess liquid and dry further by rolling in a dry towel. Use at once or store in a cool place. Rinse just before placing in dye bath. Mordants may also be applied during or after dyeing. In mordanting cotton use washing soda in place of cream of tartar.

Dyeing With Onion Skin

Place 2.5 ounces of dry, yellow onion skin in enough water to cover and boil for 15 minutes. Strain and dilute to one gallon. Immerse 4 ounces of mordanted wool in the bath and heat to boiling. Boil 30 minutes, rinse, and dry.

Dyeing With Blueberries

Mash 4 ounces of fresh or frozen blueberries and simmer in 1 gallon of water until most of the color is extracted. Clear the solution. Use to dye 4 ounces of material, starting with a cool solution and heating with gentle stirring to a simmer. Continue until the color no longer is deposited. This dye will color wool or cotton without mordant.

(Continued)

LIST 1–15. (Continued)

Dyeing With Barberry Wood, Bark, or Roots

This shrub is common in hedges and lawn plantings. The wood has a brilliant yellow color. Prepare the plant material in the form of fine chips or shavings. Extract two quart of chips in one gallon of boiling water for 30 minutes or until most of color is extracted. Dilute to one gallon. Dye 4 ounces of mordanted wool as for onion skins.

LIST 1–16. EXAMPLES OF ENDANGERED PLANTS

There are about 310,000 species of known plants. Many plant species are being threatened with extinction (dying out as a species). Species extinction is a natural process, but human intervention or activity such as destruction of habitat, particularly of the rain forests, and over-collecting have escalated this natural process. The threatened plants have provided us with improved crops, about 50 percent of our medications, gums, waxes, fibers, timber, oils, and dyes. The "threatened" status is further categorized as:

- *Endangered*—in danger of extinction as a species unless conservation measures alleviate the causes.

- *Threatened*—in danger of becoming endangered as a species unless conservation measures alleviate the causes.

- *Rare*—while not threatened or endangered, these are at risk as a species mostly due to small world populations.

Examples of Endangered Plants and Their Range

COMMON NAME	SCIENTIFIC NAME	HISTORIC RANGE
Arizona agave	*Agave arizonica*	Arizona
Aleutian shield-fern	*Polystichum aleuticum*	Alaska
ashy dogweed	*Thymophylla tephroleuca*	Texas
big-leaf palm	*Marojeja darianii*	Madagascar
bois de prune blanc	*Drypetes caustica*	Mauritius
bunched arrowhead	*Sagittaria fasciculata*	North and South Carolina
Brady pincushion cactus	*Pediocactus bradyi*	Arizona
caiapia	*Dorstenia albertorum*	Brazil
cacaode Monte	*Herrania balaensis*	Ecuador
caoba	*Persea theobromifolia*	Western base of Andes, Ecuador
Cooley's water-willow	*Justicia cooleyi*	Florida
Costa Rican jatropha	*Jatropha costaricensis*	Costa Rica
Cumberland sandwort	*Arenaria cumberlandensis*	Kentucky, Tennessee
Diamond Head schiedea	*Schiedea adamantis*	Hawaii
Drury's slipper orchid	*Paphiopedilum druryi*	India
dwarf naupaka	*Scaevola coriacea*	Hawaii
elfin tree fern	*Cyathea dryopteroides*	Puerto Rico
four-petal pawpaw	*Asimina tetramera*	Florida
Florida torreya	*Torreya taxifolia*	Florida, Georgia
Florida zizphus	*Zizphus celata*	Florida
golden gladiolus	*Gladiolus aurea*	South Africa
Grantham's camellia	*Camellia granthamiana*	Hong Kong, China
green pitcher-plant	*Sarracenia oreophila*	Alabama, Georgia, Tennessee

(Continued)

LIST 1–16. (Continued)

COMMON NAME	SCIENTIFIC NAME	HISTORIC RANGE
Hamilton's gunnera	*Gunnera hamiltonii*	New Zealand
Harper's beauty	*Harperocallis flava*	Florida
Hawaiian vetch	*Vicia menziesii*	Hawaii
horseshoe fern	*Marattia salicina*	Australia
Johnston's frankenia	*Frankenia johnstonii*	Texas, Mexico
Kauai hau kuahiwi	*Hibiscadelphus distans*	Hawaii
Kauai silversword	*Argyroxiphium kauense*	Hawaii
Knowlton cactus	*Pediocactus knowltonii*	New Mexico, Colorado
Lloyd's hedgehog cactus	*Echinocereus lloydii*	Texas
Mauritian crinum lily	*Crinum mauritianum*	Mauritus
Minnesota trout lily	*Erythronium propullans*	Minnesota
Missouri bladderpod	*Lesquerella filiformis*	Missouri
mogumber bell	*Darwinia carnea*	Southwest Australia
mountain sweet pitcher plant	*Sarracenia rubra ssp.jonesii*	North and South Carolina
na'u (Hawaiian gardenia)	*Gardenia brighamii*	Hawaii
Navasota ladies'-tresses	*Spiranthes parksii*	Texas
Nichol's Turk's head cactus	*Echinocactus horizonthalonius var. nicholii*	Arizona
papyrus	*Cyperus papyrus hadidi*	Egypt
persistent trillium	*Trillium persistens*	Georgia, South Carolina
pygmy fringe-tree	*Chionanthus pygmaeus*	Florida
reflect trillium	*Trillium reliquum*	Alabama, Georgia, South Carolina
robin's cinquefoil	*Potentilla robbinsiana*	New Hampshire, Vermont
San Rafael cactus	*Pediocactus despanii*	Arizona
scrub blazingstar	*Liatris ohlingerae*	Florida
Sicilian fir	*Abies nebrodensis*	Sicily, Italy
Short's goldenrod	*Solidago shortii*	Kentucky
snakeroot	*Eryngium cuneifolium*	Florida
Texas bitterweed	*Hymenoxys texana*	Texas
Tobusch fishhook cactus	*Ancistrocactus tobuschii*	Texas
Todsen's pennyroyal	*Hedeoma todsenii*	New Mexico
tumamoc globe-berry	*Tumamoca macdougalii*	Mexico
uhiuhi	*Caesalpinia kavaiense*	Hawaii
underground orchid	*Rhizanthella gardneri*	Southwestern Australia
Vahl's boxwood	*Buxus vahlii*	Puerto Rico
Wheeler's peperomia	*Peperomia wheeleri*	Puerto Rico
white gum	*Eucalyptus argophloia*	Australia
wireweed	*Polygonella basiramia*	Florida

NOTE: This list is long but identifies fewer than half of the plants that are known to be endangered. As the destruction of habitat continues, more plants will be added to this list, and more plants will become extinct.

The Science Teacher's Book of Lists, © 1993 by Prentice Hall

LIST 1–17. TROPICAL RAIN FORESTS: WHAT AND WHERE THEY ARE

Tropical rain forests are what most of us think of as jungles. Rain forests are hot and humid ecosystems full of thousands of types of plants and animals that live together in an area that receives more than 60 inches of rain a year and where the temperatures range between 70° and 85°F. They are located in a belt around the earth located north and south of the Equator, mostly between the Tropic of Cancer and the Tropic of Capricorn. These rain forests supply us with everyday products including wood for furniture, rubber for tires, sneakers and erasers; chemicals for medications and dyes; plants for food, oxygen and fiber; and cooling protection from the sun's hot rays.

Rain forests are located in more than seventy countries but more than half of them are located in three countries: Brazil, Zaire, and Indonesia.

Location of Some Rain Forests

Berwanda	Uganda	Melanesia	Guatemala
Cameroon	Zaire	Pakistan	Guyana (Guiana)
Ethiopia	Queensland/ Australia	Papua New Guinea	Honduras
Gabon		Philippines	Mexico
Ghana	Bangladesh	Sri Lanka	Nicaragua
Guinea	Borneo	Thailand	Panama
Ivory Coast	Brunei	Vietnam	Peru
Kenya	Burma	Belize	Surinam
Liberia	Cambodia	Bolivia	Venezuela
Madagascar	India	Brazil	Florida Mangroves/ USA
Nigeria	Indonesia	Colombia	
Nepal	Java	Costa Rica	Hawaii/USA
Rwanda	Kalimantan	Ecuador	Puerto Rico
Sierra Leone	Kampuchia	El Salvador	Washington/USA
Tanzania	Laos	French Guiana	
	Malaysia		

Aerial roots of an orchid on the branch of a tree

LIST 1–18. SOME PLANT PRODUCTS OF THE TROPICAL RAIN FORESTS

More than half of the world's plant species grow in the tropical rain forests. These tropical plants supply products or raw materials for many of the products that we use daily such as food, chewing gum, wooden furniture, sneakers, and tires. They also supply about half of our prescription medicines. Chemists continue to investigate rain forest plants to identify new sources of products, especially new medicines to treat cancer, heart disease, and other diseases and health problems.

Some Canes and Fibers From the Rain Forests

bamboo—cane furniture, shades, mats, baskets, ropes, fabrics, chopsticks, screens; edible shoots

jute—burlap sacks, rope, twine

kapok—heat and sound insulation, in life-saving equipment, used to be used in pillows and upholstery

kenaf—jute substitute

toquilla palm—Panama hats

ramie—yarn-like material knitted with other fibers

rattan—furniture, split and woven for seats, baskets, blinds

roselle—jute substitute

urena—jute substitute

Some Essential Oils From the Rain Forests

bay oil—perfume, men's cologne and after shave, table sauces

oil of camphor—carminative to relieve colic or griping, stimulant in medicines, insect repellent

oil of cascarilla—used in medical preparations, especially for stomach bitters; spicy flavor similar to nutmeg, clove, and thyme used for flavor in confections and drinks

coconut oil—confections, soap, lotions

East Indian sandalwood oil—perfumery, soap, candles; blends well with other oils

eucalyptus oil—medical preparations, cough medicines, and throat lozenges; perfumery, insect repellent, tanning agent

guaiac oil—perfumery, fixative for less stable fragrances

oil of lime—flavoring in non-alcoholic drinks, ice cream, confectionery, scenting of soaps and bath oils

oil of palm—baked goods

(Continued)

The Science Teacher's Book of Lists, © 1993 by Prentice Hall

LIST 1–18. (Continued)

oil of petigrain—cosmetics and soaps for refreshing orange-like scent

patchouli oil—perfumery, soap

rosewood oil—perfumes, cosmetics, flavorings

oil of star anise—flavoring for oral pharmaceuticals, confectionery, anisette drinks; scenting for soaps and cosmetics; cough expectorant

ylang-ylang oil—"extra" or highest grade used in finest French perfumes; other grades used in cosmetics and soaps

Some Gums and Resins From the Rain Forests

balata—golf ball covers, adhesives, waterproofing fabrics, backing in shoes

chicle gum—chewing gum, confectionery

copal—a group of resins used in paint, varnish, printing ink

dammar—a group of resins used in varnish, lacquer, wallpaper, white enamels

pine oleoresin—turpentine, rosin, paint, pharmaecuticals, perfumery, insecticide

rubber—balls, balloons, boots, condoms, erasers, foam rubber, rubber bands, grips on handles, tubing, sneakers, tires, white rectangle on pitcher's mound

Some Pharmaceuticals

diosgenin—used to produce a birth control pill, sex hormones, steroids and medications for asthma and rheumatoid arthritis

gambier—used to treat diarrhea in the past; little medical use now

ipecacuanha root—used as an emetic, an expectorant, and to treat amoebic dysentery

logwood—dye used to stain tissues for microscopic study

quinine—used to treat malaria, pneumonia, and as an antipyretic, to lower fever

reserpine—used as a sedative and in the treatment of hypertension

sappanwood—used for the treatment of dysentery and skin problems

strophanthus—used in the treatment of circulatory and heart conditions

Fruit of *Drylbalanops*, a resin-producing tree

LIST 1–19. SOME FOODS, SPICES, AND HOUSE PLANTS FROM THE RAIN FORESTS

Foods	*Spices*	*Plants*
avocado	allspice	African violet
banana	black pepper	aluminum plant
Brazil nut	cassia	anthurium
cashew nut	cayenne	begonia
coconut	chili pepper	bird's nest fern
coffee	chocolate	bromeliad
cola	cinnamon	Christmas cactus
corn	clove	dracaena
grapefruit	ginger	fiddle leaf fig
guava	mace	flaming sword
heart of palm	nutmeg	Joseph's coat
lemon	paprika	kentia palm
lime	turmeric	orchid
macadamia nut	vanilla	philodendron
mango		prayer plant
orange		rubber plant
papaya		snake plant
passion fruit		sweetheart vine
peanut		Swiss cheese plant
pepper		umbrella tree
pineapple		
potato		
rice		
sweet potato		
tangerine		
tapioca		
yam		

LIST 1–20. SELECTED RAIN FOREST TIMBERS AND SOME USES

AFRICA	*SOUTH AMERICA*	*SOUTHEAST ASIA*
abura	balsa	amboyna
afara	basralous	balau
African mahogany	Central American	kapur
afzelia	mahogany	kempas
agba	crabwood	mengkulang
ayan	greenheart	teak
dahoma	mora	white seraya
ekki	sucupira	
gaboon		
gedu nohor		
guarea		
okan		

Uses of African Timbers

PLANT	*USES*
abura	Interior woodwork and furniture.
afara	In furniture: frames, table and chair legs, veneer. Stretchers, interior work, and plywood.
African mahogany	Fine furniture and reproductions. In boat building: planks, deck-housing, and cabins.
afzelia	Joinery in staircases, window frames, counter tops, and flooring; vats for chemicals.
agba	An alternative to oak in joinery and furniture making. In boat building: planks and laminated frames.
ayan	Piles and decking of wharfs. Heavy-duty factory flooring.
dahoma	Workbenches and heavy construction use.
ekki	Heavy construction: piles and decks for piers, jetties, harbor works, bridges, wharfs; heavy-duty flooring, framing.
gaboon	Plywood used for drawer panels, partitions, backs of chests.
gedu nohor	In boat building: deck planks, cabin construction, and fittings.

LIST 1–21. THREATS TO TROPICAL RAIN FORESTS

Tropical rain forests are found in tropical Asia, Australia, Africa, Central America, and South America. These rain forests are home to more than half of the world's species of animals and plants. These tropical plants supply us with about half of today's prescription medicines. They also supply raw products used to make many items that we use daily, such as sneakers and rubber bands. Rain forests help keep the temperature of Earth moderate and prevent floods, droughts, epidemics, and other natural disasters. Through the process of photosynthesis, the green plants release oxygen into the air. Without the rain forests, we would lose the medicines, useful products, and protection they provide. Rain forests are under attack now. The World Wildlife Fund reports that in 1990, rain forests were being deforested at an estimated rate of 50 acres per minute. *Deforestation or destruction of the rain forest habitat is the primary cause of extinction and possible extinction of thousands of plants and animals.*

Behaviors contributing to the deforestation of the rain forests include:

- Slash-and-burn agriculture
- Commercial logging
- Clearing for ranching and farming
- Clearing for hydro-electric projects
- Illegal trade in rain forest plants and animals or their products
- Overhunting or overcollecting of rain forest plants and animals for commerce

Laelia purpurata

The Science Teacher's Book of Lists, © 1993 by Prentice Hall

LIST 1–22. CARNIVOROUS PLANTS: PLANTS THAT CONSUME ANIMALS

There are close to 600 species of plants that consume animals. They range in size from small plants which attract insects to 2-foot high sundews and 3-foot high pitcher plants which lure, trap, and digest rodents, small birds, frogs, and lizards. These carnivorous plants attract their prey with alluring fragrances, attractive blossoms, and/or bright colors, then trap and digest them. Those that do not produce digestive fluids have bacteria which cause the prey to decay. The "digested" materials are then absorbed by the plant and used for growth. Different species have different trapping mechanisms and digestive processes. Scientists infer that these photosynthetic, carnivorous plants have evolved to supplement nutrients, especially nitrogen and minerals, lacking in the soils, waters, or mosses in which these plants grow. Many live in bogs. Thus, the plants supplement their "diet" with small animals, mostly insects and spiders. They cannot consume humans, except in science fiction. There are seven families of carnivorous plants and fifteen genera.

Carnivorous Plants

FAMILY (7) GENUS (15) SPECIES	NO. OF SPECIES	COMMON NAME	TYPE OF TRAP
1. Byblidaceae		Rainbow Plant	Passive flypaper
(1) *Byblis*	2	Rainbow Plant	
B. gigantea		Giant Rainbow	
B. liniflora		Lesser Rainbow	
2. Cephalotaceae			
(2) *Cephalotus*	1	Western Australian	Passive pitfall
C. follicularis		Pitcher Plant	
3. Dioncophyllaceae			
(3) *Triphyophyllum*	1	Fly catcher	Passive flypaper
4. Droseraceae			
(4) *Aldrovanda*	1	Waterwheel Plant	Active fly trap
A. vesiculosa			
(5) *Dionaea*	1	Venus Fly Trap	Active fly trap
D. muscipula			
(6) *Drosera*	120	The Sundews	Semi-active
D. anglica			
D. binata			
D. capensis			
D. filiformis			
D. heterophylla			
D. intermedia			
D. pallida			
D. rotundifolia			
D. sulphurea			
D. trinervia			
D. villosa			
(7) *Drosophyllum*	1	Portuguese Sundew	Semi-active

(Continued)

The Science Teacher's Book of Lists, © 1993 by Prentice Hall

LIST 1–22. (Continued)

The Science Teacher's Book of Lists, © 1993 by Prentice Hall

FAMILY (7) GENUS (15) SPECIES	NO. OF SPECIES	COMMON NAME	TYPE OF TRAP
5. Nepenthaceae		Pitcher Plants	Passive pitfall
(8) *Nepenthes*	71	Tropical pitcher	
N. ampullaria		Monkey Cup	
N. gracilis		Monkey's Rice Pot	
N. khasiana			
N. rafflesiania			
6. Sarraceniaceae		Pitcher Plants	Passive pitfall
(9) *Darlingtonia*	1	Cobra Lily	
D. californica			
(10) *Heliamphora*	6	South American Sun Pitcher	
H. heterodoxa			
H. nutans			
(11) *Sarracenia*	9	Trumpet Pitchers	
S. flava		Huntsman's Horn	
S. leucophylla		White Trumpet	
S. psittacina		Parrot Pitcher	
S. purpurea venosa		Southern Pitcher Plant	
7. Lentibulariacea			
(12) *Genlisea*	14	Forked Traps	Passive
(13) *Pinguicula*	50	Butterworts	Passive flypaper
P. alpina		Alpine Butterwort	
P. grandiflora		Irish Butterwort	
P. villosa		Arctic Butterwort	
P. vulgaris			
(14) *Polypompholyx*	2	Pink Petticoats	Active mousetrap suction type
(15) *Utricularia*	300	Bladderworts	
U. sandersonii			
U. vulgaris		Greater Bladderwort	Suction type

Nepenthes
villosa

LIST 1–23. CARNIVOROUS PLANTS GROUPED BY THE WAY THEY TRAP THEIR PREY

Carnivorous plants trap their prey in different ways that can be classified as: active, semi-active, and passive. Common names of carnivorous plants vary from country to country. Thus, the scientific name used by all countries is also given. The scientific name is always in italics when printed and underlined when written by hand.

I. ACTIVE TRAPS
   A. Those that detect prey with trigger hairs and snap shut.
      Venus Fly Trap, *Dionaea muscipula*
      A miniature aquatic fly trap, *Aldrovanda vesiculosa*
   B. Those that trap by suction.
      Bladderworts, *Utricularia*

II. SEMI-ACTIVE TRAPS
   A. Those that trap with a sticky fluid on the tentacles. As the prey struggles to get away, its movements cause more sticky fluids to flow, which triggers a slow tightening of tentacles around the prey.
      Sundew, *Drosera*
      Portuguese Sundew, *Drosophyllum*
   B. Those that trap with sticky fluid and the struggle of the prey triggers the leaves to roll up to form a cup for digestive fluids.
      Butterwort, *Pinguicula*.

III. PASSIVE TRAPS
   A. Those that lure their prey with a sweet nectar to a pitcher of fluids.
      Pitcher plants
         Trumpet Pitchers, *Sarracenia*
         Western Australian Pitcher Plants, *Cephalotus follicularis*
         South American Sun Pitchers, *Heliamphora heterodextra*
         Cobra Lily, *Darlingtonia californica*

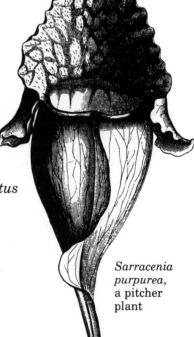

Sarracenia purpurea, a pitcher plant

LIST 1–24. SEXUAL REPRODUCTION IN PLANTS

Sexual reproduction or fertilization means the union of egg and sperm. In the case of plants, this occurs as a result of pollination, when pollen from the anther of the stamen (male organ) reaches the stigma of the pistil (female organ). This sexual union usually results in seeds.

Bisexual Flowers

In some plant species, the flower contains both the male (stamen) and female (pistil) reproductive organs. These flowers are classified as bisexual. Most of these flowers are capable of self pollination.

Examples of Bisexual Flowers Are:

- Marigolds
- Zinnia
- Sundews
- Most pitcher plants with the exception of the *Nepenthes* or Monkey Cup
- Sunflowers

Unisexual Flowers

In some plant species, the flower of an individual plant contains only the male (anther) or female (pistil) sexual organ. These types of flowers are classified as unisexual. These flowers are not capable of self-pollination and require assistance from the animal community, the wind, or both.

Examples of Unisexual Plants Are:

- Holly
- Kiwi vine
- Most drupe trees
- Nepenthes or Tropical Pitcher Plant or Monkey Cup

The Science Teacher's Book of Lists, © 1993 by Prentice Hall

LIST 1–25. ASEXUAL OR VEGETATIVE REPRODUCTION IN PLANTS

Asexual reproduction in plants does not require the union of sperm and egg to produce a seed and then a plant. Instead, some plants have nonsexual or asexual ways of producing not a seed, but a plantlet.

Examples of Asexual Reproduction in Plants

Budding: New plantlets form on plant organs such as:

leaves—flat, thin, expanded organs growing from the stem of a plant; for example, Venus fly trap, sundews, and butterworts

stems—the main, aboveground stalk or trunk of a plant; for example, some sundews and butterworts

roots—base of the plant that draws in water and nourishment and stores food; for example, some sundews

runners—aboveground stems; for example, strawberry, and some sundews and gutterworts

rhizomes—horizontal underground stems; for example, sensitive fern, Western Australian pitcher plant, and cobra lily

Cuttings: New plantlets form from cuttings, which include both stems and a few leaves; for example, African violets, geraniums, forsythia, pussy willows, philodendron, sundews, impatiens, and spider plants.

NOTE: Cuttings make excellent class projects. To help each cutting survive:

- Fill a clear jar with water.
- Cover it with clear cellophane wrap.
- Secure in place with a rubber band.
- Make a hole in the clear wrap.
- Insert the stem through the hole.
- Place where the cutting will not get cold and will receive 6 to 12 hours of light a day.

LIST 1–26. IMMIGRANT PLANTS

Many of the plants that we observe about us are not native to our area. Botanists estimate that there are about 3,000 plant species growing wild in North America that originated in other countries. Many of these were introduced to the United States by people interested in plants, especially for their own homes and gardens. Other plants and seeds arrived in ships, planes, and animals transported to North America. Some botanists are concerned that these immigrant plants will force out native plants, interfere with biodiversity, and disrupt the natural ecosystems. Examples of common plants that are not native to North America but are immigrant plants:

Ailanthus of China, or tree of heaven
Chicory, European
Chickweed, European
Clover, white and red, European
Cocklebur, European
Crabgrass, European
Dandelion
Day lily, European
Eucalyptus, Australian
Japanese honeysuckle
Japanese kudzu
Norway maple
Oxeye daisy, European
Queen Anne's lace, European

Timothy (a kind of hay grass)
Tumbleweed
Salt-spray rose
Rye grass, European
Wild onion

The Science Teacher's Book of Lists, © 1993 by Prentice Hall

LIST 1–27. SOME POISONOUS PLANTS

Most of the hundreds of thousands of known plants are harmless. However, there are hundreds of plants that are poisonous to animals and people. Some cause reactions when touched, such as poison ivy, and some cause sickness or death when eaten, such as foxglove. Only specific parts of some plants are poisonous while other parts may even be edible. All people do not react the same to various plants, just as many have allergies while others do not.

The following lists contain the names of only some of the plants commonly poisonous to people in some way. However, if a plant is not in the list, do not assume that it is therefore safe to handle or eat!

NAME	SCIENTIFIC NAME	SENSITIVITY
Blue thistle	*Echium vulgare*	Common
Cursed crowfoot	*Ranunculus sceleratus*	Common
English ivy	*Hedera helix*	Some individuals
Ginkgo tree, (fruit)	*Ginkgo biloba*	Some individuals
Jack-in-the-pulpit	*Arisaema triphyllum*	Some individuals
Iris	*Iris versicolor*	Some individuals
Moosewood	*Dirca palustris*	Some individuals
Motherwort	*Leonurus cardiaca*	Some individuals
Oleander	*Nerium oleander*	Some individuals
Osage-orange	*Maclura pomifera*	Some individuals
Pawpaw	*Asimina triloba*	Some individuals
Poison ivy	*Rhus toxicodendron*	Common[a]
Poison sumac	*Rhus vernix*	Common
Primrose	*Primula sinensis* and *malacodies*	Some individuals
Scarlet pimpernel	*Anagallis arvensis*	Some individuals
Showy lady's slipper	*Cypripedium reginae*	Some individuals
Stinging nettles	*Urtica dioica*	Common
Tall field buttercup	*Ranunculus acris*	Common
Yellow lady's slipper	*Cypripedium parviflorum*	Some individuals

The Science Teacher's Book of Lists, © 1993 by Prentice Hall

[a]Poison oaks, *Rhus quercifolia* and *diversiloba*, which are similarly poisonous, are considered by many naturalists to be variations or subspecies of poison ivy.

LIST 1–28. EXAMPLES OF PLANTS THAT HAVE POISONOUS PARTS

NAME	SCIENTIFIC NAME	POISONOUS PARTS
Aconite	*Aconitum napellus*	Leaves, roots, seeds
American yew	*Taxus canadensis*	Wood, bark, leaves, seeds
Belladonna	*Atropa belladonna*	Berries
Black nightshade	*Solanum nigrum*	Unripe berries
Castor bean	*Ricinus communis*	All parts
Chokecherry	*Prunus virginiana*	Leaves, seed pits
Christmas berry	*Photina arbutifolia*	Leaves
Climbing bittersweet	*Celastrus scandens*	Leaves, berries
Daphne	*Daphne mezereum*	Bark, leaves, fruit
Death camas	*Zygadenus paniculatus*	All parts
Elderberry	*Sambucus canadensis*	Unripe berries
False jessamine	*Gelsemium sempervirens*	All parts
Fools parsley	*Aethusa cynapium*	Leaves, roots
Foxglove	*Digitalis purpurea*	Leaves, seeds
Goldenseal	*Hydrastis canadensis*	Leaves, roots
Holly	*Ilex opaca*	Berries
Horse chestnut	*Aesculus hippocastanum*	Leaves, seeds
Horse nettle	*Solanum carolinense*	Berries
Indian hemp	*Cannabis sativa*	Leaves, seeds
Iris (blue flag)	*Iris versicolor*	Roots
Japanese yew	*Taxus cuspidata*	Most parts
Jimsonweed	*Datura stramonium*	All parts
Lily-of-the-valley	*Convallaria majalis*	Leaves, flowers, roots
May apple	*Podophyllum peltatum*	Roots, unripe fruit
Mescal bean	*Sophora secundiflora*	Seeds
Mistletoe	*Phoradendron flavescens*	Berries
Moonseed	*Menispermum canadense*	Fruit
Narcissus	*Narcissus poeticus*	Bulbs
Oleander	*Nerium oleander*	Leaves
Poinsettia	*Euphorbia pulcherrima*	Leaves, stem, sap
Poison (water) hemlock	*Conium maculatum*	All parts
Pokeweed	*Phytolacca americana*	Roots, other parts of mature plant
Precatory bean	*Abrus precatorius*	Seeds
Wild black cherry	*Prunus serotina*	Leaves, seed pits

The Science Teacher's Book of Lists, © 1993 by Prentice Hall

LIST 1–29. SOME WILDFLOWERS AND THEIR FAMILIES

NAME	FAMILY	NAME	FAMILY
Black-eyed Susan	Daisy	Rush aster	Daisy
Bloodroot	Poppy	Showy lady's slipper	Orchid
Buffalo clover	Pea	Slender arrowhead	Arrowheads
Caraway	Parsley	Small pond-lily	Lily
Catnip	Mint	Small white lady's slipper	Orchid
Chicory	Daisy	Smooth false foxglove	Snapdragon
Common strawberry	Rose	Spatulated-leaf sundew	Sundew
Common wood sorrel	Wood-sorrel	Spotted wintergreen	Wintergreen
Cowbane	Parsley	Spring Forget-me-not	Forget-me-not
Dutchman's-breeches	Poppy	Solomon's seal	Lily
Dwarf ginseng	Ginseng	Star-of-Bethlehem	Lily
Field pansy	Violet	Swamp honeysuckle	Heath
Garlic mustard	Mustard	Sweet white violet	Violet
Horseradish	Mustard	Three-toothed cinquefoil	Rose
Indian hemp	Dogbane	Trumpets	Pitcher-plant
Indian pipe	Wintergreen	Watercress	Mustard
Ivy-leagued morning glory	Morning glory	Water dragon	Lizard's tail
Jimsonweed	Tomato	White clover	Pea
Labrador-tea	Heath	White milkweed	Milkweed
Lily-of-the-valley	Lily	White trillium	Lily
Mayapple, Mandrake	Barberry	White trout lily	Lily
Moccasin flower	Orchid	White water-buttercup	Buttercup
Pokeweed, poke	Pokeweed	Wild chamomile	Daisy
Prickly pear	Cactus	Wood strawberry	Rose
Queen Ann's lace	Parsley	Yarrow	Daisy
Round-leafed sundew	Sundew	Yucca	Lily

LIST 1–30. SOME COMMON FAMILIES
OF SHRUBS AND WOODY VINES
AND EXAMPLES OF EACH

Arrowwood Family

High cranberry bush
Toothed arrowwood
Sheepberry

Barberry Family

Common barberry

Crowfoot Family

Virgin's bower
Purple clematis

Dogwood Family

Alternate-leafed dogwood
Flowering dogwood

Heath Family

Huckleberry
Mountain blueberry
Mountain cranberry
Rhododendrons
Azaleas

Honeysuckle Family

Swamp honeysuckle
Red-berried elder

Holly Family

Winterberry
Mountain holly

Laurel Family

Spicebush

Oak Family

Green alder
American hazelnut

Pine Family

Common juniper
American yew

Rose Family

Chokeberry
Three-toothed cinquefoil
Red raspberry
Black raspberry

Saxifrage Family

Smooth gooseberry
Red currant

Sumac Family

Poison ivy
Poison sumac

Sweet-gale Family

Sweet fern
Sweet gale

Vine Family

Fox grape
Virginia creeper

Willow Family

Pussy willow
Prairie willow

Witch-hazel Family

Sweet gum
Witch hazel

The Science Teacher's Book of Lists, © 1993 by Prentice Hall

Flowering dogwood

LIST 1–31. WRITING THE SCIENTIFIC NAMES OF PLANTS

When writing the scientific names of plants, scientists generally use the binomial system for naming organisms based on the system developed in the eighteenth century by Carolus Linnaeus, a Swedish botanist whose original name was Carl von Linne. The first part of the name denotes the genus and is written with a capital letter. The second part of the name denotes the species and is written with a lower-case letter. When in type, these words are italicized, as in *Rudbeckia hirta*. When hand-written these words are always underlined.

COMMON NAME	GENUS	+	SPECIES	=	SCIENTIFIC NAME
Aromatic aster	Aster		oblongifolius		*Aster oblongifolius*
Black-eyed Susan	Rudbeckia		hirta		*Rudbeckia hirta*
Catnip	Nepeta		cataria		*Nepeta cataria*
Common buttercup	Ranunculus		acris		*Ranunculus acris*
Common dandelion	Taraxacum		officinale		*Taraxacum officinale*
Common sunflower	Helianthus		annuus		*Helianthus annuus*
Downy yellow violet	Viola		pubescens		*Viola pubescens*
Leafy white orchis	Habenaria		dilatata		*Habenaria dilatata*
Moccasin flower	Cypripedium		acaule		*Cypripedium acaule*
Red clover	Trifolium		pratense		*Trifolium pratense*
Round-leaf sundew	Drosera		rotundifolia		*Drosera rotundifolia*
Showy lady's slipper	Cypripedium		reginae		*Cypripedium reginae*
Small pond-lily	Nuphar		microphyllum		*Nuphar microphyllum*
Snow trillium	Trillium		nivale		*Trillium nivale*
Tumbleweed	Amaranthus		graecizans		*Amaranthus graecizans*
White trout-lily	Erythronium		albidum		*Erythronium albidum*
Wild carrot	Daucus		carota		*Daucus carota*
Wild radish	Raphanus		raphanistrum		*Raphanus raphanistrum*
Yarrow	Achillea		millefolium		*Achillea millefolium*
White oak	Quercus		alba		*Quercus alba*

LIST 1–32. FRANKINCENSE AND MYRRH

Gold, frankincense, and myrrh are known as the gifts that the three kings gave to Jesus on the occasion of His birth. Gold is a precious metal, but what are frankincense and myrrh? They are plant resins, which were valued by everyone for their medical purposes, but affordable by few. In today's values, frankincense is worth about $500 a pound and myrrh about $4,000 a pound! Truly, the gift of kings.*

Frankincense

- Listed in the Egyptian Papyrus Ebers, a list of prescriptions, dated 1500 B.C.

- Resin from scrubby, camel-high trees, best source, *Boswellia carteri*.

- Trees grow in northeast Africa and southwest Arabia.

- Tree grows best in limestone soil.

- Best comes from Oman desert.

- To harvest, gashes are made in the bark. A milky sap oozes out to cover each gash and hardens in about a week.

- Pale-colored sap tastes sweet.

- One tree can yield about 10 pounds of resin per year.

- Egyptians burned the resin in homes and temples and chewed it to heal sore gums.

- Chinese used it to treat respiratory illnesses.

- Romans made an oil for treatment of skin problems including wounds.

- Modern research shows that the resin has antiseptic, antifungal, and anti-inflammatory properties and contains flavonoids which dilate the bronchi in the lungs.

Myrrh

- Listed in the Egyptian Papyrus Ebers.

- Resin from a shaggy, thorn tree, best source, *Commiphora myrrha*.

- Trees grow in northeast Africa, southwest Arabia, and India.

- Tree grows best in basaltic soil.

- Has a wide range.

- To harvest, dark-colored globules of sap, which form to protect cracks in the brittle bark, are gathered.

- Dark-colored sap tastes bitter.

- Egyptians used resin to embalm royal mummies.

- Chinese mixed it with mother's milk for diaper rash.

- Romans added it to perfumes.

- Modern research indicates that extracts from Indian myrrh might be helpful in preventing arteriosclerosis and heart disease and lowering cholesterol and weight.

*Adapted from "Three Wise Gifts," Donna Johnson, *National Wildlife Magazine*, National Wildlife Federation, Vienna, Virginia, December–January 1992.

The Science Teacher's Book of Lists, © 1993 by Prentice Hall

LIST 1–33. SOME PLANT SUPERLATIVES

- **Biggest cactus:** Saguaro cactus of the Arizona and Mexican deserts; grows to a height of 16m (52.4 ft.)
- **Tallest tree:** Coast Redwood in California; a height of 111.6 m (365 ft.)
- **Tree with largest circumference:** Banyan tree of India and Ceylon has a main trunk that is 30 feet in circumference and has about 230 smaller trunks; the multiple trunks of one tree can cover an area of about 1,000 square feet.
- **World's Largest Banyan Tree:** Shades Lahaina's town square in Maui, Hawaii.
- **Tree with the largest single trunk:** Baobab of Africa has a tree trunk that reaches a diameter of more than 30 feet. It grows to a height of 60 feet.
- **Largest seed:** Palm trees; those of the Seychelles Islands weigh up to 50 lbs.
- **Oldest tree:** Bristlecone pines of California and Nevada, about 5,000 years old.

ANIMALS

LIST 2-1. INTRODUCTION TO THE FIVE KINGDOMS

For hundreds of years scientists have classified living organisms into two groups, plants and animals. But the electron microscope has provided observations that demonstrate that living organisms are more diverse and do not neatly fit into one of two groups. The most widely used system of classification, the Five Kingdoms, is based upon the work of R.H. Whittaker. As new observations occur, one can expect modifications to this system of classification.

KINGDOM	DESCRIPTION	EXAMPLES
1. Prokaryotae (Monera)	Single cell with nuclear material scattered due to lack of nuclear membrane	Bacteria
2. Protista	Single cell with a membrane-bound nucleus	Algae, protozoa, slime molds, water molds
3. Fungi	Unicellular or multicellular, cannot move, cannot make food; absorbs food from other organisms, living or dead	Mushrooms, molds, yeasts
4. Animalia	Many specialized cells which work together; obtain food from plants, animals, or both	Vertebrate, invertebrate
5. Plantae	Many specialized cells with chlorophyll; chemically produce their own food	Mosses, ferns, cone-bearing plants, flowering plants

LIST 2–2. THE FIVE KINGDOMS OF LIVING ORGANISMS

For the purposes of study and identification, scientists classify living organisms into kingdoms based on physical characteristics, behavior, and place in nature. Before the development of modern microscopes, scientists classified the living world into two kingdoms, Plants and Animals. During the 1960s, new information gained about organisms by biochemical and electron-microscopical investigations indicated a need for more than two kingdoms. The five-kingdom system developed by Robert H. Whittaker in 1959 gained support. Generally speaking, biologists currently classify all organisms into one of five kingdoms. The classification system continues to be modified as technology permits closer observations of organisms.

Animalia Kingdom (Animals)

- Animals are made up of many cells which form tissues, organs, and complex systems.
- Animal cells lack a cell wall, but are surrounded by plasma membranes.
- Animals cannot make their own food.
- Animals get energy by eating plants, animals, or both.
- Most animals can move by muscular contraction.
- Generally speaking, animals can reproduce their own kind.
- All animals carry out life processes to survive.
- Examples: insects, jellyfish, birds, fish, amphibians, reptiles, mammals.

Plantae Kingdom (Plants)

- Plants are made up of cells.
- Plant cells have cell walls made of cellulose.
- Plants make their own food through the process of photosynthesis.
- Most plants cannot move on their own.
- Plants have multicellular reproductive organs.
- Plants pass through distinct developmental stages.
- Within the plant kingdom, plants are grouped into two groups: bryophytes, or nonvascular plants, and tracheophytes, or vascular plants. Mosses are examples of nonvascular plants, maple trees, pine trees, blackberry bushes, daisies, and daffodils are examples of vascular plants.

Fungi Kingdom (Fungus)

- Fungi are made up of one cell or many cells.
- Fungus cells have cell walls.

The Science Teacher's Book of Lists, © 1993 by Prentice Hall

(Continued)

LIST 2-2. (Continued)

- Fungi cannot make their own food.
- Fungi get food from other living organisms.
- Fungi are decomposers.
- Some fungi are parasites.
- Examples: molds and yeasts.

Protista Kingdom (Protists)

- Protists are one-celled or simple multicellular organisms.
- They live in water or in moist places.
- Most protists require a lens or microscope to be seen.
- Some protists are animal-like, without a cell wall, such as amoebas.
- Some protists are plant-like, with a cell wall, such as diatoms.
- Some protists are both plant-like and animal-like, such as *Euglena*.
- Examples: protozoa, water molds, slime molds, green algae, red algae.

Prokaryotae Kingdom—Formerly Monera Kingdom (Moneran)

- Prokaryotae (Monerans) are one-celled organisms that lack a nuclear membrane but have nuclear material throughout the cytoplasm.
- Prokaryotae can be seen only with the aid of a microscope.
- Some are photosynthetic.
- Most live off soil or water which contain organic components.
- Some are parasitic.
- Examples: bacteria, blue-green algae.

The Science Teacher's Book of Lists, © 1993 by Prentice Hall

NOTE: Viruses are not yet classified. They do not reproduce themselves; the host cell reproduces them. They do not metabolize, they are not made of cells as all living organisms are, and not all have DNA. On the other hand, they do exhibit the mechanics of genetic adaptation, which is suggestive of life. Consequently, their living status is highly questionable.

LIST 2–3. MOLLUSK CLASSIFICATION

The six major classes of living mollusks, soft-bodied animals lacking joints and sometimes possessing an internal or external shell, are:

GROUP	COMMENT
1. Gastropoda (univalves)	Possess one shell. Examples: conch, snails, murex, cones, limpets, periwinkles, whelks.
2. Bivalvia (bivalves)	Possess two shells. Examples; oysters, clams, cockles, mussels, scallops.
3. Cephalopoda	Possess an internal shell and a strong beak-like mouth. Examples: octopus, squid, nautilus.
4. Amphineura	Have a segmented shell. Known as coat-of-mail shells. Example: chitons.
5. Scaphopoda	Also called tusk shells.
6. Monoplacophora	Have flat, bilateral symmetry; a primitive form. Also called gastroverms.

An octopus

A volute

The Science Teacher's Book of Lists, © 1993 by Prentice Hall

LIST 2–4. EXAMPLES OF MAJOR ANIMAL GROUPINGS

Scientists have divided the animal kingdom into groups and subgroups based on physical traits and behavior. Accordingly, the animal kingdom is divided into groups or subkingdoms, called phyla. Each phylum is divided into classes. Classes are divided into orders. Orders are divided into families. Families are divided into genera. Each genus is divided into species. Examples:

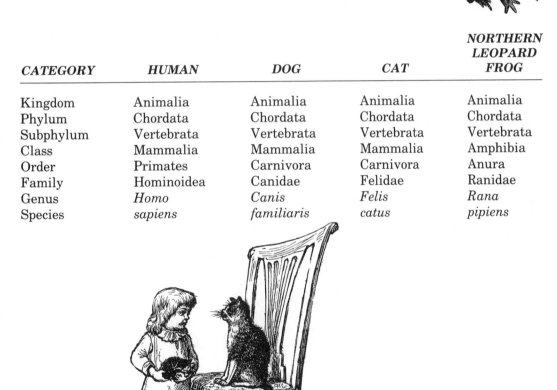

CATEGORY	HUMAN	DOG	CAT	NORTHERN LEOPARD FROG
Kingdom	Animalia	Animalia	Animalia	Animalia
Phylum	Chordata	Chordata	Chordata	Chordata
Subphylum	Vertebrata	Vertebrata	Vertebrata	Vertebrata
Class	Mammalia	Mammalia	Mammalia	Amphibia
Order	Primates	Carnivora	Carnivora	Anura
Family	Hominoidea	Canidae	Felidae	Ranidae
Genus	*Homo*	*Canis*	*Felis*	*Rana*
Species	*sapiens*	*familiaris*	*catus*	*pipiens*

LIST 2–5. WRITING THE SCIENTIFIC NAMES OF ANIMALS

The scientific name of an animal or plant is made up of two "Latinized" words. The first word names the genus to which the animal belongs. This is the generic name and is written with a capital letter. The second word identifies the species to which the animal belongs. It begins with a lower case letter. The genus and species names are always underlined when written by hand and italicized when printed. This system of naming plants and animals by a two-word name to identify the genus and species was a contribution of Carolus Linnaeus (1707–1778), a Swedish botanist whose original name was Carl von Linne.

COMMON NAME	GENUS	+	SPECIES	=	SCIENTIFIC NAME
Human	Homo	+	sapiens	=	*Homo sapiens*
Dog	Canis	+	familiaris	=	*Canis familiaris*
Cat	Felis	+	catus	=	*Felis catus*
Spanish lynx	Felis	+	pardina	=	*Felis pardina*
Tiger	Panthera	+	tigris	=	*Panthera tigris*
Jaguar	Panthera	+	onca	=	*Panthera onca*
Leopard	Panthera	+	pardus	=	*Panthera pardus*
Bullfrog	Rana	+	catesbeiana	=	*Rana catesbeiana*
Cameroon toad	Bufo	+	superciliaris	=	*Bufo superciliaris*
Houston toad	Bufo	+	houstonensis	=	*Bufo houstonensis*
Nile crocodile	Crocodylus	+	niloticus	=	*Crocodylus niloticus*
Caiman	Caiman	+	crocodilus	=	*Caiman crocodilus*
Jamaican boa	Epicrates	+	subflavus	=	*Epicrates subflavus*
Puerto Rican boa	Epicrates	+	inornatus	=	*Epicrates inornatus*
Jamaican iguana	Cyclura	+	collei	=	*Cyclura collei*
Mona iguana	Cyclura	+	stejnegeri	=	*Cyclura stejnegeri*
Desert monitor	Varanus	+	griseus	=	*Varanus griseus*
Komodo dragon	Varanus	+	komodoensis	=	*Varanus komodoensis*
Aquatic box turtle	Terrapene	+	coahuila	=	*Terrapene coahuila*
Peregrine falcon	Falco	+	peregrinus	=	*Falco peregrinus*
Piping plover	Charadrius	+	melodus	=	*Charadrius melodus*
Audouin's gull	Larus	+	audouinii	=	*Larus audouinii*
Relict gull	Larus	+	relictus	=	*Larus relictus*
Crayfish	Cambarus	+	zophonastes	=	*Cambarus zophonastes*
Tooth cave spider	Leptoneta	+	myopica	=	*Leptoneta myopica*
Snail darter fish	Percina	+	tanasi	=	*Percina tanasi*

LIST 2–6. ANIMAL FAMILY NAMES

ANIMAL	*PLURAL*	*MALE*	*FEMALE*	*YOUNG*	*GROUP*
Bear	Bears	Boar	Sow	Cub	Sloth
Buffalo	Buffaloes	Bull	Cow	Calf	Herd
Cat	Cats	Tom	Queen	Kitten	Clowder
Cow	Cattle	Bull	Cow	Calf	Herd
Chicken	Chickens	Rooster	Hen	Chick	Flock
Goose	Geese	Gander	Goose	Gosling	Flock
Deer	Deer	Buck	Doe	Fawn	Herd
Dog	Dogs	Dog	Bitch	Pup	Pack
Duck	Ducks	Drake	Duck	Duckling	Flock
Elephant	Elephants	Bull	Cow	Calf	Herd
Fox	Foxes	Reynard	Vixen	Pup	Skulk
Goat	Goats	Billy	Nanny	Kid	Herd
Horse	Horses	Stallion	Mare	Foal/colt	Herd
Kangaroo	Kangaroos	Buck	Doe	Joey	Mob
Lion	Lions	Lion	Lioness	Cub	Pride
Moose	Moose	Bull	Cow	Calf	Herd
Pig	Pigs/swine	Boar	Sow	Piglet	Sounder
Seal	Seals	Bull	Cow	Calf	Pod
Whale	Whales	Bull	Cow	Calf	Pod/Gam

LIST 2–7. ANIMAL FAMILY AND GROUPING BEHAVIOR

Animals live in families, herds, or groups or as solitary individuals depending upon which grouping behavior that has developed as the most efficient way for that animal to survive, reproduce, and raise young. Listed below are types of animal families and grouping behaviors with some specific examples.

NAME OF BEHAVIOR	EXPLANATION OF BEHAVIOR	TYPICAL ANIMALS
Solitary	Male and female live alone except during mating season.	Leopards; bears; pandas; raccoons; bullhead fish; many snakes
Pair	Pair stays together, raise young.	Most bird species; beavers; jackals; foxes; gibbons; nesting fish, cichlids
Family	An extension of the pair; young stay with parents until they are fully or nearly grown, but leave or are driven away to form their own group when they mature.	Chimpanzees
Harem	One dominant male with several females	Monkeys; fur seals; deer; hamadryas baboons
Matriarchy	Females and young stay together, males are allowed in the group during the mating season only; one dominant female.	Elephants
Oligarchy	Strong, powerful males protect shared females and young.	Common baboons
Arena	All-male group; males display in an "arena" for females.	Birds such as Ruffs and Black Grouse
Hierarchy or pecking order	Individuals rise to the top of the group.	Wolves
Aggregation	Huge gatherings, usually for migration sometimes for hibernation	Wildebeest; salmon; Canada geese; zebras; caterpillars; many hibernating snakes
Caste System	Division of labor	Ants; bees; termites; wasps

Adapted from: Morris, Desmond, *Animal Watching*, Crown Publishers, New York, 1990.

LIST 2-8. ANIMALS WITH MISLEADING COMMON NAMES

The common name of many animals can be misleading!

Ceylon frogmouth—*Batrachostomus moniliger*, is a bird.

Flying fish—*Parexocoetus mesogaster*, do not fly, but glide.

Flying squirrels—*Idiurus zenkeri* do not fly, but jump and glide.

John Dory—*Zeus faber*, is a fish.

Killer whales—are not whales, but dolphins.

Koala bears—*Phascolarctos cinereus*, are not bears, but marsupials.

Galliwasp—*Diploglossus lessorae*, is not a wasp but a lizard.

Giant panda bears—*Ailuropoda melanoleuca*, were once thought to be bears, but are now considered to be more closely related to raccoons than bears. They are now referred to as giant pandas.

Glass snake—*Ophisaurus apodus*, is not a snake, but a lizard.

Groundhogs—*Marmota monax*, are not hogs. "Groundhog" is another name for the woodchuck, a rodent.

Guinea pigs—*Cavia cobaya*, are not pigs, but rodents.

Horned toad—*Phrymosoma cornutum*, is not a toad. It is a lizard.

Mudpuppy—or water dog, *Necturus maculosus*, is not a puppy or a dog, but an amphibian.

Nightjars—make up a family of specialized nocturnal birds, including the Common Poor-will. There are about 67 species.

Prairie dogs—*Cynomys ludovicianus*, are not dogs, but rodents related to woodchucks.

Red bishop—*Euplectes orix*, is a bird belonging to the weaver family.

Roach—*Rutilus rutilus*, is one of the cypriniform fishes.

Sandfish—*Scincus philbyi*, is not a fish but a desert skink, a type of lizard.

Sea cows—are not cows but any of several sea mammals, such as the dugong or manatee.

Sea cucumbers—*Stichopus californicus*, are not cucumbers or plants. They are a group of echinoderms (small sea animals with hard, spiny shells) with bodies shaped like cucumbers.

Seahorse—*Hippocampus obtusus*, is not a horse, but a small semitropical fish.

Slowworm—*Anguis fragilis*, is not a worm, but a lizard.

Starfish—*Asterias forbesi*, are not fish. They belong to a group of invertebrates known as echinoderms.

Striped burrfish toad—*Chilomycterus schoepfi*, is not a toad but a fish.

(Continued)

LIST 2–8. (Continued)

Tasmanian devil—*Sarcophilus harrisi*, is a marsupial

Titmouse—is not a mouse, but a bird. There are the tufted titmouse, *Parus bicolor*, the plain titmouse, *Parus inornatus*, and bridled titmouse, *Parus wollweberi*.

Weedy seadragon—*Phyllopteryx taeniolatus*, is a type of seahorse.

Winged dragon—*Pegasus volitans*, is not a dragon, but a fish.

LIST 2–9. PLAYING POSSUM

In the animal world there is a wide variety of survival techniques. One interesting and seemingly dangerous survival technique that has been observed is that of "playing possum" or playing dead. The threatened animal suddenly collapses and remains still even when poked or bitten. Only when the threat is gone will the "actor" flee to safety.

The term "playing possum" comes from the American opossum, which is well known for playing dead. Opossums have been observed to remain perfectly still even when bitten hard. Some other animals that have been observed playing possum are:

African ground squirrel
Eastern hognose snake
Bullfrog
Chameleons
Grass snake
Small boa constrictors
Some beetles
Some grasshoppers

Stick insects
Some spiders
Some toads
South American foxes
West Indian wood snake

Playing possum

The Science Teacher's Book of Lists, © 1993 by Prentice Hall

LIST 2–10. REGENERATION, THE ABILITY TO REPLACE INJURED OR LOST PARTS

If a person suffers the loss of an arm or leg, the human body cannot grow a new one. Mammals and birds do not have the ability to regenerate lost parts. But some other members of the animal kingdom have the ability to regenerate lost or injured organs or appendages. Some examples are:

- Crabs
- Crocodiles are able to regenerate the tip of a lost tail.
- Hydra
- Lizards are able to sacrifice a tail or skin to escape predators and regrow a new one.
- The natural ligature salamander loses its tail, which contains a poison gland, and can regrow a new tail.
- Planaria, flat worms
- Sea slugs
- Skinks and geckos are lizards which are able to shed their skin when held by a predator, leaving the predator with a mouthful of empty skin!
- Starfish can generate new arms. If an arm is severed from the starfish but is attached to a piece of the body, the arm can generate a starfish.
- Worms

A starfish regenerates an appendage

LIST 2–11. TRUE HIBERNATORS

"True hibernators" are usually defined as those animals which adapt to the shortage of food and low temperatures in winter by lowering their body temperatures to near-freezing and entering a near comatose state. Thus, they live off of fat stored for winter and cope with shortages of food and winter weather. They are:

Bat

- Bats
- Chipmunks
- Shrews
- Small rodents
- Some snakes
- Some turtles
- Woodchucks

What About Bears?

Unlike "true hibernators," which lower their body temperatures to a near-freezing comatose state, polar, grizzly, and black bears lower their body temperatures only a few degrees. This enables them to rouse themselves when their cozy winter's sleep is threatened by an intruder.

Bears devote spring and summer to feeding. A well-fed bear improves its chances of surviving the sparse food supplies of winter. Female bears need extra calories because they give birth and nurse cubs during winter.

According to naturalist and author Jeff Fair, many experts on bear hibernation generally define hibernation as "an adaptation to periods of food shortage and low environmental temperatures." A more traditional definition explains hibernation as a dormant state of decreased metabolism in which some animals pass periods of food shortage and low environmental temperatures.

Thus, whether one considers a bear a "true hibernator" depends on one's definition of hibernation.

The Science Teacher's Book of Lists, © 1993 by Prentice Hall

LIST 2–12. ANIMALS WITH PROTECTIVE PLATES, ARMOR, SPINES, OR POINTS

A variety of animal species have evolved an interesting array of "armor" for protection against predators, including man. Here are some examples.

Crab

ANIMAL	PROTECTION
Alligator	Armored scales, powerful tail and jaws
Armadillo	Armor made of horny, hinged upper covering
Armadillo lizard	Spiked armor
Bivalves (mussels, clams, oysters, etc.)	Two hard shells and a strong muscle to hold the two shells closed
Blowfish	Spines
Caiman	Armored skin, powerful jaws and tail
Crab	Armored outer shell, powerful claws.
Crocodile	Plates of bone covered with tough, horny skin, powerful tail and jaws
Echidna (spiny anteater)	Strong, sharp spikes
Elephant	Strong, one-inch thick skin, tusks
Gavial	Armored skin, powerful tail and jaws
Hedgehog	Seven thousand sharp, long, barbed quills
Hero shrew	Armored backbone that can withstand the weight of a full-grown man, even though its body is only 6 inches long
Lobster	Strong outer shell, powerful claws
Mountain devil lizard	Spines
Pangolin (scaly anteaters)	Armor made of large, overlapping scales
Porcupine fish	Spiny scales
Rhinoceros	Thick, tough skin forms armored plates, horn(s)
Spiny catfish	Spines
Spiny mouse	Spines
Spiny pocket mouse	Sharp spines
Spiny rat	Sharp spines
Spiny sea urchin	Ball of sharp spines
Snails	One hard, tough shell
Tenrec (greater hedgehog)	Fine spines that are erected as the animal rolls into a ball
Thorny devil lizard	Sharp, strong spikes
Turtles	Armored shells; some have spikes
Univalves	One hard shell
Wild boar	Tusks

LIST 2–13. SEXUAL REPRODUCTION

Sexual reproduction means the union of egg from a female and sperm from a male. This sexual union usually results in a new individual that genetically possesses characteristics of each parent rather than being exactly like one parent. There are different types of sexual reproduction:

1. Internal Fertilization: The female carries the eggs inside her body, the male penetrates the female's reproductive system and deposits his sperm. The sperm fertilizes an egg, forming a zygote. Depending on the species, the zygote develops inside the female until it is developed enough to live outside the female's body in the case of mammals or is encased in an eggshell, after which the female lays her egg as in the case of birds and most reptiles. Examples of animals that reproduce by internal fertilization:

- Mammals
- Birds
- Some fish
- Reptiles

2. External Fertilization: The female deposits eggs and the male disperses sperm over them; or both male and female release their gametes, or reproductive cells, in proximity of each other. Fertilization takes place in water. This fertilization usually results in individuals that have genetic characteristics of both parents and are usually able to care for themselves upon hatching. Examples of animals that reproduce by external fertilization:

- Amphibians
- Clams
- Barnacles
- Some fish
- Colonial coelenterates
- Tunicates
- A common jellyfish or medusa, which (in the polyp stage) can also reproduce by asexual budding.

3. Cross-Fertilization: Cross-fertilization requires two individuals each having both male and female reproductive organs. Animals with both female and male sex organs are known as hermaphrodites. Two hermaphrodites position themselves side by side and exchange sperm. Examples of animals that reproduce by cross-fertilization are:

- Earthworms
- Marine annelids
- Green hydras (can also reproduce by budding)
- Planerians
- Snails
- Most sponges

4. Self-Fertilization: Some animals that have both male and female reproductive organs (hermaphrodites) are capable of getting their own sperm to their own eggs. However, not all hermaphrodites are capable of self-fertilization. This is a necessary adaptation for animals that live solitary lives, such as:

- Tapeworms
- Green hydras

The Science Teacher's Book of Lists, © 1993 by Prentice Hall

LIST 2–14. ASEXUAL REPRODUCTION

Asexual reproduction means reproduction without sex; there is no union of sperm and egg. In asexual reproduction, the offspring is usually a copy of the one parent. There are different types of asexual reproduction:

1. Fission: The parent divides into two animals. Example:

- *Trichoplax adhaerens*, the simplest of animals, reproduces both sexually and asexually; large trichoplaxes simply divide by fission into two animals

2. Budding: A small part of the parent's body separates from the rest, forming a new individual or colony. Examples:

- Green hydra, can also reproduce by cross-fertilization
- *Aurelia*, a common jellyfish known as the medusa, can also reproduce by external fertilization by releasing eggs and sperm in water.

LIST 2–15. REPRODUCTIVE CYCLE
FOR MAMMALS

1. A sperm fertilizes an egg.
2. The fertilized egg develops into a zygote.
3. The zygote develops into an embryo.
4. The embryo develops into a fetus.
5. A baby is born.
6. The baby grows into a child.
7. The child grows into an adolescent (sub-adult in nonhumans).
8. The adolescent becomes an adult.
9. Adults and most adolescents are capable of beginning the cycle by mating.

LIST 2–16. STAGES OF COMPLETE METAMORPHOSIS

Some insects, such as the monarch butterfly, follow a developmental pattern known as complete metamorphosis, during which they undergo four major developmental stages.

1. Adult female lays a fertilized egg.
2. The fertilized egg develops into a larva.
3. The larva changes into a pupa.
4. An adult emerges from the pupa.
5. The adult begins the cycle again by mating.

Swallowtail

LIST 2–17. STAGES OF INCOMPLETE METAMORPHOSIS

Some insects, such as the chinch bug, follow a developmental pattern with fewer stages than those which go through complete metamorphosis. This development in three or fewer stages is known as incomplete metamorphosis.

1. Adult female lays a fertilized egg.
2. A nymph hatches from the egg. It is generally a small version of the adult.
3. An adult, which results from the growth of the nymph, develops wings and by stages becomes capable of beginning the cycle of life anew.

The Science Teacher's Book of Lists, © 1993 by Prentice Hall

LIST 2–18. COLORFUL WARNINGS: PREDATOR BEWARE

Most animals are marked in such a way that they blend in with their surroundings. This provides them with a form of protective coloring that helps them survive as a species. Why then are there many animals with bright, colorful markings? Colorful markings help some species attract a mate and help others blend in with colorful surroundings, but most often bright, colorful markings serve as a warning to predators. The colors yellow, orange, black, red, and blue are frequently the colors displayed by many animals with stings, poison glands, or venomous bites.

- Butterfly: monarch
- Caterpillar: monarch
- Frogs: Kokoi frogs (also known as poison-arrow frogs)
- Fish: lionfish, stingrays, and wasp fish
- Jellyfish: Portuguese man-of-war
- Lizards: beaded lizard, gila monster
- Oriental fire-bellied toad
- Sea slugs and many of the marine mollusks without external shells
- Snakes: coral snakes, sea-snakes of the Indo-Pacific region
- Spiders: the most dangerous is the black widow, with her red hourglass
- Wasps

Sea slug

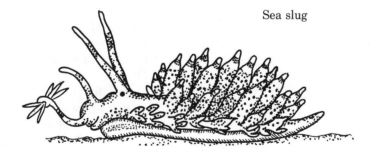

LIST 2–19. VENOMOUS AND POISONOUS ANIMALS

Venomous animals are those that have glands which produce a venom or poison which is transmitted to its prey chiefly through biting or stinging. These animals use their venom to immobilize prey which they can consume immediately or later. The major use of the venom is for obtaining food, but these animals will use their venom for self-defense, particularly if cornered.

Poisonous animals have poisons on or in their bodies. The poison is transmitted when the poisonous animal is touched, bitten, or ingested. Generally, poisonous animals do not use their poison to obtain food.

There are over 400 venomous snakes, about 500 "poison-tongue" cone shells, eight genera of deadly scorpions, and thousands of other known poisonous animals, as well as many animals whose poisons are not understood. It is impossible to provide a comprehensive list here. Therefore, do not assume that if an animal's name is absent from this list, it is safe to handle and is not venomous or poisonous to humans.

EXAMPLES OF VENOMOUS ANIMALS

Box jellyfish or sea wasp
Cone shells, mollusks
  Textile cone
  Worm-eater cone shells
  Fish-eater cone shells
Duck-billed platypus (male has spurs
  connected to venom glands)
Blue-ringed octopus
Portuguese man-of-war
Sea slugs
Scorpions
Snakes
  Asian kraits
  Australian tiger snakes
  Boomslang
  Cobras
  Copperheads
  Coral snakes
  Mambas
  Rattlesnakes
  Sidewinders
  Sea snakes
  Taipans
  Vine snake
Short-tailed shrew
Spiders
  Black widow, female
  Brown recluse
Lizards
  Gila monster
  Mexican beaded lizard

EXAMPLES OF POISONOUS ANIMALS

Crown-of-thorns starfish
Fish
  Lionfish
  Scorpionfish
  Stonefish
  Toadfish
Golden arrow-poison frog
Kokoi frogs (poison-arrow frog)
Lizards
Marine ribbon worms
Red sponge
Red Pacific salamander
Toads
  Buff marine toad
  Bufo toads
  Spadefoot toads
Salamanders

Snake with
fangs that
inject venom

LIST 2–20. LITTER SIZE, GESTATION PERIOD, AND HABITAT OF SOME WILD DOGS

Dogs belong to the order carnivora. That is, they are generally carnivorous, or flesh-eating predators. They belong to the *Canidae* family. Canids possess physical characteristics which enable them to hunt. They have a muscular, long-legged body, which is built for a high-speed chase over a short distance and for endurance on a long-distance hunt. Their large, triangular ears (which can turn without moving the head) provide a keen sense of hearing. Dogs also have an excellent sense of smell. Some canines hunt in packs (the wolf and African hunting dog); others hunt alone (the fox). Males and females usually look alike, with the male being slightly larger than the female. Dogs have claws that are not retractable.

WILD DOG	PUPS/LITTER	GESTATION PERIOD	HABITAT
Arctic fox	4–11	51–57 days	Tundra, woodland
Coyote	3–10	63–65 days	Prairie, woodland
Dhole	2–6	63 days	Forest, woodland
Dingo	4–5	63 days	Desert, forest
Fennec fox	2–5	50–51 days	Desert, semi-desert
Gray wolf	3–8	63 days	Tundra, steppe, woodland, forest
Hunting dog of Africa	2–16	69–72 days	Savanna, plains, semi-desert, mountains
Maned wolf	1–5	About 60 days	Grassland, swamp edge
Raccoon dog	6–8	About 60 days	Forest, near rivers and lakes
Red fox	4	51–63 days	Woodland, open country

A fox

LIST 2–21. LITTER SIZE, GESTATION PERIOD, AND HABITAT OF SOME WILD CATS

Cats belong to the order Carnivora, flesh-eating predators, and the Felidae family. There is considerable disagreement about the organization of the cat family. All cats possess physical characteristics for hunting. They have a body that is muscular and flexible, and they possess excellent senses of hearing and smell. Cats generally overpower their prey and kill it with a bite to the neck. Some hunt in groups (lions); some hunt alone (panthers). Large cats roar and do not purr; small cats purr and do not roar. Offspring of the domestic cats can and do survive in the wild. These are known as "feral" cats. Most cats have retractable claws; the cheetah is an exception.

WILD CATS	CUBS/LITTER	GESTATION PERIOD	HABITAT
Bobcat	1–6	About 50 days	Chaparral, brush swamp, forest
Caracal	2–3	About 70 days	Savanna, plains
Cheetah	2–4	91–95 days	Open country, desert, savanna
Clouded leopard	1–5	86–92 days	Forest
Jaguar	1–4	93–105 days	Forest, savanna
Leopard	1–6	90–112 days	Desert, forest, plains, mountain
Lion	1–6	102–113 days	Savanna
Lynx	2–3	About 63 days	Coniferous forest, scrub
Mountain lion	2–4	92–96 days	Mountains, forest, swamp, grassland
Ocelot	2–4	About 70 days	Humid forest, brush, marsh
Pallas's cat	5–6	Not known	Steppe, desert, mountainside
Pampas cat	1–3	About 70 days	Grassland, forest
Serval	1–4	67–77 days	Savanna, plains, woodland
Snow leopard	2–5	98–103 days	Mountainside, forest
Wild cat	2–3	63–69 days	Forest, scrub, savanna, plains, semi-desert

A cheetah

The Science Teacher's Book of Lists, © 1993 by Prentice Hall

LIST 2–22. BIRDS THAT DON'T FLY

All birds are warm-blooded and possess feathers and wings, but not all birds can use their wings to fly. Most ornithologists, scientists who study birds, theorize that all birds could originally fly. But some birds no longer needed to fly to survive and became flightless. Here are some names of birds that do not fly. Ornithologists usually capitalize the first letter of all parts of a bird's name.

Ostrich

Ostriches, which are the largest living birds. They can run up to 27 miles per hour. The American Ostrich looks like the African Ostrich but is smaller and has three toes rather than two.
Emu—six foot tall, non-flying, Australian bird.
The Brown Kiwi
The Gray Kiwi
The South Island Kiwi
Cassowaries—large, strong birds that can disembowel a lion with their spiked toe.

The Great Auk, now extinct

Takahe

Giant Wood Rail

Common Moorhen

Water Rail

Corncrake

Penguins

Flightless Cormorant

Flightless Grebe

Owl Parrot—(also known as Kakapo)

Great Auk (extinct)—It lived until the mid 1800s, when the last two known Great Auks were shot and killed.

Dodo (extinct)—It was a large land bird with hooked bill and short neck and legs. It was slow and fearless.

Elephant Bird (extinct)—It was larger than an Ostrich.

Moa (extinct)—It was a large, long-necked bird, native to New Zealand.

LIST 2–23. PENGUINS

Penguins are aquatic birds that use their wings to "fly" underwater. These flightless birds have developed in an interesting variety. Penguins are near-sighted and have almost no binocular vision. Most live in Antarctica; all live in the southern hemisphere. Here is a list of names and characteristics of some Penguins:*

Adelie Penguins—are very sociable, are usually seen in groups, are curious, and lack fear of people.

Black-Footed (Jackass) **Penguins**—make a braying sound similar to a jackass.

Chinstrap Penguins—have the marking of a black strap under the chin.

Emperor Penguins—are the largest of the Penguin family.

Erect-Crested Penguins—have a bright yellow erect crest.

Fjordland Crested Penguins—have a yellow crest and red eyes.

Galapagos Penguins—are one of the rarest and smallest of Penguins. They live on the Galapagos Islands, which means it lives farther north than any of the other Penguins.

Gentoo Penguins—live in small groups, prefer nests of grass rather than rocks.

King Penguins—are striking and sleek, each with outstanding gold markings about its head, bill, and bib.

Littler Blue (Fairy) **Penguins**—are the smallest and only nocturnal Penguins. They are the only ones that nest in Australia.

Macaroni Penguins—have yellow feathery "eyebrows" and red eyes and nest on rocky hillsides.

Magellanic Penguins—are named after Ferdinand Magellan. They nest in underground burrows.

Rock Hopper Penguins—have red eyes and spiked feathers on their heads. They hop from rock to rock when on land.

Snares Island Penguins—possess bright yellow crests on each side of their heads and have red eyes.

Yellow Eyed (Cookie) **Penguins**—are about thirty inches tall, and are the only penguins that do not live in colonies.

The Science Teacher's Book of Lists, © 1993 by Prentice Hall

Adapted from: Gorman, James, *The Total Penguin*, Prentice Hall Press, New York, 1990.

LIST 2-24. RAPTORS, BIRDS OF PREY

Raptors, or birds of prey, are generally birds with a strong notched beak, sharp talons, excellent vision, and strong wings, such as eagles, hawks, owls, and vultures (although some vultures lack strong grasping talons and they only rarely take live prey).

Raptors range in size from small falcons and owls that are no bigger than a sparrow to the 4-foot-long Andean Condor with a wingspan of 10 feet. Their styles of flight include the spectacular soaring of eagles and vultures, the noiseless flight of owls, and the 200-miles-per-hour dive of the Peregrine Falcon. There are over 200 species of hawks which are diurnal (hunt by day), and about 135 species of owls, which are nocturnal (hunt by night). Most owls and hawks regurgitate pellets of fur, bones, and other undigestible matter from their prey. When writing names of birds, ornithologists capitalize all parts of the common name.

When writing the scientific name, the standard procedure is to capitalize the name of the genus but not the name of the species. Underline both when handwriting and italicize both when printing.

COMMON NAME	SCIENTIFIC NAME	SIZE IN LENGTH
American Kestrel	*Falco sparverius*	9–12 in. (23–30 cm)
Andean Condor	*Vultur gryphus*	4 ft. (120 cm)
Bald Eagle	*Haliaeetus leucocephalus*	30–43 in. (75–108 cm)
Barn Owl	*Tyto alba*	14–20 in. (35–50 cm)
Barred Owl	*Strix varia*	17–24 in. (43–60 cm)
Bateleur	*Terathopius ecaudatus*	25 in. (63 cm)
Crested Caracara	*Caracara cheriway*	20–25 in. (50–63 cm)
Egyptian Vulture	*Neophron percnopterus*	25 in. (63 cm)
Elf Owl	*Micrathene whitneyi*	6 in. (15 cm)
Everglade Kite	*Rostrhamus sociabilis*	17–19 in. (43–48 cm)
Golden Eagle	*Aquila chrysaetos*	30–40 in. (75–100 cm)
Great Grey Owl	*Strix nebulosa*	24–33 in. (60–83 cm)
Great Horned Owl	*Bubo virginianus*	18–25 in. (45–63 cm)
Harpy Eagle	*Harpia harpyja*	3 ft. (90 cm)
Long-Eared Owl	*Asio otus*	13–16 in. (33–40 cm)
Marsh Hawk	*Circus cyaneus*	17.5–24 in. (44–60 cm)
Osprey	*Pandion haliaetus*	21–24.5 in. (53–61 cm)
Peregrine Falcon	*Falco peregrinus*	15–20 in. (38–50 cm)
Prairie Falcon	*Falco mexicanus*	17 in. (43 cm)
Red-Tailed Hawk	*Buteo jamaicensis*	19–25 in. (48–63 cm)
Saw-Whet Owl	*Aegolius acadicus*	7–8.5 in. (18–21 cm)
Screech Owl	*Otus asio*	7–10 in. (18–25 cm)
Snowy Owl	*Nyctea scandiaca*	20–27 in. (50–68 cm)
Turkey Vulture	*Cathartes aura*	26–32 in. (65–80 cm)

Rhino

LIST 2–25. FACTS ABOUT ENDANGERED SPECIES

- A species is a group of plants or animals that can interbreed and produce fertile offspring.
- *Endangered species* are plants and animals that are in immediate danger of dying out as a species and require protection to survive as a species.
- *Threatened species* are plants and animals that are low in number and are likely to become endangered as a species, without help to stop the decline in their numbers.
- *Vulnerable species* are plants and animals that are liable to become threatened as a species if their numbers continue to decline at the present rate.
- *Rare species* are plant and animal species that are at risk because their population is small.
- *Out-of-danger species* are plant and animal species that were listed in one of the above classifications but are out of danger because of effective conservation.
- *Indeterminate species* are plants and animals that are assumed to be endangered, vulnerable, or rare but about which there are insufficient data to classify them.
- The causes of extinction can be classified as natural or human.
- Natural causes of extinction are floods, fires, volcanic eruptions, diseases, ice ages, gigantic and/or multiple crashing meteors, and loss of food or habitat required by species which is totally dependent on that food or habitat.
- Human causes of extinction are destruction of habitat, overhunting, overcollecting, and the use of pesticides and pollutants.
- The primary cause of modern-day extinction and endangerment is the destruction of habitat to clear the land and fill in wetlands for human uses such as building ranches, farms, homes, roads, shopping centers, places of business, and urban centers.
- The rate of extinction in 1970 was one species per day.
- The rate of extinction in 1990 was one species per hour.
- One million species will become extinct before the year 2000, if current land-use development continues, according to predictions by the World Wildlife Fund.
- Up to 20 million acres of forest are cleared each year in the tropics for agriculture.

(Continued)

The Science Teacher's Book of Lists, © 1993 by Prentice Hall

LIST 2–25. (Continued)

- Deforestation rates are estimated at 50 acres per minute. This destruction of habitat is the primary threat to plant and animal species of the rain forest.

- Animals are monitored by the International Union for Conservation of Nature and Natural Resources (IUCN), Conservation Monitoring Centre, Cambridge, England.

- International trade in wild animals and plants is guided by Convention on International Trade in Endangered Species of Wild Fauna and Flora (CITES).

- The United States ratified CITES in 1975; at present, more than one hundred nations have agreed to follow the CITES guidelines for international trade in wild animals, their parts, and plants.

- The U.S. Endangered Species Act of 1973 makes it illegal and punishable by a heavy fine and a jail sentence to hunt, buy, and sell endangered species and their body parts or products. Other countries have similar laws.

LIST 2–26. BUYER BEWARE! ENDANGERED SPECIES, PRODUCTS, AND PETS

The beautiful and useful products derived from wild animals have caused many animals to be hunted to extinction and others to be hunted to near extinction. The demand for exotic pets and animals for zoos and research have threatened other species. Consequently, many nations have passed laws banning the sale of endangered species and their products. It is essential to eliminate or manage the profitable market for these species and their products to provide them with a chance to increase their numbers enough to survive.

Examples of Economic Threats to Endangered Species

EXAMPLES OF ENDANGERED SPECIES	EXAMPLES OF PRODUCTS
All sea turtles: Hawksbill, Leatherback, Green, Atlantic Ridley, Loggerhead, Olive Ridley	Tortoiseshell jewelry and eyeglass frames are made from the shell; cosmetics are made from sea turtle oil; leather boots are made from the skin; food products including meat, eggs, and turtle soup are made from meat and bones. Turtles are also stuffed as curios.
African elephant; Indian elephant	Tusks are used for carving ivory products. In the past, tusks were made into billiard balls and white piano keys. These are now made of plastic. Today ivory tusks are carved into jewelry and curios. There is disagreement about its status: the U.S. lists the African elephant as "threatened," CITES recognizes the need to upgrade to "endangered."
All large cats in the wild: Clouded leopard, Leopard, Snow leopard, Jaguar, Tiger, Lion, Ocelot, Cheetah	Pelts are made into fur coats, hats, purses, rugs, and wall hangings. Heads are mounted for trophies.
Large animals: Black bears, Grizzly bears, Polar bears, Elephants, Gray wolves, Grevy's Zebra	Vacations that feature hunting big game for trophies and pelts. Some cultures value bear parts and gall bladder and fluids for medical purposes.
Whales: Humpback, Right, Sperm, Blue Bowhead	Oil is used to produce a variety of products such as cosmetics and machine oil; bones are decorated and carved and sold as scrimshaw.
Philippine Eagle	Stuffed birds are sought for trophies to be displayed in private homes in the Philippines.
Ostrich; song birds	Feathers are used for decorations and fashion items.
Exotic birds: Macaws, Parrots, Quetzal	Exotic birds are captured live to sell for pets. Many die during transportation; others die because their owners do not understand their nutritional and health care needs.

(Continued)

The Science Teacher's Book of Lists, © 1993 by Prentice Hall

LIST 2–26. (Continued)

EXAMPLES OF ENDANGERED SPECIES	EXAMPLES OF PRODUCTS
All rhinoceroses: Black, Indian, Sumatran, Javan, Square-lipped	Horn of the rhinoceros sought as a trophy and by some cultures as a medicine, and to use for handles of daggers.
Reptiles: Caimans, Lizards, Pythons, Cobras, Gavials, Crocodiles, Iguanas, Pythons, Boa constrictors, Chinese alligator	Skins are used as leather to make belts, wallets, map cases, purses, briefcases, boots, and shoes; reptiles are also stuffed for display. Some are captured live to sell as exotic pets.
Primates: Yellow-tailed woolly monkey, Squirrel monkey, Black colobus, Orangutan, Mentawai macaque, Long-tailed macaque, Javan gibbon	Captured for pets or killed for skins.
Chimpanzee, Buffy-headed marmoset, Golden-rumped lion tamarin, Cotton-top tamarin	Sought after for pets, zoos, and medical research.
Gorilla	Ashtrays are made from the hands of gorillas. Heads are mounted as trophies.

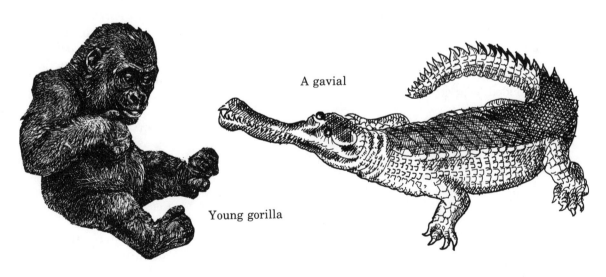

A gavial

Young gorilla

LIST 2–27. EXAMPLES OF ENDANGERED MAMMALS AND THEIR RANGE*

COMMON NAME	SCIENTIFIC NAME	RANGE
African wild ass	*Equus africanus*	Northeast Africa
American manatee	*Trichecus manatus*	Atlantic coastal waters of Florida, Caribbean, South America
Arabian oryx	*Oryx leucoryx*	Southeast Saudi Arabia
Asian elephant	*Elephas maximus*	South-central and southeast Asia
Aye-aye	*Daubentonia madagascariensis*	Madagascar
Bactrian camel	*Camelus ferus*	China, Mongolia
Banteng (Bovid)	*Bos javanicus*	Southeast Asia
Baluchistan bear	*Ursus thibetanus gedrosianus*	Iran, Pakistan
Beaver	*Castor fiber birulai*	Mongolia
Black-footed ferret	*Mustela nigripes*	Alberta, Canada to North Texas
Black rhinoceros	*Diceros bicornis*	Sub-Saharan Africa
Black spider monkey	*Ateles paniscus*	Costa Rica, Panama
Blue whale	*Balaenoptera musculus*	All oceans
Brown bear	*Ursus arctos pruinosus*	China (Tibet)
Bobcat	*Felis rufus escuinapae*	Central Mexico
Bowhead whale	*Balaena mysticetus*	Arctic Ocean/coastal waters
Brown hyena	*Hyaena brunnea*	Southern Africa
Cheetah	*Acinonyx jubatus*	Africa, East Iran, India
Chimpanzee	*Pan troglodytes*	Africa: Guinea to Zaire, Uganda and Tanzania
Chinchilla	*Chinchilla laniger*	Bolivia, Chile
Clouded leopard	*Neofelis nebulosa*	Nepal to South China, Taiwan, Sumatra, Borneo
Common wooly monkey	*Lagothrix lagothricha*	Upper Amazon basin
Dhole (Asiatic wild dog)	*Cuon alpinus*	East Asia, south to Sumatra and Java
Drill	*Mandrillus leucophaeus*	Equatorial West Africa
Dugong	*Dugong dugon*	Coast of Southeast Africa, Red Sea, Indian Ocean to North Australia
Giant armadillo	*Priodontes maximus*	Venezuela to North Argentina
Giant otter	*Pteronura brasiliensis*	Venezuela to Argentina
Gibbons	*Hylobates spp.*	China, India, Southeast Asia
Golden lion tamarin	*Leontopithecus rosalia*	Southeast Brazil coastal forest

(Continued)

Major source: "Endangered & Threatened Wildlife and Plants," issued by the United States Departments of the Interior and Fish and Wildlife, April 15, 1990.

LIST 2–27. (Continued)

COMMON NAME	SCIENTIFIC NAME	RANGE
Gorilla	*Gorilla gorilla*	Central and Western Africa
Gray wolf	*Canis lupus*	East Europe, east to India, Russia, Canada, U.S., Mexico
Humpback whale	*Megaptera novaeangliae*	All oceans, coastal waters
Indian rhinoceros	*Rhinoceros unicornis*	Nepal, northeast India
Jaguar	*Panthera onca*	Southwest U.S., North Mexico, Central and South America to North Argentina
Leopard	*Panthera pardus*	Siberia to Korea, Sri Lanka, Java, Middle East, Africa
Malayan tapir	*Tarpirus indicus*	Southeast Asia, Burma to Malaysia, Sumatra
Maned wolf	*Chrysocyon brachyurus*	Brazil, Bolivia, Uruguay, Paraguay, North Argentina
Numbat	*Myrmecobius fasciatus*	Southwest Australia
Ocelot	*Felis pardalis*	Arizona, Texas, Mexico, Central and South America, Argentina
Onager (Asiatic wild ass)	*Equus hemionus*	Iran, Afghanistan, Russia, Madagascar
Orangutan	*Pongo pygmaeus*	Sumatra, Borneo
Pampas deer	*Ozotoceros bezoarticus*	Brazil, Paraguay, Uruguay, North Argentina
Pygmy chimpanzee	*Pan paniscus*	Zaire
Pileated gibbon	*Hylobates pileatus*	Southeast Thailand
Pink fairy armadillo	*Chlamyphorus truncatus*	Central western Argentina
Proboscis monkey	*Nasalis larvatus*	Borneo
Pronghorn	*Antilocapra americana*	Central Canada, Western U.S., Mexico
Rabbit-bandicoot	*Macrotis lagotis*	Central and northwestern Australia
Red colobus monkey	*Colobus badius*	Kenya
Ring-tailed rock wallaby	*Petrogale xanthopus*	Central and eastern Australia
Snow leopard	*Panthera uncia*	Pakistan, Afghanistan, north to Russia, Himalayas, China
Sumatran rhinoceros	*Dicerorhinus sumatrensis*	Burma, Thailand, Malaysia, Sumatra, Borneo, Laos
Tiger	*Panthera tigris*	Siberia to Java and Bali

(Continued)

LIST 2–27. (Continued)

COMMON NAME	SCIENTIFIC NAME	RANGE
Volcano rabbit	*Romerolagus diazi*	Slopes of volcanoes southeast of Mexico City
Woolly lemur	*Avahi laniger*	East and northwest Madagascar
Wooly spider monkey	*Brachyteles arachnoides*	Brazil
African elephant†	*Loxodonta africana*	Sub-Saharan Africa

†Listed by CITES (Convention on International Trade in Endangered Species of Wild Fauna and Flora 1989), not the "Endangered & Threatened Wildlife and Plants" issued by the United States Departments of the Interior and Fish and Wildlife, April 15, 1990.

NOTE: Although many endangered species have been listed, this list represents fewer than half of the species identified as endangered. In addition, there are species that have not yet been discovered and many of these may become extinct before they are discovered due to the destruction of habitats, especially that of the rain forests.

The Science Teacher's Book of Lists, © 1993 by Prentice Hall

LIST 2–28. EXAMPLES OF ENDANGERED BIRDS AND THEIR RANGE*

NAME	SCIENTIFIC NAME	RANGE
Abbott's Booby	*Sula abbotti*	Christmas Island, Indian Ocean
Akepa	*Loxops coccinea*	Hawaii: Maui, Kauai
Andean Condor	*Vultur gryphus*	Columbia to Chile and Argentina
Arabian Ostrich	*Struthio camelus syriacus*	Jordan, Saudi Arabia
Audouin's Gull	*Larus audouinii*	Mediterranean Sea
Azores Wood Pigeon	*Columba palumbus azorica*	Azores
Bald Eagle	*Haliaeetus leucocephalus*	North America
Barbados Yellow Warbler	*Dendroica petechia petechia*	Barbados
Bar-tailed Pheasant	*Syrmaticus humaie*	Burma, China
Black-Necked Crane	*Grus nigricollis*	China, Tibet
California Clapper Rail	*Rallus longirostris obsoletus*	California
California Condor	*Gymnogyps californianus*	California
Darwin's Rhea	*Pterocnemia pennata*	Argentina, Bolivia, Peru, Uruguay
Edward's Pheasant	*Lophura edwardsi*	Vietnam
Elliot's Pheasant	*Syrmaticus ellioti*	China
Everglade Snail Kite	*Rostrhamus sociabilis plumbeus*	Florida, Cuba
Forbes' Parakeet	*Cyanoramphus auriceps forbesi*	New Zealand
Galapagos Hawk	*Buteo galapagoensis*	Galapagos Islands
Galapagos Penguin	*Spheniscus mendiculus*	Galapagos Islands
Giant Scops Owl	*Otus gurneyi*	Philippines
Golden Parakeet	*Aratinga guarouba*	Brazil
Ground Parrot	*Pezoporus wallicus*	Australia
Guam Rail	*Rallus owstoni*	Guam
Harpy Eagle	*Harpia harpyja*	Mexico to Argentina
Hooded Crane	*Grus monacha*	Japan, Russia
Hawaiian Coot	*Fulica americana alai*	Hawaii
Hawaiian Goose	*Nesochen sandvicensis*	Hawaii
Hawaiian Hawk	*Buteo solitarius*	Hawaii
Imperial Parrot	*Amazona imperialis*	West Indies: Dominica
Indigo Macaw	*Anodorhynchus leari*	Brazil
Ivory-Billed Woodpecker	*Campephilus principalis*	Southeast U.S., Cuba
Kakapo (Owl Parrot)	*Strigops habroptilus*	New Zealand
Kokako	*Callaeas cinerea*	New Zealand

(Continued)

*Source: "Endangered & Threatened Wildlife and Plants," issued by the United States Departments of the Interior and Fish and Wildlife, April 15, 1990.

LIST 2–28. (Continued)

NAME	SCIENTIFIC NAME	RANGE
Nightjar or Whip-Poor-Will	*Caprimulugus noctitherus*	Puerto Rico
Palila (Honeycreeper)	*Psittirostra bailleui*	Hawaii: Mauna
Puerto Rican Pigeon	*Columba inornata wetmorei*	Puerto Rico
Peregrine Falcon	*Falco peregrinus*	Central Alaska across Northcentral Canada to central Mexico
Puerto Rican Parrot	*Amazona vittata*	Puerto Rico
Red-Browed Parrot	*Amazona rhodocorytha*	Brazil
Resplendent Quetzal	*Pharomachrus mocinno*	Mexico to Panama
Tahiti Flycatcher	*Pomarea nigra*	Tahiti
West African Ostrich	*Struthio camelus spatzi*	[Spanish] Sahara
White-Necked Rockfowl	*Picathartes gymnocephalus*	Africa: Togo to Sierra Leone
Whooping Crane	*Grus americana*	North America

Source: "Endangered & Threatened Wildlife and Plants," issued by the United States Departments of the Interior and Fish and Wildlife, April 15, 1990.

NOTE: Although many endangered species have been listed, this list represent fewer than half of the species identified as endangered. In addition, there are species that have not yet been discovered and many of these may become extinct before they are discovered due to the destruction of habitats, especially that of the rain forests.

LIST 2–29. EXAMPLES OF ENDANGERED REPTILES AND THEIR RANGE*

NAME	SCIENTIFIC NAME	RANGE
African dwarf crocodile	*Osteolaemus tetraspis tetraspis*	West Africa
Anegada ground iguana	*Cyclura pinguis*	West Indies
Aruba Island rattlesnake	*Crotalus unicolor*	Aruba
Black caiman	*Melanosuchus niger*	Amazon basin
Batagur turtle	*Batagur baska*	Southeast Asia, Bengal to Vietnam
Bolson tortoise	*Gopherus flavomarginatus*	Mexico
Caiman	*Caiman crocodilus*	Bolivia, Argentina, Peru, Brazil
Central American river turtle	*Dermatemys mawii*	Mexico, Belize, Guatemala
Chinese alligator	*Alligator sinensis*	China
Cuban crocodile	*Crocodylus rhombifer*	Cuba
Day gecko	*Phelsuma edwardnewtoni*	Mauritius
Desert tortoise	*Gopherus agassizii*	Arizona, California, Nevada, Utah, Mexico
Estuarine crocodile	*Crocodylus porosus*	South India, Indonesia, South Australia
Fiji banded iguana	*Brachylophus fasciatus*	Islands off Fiji
Galapagos giant tortoise	*Geochelone elephantopus*	Galapagos Islands
Gavial	*Gavialis gangeticus*	North India
Green sea turtle	*Chelonia mydas*	Worldwide in oceans where temp. is at least 20°C
Hawksbill (Tortoiseshell turtle)	*Eretmochelys imbricata*	Tropical Atlantic, Pacific, and Indian Oceans; Caribbean
Indian python	*Python molurus molurus*	Sri Lanka, India
Island night lizard	*Xantusia riversiana*	California
Jamaican boa	*Epicrates subflavus*	Jamaica
Komodo dragon	*Varanus komodoensis*	Indonesia
Leatherback turtle	*Dermochelys coriacea*	Worldwide in warm oceans
Mona ground iguana	*Cyclura stejnegeri*	Mona Island, Puerto Rico
New Mexico ridge-nosed rattlesnake	*Crotalus willardi obscurus*	New Mexico, Mexico
Nile crocodile	*Crocodylus niloticus*	Middle East, Africa
Plymouth red-bellied turtle	*Pseudemys rubriventris bangsi*	Massachusetts
Puerto Rican boa	*Epicrates inornatus*	Puerto Rico
Waiting Island ground iguana	*Cyclura rileyi rileyi*	Bahamas

NOTE: Although many endangered species have been listed, this list represents fewer than half of the species identified as endangered. In addition, there are species that have not yet been discovered, and many of these may become extinct before they are discovered due to the destruction of habitats, especially rain forests.

Major source: "Endangered & Threatened Wildlife and Plants," issued by the United States Departments of the Interior and Fish and Wildlife, April 15, 1990.

LIST 2–30. ENDANGERED SPECIES THAT APPEAR TO BE MAKING A COMEBACK

The efforts of many scientists and amateurs on behalf of endangered and threatened species seem to be paying off and providing some species with a chance for survival, a comeback. Here is a list of some animals that are living and reproducing in the wild, but some remain endangered. An *E* indicates that the species remains endangered; *T* indicates the species is threatened; *O* that the species is out of danger.

SPECIES ON A COMEBACK	STATUS	SPECIES ON A COMEBACK	STATUS
American Bald Eagle	E	Florida Key deer	E
American bison	O	Gray whale	O
American alligator	O	Nene (Nay-nay) Goose	E
Australian crocodile	O	Peregrine Falcon	E
Black-footed ferret	E	Puerto Rican Parrot	E
Blesbok (bovid)	O	Trumpeter Swan	E*
Bontebok (S. African bovid)	O	Wood Duck	E
California Condor	E	Whooping Crane	E

*Status may soon be changed to O.

Alligator

American bison

LIST 2–31. MANY MAGNIFICENT MARSUPIALS

A koala

Marsupials are a group of mammals that lack a placenta and have an external stomach pouch containing teats. Offspring are born prematurely, after a short gestation period, due to the lack of a placenta which would supply nourishment for development. The mother places the young in her pouch, or the young crawl there, where they attach to a teat to receive nourishment in the form of milk to complete development.

The Opossum Family: belongs to the order Marsupialia. There are over seventy species in the opossum family. They have rat-like bodies with almost hairless tails. Their defense mechanism of "playing dead" gives us the common phrase, "playing possum." The Virginia opossum is the only marsupial that lives in North America. When its young become too large for the pouch, the mother carries them on her back. Other members of the opossum family are:

- South American mouse-opossum
- Short-tailed opossum
- Colocolo
- Water opossum
- Rat opossum

The Dasyurid Family: consists of forty-nine species of marsupials ranging from the mouse-sized pygmy planigale to the cat-sized quoll and the best known, the Tasmanian devil. Other dasyurid marsupials are:

- Brown antechinus
- Fat-tailed dunnart
- Kowari
- Mulgara

The Numbat Family—consists of one species living in Australia. The numbat has a tongue like an anteater and feeds on termites and other insects.

The Marsupial Mole Family—consists of one species living in Australia, the marsupial mole. This blind marsupial is adapted for digging with shovel-like paws, but it is not a true mole.

The Koala Family—consist of one species, the koala, sometimes referred to as the "koala bear." It is not a bear. It is a tree-dwelling marsupial which lives exclusively on eucalyptus.

(Continued)

LIST 2–31. (Continued)

The Wombat Family—consists of three species living in Australia and one species in Tasmania.

The Honey Possum Family—consists of one species, the small honey possum.

The Bandicoot Family—consists of seventeen species found in Australia and New Guinea. Each member looks like a variation of a rat. They have powerful claws. Two members are Gunn's bandicoot and brown bandicoot.

The Rabbit-bandicoot Family—consists of one species.

The Phalanger Family—consists of twelve species. One member is the bush-tailed possum.

The Pygmy Possum Family—consists of seven mouse-sized species. The pygmy glider is able to glide from tree to tree in much the same way as a gliding squirrel.

The Ringtail Family—consists of twenty-two species of tree dwellers with long, prehensile tails that live in Australia and New Guinea.

The Kangaroo Family—consists of about fifty-seven species living in Australia, New Guinea, Tasmania, and Bismark Islands. Some family members are:

- Musk rat-kangaroo
- Potoroo
- Rufous rat-kangaroo
- Red-legged pademelon
- Spectacled hare-wallaby
- Quokka

- Red kangaroo
- Lumholtz's tree kangaroo
- New Guinea Forest wallaby
- Bridled nail-tailed wallaby
- Swamp wallaby

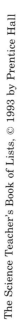

The Science Teacher's Book of Lists, © 1993 by Prentice Hall

A kangaroo and her joey

LIST 2–32. NAMES OF AMPHIBIANS

Amphibians are a class of cold-blooded vertebrates that usually begin life in the water as a tadpole with gills and later develop lungs. Even after developing lungs, they need to return to the water to keep their scaleless skin moist for purposes of respiration. Many return to the water to mate. There are three major subgroups of modern amphibians:

Urodela, or newts and salamanders. Some examples:

- Asian salamander
- Axolotl
- Dwarf siren
- Fire salamander
- Greater siren
- Hellbender
- Mudpuppy

- Olm
- Two-toed amphiuma
- Rough-skinned newt
- Warty newt
- Slimy salamander

Anura, or frogs and toads. Some examples:

- Arum lily frog
- American toad
- Bullfrog
- Boulenger's arrow-poison toad
- Common frog
- Giant toad

- Golden arrow-poison frog
- Green toad
- Northern leopard frog
- Natterjack toad
- Spring peeper
- Wallace's flying frog

Apoda, or caecilians—limbless, burrowing amphibians. Some examples:

- Panamanian caecilian
- Sao Tomé caecilian

- Sticky caecilian
- Seychelles caecilian

A frog

A toad

A Mallard duck

LIST 2–33. ANIMALS THAT MIGRATE

Many animals periodically travel a long route and return to their point of origin or migrate over long distances in search of food, water, shelter, warmer weather, a place to mate, or a place to lay eggs or raise young. Destruction of any part of the migratory route threatens the existence of the species. Examples of animals that migrate:

ANIMAL	GROUP	ANIMAL	GROUP
American Goldfinch	Bird	Loons	Bird
Arctic Tern	Bird	Monarch butterfly	Insect
Canada Geese	Bird	Red Knot	Bird
Caribou	Mammal	Robin	Bird
Dunlin	Bird	Ruddy Turnstone	Bird
Eastern Meadowlark	Bird	Salmon	Fish
Evening Grosbeak	Bird	Sandpipers	Shorebird
Flickers	Bird	Short-Tailed Shearwater	Bird
Flycatchers	Bird	Tanagers	Bird
Garden Warbler	Bird	Vireos	Bird
Green sea turtles	Reptile	Warblers	Bird
Hudsonian Gotwit	Bird	Whooper Swan	Bird
Hummingbirds	Bird	Wildebeest	Mammal
Humpback whale	Mammal	Zebras	Mammal

Note: Plural form denotes more than one species; for example, there are ten species of Vireos, fifty species of Warblers, and four species of Tanagers.

The Science Teacher's Book of Lists, © 1993 by Prentice Hall

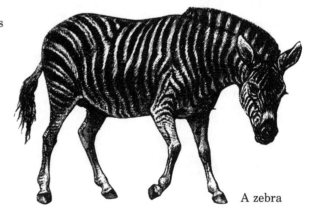

A zebra

LIST 2–34. MONSTERS, DRAGONS, AND OTHER ANIMALS STRANGER THAN FICTION

The Gila Monster is a stout, venomous lizard. Its venom is made in glands in the lower jaw and enters a victim as the gila monster chews. This monster has a short, stumpy tail in which it can store fat for use when there is a shortage of food. It resembles a beaded handbag because its head, body and tail are covered with bead-like scales of black and orange. It has adapted to the desert regions of the southwest United States by being a primarily nocturnal ground dweller, taking shelter in rocks or burrows. It feeds on small animals and the eggs of birds and reptiles. It grows to a length of about 2 feet (61 cm). Gila monsters mate in the summer and the female lays three to five eggs the following fall or winter.

The Komodo Dragon is a heavy-bodied lizard reaching a length of 10 feet (3 m) and a weight of 360 lb. It has a long, thick tail and thick, strong limbs with talon-like claws. It has a snake-like forked tongue and large jagged teeth. It lives near water and is a strong swimmer and climber. Its strength and agility enable it to feed upon wild boar, deer, pigs, and other mammals. It lives on the islands of Komodo, Flores, Pintja, and Pada. The female lays about fifteen eggs. It is an endangered species.

The Nile Monitor is a large, strong lizard reaching a length of $6\frac{1}{2}$ feet (2 m). Its strong, prehensile tail serves as a rudder for swimming and diving and as an aid in climbing trees. It lives near water, feeding on frogs, fish, snails, crocodile eggs, and young crocodiles. The Nile monitor lives in Africa from the Sahara to the Cape of Good Hope. The female lays up to sixty eggs in a termite nest.

Gould's Monitor, also known as the sand monitor, is a strong lizard reaching a length of 5 feet (1.5 cm). It varies in color, pattern, and size. Like all monitors, it has strong limbs and sharp claws. It roams from coastal forests to sandy desert areas of Australia in search of birds, mammals, reptiles, insects, and carrion. The female lays eggs.

The Medusa is metamorphic and is the reproductive cycle of the common jellyfish, which includes both sexual and asexual reproduction. The adult medusa releases eggs and sperm into the surrounding water where external fertilization takes place. Each resulting zygote develops into a ciliated larva, or planula. The planula moves about until it anchors on the ocean floor and develops into a polyp, a cylindrical body that resembles a stack of tentacled pancakes. These "pancakes" form medusae through asexual budding. The medusa then develops gonads and becomes capable of sexual reproduction.

Flatfishes are a group of fish that live on the bottom of the ocean. Being as flat as a pancake with two eyes on top are survival advantages for this group of fish. But they are not always flat and do not always have two eyes on the top of the head. They begin life in the larval stage as a thin fish resembling other fish in the way they move through the water and in that they have two eyes, one on each side of the head, and a mouth in front. But as they grow, some

(Continued)

LIST 2–34. (Continued)

interesting changes take place. They begin to flatten, the mouth moves toward the bottom and both eyes move to the top of the "pancake." This enables these fish to grub through the sandy ocean bottom while looking out for predators. These fish burrow in the sand and many can change their skin color to blend in with the sand and rocks. Examples of flatfishes:

- Atlantic Halibut
- California Halibut
- Dab
- Flounder

- Peacock Flounder
- Plaice
- Starry Flounder
- Summer Flounder

Angler Fishes are a group of fish which have developed a "fishing rod and bait." The rod is actually a modified dorsal fin spine, and the bait is a piece of skin. The angler fish moves the fin or rod so that the bait dangles in front of its mouth to lure fish within striking distance. When a fish comes close to the bait, the angler strikes. There are about 215 species of angler fish. Some examples are:

- Atlantic Footballfish
- Longlure Frogfish

- Shortnose Batfish
- Sargassumfish

The Squarespot, *Anthias pleurotaenia* is an interesting fish. It is a member of the grouper family, which lives in the western Pacific and feeds on plankton. It looks like a large goldfish, but it isn't. The interesting fact about these fish is that they are all born female. The dominant ones turn male. If too many become males, some turn back to females. This interesting adaptation contributes to the survival of this species.

Sea Horses are a group of fish that have a profile which resembles that of a horse and a prehensile tail which enables them to attach to plants. Males have a pouch on the underside of the tail. During mating the pair face each other. The female "shoots" fifty to two hundred eggs into the male's pouch as he covers them with sperm. The male then carries the eggs in his pouch until they hatch, which usually takes about a month.

Hermaphrodites are animals that have both male and female reproductive organs. Most hermaphrodites, such as earthworms and barnacles, reproduce by cross fertilization. But those that lead solitary lives, such as the tapeworm, are capable of self-fertilization.

Egg-Laying Mammals. All but three species of mammals give birth to their young live. Three unusual species of mammals lay leathery-shelled eggs. When the young hatch, they are not fully developed, are helpless, and depend on the mother for her milk and protection. These three species (of the order Monotremata) are:

(Continued)

LIST 2–34. (Continued)

- The short-nosed spiny anteater, or echidna, which places her eggs in her brood patch. There they hatch and take mother's milk by sucking it from areas of the abdominal skin.
- The long-nosed spiny anteater also places her eggs in a brood patch. Her hatchlings suck milk from special areas of the abdominal skin which form pseudonipples.
- The duck-billed platypus lays her eggs in a tunnel which she digs. The mother secretes milk on her abdomen, and the young suck it off the abdominal hairs.

Spiny anteater
or echidna

Duck-billed platypus

LIST 2–35. ANIMALS THAT USE TOOLS OR INGENIOUS BEHAVIORS

Until the early 1960s, humans were identified as the only animal to use tools. But after observations and documentation of animals in their natural settings by scientists (particularly, Jane Goodall), animals other than humans have been observed using tools or ingenious behaviors. Some examples:

Angler fish—shoot droplets of water at insects resting on branches that overhang swamps.

Beavers—build dams.

Blue sea slugs—which are not venomous, can feed on venomous marine animals such as the Portuguese man-of-war and the true jellyfish and store their venomous barbs, undigested, to later "shoot" in their own defense.

Capuchin monkeys—hammer nuts against hard surfaces to open them.

Chimpanzees—fashion and use sticks to probe nests for ants and termites.

One crab—the *Melia tesselata*, picks up a sea anemone in each claw and uses it to sting prey.

Crows and **Sea Gulls**—fly over a rocky area and drop eggs or shellfish onto the rocks to open the shells.

Doodlebugs (ant lion larvae)—construct sand traps, and wait at the bottom. When an ant approaches, the doodlebug hurls sand in the air, causing a "sand slide" and delivering the ant to the doodlebug.

Elephants—use their trunks to hold a stick which can be used as a back scratcher or as a weapon against another animal.

Egyptian Vultures—hold a stone in the beak and smash the stone on an egg to open it.

Finches—use twigs to push larvae out of tree bark.

Herons—cast insects or worms on the surface of water; then when fish investigate, the heron catches the fish.

Horses—use a stick held in the mouth as a back scratcher.

Mongooses—smash eggs against rocks to open them.

Myrmecine ants—place leaves on decaying fruits. After a leaf absorbs the juice, ants carry the enriched leaf back to the colony to be eaten.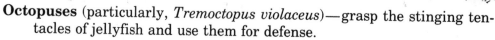

Octopuses (particularly, *Tremoctopus violaceus*)—grasp the stinging tentacles of jellyfish and use them for defense.

Sand wasps—build a nest by digging a tunnel, storing food in it for the unhatched young by placing a grub in the end of the tunnel, laying eggs on the grub, and closing the tunnel with pebbles and stones.

(Continued)

LIST 2–35. (Continued)

Sea otters—lie on their backs, place a flat stone on their chest and hammer shellfish on the flat rock to crack open the shells. They have been observed holding the stone underarm while diving for shellfish.

Skunks—throw eggs against rocks to open them.

Song Thrushes—smash snails against rocks to loosen the snail from its shell.

Spiders—build or spin webs to catch prey; diving spiders do it under water.

Woodpecker Finches—use a twig to probe, lever, and impale insects.

Elephant

Horse

LIST 2–36. THE ANIMAL CONTRACT

Zoologist and author Desmond Morris expresses his concerns about how our species abuses and exploits other species of the animal kingdom in his book, *The Animal Contract*.* Morris recognizes that human awareness and concern have been heightened, but states that animal abuse continues. He states that humans are breaking the animal contract, the basis of which is "that each species must limit its population growth sufficiently to permit other life forms to coexist with it." To address these concerns and abuses, he states that a cool-headed approach is needed and offers a new Bill of Rights for Animals:

1. No animal should be endowed with imaginary qualities of good or evil to satisfy our superstitious beliefs or religious prejudices.
2. No animal should be dominated or degraded to entertain us.
3. No animal should be kept in captivity unless it can be provided with adequate physical and social environment.
4. No animal should be kept as a companion unless it can adapt easily to the lifestyle of its human owners.
5. No animal species should be driven to extinction by direct persecution or by further increases in the human population.
6. No animal should be made to suffer pain or distress to provide us with sport.
7. No animal should be subjected to physical or mental suffering for unnecessary experimental purposes.
8. No farm animal should be kept in a deprived environment to provide us with food or produce.
9. No animal should be exploited for its fur, its skin, its ivory, or for any other luxury product.
10. No working animal should be forced to carry out heavy duties that cause it stress or pain.

"This Bill of Rights does not represent a whimsical ideal. It is practical and feasible. It is, however, very far from being implemented around the globe today."

Desmond Morris

The Science Teacher's Book of Lists, © 1993 by Prentice Hall

---

*Morris, Desmond, "The Animal Contract." (Warner Books, New York, 1991), p. 168. Printed with permission of the author.

LIST 2–37. ALTERNATIVES TO ANIMAL DISSECTION

Pat Graham, Director of the Dissection Hotline (800-922-FROG (3764)) has a teacher's guide available free of charge for teachers. It includes a list of alternatives to animal dissection as a method of teaching biology, physiology, anatomy, or zoology, some of which is listed below:

Videotapes and Slides

- The Frog Inside-Out
  Instructivision, Inc.
  3 Regent Street
  Livingston, NJ 07039
  (201) 992-9081

- Frog Dissection Explained
  Bergwall Productions
  540 Baltimore Pike
  Chadds Ford, PA 19317
  (800) 645-3565

- Dissection of the Frog
  Slide Program
  JLM Visuals
  920 Seventh Avenue
  Grafton, WI 53024
  (414) 377-7775

Anatomical Models, Charts, and Other Learning Tools

- Denoyer-Geppert Science Company
  5225 North Ravenswood Avenue
  Chicago, IL 60640
  (800) 621-1014
  Numerous charts and models of human and nonhuman animals. Biology test sheets of many animals with line drawings and anatomical parts for identification.

- Nystrom, Division of Herff Jones, Inc.
  3333 Elston Avenue
  Chicago, IL 60618
  (800) 621-8086
  Resources include laminated study prints of anatomy that students mark on for hands-on involvement; plastic zoological models of dissected perch,

(Continued)

LIST 2–37. (Continued)

frogs, earthworms, and grasshoppers; zoology charts of many common animals and human anatomy and physiology charts.

- Ward's Natural Science Establishment, Inc. (WNSE)
  5100 West Henrietta Road
  P.O. Box 92912
  Rochester, NY 14692-9012
  (800) 962-2660
  Dissection alternatives include prepared microscope slides of numerous animal cells and tissues, human anatomy models, filmstrips of dissection, slide sets of photos of whole and dissected animals, slides of live animals in their natural environments, laminated "Dissectogram" cards with color photographs of dissections, and biology charts of numerous human and non-human animals.

Computer Programs

- Software for dissection labs for use with Apple II and IIe of earthworms, clams, crayfish, grasshoppers, starfish, perch, and frogs. (Available from WNSE.)

- Operation Frog. Simulated lab dissection and reconstruction of a frog. Organs are removed, using proper sequence and instruments, and viewed in detail. Available for Apple II and Commodore 64 computers from Scholastic Software, Inc., P.O. Box 7502, 2931 E. McCarty Street, Jefferson City, MO 65102, (800) 541-5513.

- Visifrog by Ventura for the Apple II. Presents anatomical structures of the frog in high-resolution color graphics, with practice in identifying names of structures and functions. (Available from Ventura Educational Systems, 910 Ramona Ave., Suite F, Garden City, CA 93434, (800) 336-1022 (805) 473-7380.)

- Cambridge Developmental Laboratory's Educational Software catalog features a large selection of computer programs (for Apple II, Commodore 64, and IBM PC). Areas covered include general biology, botany, biochemistry, genetics, population dynamics, physiology, and anatomy. (Available from Cambridge Development Laboratory, 86 West Street, Waltham, MA 02154, (800) 637-0047.)

Books

- *General Zoology Lab Guide, Complete Version*, by J.E. Wodsedalke and Charles F. Lytle. Photographs include some taken with electron micro-

The Science Teacher's Book of Lists, © 1993 by Prentice Hall

(Continued)

LIST 2–37. (Continued)

scopes that reflect the latest knowledge of animal structure and function. (Available from WNSE.)

- *Grzimek's Animal Life Encyclopedia.* A set of thirteen volumes of animal types with photos, detailed illustrations, and plates with acetate overlays of anatomy. (Available from WNSE.)
- *The Frog Book*, by Mary C. Dickerson. Full coverage of frog physiology. (Available from WNSE.)
- *The Anatomy Coloring Book*, by W. Kapit and I.M. Elson. Contains detailed illustrations of human systems and anatomy with 142 plates of line illustrations. (Available from Harper, Collins, 1000 Keystone Industrial Park, Scranton, PA 18512, (800) 242-7737, (805) 499-1407.)
- *Zoology Coloring Book*, L.M. Elson. Detailed plates of invertebrate and vertebrate animal anatomy. (Available from Harper & Row, J.B. Lippincott.)
- Laboratory anatomy and dissection books of rats, rabbits, cats, and fetal pigs. (Available from WNSE.)

Non-Animal Projects

- Alternative Project Sheets is a collection of simple alternatives to some of the most common animal-related biology experiments and dissections. (Available from Advancement of Humane Education (NAAHE), Box 362, East Haddam, CT 06423.)
- The Harvard Biometer can replace frog pithing to study heart functions. It provides students with exercises associated with the study of the cardiovascular system, harmlessly using the students instead of frogs. The electronic biometer amplifies the heart sounds and wrist pulses of the students to demonstrate cardiac bioelectric signals. Pamphlet available: "Studying Bioelectricity and Cardiography," T. Daniel Kimbrough. (Available from Phipps & Bird, Inc., 8741 Landmark Road, Box 273324, Richmond, VA 23261.
- *Laboratory Investigations in Human Physiology*, by George K. Russell, a book of non-animal physiology lab projects for the college level. The exercises cover basic physiological phenomena by harmlessly using the students themselves as experimental subjects. (Available from The Myrin Institute, 136 E. 64th Street, New York, NY 10021, (212) 758-6457.)
- *The Endangered Species Handbook*, by Greta Nilsson. Contains numerous non-animal lab projects. (Available from The Animal Welfare Institute, P.O. Box 3650, Washington, D.C. 20007, (202) 337-2332.)

(Continued)

LIST 2–37. (Continued)

For Medical, Veterinary, Nursing, and Psychology Students

For information on alternatives to dissection in advanced training:

- Association of Veterinarians for Animal Rights, (AVAR), P.O. Box 269, Vacaville, CA 95696, (707) 451-1391.
- Physicians' Committee for Responsible Medicine (PCRM), 5100 Wisconsin Avenue, NW, Suite 404, Washington, D.C. 20016, (202) 686-2210.
- Psychologists for the Ethical Treatment of Animals (PsyETA), P.O. Box 1219, Washington Grove, MD 20880, (301) 963-4751.
- PETA Nurse Network, P.O. Box 42516, Washington, D.C. 20015-1516, (301) 770-7444 Ext. 428.

LIST 2–38. AMERICAN ASSOCIATION FOR THE ADVANCEMENT OF SCIENCE RESOLUTION ON THE USE OF ANIMALS IN RESEARCH, TESTING, AND EDUCATION*

Scientists, science educators, and science students need to address the need for science experiments on live animals. The American Association for the Advancement of Science has prepared this resolution:

Whereas society as a whole, and the scientific community in particular, supports and encourages research that will improve the well-being of humans and animals, and that will lead to the cure or prevention of disease; and

Whereas the use of animals has been and continues to be essential not only in applied research with direct clinical application in humans and animals, but also in research that furthers the understanding of biological processes; and

Whereas the American Association for the Advancement of Science supports appropriate regulations and adequate funding to promote the welfare of animals in laboratory or field and deplores any violations of those regulations; and

Whereas the American Association for the Advancement of Science deplores harassment of scientists and technical personnel engaged in animal research, as well as destruction of animal laboratory facilities; and

Whereas in order to protect the public, both consumer and medical products must be tested for safety, and such testing may in some cases require the use of animals; and

Whereas the American Association for the Advancement of Science has long acknowledged the importance and endorsed the use of animal experimentation in promoting human and animal welfare and in advancing scientific knowledge;

BE IT RESOLVED that the American Association for the Advancement of Science continues to support the use of animals in scientific research; and

BE IT FURTHER RESOLVED that scientists bear several responsibilities for the conduct of research with animals: (1) to treat their subjects with proper care and sensitivity to their pain and discomfort, consistent with the requirements of the particular study and research objectives; (2) to be informed about and adhere to relevant laws and regulations pertaining to animal research; and (3) to communicate respect for animal subjects to employees, students, and colleagues; and

(Continued)

Source: the American Association for the Advancement of Science, 1333 H Street, NW, Washington, D.C. 20005; printed with permission.

LIST 2–38. (Continued)

BE IT FURTHER RESOLVED that the development and use of complementary or alternative research or testing methodologies, such as computer models, tissue, or cell cultures, be encouraged where applicable and efficacious; and

BE IT FURTHER RESOLVED that the use of animals by students can be an important component of science education as long as it is supervised by teachers who are properly trained in the welfare and use of animals in laboratory or field settings and is conducted by institutions capable of providing proper oversight; and

BE IT FURTHER RESOLVED that scientists support the efforts to improve animal welfare that do not include policies or regulations that would compromise scientific research; and

BE IT RESOLVED that the American Association for the Advancement of Science encourages its affiliated societies and research institutions to support this resolution.

Joint Resolution Adopted by the AAAS Board and Council
February 19, 1990
Sponsored by the AAAS Committee on Scientific Freedom and Responsibility

The Science Teacher's Book of Lists, © 1993 by Prentice Hall

LIST 2–39. NATIONAL ASSOCIATION OF BIOLOGY TEACHERS GUIDELINES FOR THE USE OF LIVE ANIMALS*
(Revised January 1990)

Living things are the subject of biology, and their direct study is an appropriate and necessary part of biology teaching. Textbook instruction alone cannot provide students with a basic understanding of life and life processes. The National Association of Biology Teachers (NABT) recognizes the importance of research in understanding life processes and providing information on health, disease, medical care, and agriculture.

The abuse of any living organism for experimentation or any other purpose is intolerable in any segment of society. Because biology deals specifically with living things, professional biology educators must be especially cognizant of their responsibility to prevent the inhumane treatment of living organisms in the name of science and research. This responsibility should extend beyond the confines of the teacher's classroom to the rest of the school and community.

The National Association of Biology Teachers believes that students learn the value of living things, and the values of science, by the events they witness in the classroom. The care and concern for animals should be a paramount consideration when live animals are used in the classroom. Such teaching activities should develop in students and teachers a sense of respect and pleasure in studying the wonders of living things. NABT is committed to providing sound biological education and promoting humane attitudes towards animals. These guidelines should be followed when live animals are used in the classroom:

A. Biological experimentation should be consistent with a respect for life and all living things. Humane treatment and care of animals should be an integral part of any lesson that includes living things.

B. Exercises and experiments with living things should be within the capabilities of the students involved. The biology teachers should be guided by the following conditions:

    1. The lab activity should not cause the loss of an animal's life. Bacteria, fungi, protozoans, and invertebrates should be used for activities that may require use of harmful substances or loss of an organism's life. These activities should be clearly supported by an educational rationale and should not be used when alternatives are available.

    2. A student's refusal to participate in an activity (e.g., dissection or experiments involving live animals, particularly vertebrates) should be recognized and accompanied with alternative methods of learning. The teacher should work with the student to develop an alternative for obtaining the required knowledge or experience. The alternative

(Continued)

*Reprinted with permission from the *National Association of Biology Teachers*, 11250 Roger Bacon Drive, #19, Reston, VA 22090.

LIST 2–39. (Continued)

activity should require the student to invest a comparable amount of time and effort.

C. Vertebrate animals can be used as experimental organisms in the following situations:
1. Observations of normal living patterns of wild animals in their natural habitat or in zoological parks, gardens, or aquaria.
2. Observations of normal living functions such as feeding, growth, reproduction, activity cycles, etc.
3. Observations of biological phenomenon among and between species such as communication, reproductive and life strategies behavior, interrelationships of organisms, etc.

D. If live vertebrates are to be kept in the classroom the teacher should be aware of the following responsibilities:
1. The school, under the biology teacher's leadership, should develop a plan on the procurement and ultimate disposition of animals. Animals should not be captured from or released into the wild without the approval of both a responsible wildlife expert and a public health official. Domestic animals and "classroom pets" should be purchased from licensed animal suppliers. They should be healthy and free of disease that can be transmitted to humans or to other animals.
2. Animals should be provided with sufficient space for normal behavior and postural requirements. Their environment should be free of undue stress, such as noise, overcrowding, and disturbances caused by students.
3. Appropriate care—including nutritious food, fresh water, clean housing, and adequate temperature and lighting for the species—should be provided daily, including weekends, holidays, and long school vacations.
4. Teachers should be aware of any student allergies to animals.
5. Students and teachers should immediately report to the school health nurse all scratches, bites and other injuries, including allergies or other illnesses.
6. There should always be supervised care by a teacher competent in caring for animals.

E. Animal studies should always be carried out under the direct supervision of a biology teacher competent in animal care procedures. It is the responsibility of the teacher to ensure that the student has the necessary comprehension for the study. Students and teachers should comply with the following:
1. Students should not be allowed to perform surgery on living vertebrate animals. Hence, the administration of anesthesia and euthanasia should not be done in the classroom.
2. Experimental procedures on vertebrates should not use pathogenic microorganisms, ionizing radiation, carcinogens, drugs or chemicals

(Continued)

LIST 2–39. (Continued)

at toxic levels, drugs known to produce adverse or teratogenic effects, pain-causing drugs, alcohol in any form, electric shock, exercise until exhaustion, or other distressing stimuli. No experimental procedures should be attempted that would subject vertebrate animals to pain or distinct discomfort, or interfere with their health in any way.

3. Behavioral studies should use only positive reinforcement techniques.

4. Egg embryos subjected to experimental manipulation should be destroyed 72 hours before normal hatching time.

5. Exceptional original research in the biological or medical sciences involving live vertebrate animals should be carried out under the direct supervision of an animal scientist, e.g., an animal physiologist, or a veterinary or medical researcher, in an appropriate research facility. The research plan should be developed by the animal scientist and reviewed by a humane society professional staff person prior to the start of the research. All professional standards of conduct should be applied as well as humane care and treatment, and concern for the safety of the animals involved in the project.

6. Students should not be allowed to take animals home to carry out experimental studies.

F. Science fair projects and displays should comply with the following:

1. The use of live animals in science fair projects shall be in accordance with the above guidelines. In addition, no live vertebrate animals shall be used in displays for science fair exhibitions.

2. No animal or animal products from recognized endangered species should be kept or displayed.

LIST 2–40. ANIMAL SUPERLATIVES

- **Tallest animal:** the African giraffe, 4.5 to 6 m (14.7 to 19.6 ft.) tall.
- **Longest sleepers:** big cats sleep an average of 20 hours a day.
- **Largest and heaviest living animal:** the blue whale; weight about 175.5 tonnes (195 tons); length about 25–32 m (82–105 ft.)
- **Largest eyes:** the blue whale; 127 cm (5 inches) in diameter
- **Largest land animal:** the African elephant; average height 3.15 m (10 feet 6 inches), weight 5.58 tonnes ($6\frac{1}{4}$ tons), body length 6–7.5 m (19.75–24.50 feet), tail length 1–1.3 m (3.25–4.25 feet). Largest recorded specimen was a bull shot in Africa in 1974. In was 3.9 m (13 feet) tall and weighed 11.8 tonnes (13 tons).
- **Largest land carnivore:** the polar bear; body size about 2.2–2.5 m ($7\frac{1}{4}$–$8\frac{1}{4}$ ft).
- **Largest ears:** Male African elephant, 1.08 m (3 feet) wide.
- **Largest pinniped** (seals, walrus, and sea lions): Northern Elephant seal; 6 m (19.75 ft).
- **Largest primate:** Gorilla; 1.7–1.8 m (5.5–6 ft).
- **Largest rhinoceros:** Indian rhinoceros; body length 4.2 m (13.75 ft).
- **Smallest rhinoceros:** Sumatran rhinoceros; body length 2.5 m (8.25 ft).
- **Smallest recorded mammal:** Kitt's hog-nosed bat, also known as the bumblebee bat, weighs 1.96 g (0.07 ozs.), has a wingspan of 15 cm (6 in.).
- **Smallest bear:** sun bear of southeast Asia; height 1.1–1.4 m (3.5–4.5 ft).
- **Largest wingspan for a bat:** Bismark flying fox; wingspan of 19.6 m (6 ft).
- **Largest spiders:** Theraphosa, Lasiodora, and Grammostola of the Amazon Basin.
- **Largest crustacean:** the spider crab; length 36 m (11 ft).
- **Largest lizard:** The Komodo dragon; 3 m (10 ft).
- **Largest turtle:** leatherback; length 1.5 m (5 ft), weight 590 kg (1,300 lb.).

The Science Teacher's Book of Lists, © 1993 by Prentice Hall

(Continued)

LIST 2–40. (Continued)

- **Longest venomous snake:** King Cobra, 4–5.5 m (13–18 ft).
- **Longest snake on record:** Anaconda; 11.4 m (37.5 ft) was captured in the Amazon Jungle. Explorers have reported anacondas that measure 42 m (140 ft.).
- **Longest python:** (32 ft) was shot in Malaysia in the year 1912.
- **Longest animals ever recorded:** a ribbon snake, also known as the "boot-lace worm," washed ashore in Scotland in 1864; it measured 54 m (180 ft).
- **Fastest creature on land over short distances:** cheetah, 112 km.p.h. (69.5 m.p.h.).
- **Fastest land animal over long distances:** pronghorn antelope, 56 km.p.h. (35 m.p.h.) for 4 miles.
- **Fastest creature on two legs:** Ostrich; runs 70 kmh (44 m.p.h.).
- **Fastest creature:** Peregrine Falcon dives at speeds over 322 k.p.h. (200 m.p.h.).
- **Largest bird:** the north African Ostrich; males stand 2.7 m (9 ft) tall, weigh 155.25 kg (346 lbs.).
- **Smallest bird:** Helena's hummingbird; has a wingspan of 7.5 cm (3 in.), weight of 1.96 g (0.07 oz.) and length of 5.7 cm (2.28 in.).
- **Fastest flying animal:** spine-tailed swift; 170 km.p.h. (106.25 m.p.h.).
- **Slowest moving land animal:** three-toed sloth; ground speed of 1.8 m (6 ft.) per minute.

HUMAN HEALTH AND NUTRITION

LIST 3–1. MAJOR TERMS OF THE TEN HUMAN BODY SYSTEMS

CIRCULATORY	DIGESTIVE	ENDOCRINE	INTEGUMENTARY	MUSCULAR
heart	salivary glands	hormone	epidermis	Major types:
artery	esophagus	gland	dermis	skeletal
arteriole	stomach	pineal gland	sweat gland	smooth
capillary	duodenum	thyroid gland	sebaceous gland	cardiac
vein	pancreas	parathyroid	hair shaft	voluntary
venule	colon	gland	hair follicle	involuntary
blood	small intestine	hypothalamus	nerve ending	muscle tone
plasma	liver	adrenal gland	pore	facial
red blood cell	bile	testes	melanocyte	trapezius
white blood cell	appendix	ovaries	(pigment cell)	biceps
bone marrow	gallbladder	pancreas	nail	flexors
hemoglobin	rectum	pituitary		hamstring
	tongue	gland		gluteus
	villi			maximus
	pepsin			gluteus
	anus			medius
				deltoid
Lymphatic				muscle fiber
sub system *				contraction
lymph				lactic acid
lymphatics (vessels)				
lymph nodes				
lymph glands				
lymphatic ducts				
lymphocyte				
tonsils				
adenoids				

(Continued)

*The lymphatic system is an accessory circulatory system that is connected with blood circulation.

LIST 3–1. (Continued)

NERVOUS	REPRODUCTIVE	RESPIRATORY	SKELETAL	URINARY
neuron	*Male:*	sinus	skull	kidney
glial cell	sperm	trachea	cranium	diffusion
synapse	testes	esophagus	sternum	filtration
reflex	scrotum	lungs	rib cage	reabsorption
response	vas deferens	bronchi	vertebra	secretion
dendrite	prostate gland	bronchiole	humerus	urine
axon	penis	alveoli	clavicle	urea
receptor	testosterone	diaphragm	scapula	bladder
sensory neuron		capillary	radius	duct
motor neuron	*Female:*	gas exchange	ulna	urethra
brain	ovary	epiglottis	carpal	ureter
brain stem	clitoris	inspiration	metacarpal	glomerulus
cerebellum	vagina	expiration	phalange	nephron
cerebrum	cervix	respiration	femur	
cerebral cortex	uterus	larynx	pelvic girdle	
spinal cord	ovulation	nasal cavity	fibula	
ganglion	menstruation	pharynx	patella	
effector	vulva		tibia	
neuro- transmitter	endocrine		tarsal	
	estrogen		metatarsal	
	progesterone		cartilage	
	mammary		red marrow	
	breast		yellow marrow	
	fallopian tube		long bone	
	menopause		short bone	
	menarche		sesamoid bone	
			irregular bone	
			flat bone	

LIST 3-2. ORGAN SYSTEMS IN THE HUMAN BODY

Cells are the building blocks of living organisms. Cells form tissues. Tissues form organs. Organs work together in systems. Ten organ systems and one subsystem make up the organ systems of the human body.

SYSTEM	MAJOR COMPONENTS	FUNCTIONS
Circulatory	Heart, blood vessels, blood, lymph structures, bone marrow	Transports oxygen and nutrients; exchanges carbon dioxide for oxygen; removes wastes; maintains salt, water, and pH balance in tissues
Lymphatic	Thymus, thoracic duct, lymph nodes, spleen, lymph vessels	Returns excess tissue fluid to the blood; defends against disease; absorbs lipids from the digestive system.
Digestive	Mouth, salivary glands, esophagus, stomach, large and small intestines, liver, pancreas, gallbladder, rectum, anus	Digests and makes food useable as building materials and source of energy; eliminates non-usable materials
Endocrine	Hypothalamus, pituitary, pineal, adrenal, thyroid and parathyroid glands, ovaries, testes, pancreas	Regulates the body chemistry; with the nervous system; maintains integration and control of body functions
Integumentary	Skin, including sweat glands, hair, nails, sebaceous glands	Covers and protects body; helps regulate body temperature; receives outside stimuli
Muscular	Skeletal, cardiac and smooth muscles	Body movements, voluntary and involuntary
Nervous	Brain, spinal cord, nerves, sense organs: eyes, ears, nose, mouth	Monitors and with the endocrine system regulates body activities; receives, processes, and reacts to stimuli
Reproductive	*Female:* ovaries, uterus, vagina *Male:* testes, penis, prostate gland, vas deferens	Reproduction, secondary sex characteristics
Respiratory	Lungs, trachea, bronchi, diaphragm, larynx, pharynx, oral and nasal cavities	Exchanges carbon dioxide for oxygen and excretes carbon dioxide; enables speech
Skeletal	Bones, cartilage, ligaments	Provides body framework; protects and supports some organs; with muscles provides for movement; forms blood cells
Urinary	Kidney, bladder, ureter, urethra	Eliminates metabolic wastes; with endocrine system regulates blood chemistry

NOTE: All mammals have these ten organ systems.

LIST 3–3. MAJOR BONES OF THE HUMAN BODY

BONE(S)	DESCRIPTION	COMMENTS
Skull	Head	8 cranial bones enclose the brain; 14 bones compose the face
Rib cage	Chest	Bony cage formed by the sternum, thoracic vertebrae and 12 pairs of ribs
Sternum	Center of chest	1 bone, fusion of 3 bones
Vertebrae	Backbone sections	24 bones and two sets of fused bones (the sacrum and coccyx) support the body, enclose and support the spinal cord
Cervical	Neck	7 bones
Thoracic	Chest	12 bones
Lumbar	Back	5 bones
Sacral	Pelvis	5 fused bones
Coccygeal	Tail bone	3–5 fused bones
Clavicle	Collarbone	2 collarbones
Scapula	Shoulder blade	2 bones form the shouler or pectoral girdle
Humerus	Only long bone in upper arm	1 bone
Radius	One of two long bones in the lower arm	1 bone
Ulna	One of two long bones in the lower arm	1 bone
Carpals	Wrist bones	8 bones in each hand, glide over each other
Metacarpals	Bones in the palm of the hand and in the foot	
Phalanges	Miniature long bones of the fingers or toes	5 digits on each hand/foot
Femur	The only long bone in the upper leg	1 bone
Tibia	The long bone that runs down the front of the lower leg	1 bone, shin bone
Fibula	The long bone that runs down the back of the lower leg	1 bone
Tarsals	Ankle bones	7 gliding bones in each foot
Metatarsals	Bones of the foot	Form the metatarsal arch

The Science Teacher's Book of Lists, © 1993 by Prentice Hall

LIST 3–4. ABOUT TEETH

1. **The types of teeth that humans possess are:**
   - **Incisors**—sharp, chisel-like teeth in the front of the mouth used for cutting
   - **Canines**—pointed teeth at the corners of the mouth used for tearing and gripping.
   - **Molars and premolars**—square teeth with small cusps at the sides of the mouth used for grinding.

2. **A tooth is made up of:**
   - **The crown**—which grows out of the jaw
   - **The root**—which is embedded in the jawbone
   - **The neck**—where the crown and root meet

3. **Each tooth is made up of:**
   - **Enamel**—the hardest substance in the body; protects the tooth
   - **Dentine**—the part of a tooth made mostly of calcium located under the enamel, containing the pulp chamber and root canals
   - **Pulp**—the soft tissue surrounded by dentine which contains nerves and blood vessels that enter the root via a small channel
   - **Cementum**—covers the root and protects the underlying dentine

4. **Primary or baby teeth:**

NAME	APPROXIMATE AGE OF APPEARANCE
Central incisors	6 to 8 months
Lateral incisors	9 to 11 months
Eye teeth	18 to 20 months
First molars	14 to 17 months
Second molars	24 to 26 months

5. **Adult teeth:**

NAME	APPROXIMATE AGE OF APPEARANCE
Central incisors	7 to 8 years
Lateral incisors	8 to 9 years
Canines	12 to 14 years
First premolars	10 to 12 years
Second premolars	10 to 12 years
First molars	6 to 7 years
Second molars	12 to 16 years
Third molars	17 to 25 years, may be absent in some people

6. **The total number of teeth for adults,** not considering teeth that have been pulled or lost to accidents, is generally considered to be 32, or between 28 and 32.

The Science Teacher's Book of Lists, © 1993 by Prentice Hall

LIST 3–5. THE BRAIN: PARTS AND FUNCTIONS OF THE BODY'S COMMAND CENTER*

PARTS	*MAJOR FUNCTIONS*
Brain stem	
Medulla	Controls involuntary actions, such as heartbeat, respiration, blood pressure, swallowing, coughing, and vomiting
Pons	Controls breathing with the medulla; connects different parts of the brain with one another
Midbrain	Controls seeing, hearing and reflexes associated with sight and sound
Thalamus	Control center for incoming sensory messages
Hypothalamus	Control center for the homeostatic[a] needs of the body
Cerebellum	Coordinates fluid voluntary muscle movement; controls balance
Cerebrum	Center for thought, learning, and motor functions
Cerebral cortex (Gray matter)	Controls, with cerebellum, voluntary muscles; center for incoming information from eyes, ears, and touch; center of intelligence, emotions, and interpretation of information and messages
White matter	Provides for connections within and between the cerebral hemispheres and other parts of the brain and spinal cord

The Science Teacher's Book of Lists, © 1993 by Prentice Hall

Adapted from: Davis, P. William; Solomon, Eldra Pearl; Berg, Linda R., *The World of Biology*, Fourth Edition, Saunders College Publishing, Philadelphia, 1990, and Barhydt, Frances, *Science Discovery Activities Kit*, The Center for Applied Research in Education, West Nyack, NY, 1989.

[a]Maintenance of internal body environment, temperature, water, salt balance, and pH.

LIST 3-6. SOME DEVELOPMENTAL STAGES IN THE HUMAN EMBRYO AND FETUS

TIME FROM FERTILIZATION	*DEVELOPMENT*
36 hours	Embryo reaches two-cell stage
6 days	Cells begin to implant
2 weeks	Embryo implanted in uterine wall
	Heart tissues and blood cells are developing
3.5 weeks	Respiratory system and thyroid gland developing; heart begins to beat
4 weeks	Limbs begin; three parts of the brain are formed; eye rudiments are present
5.5 weeks	Spine and nervous system are forming
6 weeks	Heart and circulation functioning
8 weeks	Muscular development enables weak movement, all main organs are formed; brain waves are evident; liver forms blood cells; is termed a fetus; length about 1 in. (2.5 cm)
12 weeks	Lymph glands develop; skin epidermis and dermis are evident; bone marrow makes blood cells; ossification occurs; sex is detectable from the genitals; placenta is fully formed
14 weeks	Fetus can swallow, urinate, and suck thumb
16 weeks	Face possesses human features
16–40 weeks	Tremendous growth of body
21 weeks	Fetal position changes until week 28
21–23 weeks	Fingernails and toenails are complete
23 weeks	Eyelid can open and hand can grip
25 weeks	Length about 13 in. (32 cm)
40 weeks	Birth; length about 20 in. (50 cm)

LIST 3–7. THE MOTHER'S INTAKE AND ENVIRONMENT AFFECTS HER DEVELOPING BABY

INTAKE AND/OR ENVIRONMENT	POSSIBLE EFFECTS
Drugs	
Alcohol	Fetal alcohol syndrome, mentally and physically deformed; low birth weight; hyperactivity, and learning disabilities
Antibiotics	Different antibiotics cause different problems: deafness, jaundice, deformities, discolored teeth
Antihistamines	Possible physical deformities
Aspirin	An anticoagulant, can contribute to hemorrhage in newborns
Caffeine	Stimulates fetal nervous system
Cocaine	Stimulates fetal systems; heart defects, mental retardation, premature birth, cocaine-addicted baby
Cortisone	Cleft lip, increased possibility of stillbirth
Heroin	Premature birth, heroin-addicted baby, death
LSD and other psychedelics	Chromosome damage, increased risk of miscarriage
Thalidomide	Physical deformities, particularly of the limbs
Cigarette smoking	Low birth weight, higher risk of spontaneous abortion or stillbirth
German measles	Blindness, deafness, heart deformities, mental retardation
Syphilis	Birth defects, congenital syphilis, death
X rays	Higher risk of physical defects and leukemia

The Science Teacher's Book of Lists, © 1993 by Prentice Hall

LIST 3–8. EACH SYSTEM IN THE HUMAN BODY NEEDS NUTRIENTS

Each of the body's systems needs nutrients to help it operate and stay in good repair. Nutrients are digested foods. They are carried to all parts of the body by the blood. Nutrients provide three major functions:

1. The growth and repair of cells and tissues.
2. Production of energy, particularly chemical energy which is stored in the bonds of ATP, adenosine triphosphate, the energy "currency" of the cell.
3. Regulation of body processes such as respiration and excretion of wastes.

No one food or type of nutrient can provide all the materials that the body needs to function. A balanced diet is needed to provide all of the building blocks for growth and repair, energy, and regulation of systems and processes.

NUTRIENT	FUNCTION
Proteins	Provide materials needed for growth and repair of cells
Carbohydrates:	
Starches	Combine with oxygen in the cells to produce ATP and heat energy
Sugars	
Fats	Combine with oxygen in the cells to produce ATP and heat energy; fat tissue provides insulation, support, and shock absorption
Vitamins	Provide chemicals needed for body functions
Minerals	Provide chemicals needed for body functions
Water	Provides fluid for transport and reaction medium needed for body functions

LIST 3–9. THE FOUR MAJOR TYPES OF FOOD SENSITIVITIES*

Food sensitivities can range from mild to dangerous and life-threatening reactions. The four major types of food sensitivities are:

1. **Food allergies.** These reactions are true allergic reactions which involve the body's immune system. Symptoms may include hives, asthma, stomach cramps, diarrhea, and vomiting occurring immediately or hours after eating. Foods that most often cause allergic reactions include cow's milk, egg white, corn, wheat, nuts, soybeans, fish, and shellfish. The other food sensitivities are not true allergic reactions and do not involve the body's immune system.

2. **Metabolic food reactions.** These reactions result from an impaired ability to digest, absorb, or utilize food ingredients. Examples are lactose intolerance and high-fat food intolerance.

3. **Secondary sensitivities.** These are side effects to the body caused by other agents such as diseases, prescription medications, and alcohol. For example, one might take an aspirin to relieve a headache or the pain of arthritis and experience the side effect of an upset stomach.

4. **Food idiosyncrasies.** These reactions do not involve the immune system and are not fully understood. An example is sulfite sensitivity, which may include breathing difficulties, hives, and anaphylactic shock, which may be fatal if not treated.

Adapted from: "If You Have a Food Sensitivity," Barton, Lavon, University of Vermont Extension Service, Food Flash, undated.

The Science Teacher's Book of Lists, © 1993 by Prentice Hall

LIST 3–10. DEVELOPMENTAL STAGES IN HUMAN BEINGS

DEVELOPMENTAL STAGE	*TIME OF DEVELOPMENT*
Embryo	From conception to the end of the eighth week of prenatal development
Fetus	From the ninth week of prenatal development to birth
Neonate	From birth to four weeks after birth
Infant	From four weeks after birth to age two
Child	From age two to the beginning of puberty, the onset of which varies and usually begins earlier in girls
Adolescent	From puberty to adulthood; sometimes referred to as the teen years
Young adult	From the end of adolescence to about age 40
Middle-age adult	From age 40 to about age 65
Old-age adult	From age 65 to death

LIST 3–11. THE NEW FOUR FOOD GROUPS

The Physicians Committee for Responsible Medicine has developed the New Four Food Groups. It is the first major overhaul of nutrition recommendations in more than three decades. The new food groups are based on medical evidence that a meat- and dairy-centered diet, with its high cholesterol and fat content, is a chief cause of heart disease, stroke, many cancers, and other serious diseases. A diet based on a variety of foods from the new group provides plentiful nutrition and is health-promoting. None of the foods in any of the new groups contains any cholesterol, and they're all full of fiber.

VEGETABLES
Dark green, leafy vegetables such as broccoli, collards, kale, mustard and turnip greens, chicory, and bok choy are excellent sources of vitamin C, beta-carotene, riboflavin and other vitamins, iron, calcium, and fiber. Dark yellow and orange vegetables —carrots, winter squash, sweet potatoes, pumpkin—provide extra beta-carotene. Eat lots of vegetables —at least three servings a day.

WHOLE GRAINS
Bread, pasta, hot and cold cereals, corn, millet, barley, bulgur, rice, and tortillas are all rich in fiber, complex carbohydrates, protein, B vitamins, and zinc, Build each meal around a hearty grain dish.

The New Four Food Groups

LEGUMES
Peas, all kinds of beans, and lentils are good sources of protein, fiber, iron, calcium, zinc, and B vitamins. This group also includes peanuts and peanut butter, baked and refried beans, chick peas, tofu, soy milk, and tempeh. Eat two or three servings a day.

FRUITS
All fruits are rich in fiber, vitamin C, and beta-carotene. Eat three pieces of fruit a day, including at least one serving of fruit high in vitamin C, such as citrus, melons, or strawberries. Choose whole fruit over juices, which contain less fiber.

The Science Teacher's Book of Lists, © 1993 by Prentice Hall

Printed with permission of the Physicians Committee for Responsible Medicine, P.O. Box 6322, Washington, D.C. 20015

NOTE: For an interesting comparison see List 3–13, Food Guide Pyramid. It is the latest food guide developed by the United States Department of Agriculture and was published in the fall of 1992.

LIST 3–12. WHAT'S WRONG WITH MILK AND EGGS?*

Milk is a high-fat fluid designed to turn a 45-lb. calf into a 1000-lb. cow in 18 months. Humans are the only species to drink milk after infancy, and the only species to take another species' milk. Far from being "natural," this cow baby-food is totally unnatural for people, and often causes allergic reactions, digestive disturbances, and is linked to heart disease.

8 OUNCES OF WHOLE MILK	*8.45 FLUID OUNCES SOYA MILK*
34 milligrams of cholesterol	0 milligrams of cholesterol
159 calories	150 calories
2 grams of fat	4.9 grams of fat

Eggs contain one of the densest concentrations of cholesterol available. They are intended to be total life-support for a baby chick for 21 days before hatching. When people eat eggs, cholesterol pours through the bloodstream, increasing the risk of heart disease. The human body makes all the cholesterol it needs and when extra cholesterol is eaten, only 100 mg a day can be eliminated. Therefore, any more than 100 mg of cholesterol taken in each day begins clogging the arteries.

ONE EGG CONTAINS

274 milligrams cholesterol
79 calories
5.6 grams fat
1.7 grams saturated fat

The Science Teacher's Book of Lists, © 1993 by Prentice Hall

Source: "The PETA Guide to Compassionate Living," page 21, People for the Ethical Treatment of Animals, P.O. Box 45216, Washington, DC 20015. Printed with permission.

LIST 3–13. FOOD GUIDE PYRAMID: A GUIDE TO DAILY FOOD CHOICES

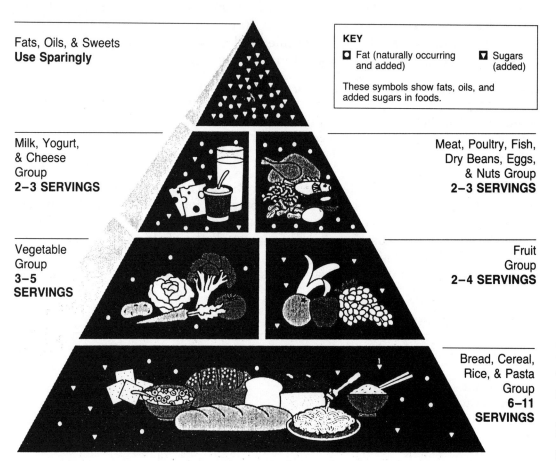

Fats, Oils, & Sweets
Use Sparingly

KEY

◻ Fat (naturally occurring and added)   ▼ Sugars (added)

These symbols show fats, oils, and added sugars in foods.

Milk, Yogurt,
& Cheese
Group
2–3 SERVINGS

Meat, Poultry, Fish,
Dry Beans, Eggs,
& Nuts Group
2–3 SERVINGS

Vegetable
Group
**3–5
SERVINGS**

Fruit
Group
2–4 SERVINGS

Bread, Cereal,
Rice, & Pasta
Group
**6–11
SERVINGS**

The Science Teacher's Book of Lists, © 1993 by Prentice Hall

LIST 3–14. A PATTERN FOR DAILY FOOD CHOICES

The U.S. Department of Agriculture and the American Red Cross have developed a food guidance plan, in which the foods are grouped according to the type of nutrients they provide. The food groups are not interchangeable, and it is important to choose a variety of foods from the five major food groups each day.

In addition to the five major food groups there is a sixth group: alcohol, fats, and sweets, to be consumed in moderation.

FOOD GROUPS	*SUGGESTED SERVINGS**
Fruits	2–4
Citrus	
Melon	
Berries	
Other fruits	
Vegetables	3–5
Dark-green leafy	
Deep-yellow	
Starchy vegetables	
Other vegetables	
Whole grain products	6–11
Breads	
Cereals	
Rice	
Pasta	
Enriched grain products	
Dairy	2–3
Milk	
Yogurt	
Cheese	
Meats/protein	2–3
Poultry	
Fish	
Dry beans	
Dry peas	
Eggs	
Nuts	
Fats, oils, sweets, and alcohol	Used occasionally, in moderation

*See List 3–18 for serving sizes.

LIST 3–15. DIETARY GUIDELINES FOR AMERICANS*

The U.S. Department of Agriculture and the U.S. Department of Health and Human Services have issued dietary guidelines for healthy Americans two years of age and over. Diseases caused by lack of vitamins and minerals are not common in the United States. But there are high rates of obesity and of certain diseases such as heart disease, high blood pressure, stroke, diabetes, and some forms of cancer. The links between diet and many of these diseases are still being investigated, but some clear correlations have been established. The guidelines are based on the data available in 1990.

- Eat a variety of foods.
- Maintain healthy weight.
- Choose a diet with plenty of vegetables, fruits, and grain products.
- Use sugars only in moderation.
- Use salt and sodium only in moderation.
- If you drink alcoholic beverages, do so in moderation.

LIST 3–16. TO DECREASE CALORIC INTAKE*

Eat a variety of foods that is low in calories and high in nutrients:

- Eat less fat and fewer fatty foods.
- Eat more fruits, vegetables, and breads and cereals—without fats and sugars added in preparation and at the table.
- Eat fewer sugars and sweets.
- Drink few or no alcoholic beverages.
- Eat smaller portions; limit second helpings.

The Science Teacher's Book of Lists, © 1993 by Prentice Hall

*Adapted from: "Nutrition and Your Health: Dietary Guidelines for Americans," Third Edition, 1990, U.S. Department of Agriculture, U.S. Department of Health and Human Services, Home and Garden Bulletin No. 232.

LIST 3–17. FOR A DIET LOW IN FAT, SATURATED FAT, AND CHOLESTEROL*

- Use fats and oils sparingly in cooking.
- Use small amounts of salad dressings and spreads, such as butter, margarine, and mayonnaise. One tablespoon of most of these spreads provides 10 to 12 grams of fat.
- Choose liquid vegetable oils most often because they are lower in saturated fat.
- Check labels on foods to see how much fat and saturated fat are in a serving.
- Have two or three servings of protein, with a daily total of about 6 ounces. Three ounces of cooked lean beef or chicken (without skin), provides about 6 grams of fat.
- Trim fat from meat; take skin off poultry.
- Have cooked dried beans and peas instead of meat occasionally.
- Moderate the use of egg yolks and organ meat.
- Have two or three servings daily of lowfat or nonfat milk or milk products.
- Choose skim or lowfat milk and fat-free or lowfat yogurt and cheese. One cup of skim milk has only a trace of fat, 1 cup of 2 percent milk has 5 grams of fat, and 1 cup of whole milk has 8 grams of fat.

LIST 3–18. WHAT'S MODERATE DRINKING?*

Women: No more than one drink a day
Women who are pregnant: no drinking
Men: No more than two drinks a day

Count as one drink:

- 12 ounces of regular beer
- 5 ounces of wine
- $1\frac{1}{2}$ ounces of distilled spirits (80 proof)

*Adapted from: "Nutrition and Your Health: Dietary Guidelines for Americans," Third Edition, 1990, U.S. Department of Agriculture, U.S. Department of Health and Human Services, Home and Garden Bulletin No. 232.

LIST 3–19. DIETARY GUIDELINES FOR AMERICANS: EAT A VARIETY OF FOODS

FOOD GROUP	ONE SERVING	RECOMMENDED NUMBER OF DAILY SERVINGS
Fruits & Vegetables	$\frac{1}{2}$ c.* diced fruit $\frac{3}{4}$ c. juice	2 or more servings of fruits
	1 med. apple, orange, banana	3 or more servings of vegetables
	1 c. raw leafy greens	
	$\frac{1}{2}$ c. other vegetable	
Grains	1 slice of bread	6 or more servings
	$\frac{1}{2}$ bun, bagel, English muffin	
	1 oz. dry cereal	
	$\frac{1}{2}$ c. cooked cereal, rice, or pasta	
Meats	3 oz. poultry, without skin	2 or 3 servings, with a daily total of 6 oz. Moderate use of organ meat and egg yolks.
	3 oz. lean beef	
	3 oz. fish	
	1 or 2 eggs	
Dairy	1 c. milk	2 or 3 servings
	1 c. yogurt	Choose skim or lowfat milk and fat-free or
	$1\frac{1}{2}$ slices of cheese	lowfat yogurt and cheese most of the time.

*c. = cup

Source: "Nutrition and Your Health: Dietary Guidelines for Americans," Third Edition, 1990, U.S. Department of Agriculture, U.S. Department of Health and Human Services, Home and Garden Bulletin No. 232.

LIST 3-20. NUTRITIONAL CALORIES*

The calories derived from the digestion of food are reported in large calories (kilogram calories, abbreviated "kcal") which are 1000 times the small calories used in much scientific work. (See list on properties of water in "Section 5: Physics.") A kilogram calorie is the heat required to raise the temperature of 1000 g of water 1°C.

Values for the three basic classes of food, carbohydrates, protein, and fat, were determined many years ago by burning typical substances in a calorimeter with oxygen. The general result was:

Carbohydrates	4	kcal/g
Protein	5.25	kcal/g
Fat	9	kcal/g

Because protein is usually incompletely digested, its value as food energy was reduced to 4 kcal/g.

These values are still used today in the calculation of the energy of foods. They are approximate and vary somewhat with the specific food source. One must know the composition of the food in terms of percentages or grams per serving weight to calculate the caloric value. Indigestible fiber and water do not count as energy sources.

Sample calculation using the above values with three cereal analyses:

Contents per 1 oz. (28.4 g)

CALORIES	*A*	*B*	*C*
Protein, g	4	3	8
Carbohydrates, g	20	23	20
Fat, g	2	1	0
Calculated calories	114	113	112
Calories on package	110	100	110

*Adapted from: Jane Brody, *Jane Brody's Nutrition Book*, Bantam Books, New York 1987, pp. 46, 56; and Ruthe Eshleman, *The American Heart Association Cookbook*, Fourth edition, David McKay, New York, 1991, pp. 497-502.

LIST 3–21. ENERGY EXPENDED BY A 150-POUND PERSON IN VARIOUS ACTIVITIES*

ACTIVITY	GROSS ENERGY SPENT IN CALORIES PER HOUR
Rest and light activity	**50–200**
Lying down or sleeping	80
Sitting	100
Driving an automobile	120
Standing	140
Domestic work	180
Moderate activity	**200–350**
Bicycling ($5\frac{1}{2}$ mph)	210
Walking ($2\frac{1}{2}$ mph)	210
Gardening	220
Canoeing ($2\frac{1}{2}$ mph)	230
Golf	250
Lawn mowing (power mower)	250
Bowling	270
Lawn mowing (hand mower)	270
Fencing	300
Rowing ($2\frac{1}{2}$ mph)	300
Swimming ($\frac{1}{4}$ mph)	300
Walking ($3\frac{1}{4}$ mph)	300
Badminton	350
Horseback riding (trotting)	350
Square dancing	350
Volleyball	350
Roller skating	350
Vigorous activity	**over 350**
Table tennis	360
Ditch digging (hand shovel)	400
Ice skating (10 mph)	400
Wood chopping or sawing	400
Tennis	420
Water skiing	480
Hill climbing (100 ft. per hr.)	490
Skiing (10 mph)	600
Squash and handball	600
Cycling (13 mph)	600
Scull rowing (race)	840
Running (10 mph)	900

The Science Teacher's Book of Lists, © 1993 by Prentice Hall

*Source: President's Council on Physical Fitness and Sports, "Exercise and Weight Control," (Washington, D.C.: U.S. Government Printing Office, 1979).

LIST 3–22. CALORIES FROM SOME COMMON FOODS*

FOOD	AMOUNT	CALORIES
Apple	1 medium	80
Apple juice	$\frac{1}{2}$ cup	60
Applesauce:		
unsweetened	$\frac{1}{2}$ cup	52
sweetened	$\frac{1}{2}$ cup	97
Asparagus	4 medium stalks	15
Avocado	$\frac{1}{2}$ 10-ounce avocado	185
Bacon	3 slices	110
Banana	1 medium	100
Bamboo shoots	1 cup	25
Bagel	$\frac{1}{2}$	80
Beans cooked:		
green, fresh or frozen	$\frac{1}{2}$ cup	15
Limas, fresh or frozen	$\frac{1}{2}$ cup	95
wax, fresh or frozen	$\frac{1}{2}$ cup	45
Beans, kidney, canned	$\frac{1}{2}$ cup	115
Beef, broiled meat only		
ground, lean	3 ounces	185
round, lean	3 ounces	160
sirloin	3 ounces	185
Beets	2	25
Blueberries, fresh, or frozen		
unsweetened	$\frac{1}{2}$ cup	40
sweetened	$\frac{1}{2}$ cup	105
Bouillon cubes	1 cube	5
Breads, 1-ounce slice		
French or Italian	1 slice	65
rye	1 slice	60
white	1 slice	70
Beer		
regular	12 fl. oz.	150
light	12 fl. oz.	95
Broccoli	1 cup	20
Brussels sprouts	1 cup	55
Butter	1 tablespoon	100
Cake		
Angel food	1 piece	125
Carrot, with cream cheese frosting	1 piece	385

(Continued)

Adapted from: "Nutritive Value of Foods," United States Department of Agriculture, Human Nutrition Information Service, Home Garden Bulletin, Number 72, 1981; and other publications of the USDA.

LIST 3–22. (Continued)

FOOD	AMOUNT	CALORIES
Coffeecake	1 piece	230
Devil's food with chocolate frosting	1 piece	235
Pound cake	1 slice	120
Sheet cake with frosting	1 slice	445
Cabbage		
Raw	1 cup	15
Cooked	1 cup	30
Chinese, raw	1 cup	10
Chinese, cooked	1 cup	20
Candy		
Caramels	1 oz.	115
Chocolate, plain	1 oz.	145
Chocolate, with peanuts	1 oz.	155
Fudge, plain	1 oz.	115
Gum drops	1 oz.	100
Jelly beans	1 oz.	105
Carrots, raw	1 cup	70
Catsup	1 tbsp.	15
Cauliflower		
Raw	1 cup	25
Cooked	1 cup	30
Celery	1 cup	20
Cheese		
American	1 oz.	105
Cheddar	1 oz.	115
Cottage cheese, 4% fat	1 cup	235
Cottage cheese, 2% fat	1 cup	205
Cream	1 oz.	100
Mozzarella (from partially skimmed milk)	1 oz.	80
Muenster	1 oz.	105
Parmesan, grated	1 oz.	130
Swiss	1 oz.	105
Chocolate		
Milk	1 oz.	145
Semi-sweet	1 oz.	145
Cookies		
Chocolate chip, commercial	4 cookies	180
Chocolate chip, home baked	4 cookies	184
Oatmeal with raisins	4 cookies	245

The Science Teacher's Book of Lists, © 1993 by Prentice Hall

(Continued)

LIST 3–22. (Continued)

FOOD	AMOUNT	CALORIES
Peanut butter	4 cookies	245
Shortbread	4 cookies	155
Sugar cookie	4 cookies	235
Corn		
Fresh	1 ear	60
Cream style	1 cup	185
Whole kernel	1 cup	165
Cucumber	6–8 slices	5
Cream		
Half-and-half	1 tbsp/cup	20/315
Light	1 tbsp/cup	30/470
Whipping		
Light	1 tbsp/cup	45/700
Heavy	1 tbsp/cup	50/820
Sour	1 tbsp/cup	25/495
Danish pastry	1 pastry	220
Doughnuts, plain	1 doughnut	210
Eggs		
Fried in butter	1 egg	95
Poached	1 egg	80
Scrambled with milk and butter	1 egg	110
Eggplant, cooked	1 cup	25
Kale	1 cup	40
Lettuce		
Boston	2 inner leaves	Trace
Iceberg	1 cup	5
Romaine	1 cup	10
Lamb		
Chops	3 oz.	235
Leg	3 oz.	205
Rib, roasted	3 oz.	315
Liver, beef	3 oz.	185
Lobster	3 oz.	80
Macaroni and cheese	1 cup	430
Margarine	1 tbsp	100
Marshmallows	1 average	25
Milk		
Whole	1 cup	150
Lowfat, 2%	1 cup	120
Lowfat, 1%	1 cup	100
Nonfat, skim	1 cup	85
Buttermilk	1 cup	100
Chocolate	1 cup	210

(Continued)

LIST 3–22. (Continued)

FOOD	AMOUNT	CALORIES
Noodles, egg, cooked	1 cup	200
Oils, vegetable, olive, etc.	1 tbsp	125
Olives, green	4 medium	20
Orange	1 medium	65
Orange juice	$\frac{1}{2}$ cup	55
Pancakes, from mix	2, 4-inch diameter	120
Peas	$\frac{1}{2}$ cup	60
Peach	1 medium	36
Peanuts, roasted	8 to 10	95
Pies		
Apple	1 piece	405
Blueberry	1 piece	380
Cherry	1 piece	410
Lemon meringue	1 piece	355
Pumpkin	1 piece	320
Pizza, cheese	$\frac{1}{8}$ of 14-inch pie	185
Popcorn, air popped	1 cup	30
Pork		
Ham	3 oz.	205
Chop, broiled	3 oz.	275
Chop, pan fried	3 oz.	335
Rib, roasted	3 oz.	270
Frankfurter	1 frankfurter	145
Potatoes		
Baked	1 medium	90
Boiled	1 medium	90
French-fried	10 pieces	155
Rice		
Brown	1 cup	230
White	1 cup	225
Rolls		
Dinner	1 roll	85
Frankfurter or hamburger	1 roll	115
Hoagie or submarine	1 roll	400
Soups,[a] canned		
Chicken-noodle	1 cup	75
Cream of chicken	1 cup	115
Cream of mushroom	1 cup	130
Minestrone	1 cup	80
Tomato	1 cup	85

(Continued)

---

[a]Check brand labels and check new low-calorie, low salt soups.

LIST 3–22. (Continued)

FOOD	AMOUNT	CALORIES
Vegetable beef	1 cup	80
Vegetarian	1 cup	70
Spinach	$\frac{1}{2}$ cup	20
Squash		
Summer	$\frac{1}{2}$ cup	15
Winter	$\frac{1}{2}$ cup	65
Strawberries	$\frac{1}{2}$ cup	25
Tangerine	1 medium	40
Tomato juice	$\frac{1}{2}$ cup	25
Tomatoes		
Fresh	1 medium	40
Canned	$\frac{1}{2}$ cup	25
Tuna, canned		
Packed in oil	6.5 oz. can	530
Packed in water	6.5 oz. can	235
Turkey		
light	4 oz.	200
dark	4 oz.	230
Walnuts	4 medium	50
Watermelon	1 cup	50
Wheat germ	1 tablespoon	15
Spaghetti	1 cup	190
Tortillas, corn	1 tortilla	210
Waffles, home-made	1 waffle	245

LIST 3–23. INFORMATION LISTED ON A BOX OF CEREAL*

Nutrition Information
(Per Serving)
Serving Size = 1 ounce ($\frac{1}{2}$ cup)
Servings Per Container = 14.5

	CEREAL	CEREAL PLUS $\frac{1}{2}$ CUP VITAMIN A & D FORTIFIED SKIM MILK
Calories	110	150
Protein, grams	2	6
Carbohydrate, grams	21	27
Fat, grams	2	4
Cholesterol, milligrams	0	0
Sodium, milligrams	160	220
	PERCENTAGE OF U.S. RECOMMENDED DAILY ALLOWANCES (USRDA)	
Protein	2	10
Vitamin A	25	30
Vitamin C	*	*
Thiamin	25	30
Riboflavin	25	35
Niacin	25	25
Folic Acid	25	25
Vitamin B-6	25	30
Vitamin D	10	25
Calcium	6	20
Iron	25	25

*Contains less than 2% of the USRDA of this nutrient.

To calculate the percentage of calories from fat $= \dfrac{\text{g of fat} \times 9}{\text{total calories}} \times 100$

Example:

Percentage of fat in cereal $= \dfrac{2 \times 9}{110} \times 100 = \dfrac{18}{110} \times 100 = 16\%$

16% of the calories in this food are fat.

Another example:

Percentage of fat in whole milk $= \dfrac{4 \times 9}{150} \times 100 = \dfrac{36}{150} \times 100 = 24\%$

24% of the calories in this food are from fat.

*Adapted from: University of Vermont Extension Service, Food Flash: "Read the Label for Value," Lavon Bartel, FS 142. The UVM Extension and the U.S. Department of Agriculture.

LIST 3–24. LABEL INFORMATION FROM SELECTED BREAKFAST CEREALS

BRAND	SERVING SIZE	CALORIES	SUGAR GRAMS	FIBER GRAMS	SODIUM MILLIGRAMS
Kellogg's All-Bran™	1 oz. about $\frac{1}{2}$ c.	50	NL	14	140
Ralston Bran Chex™	$\frac{2}{3}$ c.	90	5	5	300
General Mills Cheerios™	$1\frac{1}{4}$ c.	110	1	2	290
Kellogg's Cracklin' Oat™ Bran	$\frac{1}{2}$ c.	110	7	5	140
Nabisco Cream of Wheat™ Quick	1 oz. $2\frac{1}{2}$ Tbsp	100	.5	5	80
Nabisco Cream of Wheat™ Instant	1 packet 1 oz.	110	0	1	180
Post Grape-nuts™	1 oz. $\frac{1}{4}$ c.	110	3	2	170
Kellogg's Muselix™, with raisins, dates, almonds	1.5 oz.	160	13	3	150
Kellogg's Nutri-Grain™ Wheat	$\frac{2}{3}$ c.	100	2	3	170
Quaker Oats Oatmeal™, Instant	1 packet	90	NL	2.8	270
Kellogg's Raisin Bran™	$\frac{3}{4}$ c.	120	12	5	220
Post Raisin Bran™	$\frac{1}{2}$ c.	80	9	4	180
Kellogg's Rice Krispies™	1 c.	110	3	trace	290
Nabisco Shredded Wheat™	1 biscuit	90	0	3	10

NOTE: serving size varies, which affects the comparisons.
NL: not listed

LIST 3–25. NUTRITIONAL INFORMATION FROM SOME CANDY BAR WRAPPERS

NAME	SERVING	CALORIES	SUGAR GRAMS	FAT GRAMS	SODIUM MILLIGRAMS
Bounty™	1 bar/2 oz.	140	17	7	30
Fruit Skittles™	1 pack/2.30 oz.	270	60	2	30
Hershey's Fifth Avenue™	1 bar/2 oz.	280	38	12	130
Hershey's Milk Chocolate With Almonds™	1 bar/1.45 oz.	230	18	14	55
Hershey's Milk Chocolate™	1 bar/1.55 oz.	240	23	14	45
Hershey's Mr. Goodbar™	1 bar/1.65 oz.	270	20	18	20
Kit Kat™	1 bar/1.5 oz.	230	21	12	55
Mars Milky Way™	1 bar/NA	280	42	11	150
PB Max™	1 bar/1.48 oz.	240	20	15	150
Peter Paul Almond Joy™	1 bar/1.76 oz.	250	22	14	70
Snickers™	1 bar/NA	280	36	13	160

Note: Information was taken from individual candy wrappers.

LIST 3–26. FOUR FOOD TERMS THAT ARE HELPFUL TO KNOW*

1. **Calories** are units of measurement that express the energy you get from food. Take in more calories than you need and you gain weight. Take in too few calories and you lose weight. Being over- or underweight or having greatly fluctuating weight can contribute to health problems.

   The calories derived from the digestion of food are reported in large calories (kilogram calories) which are 1000 times the small calories used in much scientific work. A kilogram calorie is the heat required to raise the temperature of 1000 g of water 1°C, and is abbreviated kcal.

2. **Proteins** are the principal building blocks of cells. They are large, complex organic compounds made up of carbon, hydrogen, oxygen, nitrogen, and sometimes other elements such as sulfur and iron. The proteins that most directly meet the body's needs come from animal foods: meat, fish, eggs, and milk. When combined with other protein sources, protein from legumes—especially soybeans and chickpeas—is as valuable as animal protein.

3. **Carbohydrates** are compounds containing carbon, hydrogen, and oxygen, such as sugars, starches, and cellulose (fiber). Grain products, potatoes, and dry beans and peas are sources of starch. Jellies and other sweets, which are concentrated in corn syrup, fruit sugars, and refined cane and beet sugars, are sources of sugars. Fresh fruits are a more nutritious source of sugar than jellies, but one needs to keep in mind that sugar is sugar no matter the source. The sugars in fruit are not better or more healthful than the sugars in jellies or candies. The benefits provided by fruits come from the minerals they contain and fiber, especially if the skin is eaten. Fruits, vegetables, and whole-grain cereals provide fiber.

4. **Fats** are concentrated sources of calories. A gram of fat provides twice as many calories as a gram of protein or digestible carbohydrate. Some foods are pure fat, for example, shortening, cooking oil, and salad oil. Some foods are high in fat, such as cream, nuts, and bacon. Others have significant fat content, for example, whole milk and meat. Many snacks and desserts contain large amounts of fat with little other nutritional value. High fat intake has been associated with many diseases, especially heart disease, colon cancer, breast cancer, and gout.

*Adapted from: University of Vermont Extension Service, Food Flash: "Read the Label for Value," Lavon Bartel, FS 142. The UVM Extension and the U.S. Department of Agriculture.

LIST 3–27. A TRANSLATOR'S GUIDE TO FOOD LABELS*

There are a number of terms used on food labels that can be misleading or difficult to understand. Here is a glossary of the most commonly misunderstood terms and definitions.

Acidulants or acidifiers—acids that have many uses in food as flavor-enhancing agents, as preservatives to inhibit the growth of micro-organisms, and as antioxidants to prevent discoloration or rancidity. They may also be used to adjust the acidity of some foods.

Anti-caking agents—substances used to prevent powdered or granular foods from absorbing moisture and becoming lumpy. They help products like salt and powdered sugar flow freely.

Antioxidants—preservatives that prevent or delay discoloration in foods, such as cut potatoes and sliced apples. They also keep oils and fats from turning rancid. Some examples are BHA, BHT, and propyl gallate.

Bran—tough, outer coating of cereal grains (such as wheat, rye, and oats) that is separated in the refining process but is included in whole-grain products.

Calorie—unit of measure of the amount of fuel or energy a food product provides to the body. Food energy comes from three primary sources: fats, carbohydrates, and proteins.

Carbohydrates—sugars and starches that supply energy and help the body use fats efficiently. Foods with complex carbohydrates are recommended to be included for a healthful diet—whole-grain breads and cereals and dried peas and beans.

Cholesterol—fatlike substances found in foods of animal origin, but not in foods from plants. Cholesterol is essential to body functions. However, the body can make what it needs, so the amount in some people's diet is often excessive, increasing the risk of atherosclerosis and heart disease.

Emulsifiers—these agents stabilize fat and water mixtures so they will not separate. Egg yolks act as emulsifiers in mayonnaise to keep the oil from separating from the acids.

Fats—secondary source of energy and calories, they play a key role as carriers of fat-soluble vitams (A, D, E, and K). They provide the body with insulation and shock absorption.

Fiber—provides bulk or roughage in the diet. Fiber is derived from plant sources.

(Continued)

Source: "A Consumer's Guide to Food Labels," *FDR Consumer*, September 1988, HHS Publication No. (FDA) 88-2083, Department of Health and Human Services, FDA, Rockville, Maryland.

LIST 3–27. (Continued)

Flavor enhancers—help bring out the natural flavor in some foods. Some examples are monosodium glutamate (MSG), and disodium guanylate.

Flavors—naturally occurring and artificial agents used to give more taste to food. Flavoring agents include extracts from spices and herbs, as well as others that are synthetic.

Grains—Hard seed cereal plants, such as wheat, rice, corn, and rye. Whole grains contain the entire seed of the plant.

Humectants—chemicals such as glycerol, propylene glycol, and sorbitol that are added to foods to help retain moisture, fresh taste, and texture. Often used in candies.

Hydrogenated and partially hydrogenated—labeling terms that describe the process of adding hydrogen to an unsaturated fat to make it saturated. Oils may be hydrogenated to various degrees to make them suitable for use in products such as margarine.

Light or lite—labeling terms that suggest a food is lower in calories unless some other meaning is specified or obvious. Since 1980, FDA has required food labeled as "low calorie" to contain no more than 40 calories in a serving and no more than 0.4 calories per gram.

Niacin—a water-soluble B vitamin that is important for health of all body cells. The body needs it to use oxygen to produce energy.

Preservatives—substances that keep foods from spoiling, becoming rancid, or developing off-color flavors.

Refined flour—type of flour produced by milling grains to a fine consistency. Refining removes bran, fiber, and some other nutrients. Enriched flour has iron and three B vitamins added to levels required by the FDA.

Riboflavin—a water-soluble B vitamin that helps the body obtain energy from food and aids in growth, digestion, and proper functioning of the nervous system.

Sequestrants—chemicals used to bind trace amounts of metal impurities that can cause food to become discolored or rancid. EDTA is an example.

Stabilizers and thickeners—substances that give foods a smooth, uniform texture. They also protect foods from adverse conditions, such as wide temperature fluctuations and physical shock during distribution. The most common thickening agents are cornstarch and wheat starch. Other types include carrageenan, locust bean gum, agar-agar, sodium alginate, gelatin, and pectin.

Sugar-free/sugarless—common table sugar (sucrose), fructose, and corn syrup are among the types of calorie-containing sweeteners found in foods. A food can be labeled sugar-free and still contain calories from

(Continued)

LIST 3–27. (Continued)

sugar alcohols (xylitol, sorbitol, and mannitol), provided the basis for the claim is explained. Saccharin is a nonnutritive sweetener, that is, it has no calories. Aspartame (Nutrasweet™) has the same calories as sugar but is so much sweeter that only small amounts are needed to provide the desired sweetness in a product; hence, its caloric contribution is negligible. Acesulfame K, a sweetener approved by the FDA in 1988, is also noncaloric because it is not metabolized, or broken down by the body.

LIST 3-28. TOP SPORTS FOODS: SOME HEALTHFUL CHOICES*

When you're training hard, juggling school or work, exercise, and social activities plus trying to eat healthfully, you may feel frustrated that you have no time to eat the proverbial "three square meals" every day. Nevertheless, you can maintain a healthful diet. The trick is to eat a variety of nutrient-dense, lowfat snacks or meals-on-the-run.

The following list includes foods that are commonly available in a convenience store, sandwich shop, or salad bar or can be kept stocked at home. These nutritious foods guard your health within a moderate to low calorie range. Since not one of the foods is nutritionally perfect, you need to choose a variety in order to get a balance of the vitamins, minerals, carbohydrates, and proteins necessary for top performance and good health.

Foods and Nutrients

FOOD	IMPORTANT NUTRIENTS	COMMENTS
Milk, lowfat Yogurt, lowfat	Calcium, protein Riboflavin	Calcium is important throughout life to maintain strong bones. Plan to eat lowfat dairy products two to four times each day. Pizza (with lowfat mozzarella cheese) is another calcium-rich alternative.
Broccoli	Vitamins A, C	One stalk (cooked) offers 100% RDA for vitamin C. Frozen and fresh are nutritionally similar, since freezing doesn't destroy the vitamin C.
Spinach	Vitamins A, C Folic acid	Add to salads for more nutrients than offered by pale lettuce. Keep frozen spinach stocked at home for a quick dinner vegetable.
Green peppers	Vitamin C	Half a pepper offers 100% RDA of vitamin C. Add to salads and pizza, or even munch on a raw pepper for a low-calorie snack.
Tomatoes	Vitamins A, C Potassium	Boost intake by adding sliced tomatoes to sandwiches. Choose foods with tomato sauce (pizza, pasta, etc.). Drink tomato juice.
V-8 Juice™	Vitamins A, C Potassium	An easy, cook-free way to get the nutrients from eight vegetables! Keep small cans stocked for a snack or lunchtime beverage.
Baked potato	Potassium Vitamin C Carbohydrates	Be sure to eat the skin—it contains 75% of the vitamin C! For a low-calorie topping, add yogurt. Or mash with milk, for moistness without the fat and calories of butter or sour cream.

(Continued)

Source: Nancy Clark, MS, RD: Sports Medicine Brookline, Brookline, MA 02167. Used with permission.

LIST 3–28. (Continued)

FOOD	IMPORTANT NUTRIENTS	COMMENTS
Orange juice	Vitamin C Potassium Folic acid Carbohydrates	A 6-ounce serving (fresh or frozen) offers 100% RDA of vitamin C. A great post-exercise "recovery food" for potassium, "carbs," and fluid. Orange juice is nutritionally superior to many other fruit juices.
Bananas	Potassium Carbohydrates Vitamin C	To prevent over-ripening, store in the refrigerator. The skin may turn black, but the fruit will be fine. Add to cereal or eat with peanut butter and a glass of milk for a balanced, on-the-run meal.
Cantaloupe	Vitamins C, A	Half a small melon offers 100% RDA of vitamin C—and very few calories! Enjoy with lowfat cottage cheese for a quick, "lite" lunch or snack.
Chicken, Turkey	Protein	Dark meat has more nutrients, calories, and cholesterol than white; remove the skin to reduce fat, calories and cholesterol.
Lean beef	Protein Iron Zinc	Beef is among the best sources of iron and zinc. Avoid fatty meats: choose a lean roast beef sandwich rather than a greasy hamburger.
Fish, tuna	Protein Fish-oil	The oil in salmon, albacore tuna, and sardines may protect against heart disease. Avoid fried fish; use low-fat mayo with tuna, if possible.
Bran cereal	Fiber Carbohydrates	Bran is excellent for fiber (to help prevent constipation). Select "fortified" and "enriched" cereals for the most iron; drink orange juice with cereal to enhance iron absorption.
Muffins (bran, corn)	Carbohydrates B-vitamins Fiber	More nutritious than doughnuts or breakfast pastry—especially whole wheat, corn meal, and bran muffins. Top with jelly (rather than butter) for extra carbohydrates and moistness.
Bread, bagels (whole grain)	Carbohydrates B-vitamins Fiber	Dark, whole-grain breads (rye, whole wheat, oatmeal, etc.) are preferable to breads made with refined white flour. Bread is not fattening; however, butter, margarine, cream cheese, and mayonnaise are!
Pizza	Calcium Protein Vitamin A Carbohydrates	Of fast foods, thick-crust pizza with single-cheese and vegetable toppings (not pepperoni or sausage!) is preferable to burgers. If the pizza is oily, simply blot off the grease with a napkin.
Popcorn	Carbohydrates Fiber	Depending on preparation, this can be a wholesome, lowfat snack that's preferable to greasy chips. But be cautious of even "lite" commercial brands of popcorn—they can be 50% fat.

LIST 3–29. VITAMINS AND THEIR FUNCTIONS*

Vitamins are organic compounds necessary for metabolism, the chemical process through which energy and matter are made available for use by the cells and body. Vitamins can be classified into two groups: those that are fat soluble and those that are water soluble.

Vitamins, the USRDA, and Their Contributions

FAT-SOLUBLE VITAMINS	US RDA[a]	CONTRIBUTIONS
Vitamin A	5000 IU[b]	Assists in formation of healthy skin, hair, nails, mucous membranes; is a component of retinal pigments necessary for normal and night vision; essential for development of teeth and bones.
Vitamin D	400 IU	Essential for healthy bones and teeth; needed for absorption and use of calcium and phosphorus; synthesized in skin which is exposed to sunlight.
Vitamin E	30 IU	Assists in the formation of cells (especially red blood cells), muscles, and tissues; protects vitamin A and unsaturated fatty acids from oxidation; actual biochemical role not yet understood; helps healing of skin.
Vitamin K	About 1 mg	Essential for normal clotting of the blood. Helps maintain healthy bones.
WATER-SOLUBLE VITAMINS		
Thiamine (B$_1$)	1.5 mg	Helps with carbohydrate and amino acid metabolism; assists in the synthesis of chemicals in the nervous system. Helps maintain healthy appetite, skin, muscles, and nerve cells.
Riboflavin (B$_2$)	1.7 mg	Essential for cellular respiration; helps release energy from nutrients, necessary for healthy mucous membranes; important in the growth of a fetus.

(Continued)

Adapted from: Brody, Jane, *The New York Times Guide to Personal Health*, Times Books, New York, 1982; and Davis, P. William; Solomon, Eldra Pearl; Berg, Linda R., *The World of Biology*, Fourth Edition, Saunders College Publishing, Philadelphia, 1990.

[a]U.S. RDA—the recommended dietary allowance, identified by the Food and Nutrition Board of the National Research Council, as needed to maintain good health.

[b]International Unit: the internationally accepted unit recognized as the amount that produces a needed, specific biological effect.

LIST 3–29. (Continued)

WATER-SOLUBLE VITAMINS	US RDA[a]	CONTRIBUTIONS
Niacin (B_{39})	20 mg	Essential for cellular respiration; needed for healthy skin, nerves, and for the digestion of food.
Vitamin B_6	2 mg	Needed for metabolism of proteins, amino acids, and fats; assists in formation of red blood cells and maintenance of healthy skin.
Vitamin B_{12}	6 mg	Needed for metabolism of nucleic acids; assists in the formation of red blood cells and the function of the nervous system; contains cobalt; has no vegetable source; essential in preventing pernicious anemia.
Folic acid	0.4 mg	Assists in formation of red blood cells and genetic material; is especially important to women during pregnancy to prevent anemia.
Pantothenic acid	10 mg	Assists in metabolism of nutrients and formation of hormones which regulate the nervous system.
Biotin	0.3 mg	Needed for carbon dioxide fixation and releasing energy from carbohydrates.
Vitamin C	60 mg	Assists in the formation of collagen, bone matrix, tooth dentine, capillaries; protects vitamins from oxidation; may block some cancer causing agents; promotes healthy gums and skin.

LIST 3–30. SELECTED MINERALS AND THEIR FUNCTIONS

Minerals are inorganic nutrients that are required for healthy cell function and thus, a healthy body. Unlike most vitamins, they usually are not destroyed by cooking, food processing, or exposure to air.

MINERAL	SOURCES	FUNCTIONS
Calcium	Dairy products, green leafy vegetables, and "hard" drinking water	Constituent of bones and teeth; needed for muscle and nerve function and normal clotting of blood
Chlorine	Occurs in foods and in table salt, sodium chloride	Essential for fluid and acid-base balance, water balance and distribution, osmotic pressure, and muscular functioning.
Cobalt	Meat, dairy products	A component of vitamin B_{12} essential for production of red blood cells.
Copper	Liver, eggs, fish, whole wheat flour, beans	Essential for synthesis of melanin and hemoglobin
Fluorine	Usually added to municipal water supplies, in some "hard" drinking water	Component of bones and teeth, helps prevent tooth decay
Iodine	Seafoods, iodized salt	A component of thyroid hormones, which stimulate metabolic rate
Iron	Meat, nuts, egg yolks, legumes, brewer's yeast, wheat germ	Needed for hemoglobin in red blood cells, essential for oxygen transport and cellular respiration
Magnesium	Many foods: nuts, meat, fish, milk, salad greens, bananas, cocoa, dark green vegetables, dry beans and peas, whole-grain cereals	Constituent of bones; balanced with calcium, is essential for muscle and nerve function
Manganese	Whole-grain cereals, egg yolks, green vegetables	Necessary to activate enzymes, especially those needed to produce urea
Nickel	Legumes, tea, cocoa, pepper	Importance to human nutrition not yet understood
Phosphorus	Dairy, brains, kidneys, liver	Along with calcium, a building block of bones; necessary for energy transfer and storage and in metabolic processes
Potassium	In many foods: bananas, orange juice, dried fruit, peanut butter, yogurt	Important in muscles, including heart muscles, and nerve functions; is related in function to sodium and chlorine
Sulfur	Animal proteins, legumes, nuts	Found in insulin, which regulates the sugar level in the blood
Zinc	Cocoa, meat, dry beans and peas, poultry, shellfish, whole-grain cereals	Known to be a component of 70 enzymes; needed in protein digestion; may be helpful in healing wounds

LIST 3–31. UNITED STATES RECOMMENDED DAILY ALLOWANCES FOR VITAMINS*

Vitamins are organic compounds which are necessary in the diet for normal growth and healthy maintenance. They are necessary to transform foods into energy.

VITAMIN	UNIT	INFANTS (0–12 MO.)	CHILDREN UNDER 4 YRS.	ADULTS & CHILDREN OVER 4 YRS.	PREGNANT OR LACTATING WOMEN
A	IU	1500	2500	5000	8000
D	IU	400	400	400	400
E	IU	5	10	30	30
C	mg	35	40	40	60
Folacin	mg	0.1	0.2	0.4	0.8
Thiamine (B_1)	mg	0.5	0.7	1.5	1.7
Riboflavin (B_2)	mg	0.6	0.8	1.7	2.0
Niacin	mg	8	9	20	2
Vitamin B_6	mg	0.4	0.7	2	2.5
Vitamin B_{12}	mcg	2	3	6	8
Biotin	mg	0.05	0.15	0.3	0.3
Pantothenic acid	mg	3	5	10	10

IU = International Unit
mg = milligram
mcg = microgram

*Source: "Some Facts and Myths of Vitamins," *FRA Consumer*, July 1988, HHS Publication No. (FDA) 88-2117, U.S. Department of Health and Human Services, FDA, Rockville, Maryland.

LIST 3–32. CARBOHYDRATE LOADING: TIPS FOR ENDURANCE ATHLETES*

The Science Teacher's Book of Lists, © 1993 by Prentice Hall

- For two to three days prior to a marathon, triathlon, or other form of endurance that lasts more than ninety minutes of strenuous effort, you should super-fuel your muscles by eating hearty amounts of carbohydrate-rich foods. About 60%–70% of your calories should come from breads, pasta, cereal, potatoes, fruits, juices, and other high-carbohydrate choices. To slightly overeat carbohydrates is wiser than to undereat.

- In addition to eating a high-carbohydrate diet, you should exercise less to rest your muscles and allow them the opportunity to stock up on carbohydrates. The week prior to the event, gradually taper off your exercise, so that you're training only 20 minutes two and three days prior to the event, nothing the day before. Eliminate any last-minute hard training; you'll simply fatigue yourself at a time when rest would be more beneficial.

- To avoid "getting fat" due to the reduced amount of exercise, you may want to eat slightly fewer total calories. Since you'll be exercising less, you should have less of an appetite. However, the sources of calories that you do eat should be primarily carbohydrates, with small amounts of lean protein (to protect your muscles) and minimal amounts of fat.

- You'll know if you've "carbo-loaded" correctly if the scale goes up—that's water weight, not fat weight! For every one gram of carbohydrate that you store in your muscles as glycogen, you also store three grams of water. This water becomes available to you during the exercise and helps prevent dehydration.

- When selecting your diet, be careful to choose high-carbohydrate foods, not high-fat foods. The two often come together, such as butter on potato, cream cheese on bagels, and cream in ice cream.

FOODS HIGHEST IN CARBOHYDRATES	LOWER CARBOHYDRATE CHOICES
Spaghetti, noodles, macaroni with tomato sauce	Pizza, lasagna with lots of meat, cheese
Rice, potato, yams, stuffing without butter or gravy	French fries, fried rice, buttery potato
Lentils, beans, split peas	Casseroles with rich sauces and gravies
Breads, muffins, bagels—plain or with jam	Donuts, croissants, Danish pastry
French toast, pancakes, cereal	Eggs and breakfast meats
Jam, jelly, honey, syrup	Butter, margarine, cream cheese

(Continued)

Source: "Carbohydrate Loading: Tips for Endurance Athletes," Nancy Clark, MS, RD; Sports Medicine Brookline, Brookline MA 02167. Used with permission.

LIST 3–32. (Continued)

FOODS HIGHEST IN CARBOHYDRATES	LOWER CARBOHYDRATE CHOICES
Bananas, pineapple, raisins, figs, date squares, fig newtons	Cookies, cakes, baked snacks, pastries made with lots of butter
Juices: apple, grape, apricot, orange	Beer, wine, alcohol (dehydrating effect)
Blenderized fruit and juice drinks	Milk shakes, frappes
Sherbet, ice milk, yogurt	Ice cream—especially gourmet brands

- The food you eat the days before the event will fuel your muscles. The food you eat the morning of the event will help maintain a normal blood sugar level and thereby feed your brain and help you think clearly. Eat a small (<500 calorie) meal 2 to 4 hours prior to the event, such as 1 or 2 slices of toast, a small bowl of hot or cold cereal, or whatever you normally eat prior to your training runs. Don't try any new foods! Stay with the tried-and-true meals.

- You're unlikely to starve to death during endurance exercise, but you can seriously hurt yourself if you become dehydrated. Prevent dehydration by drinking extra water and juice when you carbo-load; limit alcohol (which has a dehydrating effect). Before the event, you should have to urinate frequently.

  For fluids the morning of the event:
  —Drink at least three glasses of water up to two hours before the start. (The kidneys will process this liquid in about 90 minutes, allowing time to empty the bladder pre-event.)
  —Drink one to two glasses of water 5 to 10 minutes before the start.
  —Drink whenever possible during the event. Try to consume at least one-half cup every 20 minutes.

- After the event, drink plenty of non-alcoholic fluids until your urine is clear. Eat wholesome, high-carbohydrate foods to replace the glycogen, potassium, and electrolytes. Oranges, bananas, yogurt, Fig Newtons™, potatoes, banana bread, pretzels, and juices are some appropriate "recovery foods." Enjoy the victory dinner, keeping in mind that your muscles are craving carbohydrates; feed them lots of potatoes, rolls, vegetables, fruits, and other "carbs," just as you did prior to the event. Add salt, if you crave it.

LIST 3–33. HOW TO BOOST YOUR IRON INTAKE*

- Iron is an important part of the red blood cell that helps transport oxygen from the lungs to the muscles. If you have a diet that's low in iron, you may develop iron deficiency anemia. The symptoms are weakness and rapid fatigue upon exertion.

- The Recommended Daily Allowance for iron is 10 mg for men, 18 mg for women. Women require more iron because they lose it through menstrual bleeding. The average woman consumes less than the RDA for iron.

- You can absorb the iron in meat and animal products twice as efficiently as that in vegetables. For example, although spinach is a relatively iron-rich vegetable, you can absorb only 3 percent of that iron. Animal proteins enhance the absorption of the vegetable iron when the two types of food are eaten together. Hence, if you were to eat spinach along with some chicken, meat, or fish, the animal protein would help you to better absorb the vegetable iron. Similarly, if you add lean hamburger to chili, the meat will help you to better absorb the iron in the beans.

- Vitamin C also enhances iron absorption. Try to eat foods rich in vitamin C along with meals, such as orange juice with breakfast cereal, sliced tomato on tuna sandwich, broccoli with fish. Some fruits rich in vitamin C are oranges, grapefruit, cantaloupe, kiwi, and strawberries. Vegetables rich in vitamin C include broccoli, spinach, peppers, tomato, and potato.

- Bread, cereal, and other wholesome carbohydrates are good sources of iron if the words *enriched* or *fortified* are on the food label. In general, grain products offer very little iron, and it's poorly absorbed. The iron in fortified grains supplements the little bit that occurs naturally. You can significantly boost absorption of this iron by eating a source of vitamin C with grains. For example, by having a glass of orange juice with breakfast cereal, you'll absorb 2.5 times more iron.

- When cooking use cast iron skillets and pots. They offer more nutritional value than stainless steel! For instance, the iron content of spaghetti sauce increases from 3 mg to 88 mg per half-cup of sauce when simmered in an iron pot for 3 hours.

- Milk and dairy products are poor sources of iron. Hence, if you primarily rely on cheese, yogurt, milk, and other dairy products for protein, remember that you also need to include some iron-rich foods in your diet. Vegetarians who avoid red meat have a much higher risk of becoming anemic.

- If you are not eating lean red meats, iron-enriched breakfast cereals or grains, and do not use cast iron cookware, you might want to take a simple iron supplement, such as is found in a multi-vitamin and mineral

(Continued)

Source: "How to Boost Your Iron Intake," Nancy Clark, MS, RD; Sports Medicine Brookline, Brookline, MA 02167. Used with permission.

LIST 3-33. (Continued)

pill. Taking the RDA may help protect you from becoming anemic, but remember that the iron in meats and animal foods is better absorbed.

- If you're an avid runner, you should pay particular attention to your iron intake, since runners are more prone to become anemic than other athletes, perhaps because the pounding damages blood cells or because runners often experience small blood losses via the intestinal tract.

The following list indicates the iron content of popular foods. To help determine if you meet the RDA, add up the milligrams of iron that you consume in a day.

Iron Content of Popular Foods

FOOD	*IRON (MG)*	*FOOD*	*IRON (MG)*
Liver, 4 oz. cooked	10*	Baked beans, ½ cup	2
Beef, 4 oz. roasted	6*	Kidney beans, ½ cup canned	2
Pork, 4 oz. roasted	5*	Bean curd (tofu) ¼ cake	2
Turkey, 4 oz. roasted dark meat	3*		
Tuna, 6.5 oz. canned light	3*	Cereal, 100% fortified (Total™, Just Right™), ¾ cup	18
Chicken breast, 4 oz. roasted	1*		
Fish, 4 oz. broiled haddock	1*	Kellogg's Raisin Bran™, ½ cup	18
Egg, 1 large	1	Cream of Wheat™, ½ cup cooked	9
		Wheat Chex™, ⅔ cup	4.5
Prune juice, 8 oz.	3	Spaghetti, ½ cup cooked, enriched	1
Apricots, 12 halves dried	2	Bread, 1 slice enriched	1
Dates, 10 dried	1		
Raisins, ⅓ cup	1	Molasses, 1 Tbsp. blackstrap	2
		Brewer's yeast, 1 Tbsp.	2
Spinach, ½ cup	2	Wheat germ, ¼ cup	2
Grean peas, ½ cup cooked	1		
Broccoli, ½ cup chopped	1		

*This iron is best absorbed

The Science Teacher's Book of Lists, © 1993 by Prentice Hall

LIST 3–34. A DASH OF SALT

A dash of salt adds taste to our food, but many people overuse it. In addition, salt is frequently used in processed foods, and more salt is consumed in processed foods than from the salt shaker. Thus, it is important to read the labels on processed foods to determine their sodium content.

Salt contains the element sodium which is necessary for maintaining blood volume and cellular pressure and transmitting nerve impulses. Overuse of salt has been linked to high blood pressure in many individuals. Intakes of 1,100 to 3,300 milligrams of sodium per day are considered safe and adequate for the healthy adult by the Food and Nutrition Board of the National Academy of Science's National Research Council.

One teaspoon of salt contains approximately 2,000 milligrams of sodium. Current estimates of daily sodium intake by individuals are between 2,300 to 6,900 milligrams (about 1 to 3 teaspoons or 6 to 17 grams of salt.)

The Amount of Salt in Some Common Foods and Beverages

FOOD	PORTION	SODIUM (MILLIGRAMS)
Alcoholic beverages:		
Beer	12 oz.	25
Wine:		
Red:		
Domestic	4 oz.	12
Imported	4 oz	6
White:		
Domestic	4 oz.	19
Imported	4 oz.	2
Carbonated beverages:		
Club soda	8 oz.	39
Condiments		
Butter, regular	1 tablespoon	115
Butter, unsalted	1 tablespoon	2
Garlic salt	1 teaspoon	1,850
Garlic powder	1 teaspoon	1
Soy sauce	1 tablespoon	1,029
Table salt	1 teaspoon	1,938
Breakfast sweets		
Cheese Danish	1 roll	250
Yeast doughnut	1 doughnut	99
Honey sweet roll	1 roll	119
Cookies		
Chocolate chip	2 cookies	69
Fig bars	2 bars	96
Macaroons	2 cookies	14

(Continued)

LIST 3–34. (Continued)

FOOD	PORTION	SODIUM (MILLIGRAMS)
Dairy Products		
American cheese	1 oz.	409
Blue cheese	1 oz.	396
Cheddar cheese	1 oz.	176
Grain Products		
English muffin	1 muffin	293
Instant oatmeal	$\frac{3}{4}$ cup	238
Popcorn salted	1 cup	175
Popcorn, unsalted	1 cup	1
Puffed Wheat™	2 cups	2
Spoon-sized Shredded Wheat™	$\frac{2}{3}$ cup	2
Stuffing mix	1 cup	1,131
Wheaties™	1 cup	355
Protein Products		
Cheeseburger, fast food	1 burger	709
Corned beef	3 oz.	801
Frozen fish dinner	1 dinner	1,212
Frankfurter	1 frank	639
Ham	3 oz.	1,114
Turkey roll	2 oz.	332
Soups		
Beef bouillon	1 cup	782
Beef noodle	1 cup	952
Chicken noodle	1 cup	1,106
Clam chowder, Manhattan	1 cup	1,808
Minestrone	1 cup	911
Tomato	1 cup	871
Sugars and Sweets		
Fudge, chocolate	1 oz.	54
Gum drops	1 oz.	10
Peanut brittle	1 oz.	145
Maple syrup	1 tablespoon	1
Vegetables		
Green peas, canned	1 cup	493
Green peas, frozen	1 cup	150
Fresh peas	1 cup	2
Potatoes, baked or broiled	1 medium	9
Potatoes, au gratin	1 cup	1,095
Sauerkraut, canned	1 cup	1,554
Tomatoes, stewed	1 cup	584

Source: "The Sodium Content of Your Food," U.S. Department of Agriculture, Home and Garden Bulletin Number 233, 1980.

LIST 3–35. MILK

Milk is the nutritious fluid produced by the mammary glands of all female mammals for the purpose of feeding their young. The milks of cows, goats, sheep, camels, donkeys, and zebras are used by humans around the world, as substitutes for human milk. In the Western world, cow's milk is used most often by humans. Cow's milk is treated and prepared for market in a variety of forms in the United States. These forms of milk can be grouped as: fresh sweet milks, cultured and sour milks, canned milks, and dry milks.

MILKS

Fresh Sweet Milks

Acidophilus milk—pasteurized, homogenized, chilled milk to which lactobacillus acidophilus concentrated culture has been added for those who have lactose intolerance.

Chocolate flavored—whole milk with at least 3.25% milk fat to which sugar and cocoa have been added.

Chocolate milk—whole milk with at least 3.25% milk fat to which sugar and chocolate have been added.

Concentrated milk—fresh, whole milk which has been pasteurized, homogenized, and then had $\frac{2}{3}$ of the water removed.

Fluid whole milk—milk consisting of 87% water, 3.25% milk fat, and at least 8.25% nonfat milk and other solids.

Fortified milk—milk to which vitamins A and D, riboflavin, thiamine, niacin, and sometimes iodine have been added.

Homogenized milk—pasteurized milk that has been mechanically treated to keep the fat globules evenly dispersed throughout the milk. This prevents the fat rising to the top to form cream.

Low fat milk—milk with a fat content from 0.5% to 2%. U.S. federal law requires fortification with 2,000 IU of vitamin A per quart.

Pasteurized milk—milk which has been partially sterilized by heating it to temperatures no lower than 145°F for not less than 30 minutes or 161°F for not less than 15 seconds and then promptly cooled to 40°F or lower.

Raw milk—milk that has been treated only by cooling.

Skim milk—milk with a fat content usually less than 0.5%. U.S. federal law requires fortification with 2,000 IU of vitamin A per quart.

Vitamin D milk—whole or skim milk in which the vitamin D content has been increased, usually to 400 IU per quart.

(Continued)

LIST 3–35. (Continued)

Cultured & Soured Milks

Buttermilk—milk or cream that has the fat removed but contains at least 8.25% milk solids other than fat.

Clabber—milk that has soured to the stage of firm curds but has not separated to whey.

Cultured buttermilk—pasteurized skim milk that has been soured by a lactic acid bacteria; contains at least 8.25% milk solids other than fat.

Cultured milk—milk to which a lactic acid culture has been added.

Sour milk—milk that has soured by natural or artificial means

Yogurt—whole or skimmed milk which has been fermented with a bacterial culture.

Canned Milks

Evaporated milk—whole milk from which 60% of the water has been removed under vacuum at temperatures below boiling. It is homogenized and sealed in sterilized cans. It contains at least 7.2% milk fat and not less than 25.5% total milk solids.

Sweetened condensed milk—whole milk from which about 50% of the water has been evaporated, to which refined cane and/or corn sugar are added in amounts for preservation, usually 44%. It is heated and then cooled before canning. It contains at least 8.5% milk fat and not less than 28% total milk solids.

Dry Milks

Dry whole milk—whole milk from which most of the water has been removed. It contains not less than 26% milk fat and not more than 4% moisture.

Nonfat dry milk—milk from which fat and water have been removed. Contains not more than 5% moisture and 1.5% fat by weight. Most nonfat dry milk is packaged as instant nonfat dry milk.

LIST 3-36. WHAT YOU SHOULD KNOW ABOUT FOOD POISONING ORGANISMS*

Food poisoning strikes over 2 million American every year with mild-to-severe intestinal flu-like symptoms. Due to government inspection of foods and refrigeration, many consider food poisoning a health problem of the past. Nevertheless, improper handling of food in the home is the number one cause of food poisoning in the United States today. Knowing and applying the facts about food poisoning can keep one from becoming another victim of food poisoning.

Organisms that spoil food can be classified into two groups:

1. The food poisoning bacteria that reproduce at room temperatures between 60°F to 90°F. They don't reproduce when refrigerated.

2. The food spoilage organisms, such as some bacteria, yeasts, and molds, that can reproduce at low temperatures even when refrigerated at temperatures of 40°F. Most of these organisms give off strong odors and make the food look and taste awful.

Food Poisoning Organisms

1. **Staphylococcus aureus** is a small round bacterium that is with us all of the time since it lives in our noses and on our skin.

    - *S. aureus* is usually transmitted to food by handling. At room temperatures, it begins to grow.

    - At 100°F, certain types of *S. aureus* multiply rapidly and produce a toxin or poison causing nausea, vomiting, and diarrhea, which occur 2 to 6 hours after ingesting infected food, and may last a day or two.

    - Prepared foods such as starchy foods, cooked and cured meats, cheese and meat salads should not be left out at room temperature over 2 hours.

    - Usually not serious for healthy individuals.

    - *S. aureus* is the most common cause of food poisoning in the United States.

2. **Salmonella** is the name used for some 2,000 closely related bacteria which appear as short thin rods under a microscope.

    - *Salmonella* causes more severe flu-like symptoms than *S. aureus*.

    - Symptoms of diarrhea, vomiting, and fever usually appear 12 to 36 hours after eating and may last 2 to 7 days.

(Continued)

Adapted from: "The Safe Food Bank, Your Kitchen Guide," Mary Ann Parmley, United States Department of Agriculture Food and Safety Inspection Service, Home & Garden Bulletin, Number 214, 1985.

LIST 3–36. (Continued)

- Infants, young children, the ill, and the elderly may be seriously affected.
- *Salmonella* continually cycles through the environment through intestinal tracts of people and other animals.
- *Salmonella* is often found in raw foods, such as eggs, poultry, meat, and unpasteurized milk. To prevent the growth of *Salmonella*, thaw meat and poultry in the refrigerator.
- Always wash surface and implements that have been in contact with raw meats.
- Cooking kills *Salmonella*. Follow cooking directions for temperature and time.

3. ***Clostridium perfringens*** is often called the "cafeteria germ."

- Ranks third as a cause of food poisoning in the U.S.
- Continuously cycles through the environment through the intestines of humans, other animals, the soil, and sewage.
- *C. perfringens* spores are anaerobic; that is, they grow in an environment where there is little or no oxygen.
- Produces two types:
    (a) Normal vegetative cells, which cause food poisoning.
    (b) Spores, which can survive temperatures between 70°F to 120°F and high concentration of oxygen and become normal vegetative cells when the environment is conductive.
- Symptoms of diarrhea and gas pains usually develop 8 to 24 hours after eating.
- Symptoms are mild and usually end after a day but can be serious for those with medical conditions, such as ulcer patients.
- Commonly found in foods left for long periods of time on steam tables.

4. ***Clostridium botulinum*** **or botulism** is a rod shaped bacterium which produces a deadly poison. The poison is not rare, but contracting the disease is.

- Its spores are present in water and soil.
- Grows best in a reduced-oxygen environment. Thus, improperly canned foods provide an excellent environment for its development.
- High cooking temperatures will kill the bacterial cell but higher temperatures are required to kill the spores. That is why canning is done in a pressure canner.
- Symptoms develop 12 to 48 hours after eating.

The Science Teacher's Book of Lists, © 1993 by Prentice Hall

(Continued)

LIST 3-36. (Continued)

- The poison attacks the nervous system, causing double vision, droopy eyelids, trouble swallowing, difficult breathing, and flaccid paralysis.
- Without medical attention, a victim can die of suffocation or heart failure.
- To avoid botulism, carefully examine any canned foods, especially home-canned foods. Danger signs are milky liquids that should be clear, loose lids, and swollen cans or lids.
- Don't taste suspicious foods. Even small amounts of botulinum toxin can be highly dangerous.
- Take care when throwing away suspicious foods. They can harm unsuspecting children and animals.
- There is an antitoxin which has reduced the number of deaths, but nerve damage is possible and recovery is slow.

LIST 3–37. FOR A SAFE KITCHEN

- Wash your hands before touching foods.
- Thaw meat, fish, and poultry in a refrigerator, NOT at room temperature or in warm water.
- Keep foods hot. Temperatures of 165° to 212°F reached in frying, roasting, baking, and boiling kill most food-poison producing bacteria.
- Keep countertops and work areas clean.
- Cook thoroughly.
- Don't interrupt cooking.
- Allow extra time for cooking frozen foods, generally 1½ times longer than when the food is thawed.
- Thoroughly reheat leftovers.
- Install a smoke detector and check it periodically.
- Never use water to put out a grease fire; use a dry powder like baking soda or a Class B fire extinguisher.
- Keep baking soda and/or a fire extinguisher in an easily accessible place, but not over the stove.
- When using a nonstick cooking spray, apply to the utensil over the sink and never near a hot burner or grill.
- Set timers to help you remember when to remove an item from heat.
- Do not leave the kitchen when boiling liquids are on the stove.
- Turn handles of pans toward the center of the stove to avoid dangerous spills of hot foods.
- Never leave young children unattended in a kitchen, especially when the stove is in use.
- Do not touch a pot to determine if it is hot; use pot holders and oven mitts.
- Always turn off the burner before removing the pan.
- Do not reach over a steaming pan; at a temperature of 212°F, steam can cause severe burns.
- Keep emergency numbers in sight, near the telephone.
- Do not wear loose-fitting clothing, especially a bathrobe, while cooking. These can get caught in a handle, spilling hot foods, or ignite quickly.
- Do not plug or unplug appliances with wet hands.

The Science Teacher's Book of Lists, © 1993 by Prentice Hall

(Continued)

LIST 3–37. (Continued)

- Keep appliances clean and in good working order.
- Unplug small appliances when not in use.
- Turn off food processors before inserting blades.
- Use a cutting board when cutting and slicing foods.
- When washing knives, hold them so that you can always see the blade.
- When loading knives, forks, and other sharp utensils in a dishwasher, place the pointed end down.
- Do not store food and cleaners in the same area.
- If young children are present, store cleaners, chemicals, and medications out of their reach.
- Teach children kitchen safety as you teach them to use the kitchen and to cook.

LIST 3–38. SOME PIONEERS WHOSE CONTRIBUTIONS LED TO OUR UNDERSTANDING OF THE HUMAN BODY AND DISEASES THAT AFFECT IT

SCIENTIST	*CONTRIBUTION*
Zaecharia Janssen	Between 1591 and 1608, put two lenses together and discovered that these lenses could magnify objects. This was an early microscope.
Galileo Galilei	In 1609, built an adjustable microscope with lenses in a tube.
Anton van Leeuwenhoek	From 1660 to his death in 1723, built over 200 microscopes by mounting lenses on metal frames. Some of these could magnify objects 270 times their size. Leeuwenhoek became a master observer, recording sketches and descriptions in notebooks and letters, providing the world with an introduction to microbes.
William Harvey	In 1616, explained his theory that the blood circulates from the heart to arteries all around the body through veins and then back to the heart.
Robert Boyle	In 1663, wrote about a possible link between the causes of fermentation and the causes of disease.
Robert Hooke	In 1665, in his book, *Micrographia*, Hooke wrote about observing little boxes being present in living things when observed through a microscope. He named these little boxes cells.
Louis Joblot	In 1718, observed microbes in water from a hay infusion and observed that the microbes disappeared after boiling the water. The significance of this was not understood for over a hundred years.
Edward Jenner	In the late 1790s developed vaccinations against smallpox.
Felix Dujardin	In 1835, discovered protoplasm, the living material in cells.
John Snow	In the 1850s inferred that cholera was spread by polluted water. Saved thousands from the epidemic in London by closing down a pump that delivered water polluted with sewage.
Louis Pasteur	In 1857, discovered that bacteria, in addition to yeast, can produce fermentation. Also discovered that substances that ferment could be protected from spoiling by boiling them and then sealing them to keep microbe-carrying air out.
	Proved that spoiling could not occur without living cells.
	First to disprove the spontaneous generation theory, which supported ideas such as a hair from a horse's tail could fall to the ground and spontaneously become a snake.
	Discovered the bacterium that could turn wine to vinegar.

(Continued)

The Science Teacher's Book of Lists, © 1993 by Prentice Hall

LIST 3–38. (Continued)

SCIENTIST	CONTRIBUTION
Louis Pasteur (*continued*)	Discovered that heating wine and milk to temperatures of about 55°C to 60°C (131° to 140°F) kept the wine and milk from souring. This heating process is known as pasteurization.
	Determined that the spores that Koch related to anthrax did not cause anthrax in animals when merely ingested, but did cause the deadly disease when the anthrax spore entered the blood stream.
	Demonstrated with wine, milk, beer, and silk worms that clean utensils and work area were essential to quality products.
	Immunized dogs against rabies. In 1885, gave rabies vaccinations to a boy who had been repeatedly bitten by a rabid dog and saved his life.
Joseph Lister	In the 1860s, he applied ideas of Pasteur for the need to keep areas clean. Before performing an operation, he washed his hands and cleaned his instruments.
	Experimented with different strengths of carbolic acid to kill microbes on his hands, patient's wounds, instruments, and the air. Listerine™ is named after him.
Robert Koch	In 1863, after reading Pasteur's work on fermentation, designed experiments on anthrax. He grew anthrax microbes in blood and observed their spores.
	Developed ways to grow bacteria in pure cultures and to fix bacteria on microscope slides.
	Known as the father of bacteriology.
	Koch's postulates provided a means still used to determine the causative agents of disease.
	Isolated tubercle bacillus that causes tuberculosis.
	Discovered the bacterium that causes cholera.
	With co-workers isolated microbes that cause pneumonia, meningitis, gonorrhea, streptococcus, and staphylococcus infections.
Friedrich Loffler (with Edwin Klebs)	In the late 1800's, a student of Koch who discovered the microbe that causes diptheria.
Shibasaburo Kitazato	In the late 1800's, a student of Koch who discovered the tetanus bacterium.
Arthur Nicolaier	In the late 1800's, also credited with the discovery of the tetanus bacterium.
Walter Reed	In 1900, confirmed that yellow fever was caused by the *Aedes* mosquito, and suggested methods to deal with it, including ruining the natural habitat of the mosquito.
Howard Taylor Ricketts	Began study in 1906, identified the microbe that causes Rocky Mountain Spotted Fever: *Rickettsia rickettsii*.
	Proved that ticks transmit the disease.
	Died in 1910 from typhus while investigating that disease.

LIST 3–39. SOME DISEASES AND ASSOCIATED TERMS

abscess—inflammation that may progress to an infection, as in an abscessed tooth

acute—short term, severe (illness)

alcoholism—a disease in which a person is physically and psychologically dependent on alcohol

anemia—a condition in which there is too little hemoglobin in the red blood cells, which transport oxygen

aneurysm—a sac formed by an outpouching of the wall of any blood vessel due to weakness in the wall; symptoms include pain and shock. Death may result from rupture of the outcropping

arthritis—inflammatory disease of the joints and surrounding areas

asthma—chronic but reversible narrowing of the air passages causing breathing difficulties and wheezing

atherosclerosis—"hardening of the arteries"; progressive blockage of an artery due to increased plaque formation; this reduces the artery's elasticity and is referred to as "hardening"

athlete's foot—fungus infection of the skin of the feet

bacillus—a rod-shaped bacterium

bacteria—unicellular microorganisms

benign—non-cancerous (tumor)

botulism—type of food poisoning, can be deadly

bronchitis—inflammation of the air passages, can be acute or chronic

cancer—a group of diseases characterized by uncontrolled cell growth

cataracts—cloudiness of the lens of the eye; eventually results in blindness

carcinogen—substance that causes or accelerates cancer

cholesterol—fat-like solid steroid compound found in most foods of animal origin, essential for well-being; high blood counts of low density lipoprotein (LDL) or "bad cholesterol" have been associated with heart disease

chronic—long-term illness or condition of poor health

cirrhosis of the liver—scarring disease of the liver, usually resulting from alcoholism, that eventually leads to liver failure and death

communicable—contagious (disease)

contact dermatitis—skin irritation resulting from contact with a substance to which the individual is sensitive

diabetes—a disease which interferes with the body's production of insulin

emphysema—lung disease associated with swelling of the alveoli (air sacs)

(Continued)

LIST 3–39. (Continued)

epidemic—widespread occurrence of a disease

gingivitis—inflammation of the gums

glaucoma—increased pressure in the eyeball; can be acute or chronic

hypertension—high blood pressure

hypoglycemia—abnormally low blood sugar

immunity—the body's defense against infection or disease which results in antibody formation

malignant—cancerous

meningitis—infection of the meninges, the membranes covering the brain and spinal cord

osteomyelitis—infection of the bone

osteoporosis—loss of calcium in the bones

otosclerosis—common cause of loss of hearing in adults

Parkinson's disease—progressive nervous disease in which resting muscles weaken; patient may become totally physically and mentally disabled

plantar wart—growth on the bottom of the foot caused by infection with a wart virus

pneumonia—inflammation of the lung

rheumatic fever—streptococcal infection that affects the heart

sickle-cell anemia—blood disorder in which the hemoglobin (the pigment in the blood that carries oxygen) is abnormal; hereditary

scoliosis—abnormal lateral curvature of the spine

stress—tension

tonsillitis—inflammation of the tonsils

tuberculosis—infectious bacterial disease that most often affects the lungs (pulmonary tuberculosis) but can affect other organs; once prevalent, became almost unknown in industrialized nations, but is now returning, often associated with AIDS

tumor—abnormal overgrowth of cells with no known purpose

urinary tract infection—infection of any of the parts of the system that collects and expels urine

vaccination—introduction of a small dose of an agent into the body to help build an immunity to it

LIST 3–40. SOME CHILDHOOD HEALTH CONCERNS AND DISEASES

chicken pox—is an infectious viral disease with an incubation period of ten to twenty-one days. Rare complications include encephalitis and pneumonia. Can be followed by Reye's Syndrome (see below).

diabetes mellitus—is the body's inability to produce insulin or to use insulin to metabolize glucose for energy. Insulin-dependent diabetes need carefully controlled daily injections of insulin, a well-balanced diet, exercise, and regular medical check-ups to monitor progress and possible complications. Non-insulin-dependent diabetics need a well-balanced diet, exercise, and regular medical check-ups to monitor progress and possible complications; in addition, some need a daily, oral medication to regulate the blood sugar.

dysentery—is a severe form of diarrhea due to an infection of the large bowel with the microorganism *Shigella flexneri*. Symptoms begin with a sudden rise in temperature, loss of appetite, abdominal pain, convulsions, and profuse diarrhea with mucus and blood. Can lead to malnutrition, dehydration, and death.

earaches—are one of the most common illnesses in childhood. There are basically two types: an infection of the outer ear or canal and the more serious infection of the middle ear and ear drum.

encephalitis—infection of the brain. This serious condition occasionally accompanies mumps.

enuresis—bed-wetting; generally speaking children are toilet trained between the ages of two and three years. However, bladder control while sleeping may take longer, and bed-wetting is considered normal until about age six. If bed-wetting persists, a doctor should be consulted.

fever—a temperature above the normal 98.6°F; it is not a disease but an indicator that the body is fighting an infection or possible disease; cause for concern, observation, and consultation with a doctor.

German measles—three-day measles or rubella, is relatively harmless to children but is dangerous to pregnant women whose unborn baby may be affected with a variety of conditions including blindness, deafness, heart defects, cleft palate, and brain damage. The incubation period is from fourteen to twenty-one days. After a day or two of feeling ill, the patient develops the characteristic rash and lymph nodes swell. Can be prevented by immunization.

lice—head lice, *Pediculus capitis*, are small insects that live and feed on the scalp and lay eggs (nits) at the base of a hair shaft. They are spread by contact with a person who has lice and by sharing infected combs, ear phones, etc. Shampooing with prescription shampoo followed by use

The Science Teacher's Book of Lists, © 1993 by Prentice Hall

(Continued)

LIST 3–40. (Continued)

of a fine toothed comb removes the lice and their eggs. Multiple treatments may be necessary.

measles—is one of the most contagious viral diseases known and can be serious. The symptoms are similar to those of a cold. There is an incubation period of ten to fourteen days. Within four to five days after symptoms begin, a rash of light red spots develop on face and neck and spreads to the chest and arms; vaccine is available.

mononucleosis—a viral infection of the B-lymphocytes which results in total body involvement; can last from two weeks to three or more months. It is most common among those aged 10 to 35.

mumps—a moderately contagious viral disease with an incubation period of fourteen to twenty-one days. For adults, mumps have been known to affect ovaries, testes, and pancreas. Encephalitis (see above) is an occasional complication. Can be prevented by vaccination.

poliomyelitis—is an acute infection caused by one of three polio viruses that can cause permanent paralysis of the muscles of the trunk, including those that control breathing, and the extremities. Begins with flu-like symptoms. Can be mild; can be fatal. Can be prevented with Salk and Sabin vaccines.

Reye's Syndrome—a rare but life-threatening disease that may follow chicken pox or viral respiratory illnesses; associated with use of aspirin

Rocky Mountain spotted fever—a virus which attacks the blood cells and skin, and in some cases the heart, liver, and lungs producing chills, muscular pains, and severe headaches. It is transmitted by a bite of hard-shelled ticks. Is treated with antibiotics.

Roseola—a disease with fever and rash, probably caused by a virus, may be accompanied by convulsions. The fever can be controlled with medication; occurs most often between the ages 6 months and 2 years.

strep throat—group A beta-hemolytic *Streptococcus* bacteria which infects the throat; strep throat can lead to complications of kidney infection, rheumatic fever, and scarlet fever.

teething—growth of teeth through the gums causes discomfort and pain. Ice in a moist cloth or a frozen teething ring may help with the discomfort.

whooping cough—contagious respiratory infection that usually affects infants and children who have not been immunized; severe coughing spells followed by a deep breath which makes a "whoop" sound.

LIST 3–41. DISEASES THAT COULD BE ELIMINATED BUT ARE USUALLY ASSOCIATED WITH VICTIMS OF IMPOVERISHED AND WAR-TORN COUNTRIES

beri beri—(also Beriberi) deficiency of vitamin B that produces nerve damage leading to paralysis, heart failure, and death.

bubonic plague—internal bleeding, headache, swollen glands, boils, and death caused by the bite of fleas transmitting bacteria from infected rats

cholera—an infection of the intestines by *Vibrio cholerae* that leads to dehydrating diarrhea; caused by contact with food and/or water contaminated with infected feces; on the rise in some South American countries

dysentery—infection of the bowel causing severe form of diarrhea

kwashiorkor—a form of malnutrition caused by lack of protein causing an imbalance of liquids, which produces a severely swollen belly in young children; leads to diarrhea, dehydration, and death

malaria—an infectious disease transmitted by the bite of an infected *Anopheles* mosquito which passes on parasitic protozoa, causing chills and fever.

malnutrition—lack of proper food, especially protein; can cause swollen belly, rough skin, emaciation, and death

rickets—deficiency of vitamin D that produces symptoms including softening of the bones, crippling, pain, and deformity

scurvy—deficiency of vitamin C that produces symptoms including bleeding gums, hemorrhaging, and death

yellow fever—tropical disease producing fever, jaundice, yellow skin, vomiting, and sometimes death; caused by the bite of *Aedes* mosquitos

The Science Teacher's Book of Lists, © 1993 by Prentice Hall

LIST 3–42. COMMON SKIN PROBLEMS

The skin presents the body's first defense against irritants and infections.

abscess—a swollen inflamed area in which pus gathers

acne—a common skin disorder characterized by inflammation of the sebaceous glands resulting in pimples and blackheads

boil—an inflammation which may resolve itself or may result in the collection of pus in the center

candida—fungus infections that thrive in dark moist areas of the body, like underarms, under breasts, folds in skin of overweight people, nipples of breast-feeding women, the vagina, and the groin area; associated with diaper rash, thrush mouth

carbuncle—a large boil with multiple centers of pus

herpes—an infection of skin and nerves caused by a virus that appears as a group of blisters; there are two types:

  • Type I usually infects the face and mouth and causes cold sores

  • Type II usually infects the genitals and surrounding areas

impetigo—a highly contagious bacterial infection caused by *Streptococcus* and *Staphylococcus* bacteria causing blisters that pop and ooze

ringworm—a fungus (not a worm) that attacks the skin, causing rough, raised eruptions to occur in circular patches; tinea capitis is ringworm of the head

shingles—herpes zoster, a painful blistering of the skin at the ends of nerves; associated with a reactivation of the chicken pox virus

stye—an infection or small boil on the eyelid

tinea cruris—fungus infection, ringworm of the groin, known as jock itch (see ringworm above)

tinea pedis—fungus infection, ringworm of the foot, known as athlete's foot (see ringworm above)

warts—overgrowth of skin cells brought on by viral infection

LIST 3–43. FACTS ABOUT ANOREXIA AND BULIMIA

Two major eating disorders are anorexia nervosa and bulimia nervosa. It is estimated that 1 million Americans suffer from an eating disorder and that as many as 20 percent could die from complications due to malnutrition, infection, or suicide. For more information, especially regarding treatment, consult the school nurse or your personal physician, or call your local hospital.

Anorexia nervosa

- Sometimes called the "starvation sickness," it is a complex eating disorder that usually begins during adolescence.
- Those suffering from anorexia become so obsessed with weight, thinness, and food that they deny hunger and refuse to eat.
- As malnutrition increases, bodily systems and functions are negatively affected, resulting in symptoms such as low blood pressure, slow heartbeat, and infections; ultimately the disorder becomes life-threatening.
- Females are more susceptible than males. About 90 percent of all persons suffering from anorexia are women.
- The cause is not fully understood, but the refusal to eat adequately is a sign of serious distress.
- Symptoms include: eating unusually small amounts of food, refusing to eat, abnormal weight loss, hyperactivity, depression, insecurity, nausea after eating normal amounts of food, and denial of a problem.
- Treatment requires medical, psychological, and dental care along with nutrition education and family counseling.

Bulimia nervosa

- A secretive eating disorder characterized by binge eating and purging.
- Those suffering from bulimia gorge on foods and then purge themselves by vomiting intentionally or using laxatives to rid the body of food and calories or diuretics to rid it of liquids.
- Many with eating disorders alternate between anorexia and bulimia.
- The onset has been linked to dieting begun prior to or following a major trauma.
- Symptoms include: secret eating, disappearing after eating (for purging), unusual fluctuations in weight, swollen parotid glands, abuse of drugs and/or alcohol, becoming dependent on diet pills, laxatives, and diuretics to lose weight, and dental problems.
- Treatment requires medical, psychological, and dental care along with nutrition education and family counseling.

LIST 3–44. HEALTH CARE CONCERNS OF THE HUMAN REPRODUCTIVE SYSTEMS

Some Concerns for Women

cancer—of the various female reproductive organs and breasts.

endometriosis—uterine tissue growing outside the uterus; can make the menses painful.

gonorrhea—bacterial toxin may produce redness and swelling; infects sexual organs, a variety of complications are possible such as meninges and infertility.

PMS—Pre-Menstrual Syndrome, mild to severe discomfort before the menses.

uterine fibroids—Benign tumors in the uterus; can make the menses painful.

vaginitis—infection of the vagina characterized by abnormal discharge, itching, and discomfort. There are different types of vaginal infections caused by different organisms, e.g., yeast or monilia, *Gardnerella*, and *Trichomonas*.

Some Concerns for Men

cancer—of the various male reproductive organs; testicular cancer is one of the most common cancers in men under 30; prostate cancer is more frequent in older men.

epididymitis—an infection of the epididymis (a sperm-storing structure attached to each testicle).

foreskin irritation—an irritation of the skin on or under the foreskin.

orchitis—infection of the testicles.

prostatitis—an infection of the prostate gland.

twisting of the testicles—twisting of the testicles and structures in the scrotum is not only painful but dangerous because the blood supply can be interrupted.

Some Concerns for Both Men and Women

STD (Sexually Transmitted Disease)—there are about fifteen diseases that can affect men and women and are transmitted through sexual intercourse:

- **AIDS**—acquired immunodeficiency syndrome (See "List 3–46, AIDS Vocabulary".)

(Continued)

LIST 3–44. (Continued)

- **Genital herpes** (herpes simplex Type II virus)—blisters on genitals, may cause flu-like symptoms; threat to fetus and newborns, linked to cervical cancer, no known cure.

- **Gonorrhea** (*Neisseria gonnorrhoeae*)—an infection which in early stages causes painful urination in males and is difficult to detect in females; the infection can spread causing sterility and can damage heart valves, outer coverings of the brain and spinal cord, and joints in both males and females; is treated with penicillin.

- **Nongonococcal urethritis** (NGU)—an inflammation of the urethra, usually caused by chlamydial bacteria; causes difficult urination; treated with tetracycline.

- **Pelvic Inflammatory Disease** (PID)—an infection of the reproductive organs and pelvic cavity, may lead to sterility; treated with antibiotics and surgery.

- **Syphilis** (*Treponema pallidum*)—spirochete bacterium infection, spread through lymphatic and circulatory pathways; the disease passes through different stages; brain damage can result; treated with penicillin; 33.3% of patients recover spontaneously, 5% to 10% die.

- **Trichomoniasis**—a protozoan that can be contracted from dirty toilet seats and towels; causes discharges and soreness; treated with drugs which eliminate the protozoan.

- **Yeast infections** (genital candidiasis)—symptoms are soreness and discharge; more common in females; treated with drugs.

LIST 3–45. SOME BIRTH CONTROL METHODS AND THEIR RATE OF FAILURE

METHOD	PERCENTAGE OF FAILURE WHEN USED CORRECTLY
Chance (no contraception)	90
Condom for men	2.6
Condom for women	No data available yet
Contraceptive diaphragm	3
Douche	40
Intrauterine device (IUD)	1
Oral contraceptives	0.3
Rhythm	13
Spermicides	3
Tubal ligation (female sterilization)	0.14
Vasectomy (male sterilization)	0.15
Withdrawal	9

Depo-provera (Similar hormonal principal as oral contraceptives but given in injections every 3 months or in larger doses every 6 months. Not approved for general use in the United States.)

NOTE: Lower rates of failure have been achieved by combining contraceptive methods. Higher rates of failure have occurred when a specific method is not used correctly.

LIST 3–46. AIDS VOCABULARY

AIDS—acquired immunodeficiency syndrome, a deadly disease that attacks and depresses the body's immune functions; transmitted via semen or blood containing the HIV virus, first recognized in 1981. AIDS patients die within several months to several years of cancer, pneumonia, tuberculosis, or other infections.

AIDS dementia complex—a neuropsychological disorder resulting from infection of the central nervous system by the retrovirus and characterized by progressive cognitive, motor, and behavioral dysfunction that usually ends in coma followed by death.

AIDS transmission—mainly by semen during sexual intercourse with an infected person or by direct exposure to infected blood or infected blood products, as through the use of hypodermic needles.

ARC—AIDS-related complex; symptoms include night sweats, fever, swollen lymph glands, and weight loss. ARC patients have been exposed to the HIV virus.

at risk—people with multiple sex partners (heterosexual and homosexual); intravenous drug users who share needles and their sexual partners; people who need frequent blood transfusions; and infants born to mothers with AIDS.

AZT—azidothymidine, a drug currently being tested to block HIV replication and commonly prescribed to people infected with HIV. Evidence suggests that AZT is effective in prolonging the onset of AIDS, but there are strains of the virus that are resistant to AZT.

depressed immune functions—the immune functions of body become less and less able to combat infections.

helper T cells—stimulate the reproduction of B and T cells and enhance the immune response.

HIV—human immunodeficiency virus, a retrovirus that causes AIDS; it infects helper T cells, decreasing their population, resulting in acquired immunity defects and inability to resist infection. There are two types: HIV I and HIV II.

AIDS cannot be contracted by: casual contact, casual kissing, hugging, sharing a drink, using the same bathroom facilities, or living with a person with AIDS.

The Science Teacher's Book of Lists, © 1993 by Prentice Hall

LIST 3–47. SOME ALTERNATIVES TO TRADITIONAL MEDICAL TREATMENTS

Many people, including health care providers, have become interested in alternatives to traditional medicine, leaving the use of drugs and surgery as a last resort or completely rejecting their use. Here is a list of some alternatives:

NAME OF TREATMENT	COMMENT
Acupuncture	An ancient Chinese system based on the theory that health depends upon the balance between the two energy forces within the body, Yin and Yang, which flow through the body along meridians. Needles are inserted in the skin at points along meridians to relieve pain.
Auriculotherapy	A branch of acupuncture which uses the ear as a "map" of the human body into which needles are inserted to treat specific organs.
Chiropractic	The science and art concerned with the relationship between the spinal column and the nervous system as it affects the restoration and maintenance of health, primarily using the hands to adjust misaligned or malfunctioning vertebrae; developed by D. D. Palmer in the 1890s.
Herbalism	A form of folk medicine based on the belief that certain herbs contain substances which relieve symptoms and promote good health.
Homeopathy	A system of medical treatment developed in the 1800s by German physician Samuel Hahnemann, who theorized that certain diseases could be cured by giving small doses of drugs, which in a healthy person, would produce symptoms similar to the disease.
Massage	A system of kneading parts of the body to aid circulation or to relax muscles or joints to make them more supple.
Naturopathy	A system for promoting healthy living based on the theory that ill-health can be prevented by hygienic living and a diet of "natural" foods, and of treating diseases by use of natural agents, such as air and sunshine and by rejecting drugs.
Osteopathy	A system of medical treatment developed in the 1800s by American physician Andrew Taylor Still, who theorized that disorders were caused by incorrect alignment of the bones. Today, however, many doctors of osteopathy administer drugs and medications and a few apply the massage and manipulation of the bones.
Trager® Therapy	A system of physical therapy developed in the mid-1900s by Dr. Milton Trager, who, while participating in the sport of boxing as a young man, learned the benefits of massage and developed a method of massage and exercise differing from traditional physical therapy.
Reflexology	A type of massage in which the practitioner rubs and kneads the foot using it as a "map" to adjust parts of the body to relieve pain and promote good health.

LIST 3–48. CONTROLLED SUBSTANCES—
USES & EFFECTS

Controlled Substances - *Uses &*

DRUGS/ CSA SCHEDULES		TRADE OR OTHER NAMES	MEDICAL USES	DEPENDENCE Physical
NARCOTICS				
Opium	II III V	Dover's Powder, Paregoric Parepectolin	Analgesic, antidiarrheal	High
Morphine	II III	Morphine, MS-Contin, Roxanol, Roxanol-SR	Analgesic, antitussive	High
Codeine	II III V	Tylenol w/Codeine, Empirin w/Codeine Robitussan A-C, Fiorinal w/Codeine	Analgesic, antitussive	Moderate
Heroin	I	Diacetylmorphine, Horse, Smack	None	High
Hydromorphone	II	Dilaudid	Analgesic	High
Meperidine (Pethidine)	II	Demerol, Mepergan	Analgesic	High
Methadone	II	Dolophine, Methadone, Methadose	Analgesic	High
Other Narcotics	I II III IV V	Numorphan, Percodan, Percocet, Tylox, Tussionex, Fentanyl, Darvon, Lomotil, Talwin[2]	Analgesic, antidiarrheal, antitussive	High-Low
DEPRESSANTS				
Chloral Hydrate	IV	Noctec	Hypnotic	Moderate
Barbiturates	II III IV	Amytal, Butisol, Fiorinal, Lotusate, Nembutal, Seconal, Tuinal, Phenobarbital	Anasthetic, anticonvulsant, sedative, hypnotic, veterinary euthanasia agent	High-Mod.
Benzodiazepines	IV	Ativan, Dalmane, Diazepam, Librium, Xanax, Serax, Valium Tranxexe, Verstran, Versed, Halcion, Paxipam, Restoril	Antianxiety, anticonvulsant, sedative, hypnotic	Low
Methaqualone	I	Quaalude	Sedative, hypnotic	High
Glutethimide	III	Doriden	Sedative, hypnotic	High
Other Depressants	III IV	Equanil, Miltown, Noludar, Placidyl, Valmid	Antianxiety, sedative, hypnotic	Moderate
STIMULANTS				
Cocaine[1]	II	Coke, Flake, Snow, Crack	Local anesthetic	Possible
Amphetamines	II	Biphetamine, Delcobese, Desoxyn, Dexedrine, Obetrol	Attention deficit disorders, narcolepsy, weight control	Possible
Phenmetrazine	II	Preludin	Weight control	Possible
Methylphenidate	II	Ritalin	Attention deficit disorders, narcolepsy	Possible
Other Stimulants	III IV	Adipex, Cylert, Didrex, Ionamin, Melfiat, Plegine, Sanorex, Tenuate, Tepanil, Prelu-2	Weight Control	Possible
HALLUCINOGENS				
LSD	I	Acid, Microdot	None	None
Mescaline and Peyote	I	Mexc, Buttons, Cactus	None	None
Amphetamine Variants	I	2,5-DMA, PMA, STP, MDA, MDMA, TMA, DOM, DOB	None	Unknown
Phencyclidine	II	PCP, Angel Dust, Hog	None	Unknown
Phencyclidine Analogues	I	PCE, PCPy, TCP	None	Unknown
Other Hallucinogens	I	Bufotenine, Ibogaine, DMT, DET, Psilocybin, Psilocyn	None	None
CANNABIS				
Marijuana	I	Pot, Acapulco Gold, Grass, Reefer, Sinsemilla, Thai Sticks	None	Unknown
Tetrahydrocannabinol	I II	THC, Marinol	Cancer chemotherapy antinauseant	Unknown
Hashish	I	Hash	None	Unknown
Hashish Oil	I	Hash Oil	None	Unknown

[1]Designated a narcotic under the CSA. [2]Not designated a narcotic under the CSA.

(Continued)

The Science Teacher's Book of Lists, © 1993 by Prentice Hall

LIST 3–48. (Continued)

Effects

DEPENDENCE Psychological	TOLERANCE	DURATION (Hours)	USUAL METHODS OF ADMINISTRATION	POSSIBLE EFFECTS	EFFECTS OF OVERDOSE	WITHDRAWAL SYNDROME
High	Yes	3-6	Oral, smoked	Euphoria, drowsiness, respiratory depression, constricted pupils, nausea	Slow and shallow breathing, clammy skin, convulsions, coma, possible death	Watery eyes, runny nose, yawning, loss of appetite, irritability, tremors, panic, cramps, nausea, chills and sweating
High	Yes	3-6	Oral, smoked, injected			
Moderate	Yes	3-6	Oral, injected			
High	Yes	3-6	Injected, sniffed, smoked			
High	Yes	3-6	Oral, injected			
High	Yes	3-6	Oral, injected			
High-Low	Yes	12-24	Oral, injected			
High-Low	Yes	Variable	Oral, injected			
Moderate	Yes	5-8	Oral	Slurred speech, disorientation, drunken behavior without odor of alcohol	Shallow respiration, clammy skin, dilated pupils, weak and rapid pulse, coma, possible death	Anxiety, insomnia, tremors, delirium, convulsions, possible death
High-Mod.	Yes	1-16	Oral			
Low	Yes	4-8	Oral			
High	Yes	4-8	Oral			
Moderate	Yes	4-8	Oral			
Moderate	Yes	4-8	Oral			
High	Yes	1-2	Sniffed, smoked, injected	Increased alertness, excitation, euphoria, increased pulse rate & blood pressure, insomnia, loss of appetite	Agitation, increase in body temperature, hallucinations, convulsions, possible death	Apathy, long periods of sleep, irritability, depression, disorientation
High	Yes	2-4	Oral, injected			
High	Yes	2-4	Oral, injected			
Moderate	Yes	2-4	Oral, injected			
High	Yes	2-4	Oral, injected			
Unknown	Yes	8-12	Oral	Illusions and hallucinations, poor perception of time and distance	Longer, more intense "trip" episodes, psychosis, possible death	Withdrawal syndrome not reported
Unknown	Yes	8-12	Oral			
Unknown	Yes	Variable	Oral, injected			
High	Yes	Days	Smoked, oral, injected			
High	Yes	Days	Smoked, oral, injected			
Unknown	Possible	Variable	Smoked, oral, injected, sniffed			
Moderate	Yes	2-4	Smoked, oral	Euphoria, relaxed inhibitions, increased appetite, disoriented behavior	Fatigue, paranoia, possible psychosis	Insomnia, hyperactivity, and decreased appetite occasionally reported
Moderate	Yes	2-4	Smoked, oral			
Moderate	Yes	2-4	Smoked, oral			
Moderate	Yes	2-4	Smoked, oral			

The Science Teacher's Book of Lists, © 1993 by Prentice Hall

section 4

CHEMISTRY

LIST 4–1. TERMS FREQUENTLY USED IN CHEMISTRY

absolute zero—the lowest possible temperature; the temperature at which molecules stop moving; equal to $0°K$, $-273.15°C$, or $-459.67°F$

absorb—to take in and retain

absorption spectrum—a graph showing retention of radiation by a medium over a range of wavelengths

acid—a system with a pH less than 7; substance that when added to water produces a solution in which $[H^+]$ is greater than 10^{-7} moles/L; contains hydrogen that may be replaced by a metal to form a salt; turns litmus paper red and tastes sour

acid anhydride—a nonmetal oxide that reacts with water to form an acidic solution; example: sulfur trioxide

acid-base indicator—a chemical substance that changes color when there is a change in pH; examples: litmus paper and pH paper

acid solution—an aqueous solution with pH less than 7.0 (see acid)

acid rain—rainfall that has a pH less than 5.6; usually contains H_2SO_4 and/or HNO_3

acidmeter—a hydrometer used to determine the specific gravity of an acid solution

acidophilus—growing well in an acid medium; example: acidophilus milk contains bacteria cultures that grow well in dilute acid

alcohol—a group of substances containing an OH group attached to a hydrocarbon chain having the general formula $C_nH_{2n+1}OH$; for example: C_2H_5OH, ethyl alcohol; and C_4H_9OH, butyl alcohol

alkali metals—the metals in Group IA on the Periodic Chart of Elements, such as sodium, potassium, and lithium

alkaline (base)—having a pH greater than 7; having an $[OH^-]$ that is greater than 1×10^{-7} moles/L

alloy—a mixture of two or more metals that are melted together and cooled to form a solid solution with metallic properties

amalgam—a solution of a metal in mercury

anion—an ion having a negative charge

anhydrous—a substance from which water has been removed

aromatic substance—an organic compound which contains a benzene ring; see List 4–20

atmosphere—(atm); a standard unit of pressure; equal to 101.325 kPa

atom—the smallest part of an element that maintains all of the characteristics of that element

(Continued)

LIST 4–1. (Continued)

atomic number—the number of protons in the nucleus of an atom

Avogadro's law—states that equal volumes of gases at the same temperature and pressure contain equal numbers of molecules

Avogadro's number—6.022×10^{23}, the number of discrete atoms or molecules in a mole of any substance

balanced equation—a two-part statement for a chemical reaction in which the reactants and products contain equal numbers of each kind of atom; for example: this equation for photosynthesis $6\,H_2O + 6\,CO_2 \rightarrow C_6H_{12}O_6 + 6\,O_2$ is balanced because both reactants and products contain twelve H, eighteen O, and six C atoms

base—a system with a pH greater than 7; a substance that forms an aqueous solution in which $[OH^-]$ is greater than 10^{-7} moles/L; a compound containing a metal that is combined with one or more hydroxyl radicals; turns litmus paper blue and tastes bitter

basic solution—an aqueous solution with pH greater than 7.0

binary compound—a chemical group composed of two elements often ending in "ide," such as AgCl, silver chlor<u>ide</u> and CO, carbon monox<u>ide</u>

biodegradable—substances that can be broken down into simpler substances by living things

boiling point—the temperature of a liquid at which its vapor pressure equals the applied pressure; the liquid gives off bubbles composed of its own vapors at its boiling point

bond—a linking or cohesive force between atoms

Boyle's law—states that when a sample of gas is compressed at a constant temperature, the product of the pressure and the volume remains constant

burning—rapid oxidation

buffer—a system whose pH changes only slightly when a strong acid or base is added

calorie (cal)—a unit of heat energy equal to 4.184 joules; heat to raise temperature of 1 gram of water 1°C

carbohydrate—a group of organic compounds having the general formula $C_m(H_2O)_n$; such as, glucose $C_6H_{12}O_6$ and sucrose $C_{12}H_{22}O_{11}$

catalyst—a substance that accelerates the rate of a reaction without being consumed, such as chlorophyll in the process of photosynthesis

cathode—an electrode at which reduction occurs

cation—an ion having a positive charge

chemical bond—the attractive or cohesive force that holds atoms together in a compound

The Science Teacher's Book of Lists, © 1993 by Prentice Hall

(Continued)

LIST 4–1. (Continued)

chlorofluorcarbons—(CFCs); compounds used in refrigeration devices; known to be a factor in ozone layer depletion

Celsius scale—the temperature scale on which the boiling point of water is 100° and its freezing point is 0°

centimeter—1/100 of a meter

Charles' law—states that the volume of a gas at a constant pressure is directly proportional to its absolute temperature

chemical change—a change which produces a new substance; example: two hydrogen atoms combine with one oxygen atom to produce one water molecule

chemical equations—the use of symbols and formulas to express the quantity of reactants and products of a chemical reaction; example: $2 H_2 + O_2 \rightarrow 2 H_2O$, tells us that two moles of hydrogen react with one mole of oxygen to produce two moles of water

chemical formula—the use of letters, numbers, and other symbols to write the composition of a compound; example: H_2O tells us that water is a compound made up of two atoms of hydrogen and one atom of oxygen

chemical reaction—a change that produces one or more new substances

chemical symbols—the use of letters to write the names of elements in a short form; examples: H for hydrogen and O for oxygen

chemistry—the study of the composition and synthesis of substances and the changes which they undergo

coagulation—the use of chemicals, heat, or other means to make particles clump together

coefficient—a number that shows how many moles of a substance are required or produced in a chemical reaction

colloid—a suspension that does not separate

compound—a combination of two or more elements that make up a new substance different from any of its component parts

concentrated solution—high level of solute in solution

condensation—change of state from gas to liquid

corrosion—a destructive chemical process in which metals combine with elements such as oxygen; example: iron that comes in contact with water and oxygen will undergo corrosion

covalent—a compound in which atoms share electrons nearly equally

crystallize—to separate from solution or melt as an ordered solid

cubic centimeter (cm^3)—a unit of volume equal to the volume of a cube that is one cm on each edge; one milliliter

Dalton's law—states that the total pressure of a gas mixture is equal to the sum of the partial pressure of its components

(Continued)

LIST 4–1. (Continued)

density—the property of a substance equal to its mass per unit volume; for example, water has a density of 1 gram/cm³, that is 1 cm³ of water weighs 1 gram

deuterium—a heavy isotope of hydrogen

diatomic molecule—"di" means two; a molecule containing "two" of the same atoms, such as O_2 and H_2

diffusion—the process by which one substance, by means of the kinetic properties of its particles, mixes with another; for example, freshly popped popcorn gives off particles which can be detected by smell

dilute—a weak solution containing a small amount of solute: opposite of concentrated

dissolve—to become part of a solution

distillation—conversion of a liquid to a vapor and collected again as a purified liquid; a way to recover a solute from a solution

double bond—two shared electron pairs between two bonded atoms

effusion—movement of gas molecules through a capillary or small area

electrode—a general name for an anode or cathode

electrolysis—the passing of direct electrical current through a solution, producing chemical changes at the electrodes to break down a compound

electrolyte—a substance that exists as ions in water solution, such as NaCl releasing Na^+ and Cl^- in water

electron—a negatively charged subatomic particle; carries 1 unit of negative charge and has a low mass

electrostatic forces—the forces between particles caused by their electric charges

element—a substance whose atoms are all chemically the same, having the same atomic number

emulsion—a suspension formed by two liquids

energy (E)—the property of a system related to its capacity to cause change

equilibrium—a state of balance in which rates of forward and reverse reactions are equal; thus the system does not change

ester—one of the products of the reaction between an alcohol and an acid

evaporating—changing from a liquid to a gas when the liquid is left open to the surrounding air or subject to heat

Fahrenheit scale—the temperature scale on which the boiling point of water is 212° and the freezing point is 32°

ferromagnetism—the property of being attracted to a magnetic field

filter paper—a fine textured paper used to separate undissolved solids from a liquid

The Science Teacher's Book of Lists, © 1993 by Prentice Hall

(Continued)

LIST 4–1. (Continued)

filtration—the process of separating solids from liquids by pouring the solution through a filter

First Law of Thermodynamics—states that the change in energy of a system is the sum of the heat flow into the system and the work done upon the system

flame test—observing the color imparted to a Bunsen burner flame by a sample

flotation—a separation process in which a mixture is placed in water, dense particles sink, and buoyant particles float

formula—symbols and numbers that show the relative number of atoms of the different elements in a substance

freezing—changing from a liquid to a solid

freezing point (fp)—the temperature at which a liquid and solid state can coexist at equilibrium

fusion—melting of a solid to a liquid; also the nuclear reaction in which small nuclei form a larger nucleus and in doing so release enormous amounts of energy

Graham's law—states that the rate of effusion of a gas is inversely proportional to the square root of its molar mass

gas—the form of matter that has no definite shape or volume

homogeneous—evenly mixed or the same throughout

hydrocarbon—a compound made up of hydrogen and carbon

hyroxyl radical—a group of atoms that acts as one atom, containing one oxygen atom and one hydrogen atom; OH

identify—to determine what something is

immiscible liquids—a pair of liquids that do not form a solution, such as oil and water

indicator—a dye that changes color in the presence of certain substances; for example, in acids and bases

insoluble—property of a substance that makes it incapable of dissolving; opposite of soluble

ion—an atom, or a radical that has an electrical charge because it lost or gained electrons

ionic compounds—compounds formed when atoms combine by losing or gaining electrons

ionization—separating into ions

isotopes—atoms of the same element which have different numbers of neutrons in the nucleus and therefore different atomic weights

kilogram—the equivalent of 1,000 grams

(Continued)

LIST 4–1. (Continued)

kilometer—the equivalent of 1,000 meters

limewater—a water solution of lime (calcium hydroxide); turns milky when mixed with carbon dioxide

liquid—the form of matter that has a definite volume but no definite shape

liter—the liquid equivalent of 1,000 cubic centimeters

matter—material that takes up space and has mass

melting—changing from a solid to a liquid

metals—elements that are: solid at room temperature (except for mercury), good conductors of electricity and heat, bright, shiny, and malleable

meter—the unit of measurement of length in the metric system, about 3 inches longer than 1 yard

metric system—units of measurement used by scientists and most non-scientists of the industrialized world with the exception of the United States

millimeter—1/1000 of a meter

miscible liquids—liquids that form a solution when mixed together

mixture—two or more substances mixed together physically but not combined chemically

mole—the gram-molecular weight of a molecular substance

molecular weight—the sum of the atomic weights in a molecule; the same as the formula weight

molecule—a particle formed by two or more atoms that share electrons

more active metals—metals that replace other metals in a compound

negative charge—the charge of an electron

neutral—neither acid nor base; neither positive or negative

neutralization—combining an acid and a base; produces a salt and water

nonmetals—elements that are not metals; having properties opposite metals

nucleus—the center of an atom, contains neutrons and protons

orbits—paths of electrons around the nucleus of an atom

organic compounds—compounds containing carbon

oxidation—combining with oxygen; an increase in valence; losing electrons in a chemical reaction

ozone—gas in upper atmosphere of Earth (a three-atom form of oyxgen) that absorbs most of the ultraviolet rays from the sun

periodic table—a chart that organizes information about all the elements according to similar properties, listing the element's name, chemical symbol, atomic number, and atomic weight

The Science Teacher's Book of Lists, © 1993 by Prentice Hall

(Continued)

LIST 4–1. (Continued)

period—series of elements in a horizontal row on the periodic table

physical change—a change that does not result in a new substance

polymer—commonly, an organic compound consisting mainly of a long chain of carbon atoms or carbon atoms interconnected by other atoms such as oxygen, nitrogen, or sulfur. The non-chain connecting bonds are attached to hydrogen or other substituents

positive charge—the charge of a proton

precipitate—a solid that separates from a solution because of saturation or a chemical reaction which yields an insoluble product

predict—state the expected outcome, what one thinks will happen

product—substance resulting from a chemical reaction

properties—characteristics that help identify something

proton—positively charged particle located in the nucleus of an atom

radical—a group of atoms that behave as one atom in a compound

radioactive elements—elements whose nuclei break down into other nuclei

reactant—that which is changed in a chemical reaction

reduction—removing oxygen from ore to obtain the metal; gaining electrons in a chemical reaction; decrease in valence

rusting—oxidation of iron

salt—substance produced by the reaction between an acid and a base

saturated solution—a solution that has all of the solute that it can dissolve

solid—matter in a state that has a definite shape and volume

soluble—capable of dissolving

solute—that which dissolves in a solvent

solution—a homogeneous mixture of two or more substances; water solutions are clear and will not separate when filtered

state—one of the forms of matter: solid, liquid or gas

subscript—the number written to denote the number of atoms of an element in a molecule; such as the "2" in H_2O

suspension—a cloudy mixture, usually of a solid in a liquid, which settles on standing

synfuel—a "synthetic fuel" derived from a solid or partly solid fossil fuel or from fermentation (as of grain)

ternary compounds—a chemical group composed of three elements, often ending in "ate," such as $CuSO_4$, copper sulfate and KNO_3, potassium nitrate

theory—an idea supported by scientific evidence

(Continued)

LIST 4–1. (Continued)

thermometer—a tool used to measure temperature in degrees

tincture—a solution of a solid in alcohol, often for medical use

valence—number of electrons an atom loses, gains, or shares

volume—amount of space taken up by matter

LIST 4-2. PHYSICAL AND CHEMICAL CHANGES

Matter can be changed in many ways. Discounting atomic reactions, changes in matter can be classified as physical or chemical. According to the Law of Conservation of Matter, matter can neither be created nor destroyed as a result of ordinary physical or chemical changes.

PHYSICAL CHANGES	*CHEMICAL CHANGES*
Does not result in a new substance	Does result in a new substance
Change in size and shape	More than a change in size and shape
A change in the state of matter	More than a change in the state of matter

EXAMPLES OF PHYSICAL CHANGES	***EXAMPLES OF CHEMICAL CHANGES***
Tear paper	Burn paper: produce carbon, gases, and water vapor
Chop wood	Burn wood: produce carbon, gases, and water vapor
Wet something	Burn something: produce carbon, gases, and water vapor
Add vinegar to water: produce a weak solution of vinegar and water	Add vinegar to baking soda: produce carbon dioxide
Melt chocolate	Accidentally burn chocolate: produce carbon, gases, and water vapor
Melt wax	Burn a candle: some of the melted wax travels to the top of the wick; the wax and wick combine with the oxygen in the air to produce carbon, gases, and water vapor
Mix sulfur and iron: produce a mixture of iron and sulfur	Heat a mixture of iron and sulfur: produce iron sulfide
Mix up cake batter	Bake a cake
Crack open an egg	Eat a cooked egg
Hammer a nail	Leave a wet nail exposed to the air: the iron will combine with oxygen in the air to produce iron oxide, or rust
Scrub a pan with an iron wool pad	Leave the wet iron wool pad in an open dish: rust will form
Make a mixture	Make a compound
Separate a mixture	Decompose a compound

LIST 4–3. ELEMENTS[a]

NAME	SYMBOL[b]	ATOMIC[c] NUMBER	ATOMIC[d] WEIGHT	STATE[e]	DENSITY g/cm³	VALENCE[f]
Actinium	Ac	89	(227)			3
Aluminum	Al	13	26.98	M	2.71	3,4,5,6
Americium	Am	95	(243)	M	13.67	3,4,5,6
Antimony (Stibium)	Sb	51	121.75	M	6.7	−3,0,3,4,5
Argon	Ar	18	39.95	G	1.78[g]	0
Arsenic	As	33	74.92	M	5.72	−3,0,3,5
Astatine	At	85	(210)	N		−1,1,3,5,7
Barium	Ba	56	137.34	M	3.59	2
Berkelium	Bk	97	(247)	M		3,4
Beryllium	Be	4	9.01	M	1.86	2
Bismuth	Bi	83	208.98	M	9.80	3,5
Boron	B	5	10.81	N	2.46	3
Bromine	Br	35	79.90	N, L	3.12	−1,1,3,5,7
Cadmium	Cd	48	112.40	M	8.64	2
Calcium	Ca	20	40.08	M	1.55	2
Californium	Cf	98	(251)			
Carbon	C	6	12.01	N	2.27[h]	2,3,4,−4
Cerium	Ce	58	140.12	M	6.77[h]	3,4
Cesium	Cs	55	132.91	M	1.88	1
Chlorine	Cl	17	35.45	N, G	2.98[g]	−1,1,3,5,7
Chromium	Cr	24	52.00	M	7.20	2,3,6
Cobalt	Co	27	58.93	M	8.9	2,3
Copper	Cu	29	63.55	M	8.92	1,2
Curium	Cm	96	(247)	M	13.51	3
Dysprosium	Dy	66	162.50	M	8.54	3
Einsteinium	Es	99	(254)			
Erbium	Er	68	167.26	M	9.05	3
Europium	Eu	63	151.96	M	5.26	2,3

(*Continued*)

[a]Listed alphabetically. Elements through atomic number 92 occur naturally.

[b]Latin names are given in parentheses when symbol is not from common name.

[c]Atomic number is the number of protons in the nucleus of an atom.

[d]The average relative weight of an atom as it occurs in nature compared to an arbitrary standard of 12.000 for the atomic weight of carbon. Numbers in parentheses are for the most stable isotope.

[e]G = gas; L = liquid; M = metal; N = nonmetal (at 20°C).

[f]Valence is the combining power of an element or radical. The valence number is also referred to as the oxidation state. An atom is positively electrovalent when it donates outer electrons to the formation of a bond or bonds. The valence of an atom may vary from one compound to another. In the table the valences of most metals are positive unless marked negatively. The primary valences of most metals are positive. Covalent bonds between atoms, such as the carbon-carbon bond, are formed by the sharing of a pair of electrons which may be derived from either or both of the atoms. Multiple bonds of this type can be formed between two atoms. "?" indicates some question about this valence state.

[g]Grams per liter.

[h]Two or more solid states with differing densities. One form of carbon (diamond) has a density of 3.515 while another (graphite) has a density of 2.25.

LIST 4–3. (Continued)

NAME	SYMBOL[b]	ATOMIC[c] NUMBER	ATOMIC[d] WEIGHT	STATE[e]	DENSITY g/cm³	VALENCE[f]
Fermium	Fm	100	(253)			
Fluorine	F	9	19.00	N, G	1.58[g]	−1
Francium	Fr	87	(223)	M		1
Gadolinium	Gd	64	157.25	M	7.90[h]	3
Gallium	Ga	31	69.72	M	5.91	2,3
Germanium	Ge	32	72.59	M	5.32	2,4
Gold (Aureum)	Au	79	196.97	M	19.3	1,3
Hafnium	Hf	72	178.49	M	13.31	4
Helium	He	2	4.00	N, G	1.79[g]	0
Holmium	Ho	67	164.93	M	8.80	3
Hydrogen	H	1	1.01	G	.899	−1,1
Indium	In	49	114.82	M	7.28	1,2?,3
Iodine	I	53	126.91	N	4.93	−1,1,3,5,7
Iridium	Ir	77	192.22	M	22.65	3,4
Iron (Ferrum)	Fe	26	55.85	M	7.86	2,3,4,6
Krypton	Kr	36	83.80	N, G	3.74[g]	0
Lanthanum	La	57	138.91	M	6.17	3
Lawrencium	Lr	103	(257)			
Lead (Plumbum)	Pb	82	207.2	M	11.34	2,4
Lithium	Li	3	6.94	M	0.535	1
Lutetium	Lu	71	174.97	M	9.84	3
Magnesium	Mg	12	24.31	M	1.74	2
Manganese	Mn	25	54.94	M	7.30[h]	−3 to +7
Mendelevium	Md	101	(257)			2,3
Mercury (Hydrargyrum)	Hg	80	200.59	M, L	13.59	1,2
Molybdenum	Mo	42	95.94	M	10.22	2,3,4?,5?,6
Neodymium	Nd	60	144.24	M	7.00[h]	3
Neon	Ne	10	20.18	N, G	0.90[g]	0
Neptunium	Np	93	237.05	M	20.45[h]	3,4,5,6
Nickel	Ni	28	58.71	M	8.90	0,1,2,3
Niobium	Nb	41	92.91	M	8.57	2,3,4?,5
Nitrogen	N	7	14.01	N, G	1.25[g]	−3,3,5
Nobelium	No	102	(254)			
Osmium	Os	76	190.2	M	22.61	2,3,4,6,8
Oxygen	O	8	16.00	N, G	1.33[g]	−2
Palladium	Pd	46	106.4	M	12.02	2,3,4
Phosphorus	P	15	30.97	N	1.83[h]	−3,3,5
Platinum	Pt	78	195.1	M	21.45	1?,2,3,4
Plutonium	Pu	94	239.1	M	19.82[h]	3,4,5,6
Polonium	Po	84	(210)	M	9.20[h]	2,4,6
Potassium (Kalium)	K	19	39.10	M	0.87	1
Praseodymium	Pr	59	140.91	M	6.78[h]	3,4

(Continued)

LIST 4–3. (Continued)

NAME	SYMBOL[b]	ATOMIC[c] NUMBER	ATOMIC[d] WEIGHT	STATE[e]	DENSITY g/cm³	VALENCE[f]
Promethium	Pm	61	(145)		3	
Protactinium	Pa	91	231.04	M	15.37	4,5
Radium	Ra	88	226.03	M	6	2
Radon	Rn	86	(222)	N, G	9.73[g]	0
Rhenium	Re	75	186.2	M	21.04	1 to 7
Rhodium	Rh	45	102.91	M	12.41	2 to 6
Rubidium	Rb	37	85.47	M	1.53	1
Ruthenium	Ru	44	101.07	M	12.45[h]	0 to 8
Samarium	Sm	62	150.4	M	7.54[h]	2,3
Scandium	Sc	21	44.96	M	2.99	3
Selenium	Se	34	78.96	N	4.79[h]	−2,2,4,6
Silicon	Si	14	28.09	M	2.33	2,−4,4
Silver (Argentum)	Ag	47	107.87	M	10.50	1,2
Sodium (Natrium)	Na	11	22.99	M	0.97	1
Strontium	Sr	38	87.62	M	2.60	2
Sulfur	S	16	32.06	N	2.08[h]	−2,4,6
Tantalum	Ta	73	180.95	M	16.60	2?,3,4?,5
Technetium	Tc	43	98.91	M	11.49	2 to 7
Tellurium	Te	52	127.60	M	6.24	2,4,6
Terbium	Tb	65	158.93	M	8.27[h]	3,4
Thallium	Tl	81	204.37	M	11.80[h]	1,3
Thorium	Th	90	232.04	M	11.71	4
Thullium	Tm	69	168.93	M	9.33	2,3
Tin (Stannum)	Sn	50	118.69	M	7.28	2,4
Titanium	Ti	22	47.90	M	4.51[h]	2,3,4
Tungsten (Wolfram)	W	74	183.85	M	19.35	0, 2 to 6
Uranium	U	92	238.03	M	19.05	3,4,5,6
Vanadium	V	23	50.94	M	6.1	2,3,4,5
Xenon	Xe	54	131.30	N, G	5.90[g]	0
Ytterbium	Yb	70	173.04	M	6.98[h]	2,3
Yttrium	Y	39	88.91	M	4.48	3
Zinc	Zn	30	65.37	M	7.14	2
Zirconium	Zr	40	91.22	M	6.52	2,3,4

The Science Teacher's Book of Lists, © 1993 by Prentice Hall

LIST 4–4. DETERMINING THE MOLE OF A COMPOUND

A mole of a compound is its molecular weight expressed in grams. It is a convenient number for calculating the amounts of chemicals that react with one another or are produced in a reaction and for expressing concentrations of solutions. The abbreviation of mole is mol.

To determine the mole of a compound one needs to know the atomic weight of each element. The mole of a compound is equal to the sum of the atomic/molecular weights of its elements expressed in grams.

Atomic weights can be found on the previous list, "Elements," or on a Periodic Table. Atomic weights are relative. Hydrogen being the lightest element has an atomic weight of 1. Oxygen, which is 16 times as heavy as hydrogen, has an atomic weight of 16.

Steps for Determining a Mole of a Compound

STEPS	EXAMPLE: ONE MOLE OF WATER
1. Write the formula of the compound.	H_2O
2. List the atomic weight of each element.	Atomic weights: H = 1; O = 16
3. Determine the sum of the atomic weights.	There are two hydrogen atoms and one oxygen atom. Thus: $(2 \times 1) + 16 = 18$
4. A mole is the sum of the atomic weights expressed in grams.	Therefore, one mole of water = 18 g

This information is helpful to determine the amounts of hydrogen and oxygen needed to produce water. For every 18 grams of water produced, 2 grams of hydrogen and 16 grams of oxygen are needed. Thus, if twice as much water is produced ($2 \times 18 = 36$ g), then twice as much hydrogen ($2 \times 2 = 4$ g) and twice as much oxygen ($2 \times 16 = 32$ g) are required. In the same manner any fraction or multiple of a mole can be used or produced.

Another way to look at this is the following:

WORKING WITH THE EQUATION	PROBLEM-SOLVING PROCESS
$2 H_2 + O_2 \rightarrow 2 H_2O$	Write the atomic weights: H = 1; O = 16
$(4 \times 1) + (2 \times 16) = 2[(2 \times 1) + (1 \times 16)]$	Substitute 1 for each H and 16 for each O
$4 \text{ g} + 32 \text{ g} = 2(2 + 16) = 36 \text{ g}$	4 g of H combine with 32 g of O to produce 36 g of water
$2 H_2 + O_2 \rightarrow 2 H_2O$	The balanced equation can be thought of as: 2 moles of H_2 + 1 mole of O_2 produces 2 moles of water
1 mole of water = 18 g Thus, 2 moles of water = 36 g	(See example above.)

LIST 4–5. APPLYING THE STEPS FOR DETERMINING A MOLE OF A COMPOUND

STEPS	EXAMPLE: ONE MOLE OF CARBON DIOXIDE
1. Write the formula of the compound.	CO_2
2. List the atomic weight of each element.	Atomic weights: C = 12, O = 16
3. Determine the sum of the atomic weights.	There are one atom of carbon and two atoms of oyxgen: Thus: $12 + (16 \times 2) = 44$
4. Express in grams.	Therefore, one mole of carbon dioxide = 44 g

A mole or the gram-molecular weight is 44 grams. The volume of one gram molecular weight of a gas is 22.4 liters at S.T.P. (Standard Temperature and Pressure, which is 0°C and one atmosphere pressure).

The formula CO_2 stands for a definite ratio of components. The formula does not stand for any quantity. Using the ratio, one can use any quantity needed or available.

Thus, the term "mole" is useful since it designates both weight in grams represented by the formula of a substance and the volume in liters represented by the formula of a gas.

The term "mole" is useful in representing volume in cases of gases and vapors, because one gram-molecular weight of each gas occupies 22.4 liters or a gram-molecular volume at S.T.P.

STEPS	EXAMPLE: ONE MOLE OF SULFURIC ACID
1. Write the formula of the compound.	H_2SO_4
2. List the atomic weight of each element.	2 H = 2, 1 S = 32, 4 O = 64
3. Determine the sum of the atomic weights.	98
4. Express in grams.	98 g

STEPS	EXAMPLE: ONE MOLE OF AMMONIA
1. Write the formula of the compound.	NH_3
2. List the atomic weight of each element.	1 N = 14; 3 H = 3
3. Determine the sum of the atomic weights.	14 + 3 = 17
4. Express in grams.	17 g

LIST 4–6. MOLE GAS VOLUME

The volume occupied by one mole (gram molecular weight) of a gas is 22.4 liters at 0°C and one atmosphere pressure. Accordingly:

- 1 mole, or 2 grams, of hydrogen occupies 22.4 liters.
- 1 mole, or 32 grams, of oxygen occupies 22.4 liters.
- 1 mole, or 44 grams, of carbon dioxide occupies 22.4 liters.

This can be used with Avogadro's number to calculate the average free space for one gas molecule under these conditions.

LIST 4–7. AVOGADRO'S NUMBER

Amadeo Avogadro (1776–1856) determined that one mole of gas contains 6.025×10^{23} molecules. By extension, a mole of any substance contains the same number of molecules. From this number one can calculate the mass of a molecule of any substance for which the gram-molecular weight is known.

$$\text{Mass of a molecule or atom} = \frac{\text{grams/mole of a substance}}{6.02 \times 10^{23}}$$

For carbon dioxide:

$$\text{Mass of a molecule or atom of carbon dioxide} = \frac{44 \text{ g}}{6.02 \times 10^{23}}$$

$$= 7.31 \times 10^{23} \text{ g/molecule}$$

LIST 4–8. BALANCING CHEMICAL EQUATIONS

Chemical equations are a representative of chemical reactions in the form of atomic and molecular symbols. The starting materials are written on the left and the products are on the right of a "yield" or "produce" arrow. The "+" sign means *combines or reacts with*. Since in ordinary reactions no atoms are lost or gained, a balanced equation shows the same number of atoms of the elements on each side of the equation.

Steps for Balancing Equations: ### Examples:

1. Write the equation in words.   Iron + sulfur → iron sulfide
2. Write the trial equation. $Fe + S \rightarrow FeS$
3. Determine if the equation is $1\,Fe \rightarrow 1\,Fe$
   balanced or not by determin- $1\,S \rightarrow 1S$
   ing the number of "starting
   material" and "product"   This equation is balanced.
   atoms.

Apply the Step for Balancing an Equation:

1. Write the equation in words.   Hydrogen + oxygen → water
2. Write the trial equation. $H_2 + O_2 \rightarrow H_2O$
3. Determine if the equation is $2\,H \rightarrow 2\,H$
   balanced or not by determin- $2\,O \rightarrow 1\,O$
   ing the number of "starting
   material" and "product"   This equation is not balanced. There
   atoms.   must be $2\,H_2O$ and $2\,H_2$ to balance it.
4. Balance the equation. $2\,H_2 + O_2 \rightarrow 2\,H_2O$
                                              $4\,H \rightarrow 4\,H$
                                              $2\,O \rightarrow 2\,O$

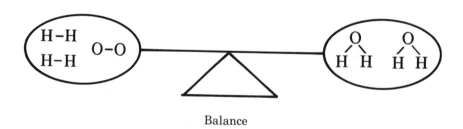

Balance

The Science Teacher's Book of Lists, © 1993 by Prentice Hall

(Continued)

LIST 4–8. (Continued)

Example of Balancing a Double Displacement Equation:

1. silver nitrate + sodium chloride → silver chloride + sodium nitrate
2. $$AgNO_3 + NaCl \rightarrow AgCl \downarrow + NaNO_3$$
3.
$$1\,Ag \rightarrow 1\,Ag$$
$$1\,N \rightarrow 1\,N$$
$$3\,O \rightarrow 3\,O$$
$$1\,Na \rightarrow 1\,Na$$
$$1\,Cl \rightarrow 1\,Cl$$

4. This equation is balanced, showing the same number of atoms of elements on each side of the equation. The downward arrow after AgCl indicates that it is a precipitate.

Example of An Oxidation-Reduction Reaction:

1. Iron oxide + carbon monoxide → iron + carbon dioxide
2. $$Fe_2O_3 + CO \rightarrow Fe + CO_2$$
3.
$$2\,Fe \rightarrow 1\,Fe$$
$$4\,O \rightarrow 2\,O$$
$$1\,C \rightarrow 1\,C$$

4. This equation is not balanced.
$$Fe_2O_3 + 3\,CO \rightarrow 2\,Fe + 3\,CO_2$$
$$2\,Fe \rightarrow 2\,Fe$$
$$6\,O \rightarrow 6\,O$$
$$3\,C \rightarrow 3\,C$$

5. Now the equation is balanced.

This is the process for obtaining iron from ore. It is called an oxidation-reduction reaction. The valence change for iron is a drop of 3; the apparent change for carbon is a gain of 2. To balance the equation the loss in valence must be made equal to the gain. Two iron atoms lose 6 valence units; therefore 3 carbon atoms are required to provide a gain of 6. When there are valence changes, balancing the equation is different but systematic.

(Continued)

LIST 4–8. (Continued)

The Equation for the Process of Photosynthesis, the Process by Which Green Plants Make Their Own Food:

1.   Water + carbon dioxide → sugar + oxygen
2. $H_2O + CO_2 → C_6H_{12}O_6 + O_2$
3. $2 H → 12 H$

     $3 O → 8 O$

     $1 C → 6 C$
4.   This equation is not balanced.

     $6 H_2O + 6CO_2 → C_6H_{12}O_6 + 6O_2$

     $12 H → 12 H$

     $18 O → 18 O$

     $6 C → 6 C$
5.   Now this equation is balanced.

LIST 4–9. TEN EXAMPLES OF BALANCED EQUATIONS

1.
$$2 \, KI + H_2O_2 \rightarrow 2 \, KOH + I_2$$
Postassium iodide + hydrogen peroxide → potassium hydroxide + iodine

2.
$$FeCl_2 + 2 \, KCN \rightarrow 2 \, KCl + Fe(CN)_2$$
Ferrous chloride + potassium cyanide → potassium chloride + ferrous cyanide

3.
$$NiCl_2 + 2 \, KCN \rightarrow 2 \, KCl + Ni(CN)_2$$
Nickel chloride + potassium cyanide → potassium chloride + nickel cyanide

4.
$$ZnCl_2 + 2 \, KCN \rightarrow 2 \, KCl + Zn(CN)_2$$
Zinc chloride + potassium cyanide → potassium chloride + zinc cyanide

5.
$$HgCl_2 + 2 \, NH_3 \rightarrow NH_4Cl + HgNH_2Cl$$
Mercuric chloride + ammonia → ammonium chloride + mercuric amide chloride

6.
$$Pb(OH)_2 + 2 \, KOH \rightarrow K_2PbO_2 + 2 \, H_2O$$
Lead hydroxide + potassium hydroxide → potassium lead oxide + water

7.
$$CuO + H_2SO_4 \rightarrow CuSO_4 + H_2O$$
Cupric oxide + sulfuric acid → copper sulfate + water

8.
$$Cu + H_2SO_4 \rightarrow H_2O + SO_2 + CuSO_4$$
Copper + sulfuric acid → water + sulfur dioxide + copper sulfate

9.
$$H_2SO_4 + 2HI \rightarrow H_2O + H_2SO_3 + I_2$$
Sulfuric acid + hydrogen iodide → water + sulfurous acid + iodine

10.
$$AgCl + 2 \, KCN \rightarrow KAg(CN)_2 + KCl$$
Silver chloride + potassium cyanide → potassium silver cyanide + potassium chloride

LIST 4–10. ELEMENTS, COMPOUNDS, MIXTURES, AND SOLUTIONS

ELEMENTS

A pure substance made of one kind of atom

Chemically combine to produce compounds

Have a chemical symbol

Have individual properties

Cannot be divided into other simpler substances

COMPOUNDS

Substance made of two or more atoms or radicals that are chemically combined

Have a chemical formula

Have properties which are not like the component elements

Can be broken down, or decomposed, by chemical means

MIXTURES

All mixtures are not solutions

Made of two or more substances mixed together which:

- Do not mix evenly
- Generally separate when filtered
- Are not transparent (water mixtures)

Do not have a chemical symbol

Can be separated by physical means

Can be a mixture of solids, liquids, and gases

Substances keep their properties in mixture

SOLUTIONS

All solutions are a special kind of mixture

Made of two or more substances mixed together which:

- Do mix evenly or homogeneously
- Do not separate when filtered

- Are transparent (water solutions)

Do not have a chemical symbol or formula

Can be separated by physical means

Can be a solution of solid, liquids, and gases

Examples of metals in solution: Brass = copper + zinc; bronze = copper + tin

Substances do not always retain their physical properties in solution; for example salt loses the property of being a solid when forming a solution with water. However, two or more gases can mix to form a solution and retain the property of being a gas. Example, air.

The Science Teacher's Book of Lists, © 1993 by Prentice Hall

LIST 4–11. SUBSTANCES SOLUBLE AND INSOLUBLE IN WATER

Substances that dissolve in water are said to be *water soluble*. Those that do not dissolve in water are said to be *insoluble*. To determine if a substance is water soluble, fill a test tube half way with water, place at least ¼ teaspoon of the substance in the water. Place a stopper in the tube and shake the tube. If the substance mixes evenly and disappears, forms a transparent solution, and will not separate when filtered, then the substance is said to have formed a solution with the water, or is water soluble.

Liquids that form solutions with water are called *miscible with water*. Liquids that do not form solutions with water are called *immiscible*. The substance dissolved in solution is called the *solute*. The substance causing the dissolving is called the *solvent*.

Water Soluble	Insoluble in Water
Sugar	Stones
Salt	Iron filings
Potassium dichromate	Iron or aluminum nails
Alcohol	Sulfur
Vinegar	Cooking or salad oil
Powdered soft drinks	Motor, heating oil
Carbon dioxide	Benzene
Food coloring	Cream
Copper sulfate	Noodle soup (Solid and oil parts)
Apple juice	Vegetable soup (Solid and oil parts)
Club soda	French dressing

LIST 4–12. LIQUID SOLUTIONS, SUSPENSIONS, AND EMULSIONS

- *Liquid solutions* are clear mixtures that form when one or more substances dissolve into another.
- *Suspensions* are cloudy mixtures that form when two or more substances mix but do not dissolve.
- *Emulsions* are a suspension of two liquids.

General Properties of Liquid Solutions, Suspensions, and Emülsion

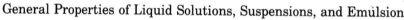

SOLUTIONS	SUSPENSIONS	EMULSIONS
Homogeneous mixture of two or more substances	Mixture of two or more substances	A suspension of two liquids
Clear liquid	Cloudy liquid	Cloudy liquid
Do not separate on standing	May settle on standing	Do not separate on standing
Do not separate when filtered	Can separate when filtered	Do not separate when filtered
Particles are molecular in size	Particles are much larger than molecules	Particles are not molecular
Particles dissolve	Particles do not dissolve	Particles do not dissolve

Examples

SOLUTIONS	SUSPENSIONS	EMULSIONS
Sugar in water	Starch in water	Mayonnaise
Salt in water	Calamine lotion	Homogenized whole milk
Carbonated soda	Italian salad dressing	French dressing
Apple juice in water	Clay in water	Skin lotions
Food coloring in water	Powdered paint in water	Thousand Island dressing
Vinegar in water	Corn starch in water	Margarines
Alcohol in water	Peanut butter	Fertilizers/fish oil
Alka-Seltzer® in water	Laundry blueing in water	
Iodine in alcohol	Pepto-Bismol®	

LIST 4–13. ACIDS AND BASES

- *Acids* are chemical compounds made up of nonmetallic elements or radicals combined with hydrogen. They react with metals to release hydrogen and have a pH less than 7. They turn litmus paper red. Those that are safe to taste have a sour taste.

- *Bases* are compounds made up of metallic elements or radicals combined with hydroxyl radicals. They are formed when some metals react with water and have a pH above 7. They turn litmus paper blue. Those that are safe to taste have a bitter taste. Those that are safe to touch feel slippery.

- Substances that are neither an acid nor a base are called *neutral*. They have a pH of 7 and do not change the color of litmus paper. Water is an example of a neutral substance.

Properties of

ACIDS	*BASES*
Contain hydrogen	Contain hydrogen and oxygen
Contain hydrogen ions, hydrogen atoms with a plus charge, that combine with a nonmetallic element or radical	Contain hydrogen and oxygen combined into a hydroxyl radical (OH)
React with metals to produce hydrogen	Are formed and hydrogen is released when some metals are placed in water
Can be dangerous chemicals	Can be dangerous chemicals
Those that are safe to taste, taste sour (vinegar)	Those that are safe to taste, taste bitter
Do not feel slippery	Feel slippery (soap)
Turn litmus paper red	Turn litmus paper blue
Turn phenolphthalein colorless	Turn phenolphthalein pink
Turn methyl red, red	Turn methyl red, yellow
Turn congo red, blue	Turn congo red, red
Turn bromthymol blue, yellow	Turn bromthymol blue, blue

EXAMPLES OF ACIDS AND THEIR FORMULAS	*EXAMPLES OF BASES AND THEIR FORMULAS*
Acetic acid, CH_3COOH	Potassium hydroxide, KOH
Boric acid, H_3BO_3	Magnesium hydroxide, $Mg(OH)_2$
Carbonic acid, H_2CO_3	Calcium hydroxide, $Ca(OH)_2$
Hydrochloric acid, HCl	Sodium hydroxide, $NaOH$
Sulfuric acid, H_2SO_4	Ammonium hydroxide, NH_4OH

(Continued)

LIST 4–13. (Continued)

Two sample reactions with acids and bases that yield familiar household substances:

(1)   Chemically producing table salt:

$$acid + base \rightarrow salt + water$$

$$hydrochloric\ acid + sodium\ hydroxide \rightarrow sodium\ chloride + water$$

$$HCl + NaOH \rightarrow NaCl + H_2O$$

(Table salt)

(2)   Chemically producing Milk of Magnesia:

$$metal + water \rightarrow base + hydrogen$$

$$magnesium + water \rightarrow magnesium\ hydroxide + hydrogen$$

$$Mg + 2\ H_2O\ (hot) \rightarrow Mg(OH)_2 + H_2$$

(Milk of Magnesia)

LIST 4–14. ACIDITY SCALE (pH) AND ACID RAIN

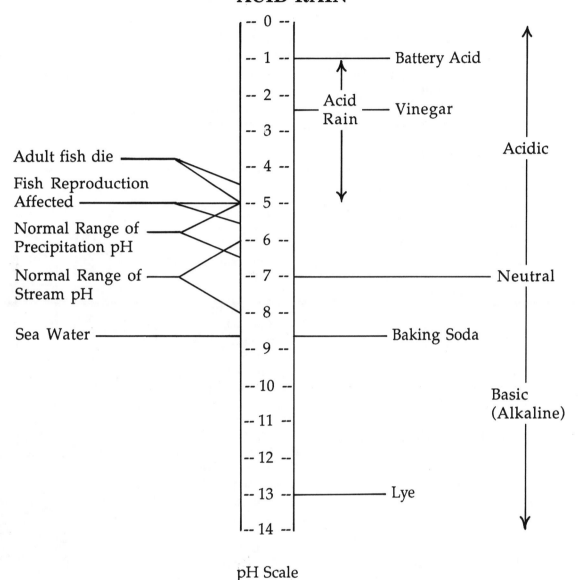

pH Scale

Acids produce high concentrations of hydrogen ions (H^+); bases give low concentrations. The pH scale is a way of expressing those concentrations. One would think that acids would yield higher numbers. However, the pH value is the reciprocal of the logarithm of the hydrogen ion concentration.

The pH can be measured by use of compounds that change color with acidity. These substances are sometimes impregnated in paper. These are called indicator papers. The pH is also commonly determined with special electrical instruments.

LIST 4–15. COMPOSITION OF SUBSTANCES ABOUT THE HOUSEHOLD

Many household items are complex mixtures, natural or artificial. An attempt has been made to list substances which (1) are wholly one material, (2) contain major amounts of a chemical, or (3) have a recognizable ingredient which provides the product's effect.

The ingredients in many products are listed on the label. Some of these words and abbreviations are given at the end of the list.

PRODUCT	*COMPOSITION*

Food and Food Ingredients

Water	Hydrogen oxide, H_2O
Salt	Sodium chloride, $NaCl$
Cane/brown/confectioner's sugar	Sucrose, $C_{12}H_{22}O_{11}$
Molasses	Impure sucrose and water
Maple syrup	Sucrose
Corn syrup	Glucose and water, $C_6H_{12}O_6$
Honey	Levulose, glucose and some sucrose
Fructose	A six-carbon sugar, $C_6H_{12}O_6$
Sacharrin	ortho-Benzoyl sulfimide, $C_7H_5O_3NS$
Aspartame (Nutrasweet™)	Dipeptide of two amino acids, penylalanine and aspartic acid
Ascorbic acid (vitamin C)	$C_6H_8O_6$
Cream of tartar	Acid potassium tartrate, $KC_4H_5O_6$
Baking soda	Sodium bicarbonate, $NaHCO_3$
Baking powder	May be baking soda, sodium aluminum sulfate, $NaAl(SO_4)_2$, and calcium acid phosphate, $CaHPO_4$
Cornstarch	Polymers of glucose
Oil of wintergreen	Methyl salicylate, $HO(C_6H_4)CO_2CH_3$
Oil of peppermint	Menthol, $C_{10}H_{19}OH$ and menthene, $C_{10}H_{18}$
Oil of clove	Eugenol, $C_{10}H_{12}O_2$
Pennyroyal	Pulegone/menthenone, $C_{10}H_{16}O$ (isomer with camphor)
Vanilla	Vanillin, $(CH_3O)C_6H_3(OH).CHO$
Vinegar	Aqueous acetic acid, CH_3COOH
Wines	Aqueous ethyl alcohol, CH_3CH_2OH
Milk	A dispersion of protein (casein), lactose, and fat
Carbonated drinks	Water with dissolved carbon dioxide, CO_2

(Continued)

The Science Teacher's Book of Lists, © 1993 by Prentice Hall

LIST 4–15. (Continued)

PRODUCT	*COMPOSITION*
Coffee	Caffeine (alkaloid), $C_8H_{10}O_2N_4 \cdot H_2O$
Tea	Theobromine (alkaloid), $C_7H_8O_2N_4$ and tannins
Oils and fats	Long chain fatty acid esters of glycerin*

Medicines and Personal Care

Aspirin	acetyl salicylic acid
Ibuprofen	2-(para-Isobutylphenyl) propionic acid
Acetaminophen	para-Acetaminophenol; $CH_3CONH(C_6H_4)OH$
Antiacids	Often contain calcium carbonate $CaCO_3$, magnesium hydroxide $Mg(OH)_2$, or aluminum hydroxide $Al(OH)_3$
Styptic pencil	Alum, $KAl(SO_4)_2$
Milk of magnesia	A dispersion of magnesium hydroxide, $Mg(OH)_2$
Phenolphthalein	A phenol derivative of phthalide, $C_{20}H_{16}O_4$
Tincture of iodine	Elemental iodine in ethyl alcohol
Wart removers	Salicylic acid or trichloroacetic acid, Cl_3CCOOH
Rubbing alcohol	Isopropyl alcohol, 70% in water, $(CH_3)_2CHOH$ or C_3H_8O
Calamine solution	Suspension of zinc oxide, ZnO
Epsom salts	Magnesium sulfate, $MgSO_4$
Glauber's salt	Sodium sulfate hydrate, $Na_2SO_4 \cdot 10 \ H_2O$

Insect Repellants

Citronella	From a grass; mixed oxygenated monoterpenes: citronellal, citronellol, and geraniol
Pennyroyal	Pulegone; see flavors

Petroleum Fluids

	Hydrocarbon products of varying molecular weights derived from petroleum oil or synthesized
Propane	Compound with three carbon atoms, C_3H_8
Butane	Compound with four carbon atoms, C_4H_{10}
Lighter fluid	Mixture: 5 to 6 carbon atoms

(Continued)

*The fatty acids have different numbers of carbon atoms and also differ in the number of double bonds (unsaturation) in the chain. They are classed as saturated (no double bonds), monounsaturated (one double bond), and polyunsaturated (more than one double bond). Partially hydrogenated means that some of the double bonds have been removed by reaction with hydrogen.

LIST 4–15. (Continued)

PRODUCT	COMPOSITION
Gasoline	Mixture with additives: about 6–12 carbon atoms, boiling point range 60–225°C
Kerosene	Mixture: about 10–22 carbon atoms, boiling point range 150–300°C
Fuel oil	Similar to kerosene; less refined
Mineral oil	Mixture: boiling point above 370°C
Lubricating oils	Mineral oils with additives
Lubricating greases	Oils with soaps
Candle/canning wax (paraffin)	Mixture: 20–36 carbon atoms; melting point 46–68°C

Cleansers and Antiseptics

Soaps	Pure soaps are salts of fatty acids such as sodium stearate $NAC_{18}H_{35}O_2$; many contain additives of various kinds
Detergents	Complex mixtures of dispersing agents and additives
Laundry starch	Glucose polymers (amylose a sugar and amylopectin)
Chloride of lime	Calcium hypochlorite, $Ca(ClO)_2$
Drain cleaners	Commonly lye (sodium hydroxide, $NaOH$) with sodium hypochlorite, $NaClO$

Bleaches

Chlorine	Sodium hypochlorite, $NaClO$
Nonchlorine	Sodium peroxyborate, $NaBO_3.H_2O$ or $NaBO_2.3H_2O.H_2O_2$
Window cleaners	May be ammonia water with a small amount of detergent; some contain an alcohol, methoxyethanol, $CH_3O(CH_2)_2OH$

Automotive Products

Antifreeze	Primarily ethylene glycol, $HO(CH_2)_2OH$
Windshield washer liquid	Usually methyl alcohol, CH_3OH (very poisonous)

Garden and House Plants

Plant foods (salt type)	Mixtures of ammonium phosphate, ammonium sulfate, potassium phosphate, potassium nitrate, potassium chloride, and sometimes urea
Lime	Calcium hydroxide, $Ca(OH)_2$

(Continued)

The Science Teacher's Book of Lists, © 1993 by Prentice Hall

LIST 4–15. (Continued)

The Science Teacher's Book of Lists, © 1993 by Prentice Hall

PRODUCT	COMPOSITION
Ground limestone	Calcium carbonate, $CaCO_3$
Insecticidal soap	Potassium salts of fatty acids
Flowers of sulfur	Powdered elemental sulfur

Crafts and Shop

Paint removers	Often contain methylene chloride, CH_2Cl_2; others based on lye, NaOH

Metal Alloys

Brass	Copper with zinc
Bronze	Copper with zinc and small amounts of lead, or copper with tin and small amounts of other metals
Solder	Typically tin with lead and/or other metals
Pewter	Tin with copper, bismuth, and antimony
Stainless steel	Primarily iron with chromium
Soldering flux	Rosin or ammonium chloride, NH_4Cl
Plaster of paris	Dehydrated gypsum (calcium sulfate), $CaSO_4$
Pencil lead	Graphite (crystalline carbon) and clay

Paper — Cellulose fiber from cotton or wood pulp

Adhesives

Casein	Milk protein with modifiers
White glues	Often dispersions of vinyl acetate polymers
Mucilage	A vegetable gum in water
Rubber cement	Natural or synthetic rubbers in a solvent
"Duco" cement	Nitrocellulose in a solvent such as amyl acetate

LIST 4–16. PHYSICAL PROPERTIES OF WATER

PROPERTY	VALUE[a]	CONDITIONS
Boiling point	100°C/212°F	Pressure, 101.325 kPa[e]
Freezing or fusion point	0°C/32°F	Pressure, 101.325 kPa
Heat of fusion	79.7 cal/g	Melting point, 0°C
Heat of vaporization	539.1 cal/g	Boiling point, 100°C
Heat capacity[b]	1.0 cal/g	0–100°C: 101.325 kPa
Heat capacity of ice[c]	0.5 cal/g	−30–0°C
Density of ice	0.9168 g/cm^3	0°C
Density of water[d]	0.999841 g/cm^3	0°C
	0.999965	3.0°C
	0.999973	3.8 to 4.2°C
	0.999965	5.0°C

[a]Calories are 15° calories, the heat required to heat one gram of water from 14.5 to 15.5°C at 101.325 kPa.

[b]Heat required to raise temperature of water 1°C. More sharply defined values are known.

[c]Heat required to raise the temperature of ice 1°C. Heat capacity values are lower at lower temperatures. More sharply defined values are known.

[d]Water attains a maximum density at 3.95°C.

[e]kPa represents a kilopascal. This is the currently-used standard for pressure.

LIST 4–17. MOLAR FREEZING POINT DEPRESSION FOR SEVERAL SUBSTANCES

The freezing point of liquids are depressed by dissolved substances. The depression is characteristic of the liquid and dependent on the concentration of the dissolved substance and the number of species, such as ions, generated by the solute.

SOLVENT	FREEZING POINT °C	MOLAR FREEZING POINT DEPRESSION[a] °C
Acetic acid (100%)	16.7	3.9
Benzene	5.5	5.12
Camphor	178.4	40.0
Cyclohexane	6.5	20.0
Naphthalene (moth balls)	80.2	6.9
Phenyl salicylate	43.0	12.3
Stearic acid	69.0	4.5
Water	0	1.86

[a]Freezing point depressions are for one gram-molecular-weight of dissolved substance in 1000 g of solvent. Freezing point depression is proportional to the concentration of solute and can be used as a method of determining molecular weight or approximate degree of ionization of the solute.

This effect is used in salts put on icy roadways and sidewalks, in automobile antifreezes, and in the ice-salt mixtures used in ice cream freezers.

LIST 4–18. THE CHEMISTRY OF CARBON

Of all the elements, carbon has a unique ability to bond with itself to form stable compounds. This combining power, together with the incorporation of a number of other elements, has resulted in the formation of several million known natural and synthetic substances that contain carbon. Some of the other elements commonly combined with carbon are hydrogen, oxygen, nitrogen, chlorine, and sulfur. Carbon compounds are the basic components of living organisms. The field of carbon compounds and their synthesis, behavior, and properties is called organic chemistry. Our purpose here is to provide a simple introduction to some of the facets of organic materials.

Groups of Well-Known Organic Compounds

Plastics and rubber	Many medicines
Natural and synthetic fibers	Gasoline and oils
Proteins	Soaps
Carbohydrates (sugars)	Alcohols
Many dyes	Many acids

There are examples of organic compounds in other lists without much explanation. The explanations and basic principles here may help with their interpretation.

Carbon has a valence or combining power of four, and all four bonding points must be satisfied in some way. Ordinarily, the bonding forces are arranged so that they form the points of a four sided figure, a tetrahedron, but they are often distorted in position to accommodate other configurations. The nature of bonds formed between carbon atoms or with other elements is usually through shared electrons, wherein outer electrons from one atom are shared with those of another atom.

Chemists represent the structure of compounds in a number of ways by writing symbols for the elements and lines for bonds. For many substances, the simplest method on paper is to write a group of symbols and bonds without trying to indicate the true arrangement in space or the angles of the bonds. Sometimes the bonds are not shown if the attachment of the atoms is clear. Some symbols are: C = carbon, H = hydrogen, O = oxygen, S = sulfur, Cl = chlorine, and F = fluorine.

The Science Teacher's Book of Lists, © 1993 by Prentice Hall

LIST 4–19. SELECTED STRUCTURAL FORMULAS OF COMPOUNDS USING GROUPS OF SYMBOLS AND LINES

```
      H
      |
   H-C-H          Methane
      |
      H
```
Methane

```
      H
      |
   H-C-O-H        Methyl alcohol[a]
      |
      H
```
Methyl alcohol[a]

```
   H H
   | |
   H-C-C-H        Ethane
   | |
   H H
```
Ethane

```
   H H
   | |
   H-C-C-O-H      Ethyl alcohol
   | |
   H H
```
Ethyl alcohol

```
   H H H
   | | |
   H-C-C-C-H      Propane
   | | |
   H H H
```
Propane

```
   H H H
   | | |
   H-C-C-C-O-H    Propyl alcohol
   | | |
   H H H
```
Propyl alcohol

```
      H
      |
   H-C-C-O-H      Acetic acid[b]
      |  ||
      H  O
```
Acetic acid[b]

```
   H H     H
   | |     |
   H-C-C-O-C-C-H
   | |     ||  
   H H     O H
```
Ethyl acetate (a liquid used as a solvent in lacquers)

(Continued)

[a]The -O-H group alone signifies an alcohol.

[b]The -C-O-H group indicates an acid.
        ||
        O

An organic acid is written

   -COOH   or   -C-O-H
                     ||
                     O

One oxygen is double-bonded. The first formula looks like a peroxide but is commonly accepted.

LIST 4–19. (Continued)

$$\begin{array}{ccccc} H & O & H & H \\ | & || & | & | \\ H-C-C-C-C-H \\ | & & | & | \\ H & & H & H \end{array}$$

Methyl ethyl ketone (a solvent and intermediate in synthesis; reported to be used in the purification of cocaine.)

$$\begin{array}{ccc} H & H & H \\ | & | & | \\ H-C-C-N-H \\ | & | \\ H & H \end{array}$$

Ethyl amine

$$\begin{array}{cc} H & H \\ | & | \\ H-N-C-C-O-H \\ | & || \\ H & O \end{array}$$

Glycine (an amino acid)

$$\begin{array}{c} Cl \\ | \\ H-C-Cl \\ | \\ Cl \end{array}$$

Chloroform (an anesthetic)

$$\begin{array}{c} Cl \\ | \\ Cl-C-Cl \\ | \\ Cl \end{array}$$

Carbon tetrachloride (a toxic cleaning solvent)

$$\begin{array}{cc} F & F \\ | & | \\ F-C-C-Cl \\ | & | \\ F & F \end{array}$$

A chlorofluorcarbon (CFC) used in refrigeration devices. Compounds of this class are known to be a factor in ozone layer depletion.

$$\begin{array}{ccc} H & \left(\begin{array}{c}H\end{array}\right) & O \\ | & | & || \\ H-C- & \left(\begin{array}{c}C\end{array}\right) & -C-O-H \\ | & | \\ H & \left(H\right)_{16} \end{array}$$

Stearic acid (the sodium salt is a soap)

(Continued)

The Science Teacher's Book of Lists, © 1993 by Prentice Hall

LIST 4–19. (Continued)

A formula written with parenthesis is a way of condensing structures having a large number of repeated units. Stearic acid is described as saturated. A similar acid with one double bond is monounsaturated. An acid with two or more double bonds per molecule is polyunsaturated.

LIST 4–20. AROMATIC COMPOUNDS

Carbon is capable of forming a large number of ring compounds. Six-membered ring compounds with unsaturation equivalent to alternating single and double bonds are classified as aromatic.

Examples of Aromatic Compounds

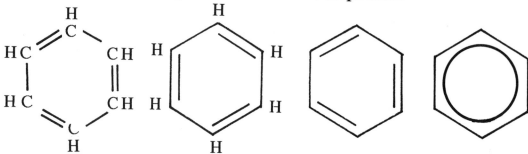

Four ways of representing the structure of benzene. In the third and fourth types any unsubstituted corner is considered to bear a hydrogen atom. The third type of formula is used below.

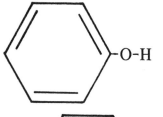 Phenol (a disinfectant and component of some gargles)

 Para-dichlorobenzene (moth flakes)

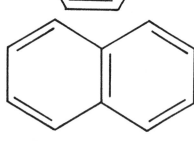 Naphthalene (moth balls)

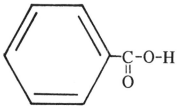 Benzoic acid (the sodium salt is a food preservative)

(Continued)

LIST 4–20. (Continued)

Examples of More Complex Molecules

Saccharin

Aspirin

LIST 4–21. GIANT MOLECULES

The very large molecules of plastics, rubber, and like materials usually consist of long chains of repeated units called *polymers*. They may also contain combinations of different units. As with stearic acid above, the repeating unit is enclosed in brackets with a subscript, which might be 10 to 100 or more.

$$H-\left[\begin{array}{c} H\ \ H \\ |\ \ \ | \\ -C-C- \\ |\ \ \ | \\ H\ \ H \end{array}\right]_x -H \qquad \text{Polyethylene (a common film and plastic)}$$

$$H-\left[\begin{array}{c} H\ \ H\ \ \ \ \ \ H \\ |\ \ \ |\ \ \ \ \ \ | \\ -C-C=C-C- \\ |\ \ \ \ \ \ \ \ \ \ \ | \\ H\ \ \ \ \ \ \ \ \ \ H \\ \ \ \ \ \ \ CH_3 \end{array}\right]_x -H \qquad \text{Polyisoprene (natural rubber)}$$

$$H-O-\left[\begin{array}{c} H\ \ H \\ |\ \ \ | \\ -C-C-O-C-\bigcirc-C- \\ |\ \ \ |\ \ \ \ \ \|\ \ \ \ \ \ \ \ \ \ \| \\ H\ \ H\ \ \ \ O\ \ \ \ \ \ \ \ \ O \end{array}\right] -O-H \qquad \begin{array}{l}\text{Poly(ethylene tereph-}\\ \text{thalate) (used in films}\\ \text{and fibers and called}\\ \text{polyester for short)}\end{array}$$

$$H-\left[\begin{array}{c} H\ \ H \\ |\ \ \ | \\ -N-C-C- \\ |\ \ \ \ \ \| \\ H\ \ \ \ O \end{array}\right]_x -O-H \qquad \begin{array}{l}\text{Polyglycine (a polyamino acid akin to a protein.)}\\ \text{Proteins are composed of many different amino}\\ \text{acid units.}\end{array}$$

LIST 4–22. ISOTOPES OF CHEMICAL ELEMENTS

Atoms of the elements are composed of a nucleus of protons (positively charged and having appreciable mass) and neutrons (about equal in mass with no charge) surrounded by electrons (negative charges with very little mass and equal in number to the protons). The number of protons is the *atomic number*, and the sum of mass of the protons and neutrons is the *atomic mass* or *weight*. (See List 4–3, Elements.)

Isotopes of an element are atoms in which the number of protons and electrons is the same but the number of neutrons is different. Thus the chemical properties are not changed, although the atomic weight is different and physical properties are slightly different.

Isotopes are designated by the symbol or name together with a number for the sum of the protons and neutrons added as a suffix or a superscript. For example, normal carbon is carbon-12 or C^{12}. Two isotopes of carbon are C^{13} and C^{14}. The isotope is classed as stable if it does not exhibit radioactive decay and is classed as radioactive, or a radioisotope, if it does.

The existence of isotopes is the reason why the atomic weights of the elements are not all even numbers.

Examples of Some Isotopes

ATOM	PROTONS	NEUTRONS	ELECTRONS	HALF-LIFE[a]
Hydrogen	1	0	1	
Hydrogen-2 (deuterium)	1	1	1	
Hydrogen-3 (tritium)	1	2	1	12.5 y
Carbon-12	6	6	6	
Carbon-13	6	7	6	
Carbon-14[b]	6	8	6	5370 y
Oxygen-16	8	8	8	
Oxygen-18	8	10	8	
Sulfur-32	16	16	16	
Sulfur-35	16	19	16	87.4 d
Potassium-39	19	20	19	
Potassium-40	19	21	19	1.25×10^9 y
Colbalt-56	27	29	27	
Colbalt-60	27	33	27	5.27 y
Rubidium-85	37	48	37	
Rubidium-87	37	50	37	4.88×10^{10} y

(Continued)

[a]d = days; y = years. Half-life is the time required for one half the radioactive material to decompose. A knowledge of the amounts of product(s) and remaining radioactive isotope permits calculation of a time for the beginning and stage of decay.

[b]Carbon-14 is generated in the upper atmosphere by the impact of carbon dioxide with cosmic ray particles.

LIST 4–22. (Continued)

Uses of Isotopes

Isotopes, both stable and radioactive, are useful in many ways. They can be detected by various modern instrumental methods. Examples of uses are:

- Tracking the course of chemical reactions.
- Studying biological and metabolic processes.
- Determining fertilizer needs of plants and crops.
- Labeling of drugs.
- Tracing oil flow in pipelines.
- Study of friction and corrosion of metals.
- Study of uniformity of mixing as in wood pulp for paper manufacture.
- Dating archaeological remains with carbon-14.
- Tracing the geological history of natural waters.
- Dating the age of fossils, rocks, and meteorites.

PHYSICS

LIST 5–1. ABOUT PHYSICS

Physics is the science that investigates matter and energy and their inter-actions. The major branches of physics are linked by concepts in energy, mass, motion, forces, magnetism and charge. The major branches of physics are:

Traditional Physics

- Acoustics
- Atomic physics
- Electricity and magnetism
- Heat
- Mass
- Mechanics
- Optics

The New Physics

- Particle physics

LIST 5–2. PHYSICS VOCABULARY

absolute zero—the temperature at which the average kinetic energy of a gas molecule is zero, equal to $-460°F$, $-273°C$, or $0°K$

absorb—to take in (not reflect) or incorporate

absorption—the process by which radiant energy is taken in and transformed into other forms of energy

acceleration—the rate of change of velocity; an object is accelerated when its speed or direction is changed

acoustics—the study of sound

alternating current—electrical current that continually changes direction in a circuit

ammeter—a meter for measuring electrical current

ampere—unit for measuring electrical current corresponding to the passage of one coulomb of electric charge per second; the symbol is A.

amplitude—maximum displacement of a body undergoing harmonic motion from its equilibrium position; width of a sound's wave pattern

Archimedes' principle—states that the loss of weight of an object in water is equal to the weight of the water it displaces

antimatter—for every particle of matter there is an opposite or antiparticle with opposite properties; when matter and its antimatter meet they can annihilate each other, producing energy; examples: protons and antiprotons and quarks and antiquarks

atom—smallest part of an element that still has all the chemical and physical properties of the element

battery—two or more electrical cells connected together; "battery" is also commonly used for a single electrical cell

big bang theory—holds that the universe began 10 to 20 billion years ago under a state of tremendous temperatures and density, then exploded outward, marking the beginning of time, and has been cooling and expanding to its present state

binary stars—two stars which move in elliptical orbits about their common center of mass

black hole—a region in space from which light cannot escape a strong gravitational field; believed to form from the gravitational collapse of a massive star

boiling point—temperature at which a liquid forms bubbles of its vapor within the mass; occurs when liquid's vapor pressure equals the atmospheric pressure

Celsius scale—temperature scale of 100 equal divisions between the ice point, at $0°$, and the steam point, at $100°$

The Science Teacher's Book of Lists, © 1993 by Prentice Hall

(Continued)

LIST 5–2. (Continued)

centimeter—a unit of measure equal to $\frac{1}{100}$ of a meter, abbreviated cm

chaos theory—states that simple nonlinear systems can behave in ways that are so complex that long-term predictability is impossible; see List 5–23, Chaos Theory

charged body—an object with a loss or gain of electrons; since an electron has a negative charge, a gain of electrons produces a negative charge and a loss of electrons produces a positive charge

chord—three or more notes sounded together chosen by the rules of harmony (otherwise it's a discord)

closed circuit—a complete path along which electrons flow; appliances perform in a closed circuit and shut down in an open circuit.

concave lens—lens that curves inward in the center and is thicker at the edges; See List 5–20, Three Basic Types of Lenses

condensation—change of state from gas to liquid

conduction—movement of heat energy caused when molecules bump into each other

conductor—material through which heat or electricity travels easily

contract—to get smaller

convection—the way heat travels through liquids and gas, with hot molecules rising and cold molecules falling

convex lens—lens that is thicker in the center than at the edges

coulomb—a fundamental unit of electrical charge equal to the quantity of charge transferred in one second by a steady current of one ampere; abbreviated C

decibel—a unit of measurement for the loudness of sound; abbreviated dB

degree—unit of measurement of temperature or arc

dense—having density

density—relationship between mass and volume

dry cell—electrical cell with a moist, nonliquid, electrolyte

echo—sound that is reflected by an object

effort—force applied against inertia; force needed to perform work

electrical charge—a gain or loss of electrons (see charged body)

electrical circuit—closed path of an electrical current

electrical current—the rate of flow of electrons past a given point in an electrical circuit

electrical current, alternating—a flow of electrons that reverses its direction of flow at regular intervals

(Continued)

LIST 5–2. (Continued)

electrical current, direct—a steady flow of electrons in one direction

electrical energy—energy caused by moving charges

electrode—negative or positive terminal of an electrical cell

electromagnet—a magnet that is made when electricity passes through a coil of wire, which is wrapped around a nonmagnetic bar of iron

electromagnetic spectrum—the entire range of radiation extending in frequency approximately from 10^{23} to 0 cycles per second; this includes, in order of decreasing frequency: cosmic-ray photons, gamma rays, X rays, ultraviolet radiation, visible light, infrared rays, microwaves, radio waves, heat, and electric current

electron—a negatively charged particle of an atom, having very small mass and orbiting around the nucleus of an atom

electron shell—a region about an atomic nucleus within which electrons move; there may be several such regions

energy—the ability to do work

evaporation—change of state at the surface of the liquid as it changes to a gas

expand—to get larger

Fahrenheit scale—temperature scale on which water boils at 212° and freezes at 32°

filament—the thin wire inside a light bulb which glows when electricity moves through it

filter—(a) material that permits some particles to pass through and prevents others; (b) material which transmits some colors of light and blocks others

fluid—matter that flows

force—a push or a pull; an influence on a body which causes the body to be accelerated

freezing—changing from a liquid to a solid

freezing point—temperature at which a liquid changes to a solid

frequency—number of vibrations per unit of time; also, the number of waves passing a point per unit of time

friction—force that resists the movement of one object over another, resulting in heat

fuel—material that is burned to produce heat energy

fulcrum—point at which a lever is supported

galvanometer—a meter that measures small electrical currents

gas—form of matter that lacks definite shape or volume

The Science Teacher's Book of Lists, © 1993 by Prentice Hall

(Continued)

LIST 5–2. (Continued)

generator—a machine made of a coil of wire and a magnet that changes mechanical energy into electrical energy when the coil or magnet moves

gram—unit of measurement of mass in the metric system; equal to 0.032527 ounce

grand unified theory—mathematical scheme in which the gravitational, electromagnetic, weak, and strong nuclear forces are unified into a consistent description

gravity—the force of attraction between two massive bodies that is directly proportional to the product of their masses and inversely proportional to the square of the distance between them; force that pulls towards the center of a planet or other heavenly body

greenhouse effect—trapping and building up of heat in the atmosphere due to accumulation of CO_2

hadron—objects made up of quarks and/or anti quarks; see List 5–11, The Quark Theory

half-life—the time required for half of the number of nuclei in a radioactive material to decay

heat—a form of energy produced by the random motion of atoms and molecules

hertz—unit for measuring frequency, equal to one cycle per second; abbreviated Hz

hydroelectric energy—electrical energy produced when moving water turns either the coil of wire or the magnet in a generator

hypothesis—a scientific generalization lacking unrefutable data, usually used to begin a serious investigation; the data either support or nullify the hypothesis

image—reflection in a mirror or viewed through a lens

inclined plane—tilted surface

induced current—electrical current that is produced by cutting the lines of force in a magnetic field

induced magnetism—magnet made by touching a nonmagnetic object to a magnetic one

inertia—the resistance of a body to any change of its state of motion

infrared light—light with wavelengths that are longer than red light waves but shorter than radio waves; invisible to the human eye

insulator—material electrons do not move through easily, thus, not a good conductor of electricity

ion—an atom, or chemically combined group of atoms, having a charge caused by an excess or reduction of electrons

(Continued)

The Science Teacher's Book of Lists, © 1993 by Prentice Hall

LIST 5–2. (Continued)

joule—one newton-meter of work; a unit of energy equal to work done by a force of one newton over a distance of one meter; equal to 10^7 erg; abbreviated J

Kelvin scale—absolute temperature scale, roughly equal to Celsius temperature plus 273 degrees

kilocalorie—the amount of heat needed to raise the temperature of one kilogram of water one degree Celsius; 1,000 calories; also equal to one food calorie; abbreviated kcal

kilogram—unit of mass equal to 1,000 grams; abbreviated kg

kiloliter—a unit of volume equal to 1000 liters or one cubic meter; equal to 264.2 gallons; abbreviated kl

kilometer—unit of length measurement equal to 1,000 meters; equal to 3,280.8 feet; abbreviated km

kilowatt—unit of electrical power equal to 1,000 watts; abbreviated kW

kilowatt hour—unit of electrical energy or work equal to that done by one kilowatt in one hour; abbreviated kWh

kinetic energy—energy of motion

lens—curved piece of glass or other transparent material; used to enhance vision in eyeglasses, microscopes, and telescopes

lever—a simple machine with a fulcrum, effort arm, and resistance arm; used to change force and make work easier

light—electromagnetic radiation that is visible to the eye

light-year—distance that light travels in one year, approximately 10^{16} meters

lines of force—invisible field about a magnet that can be observed by placing a magnet under a cover and sprinkling the cover with iron filings; lines represent the density of a vector field; density of lines indicates strength of the force field

liquid—form of matter that has definite volume but no definite shape

liquid crystal—substances intermediate in their properties between liquid and crystals; there is a variety of types of structures; they can grow like crystals

liter—unit of volume in the metric system that is equal to 1,000 cubic centimeters, equal to about 1.06 quarts; abbreviated l

luminous—emitting light, especially self-generated light

magnet—an object that attracts iron; when suspended freely, lines up with the magnetic poles of a planet

magnetic field—magnetic lines of force about a magnet

magnetize—to make into a magnet

(Continued)

LIST 5-2. (Continued)

manometer—instrument for measuring pressure of a fluid

mass—amount of matter in an object; measured by its inertia or by placing on a balance

mass number—total number of protons and neutrons in an atomic nucleus

matter—anything that has mass

mechanical advantage—the number that identifies how many times a machine multiplies the effort used

medium—a substance through which a wave is carried; for instance, air and water are media for sound waves

metals—elements that are solid at room temperature (except for mercury), are good conductors of heat and electricity, and are bright, shiny, and malleable

melting—changing from a solid to a liquid

meter—unit of measurement of length in the metric system equal to 100 centimeters or 39.37 inches; abbreviated m

metric system—the "International System of Units"; a system of units of measurement based on the powers of ten with the meter, gram, liter, and second used as base units; used by scientists and most nations of the world

millimeter—unit of measurement in the metric system equal to $\frac{1}{1000}$ of a meter or 0.039 inch; abbreviated mm

mole—the molecular weight of a substance expressed in grams; the mole of a compound is equal to the sum of the atomic/molecular weights of its elements expressed in grams; abbreviated mol

molecule—smallest particle of a substance that can exhibit the chemical properties of that substance

negative charge—the charge of an electron

neutral—having no charge

neutron—constituent of the nucleus of an atom having mass but no charge

newton—unit of force required to accelerate a kilogram of mass one meter per second^2; abbreviated N

nuclear energy—energy of the nucleus of an atom, released when any of the mass of the atomic nucleus is converted to energy, as occurs during nuclear fission (splitting) or nuclear fusion (joining)

nuclear fission—a nuclear reaction in which the heavy nuclei of atoms are split into nuclear fragments, releasing tremendous amounts of energy

nuclear fusion—a nuclear reaction in which the light nuclei of atoms join together to form a heavier nucleus, producing tremendous amounts of energy

(Continued)

LIST 5–2. (Continued)

nucleus—center of the atom, composed of protons and neutrons

ohm—unit of electrical resistance; equal to the resistance of a conductor in which a current of one ampere is produced by a potential of one volt across its terminal; symbol Ω

opaque materials—materials that block light

open circuit—incomplete electrical path in which electricity cannot flow and appliances will not perform

orbit—path of electrons around the nucleus of an atom (also referred to as a "shell"); also, path of a planet around its star or moon around its planet

overtones—extra frequencies that give sound its quality

parallel circuit—circuit that has multiple paths for electrons

photon—see quantum

pitch—how high or low a sound is, determined by its frequency

pole—end of a magnet where the magnetic force is strongest

pollutants—substances harmful to the environment

positive charge—the charge of a proton; a body which loses electrons or gains protons has a positive charge

potential energy—stored energy that can be converted into other forms of energy; for instance, a match, which has stored chemical energy in the match head, which can be released by striking the match giving off heat and light energy

power—the rate at which work is done

pressure—amount of force on a specific area, commonly expressed in pounds per square inch, dynes per square centimeter, or newtons per square meter

prism—triangular piece of glass capable of breaking white light into the spectrum of visible colors

probability—the likelihood of events; the ratio of the number of specific outcomes to the total number of outcomes

properties—characteristics that identify an object or substance

proton—positively charged constituent of the nucleus of an atom; built from three quarks

pulley—simple machine made of a wheel and axle used to make work easier by changing the direction of force

quantum—the unit of energy associated with each given frequency of radiation; a photon

quantum jump—jump of an electron between levels of an atom due to absorption or release of energy

The Science Teacher's Book of Lists, © 1993 by Prentice Hall

(Continued)

LIST 5-2. (Continued)

quantum numbers—numbers that describe each of possible energy levels of an atom

radar—radio detecting and ranging; instrument that sends out high-frequency radio waves and then receives them up after they have been reflected off an object, to determine the distance and direction of the reflecting object

radiant energy—energy released as electromagnetic radiation

radiation—the process in which energy in the form of heat, light, or high energy particles are released from atoms as they undergo internal change; radiation from radium and other radioactive materials is used in treatment of some diseases

radiometer—a device made of white paddles, which reflect light, and black paddles, which absorb light, transforming light energy to mechanical energy by turning the paddles about a spindle, in a partial vacuum

radon—colorless, radioactive gas given off in the decay of radium in rocks and soil; is used as a source of radiation in radiotherapy and research; abbreviated Rn

ray—a stream of particles given off by a radioactive substance; a straight line along which energy travels from its source to any given point; also electromagnetic radiation such as X rays and light beams

reflected light—light that is bounced off an object

refraction—the bending of light as it passes from one medium to another

repel—force that pushes away

resistance—measure of how easy or hard it is for electrical current to flow through an object; force that acts against levers

resistance arm—distance from the fulcrum to which the resistance acts upon the lever

series circuit—an electrical circuit that has one path for the electrons

short circuit—an electrical circuit through a negligible resistance which usually carries a normal load and overloads the circuit

solar cell—device that produces electricity when sunlight shines on it; photovoltaic cell; see List 5-9, An Overview of Electricity

solar collector—device that collects solar energy

solar energy—energy from the sun

solid—state of matter that has a definite shape and volume

sonar—sound navigation ranging; instrument that transmits high-frequency sound waves in water and registers the vibrations reflected back to determine objects and their distances underwater

(Continued)

LIST 5-2. (Continued)

sound—a form of energy (in the form of vibrations) that travels by waves and is detected by hearing organs

speed—the rate of motion; expressed as the distance an object moves in a period of time, such as miles per hour

static electricity—the build up of electrical charges

state—a form of matter, either solid, liquid, or gas

strong force—the force which binds subatomic particles in the nuclei, the forces between hadrons (objects made of quarks and/or antiquarks: protons, neutrons, and antiprotons)

superconductor—a material that loses its electrical resistance when it is at very low temperatures

temperature—a measure of the intensity of heat or cold (or the average kinetic energy of molecules) in degrees on a standard scale

tension—tightness of a string or spring caused by force

terminal—negative or positive end of an electric cell

theory—an idea based on scientific research and data

thermometer—instrument for measuring temperature in degrees

transparent—medium through which visible light readily passes

translucent materials—materials that permit some light to travel through them, but do not provide a clear image

ultraviolet light—invisible light with wavelengths shorter than violet

unit—amount used to measure objects and properties

vacuum—absence of matter

valence—the number of electrons an atom can lend or borrow when combining with other atoms into molecules

velocity—the speed and direction of a moving object

vibrate—back and forth motion; usually expressed in movements per unit of time

visible spectrum—visible colors of light as seen in a rainbow: red, orange, yellow, green, blue, and violet

volt—unit of measurement for electrical potential difference; abbreviated V

voltage—electromotive force or potential difference

voltmeter—instrument that measures voltage

volume—amount of space taken up by matter

Watt—unit of power equal to one joule per second; abreviated W

weak force—one of the fundamental forces of nature, manifested in the emission of electrons or protons in the radioactive decay of nuclei; the weak force is only 10^{-13} as great as the strong force

(Continued)

The Science Teacher's Book of Lists, © 1993 by Prentice Hall

LIST 5–2. (Continued)

weight—force of gravity on an object

wet cell—electrical cell that has a liquid electrolyte

work—the force acting to move an object through a distance; expressed as
force × distance, or in newton-meters or joules

LIST 5–3. STATES OF MATTER

Matter is anything that takes up space and has mass. It is made up of atoms or molecules and exists as a solid, liquid, or gas. A change from one state of matter to another is always a physical change. The Law of Conservation of Matter states that matter can neither be created nor destroyed by ordinary physical or chemical changes.

A Look at the Three States of Matter

SOLIDS	LIQUIDS	GASES
Have definite shape and definite volume	Have a definite volume but no definite shape	Have no definite volume and no definite shape
Molecules are tightly packed, cannot move easily, and vibrate in place	Molecules are less tightly packed, slide over each other and easily change place, fill the shape of the container	Molecules are not packed together and spread out to fill the shape of the container
Expand when heated	Expand when heated	Expand when heated
Contract when cooled	Contract when cooled; (water is an exception, it expands when cooled)	Contract when cooled

(Continued)

NOTE: All substances do not exist in all three states; for example, dry ice (CO_2) exists as a solid and a gas, not as a liquid. This property makes dry ice more desirable than ice for packing, storing, and transporting ice cream.

LIST 5–3. (Continued)

Examples of Substances and the States of Matter in Which They Normally Exist

SOLID FORM (NAME)	LIQUID FORM	GASEOUS FORM
Ice Melts 0°C	Water Boils 100°C	Steam or water vapor
Dry ice (Carbon dioxide)	None at room temperature and atmospheric pressure	Colorless, odorless
Moth flakes (para-dichlorobenzene) Melts 53.1°C	Boils 174°C	Odoriferous vapors
Moth balls (naphthalene) Melts 80.6°C	Boils 218°C	None
None	Gasoline	Gasoline fumes
None	Alcohol	Alcohol fumes
Acetic acid (100%) Melts 16.6°C	Boils 118°C	Acid vapor
Benzoic acid Melts 122.4°C	Boils 249°C	Acid vapor
Zinc chloride Melts 283°C	Boils 732°C	Corrosive vapor
Silver Melts 961°C	Boils 2212°C	None

NOTE: Scientist recognize another phase of matter, plasma—highly ionized gas such as neon and the surface gases of the sun and other stars. Plasma is rare on Earth but plentiful in the universe.

Caution: If experiments are done with these materials (except water), only small amounts should be used and care taken to avoid breathing fumes and receiving burns.

LIST 5–4. MEASURING MATTER

LINEAR MEASURE	*MASS*	*VOLUME*	*TEMPERATURE*

Metric System Instruments and Basic Units

Meter stick	*Balance*	*Graduated cylinder*	*Thermometer*
Kilometers	Kilograms	Liters	Degrees Celsius
Meters	Grams	Milliliters	
Centimeters	Milligrams		
Millimeters			

English System Instruments and Units

Yard stick	*Balance*	*Measuring cup*	*Thermometer*
Yards	Pounds	Gallons	Degrees Fahrenheit
Feet	Ounces	Quarts	
Inches		Pints	
		Cups	
		Ounces	

The Science Teacher's Book of Lists, © 1993 by Prentice Hall

LIST 5–5. SIMPLE MACHINES

Simple machines are devices that make work easier by changing the amount or the direction of force.

Simple machines can help by:

- Increasing force that enables us to lift heavy objects.
- Changing the direction of the force that enables us to move objects in different directions.
- Increasing the speed of a force to enable us to move things farther or faster.

Formula to calculate work: $W = F\,D$
$$\text{Work} = \text{force} \times \text{distance}$$

Simple Machines

Levers   **Inclined planes**

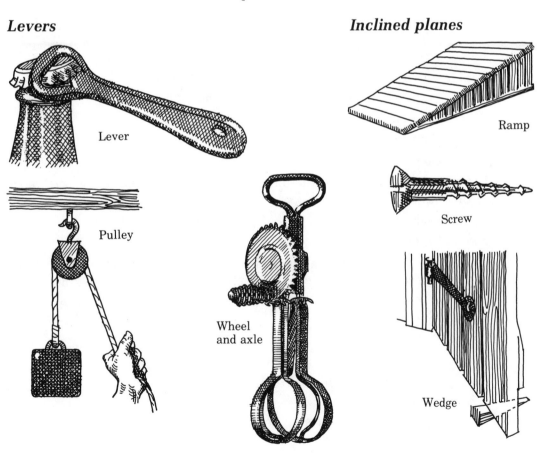

Lever

Pulley

Wheel and axle

Ramp

Screw

Wedge

LIST 5–6. SIX CLASSES OF SIMPLE MACHINES WITH DEFINITIONS AND EXAMPLES

1. **Inclined plane**—consists of a plane surface which is tilted or inclined. Using an inclined plane to move a heavy object takes less force than lifting it directly. Examples:

   Ramp for loading and unloading

   A switchback road

   Sliding board

   Water slide

   Ladder

2. **Wedge**—consists of two inclined planes and is usually used to cut or break things apart. Wedges move objects by being forced under or between them. They alter the direction of a force applied to them. When you push down on a wedge, it pushes out on the two planes that it is in between. Examples:

   Log splitter (a wedge used with a sledge hammer to split logs)

   Axe heads

   Cutting edges of chisels, knives, and scissors

   Points of nails, needles, pins, and moly bolts

   Tip of a screw driver

   Tines of forks

   Door stops

3. **Screw**—consists of an inclined plane wound about a post. Screws can lift things. Examples:

   Jackscrew

   Piano stool

4. **Lever**—There are three types of levers that are classified according to their three parts: the fulcrum, the effort arm, and the resistance arm.

   (1) *First class levers*—the fulcrum is between the resistance and the force. Examples:

      Car jacks

      Crowbars

      Hammer claw used to pull out
      nails

      Balance for massing or weighing
      objects

      Hedge trimmers

      Pliers

The Science Teacher's Book of Lists, © 1993 by Prentice Hall

(Continued)

LIST 5–6. (Continued)

Pruning shears

Scissors

Seesaws

Wire cutters

(2) *Second class levers*—the resistance is between the fulcrum and the force. Examples:

Garlic presses

Wheelbarrows

(3) *Third class levers*—the force is between the resistance and the fulcrum. Examples:

Brooms

Tweezers

5. **Pulleys**—consists of a grooved wheel (or wheels) that spins on a fixed axis with a rope or chain moving over the wheel. There are two types of pulleys:

(1) *Fixed pulleys*—wheel(s) and rope are fixed in place. They make lifting easier by changing a push to a pull. Examples:

Clotheslines

Flagpoles

Mini blinds

Lifting hay into a hayloft

Sailboats, to raise the sails

(2) *Movable pulleys*—wheel(s) and rope are attached to and move with the resistance. They make work easier by changing the force. Example:

Block and tackle—consists of fixed and moveable pulleys. It makes work easier by changing the direction of force and decreasing the force.

6. **Wheel and axle**—consists of a wheel that turns around a rod or axle. Turning one turns the other. Examples:

Airplane propellers

Blades on a helicopter, electric fan

Doorknob

Handlebars on a bicycle

Wheels on wagons, car, bicycles, etc.

Wheels and axles with teeth that fit into one another are called gears.

(Continued)

LIST 5–6. (Continued)

As one gear turns, it turns the gears that it touches. Gears are used in:
  Bicycles
  Can openers
  Cars and trucks
  Mechanical clocks and watches; these gears cause the tick-tock.

Several simple machines working in conjunction with each other create *compound machines.* Examples:
  Bicycles
  Can openers
  Cars and trucks
  Helicopters
  Music boxes
  Pencil sharpeners

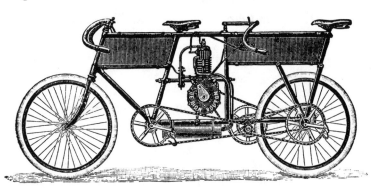

LIST 5–7. ABOUT MAGNETS

Magnets are made of a combination of iron, steel, nickel, and/or cobalt. Iron by itself usually does not make a strong magnet and loses its magnetism easily. When iron is chemically combined with carbon and metals such as nickel and chromium, it makes the alloy steel. When magnetized, steel makes excellent magnets.

The Law of Magnetism states that like poles repel and opposite poles attract.

To Observe a Magnetic Force Field

1. Place a magnet in a clear plastic bag and seal. This protects the magnet and keeps it clean of iron filings.

2. Place the magnet, in the bag, on a flat surface.

3. Sprinkle iron filings over the entire magnet. Different shaped magnets have different force field patterns.

- In 1820, Hans Christian Oersted connected a wire to a battery and noticed that the needle on a nearby compass moved, thus discovering that there is a relationship between electricity and magnetism.

- After reading about Oersted's discovery, Michael Faraday reasoned that if a magnetic needle moved when a current was sent through a conductor, then something should happen in a conductor if a magnet is moved near it.

Thus,

- Electricity can be used to produce magnetism, as in electromagnets.
- Magnetism can be used to produce electricity, as in generators.

When the force field of a magnet has a coil of wire moved through it, electrons flow through the wire, producing electricity. This is the principle upon which most modern electric generators work.

LIST 5–8. AN OVERVIEW OF MAGNETISM

Classification of Selected Metals

MAGNETIC	*NONMAGNETIC*	
Iron	Aluminum	Lead
Steel	Silver	Copper
Cobalt	Gold	Zinc
Nickel	Mercury	Tin
	Sodium	

A Common Misconception About Magnetism

Many people have the misconception that all metals are magnetic. Only three naturally occurring metals are magnetic. They are iron, nickel, and cobalt. Steel, an alloy, can also be magnetized. Some stainless steels are not magnetic or only slightly so.

Shapes of Magnets

Through the processes of heating and molding, magnets can be made in different shapes. The most common shapes are:

- Bar
- U
- Horseshoe
- Circle
- Square
- Doughnut

Electromagnets are used in:

- Telephones
- Doorbells
- Buzzers
- Junkyard cranes
- St. Louis Motors
- Smoke detectors
- Fire alarms

LIST 5–9. AN OVERVIEW OF ELECTRICITY

Scientists theorize that electricity is a flow of electrons, negatively charged particles that orbit about the nucleus of an atom. The electrons can build up on objects causing the "receiving" object to have a negative charge and the "sending" object to have a positive charge. The buildup and/or deficiency of charges is known as static electricity. In addition, electrons can be induced to flow through a conductor. When they do so, the result is current electricity.

Classes of Electricity

STATIC:	*CURRENT:*
A buildup or deficiency of electrons.	A flow of electrons in a conductor through a closed circuit.
Examples:	Examples:
• "static cling" in clothes	• glowing lights and neon signs
• rubbing balloons with wool	• laser printers printing a document
• "shock" on touching a doorknob after walking across a wool rug	• electric pencil sharpeners
• lightning	• stereos playing music

GOOD CONDUCTORS OF ELECTRICITY	*POOR CONDUCTORS (INSULATORS)*
Metals	Nonmetals
Water containing impurities	Pure water*, no impurities
Living trees (containing sap), wet wood	Dry wood
Animals, including people	Glass
Liquid cleaners	Plastics
	Rubber

Current electricity is produced when electrons flow through a conductor. It can be produced and/or induced by:

Chemical Reactions: which take place in:

• wet cells   • dry cells   • batteries

(Continued)

---

*In everyday life we rarely encounter pure water. For reasons of safety, one needs to assume that water contains impurities which make it an excellent conductor.

Generalization: Substances that are good conductors of electricity are also conductors of heat.

LIST 5–9. (Continued)

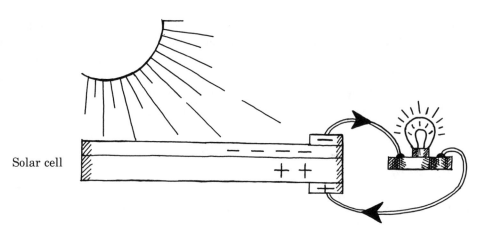

Solar cell

Moving a Magnet Near a Conductor: which is the principle upon which all electrical generators operate. A coil of wire or a magnet is moved by a turbine that is moved by a source of heat or kinetic energy derived from:

- fossil fuels
- wind power
- hydro power
- geothermal power
- solar-thermal systems
- nuclear power

Solar Cells: which are made of semiconductors such as silicon, which absorb sunlight causing a buildup of electrons on the front of the solar cell. When a conductor is attached to the front and back of the cell, electrons flow from the front of the cell, through the conductor, to the back of the cell.

LIST 5–10. DO'S AND DON'TS FOR ELECTRICAL SAFETY

Do's

Stay away from power lines.

Call the power company to retrieve model airplanes or kites caught in a tree near power lines.

Call the power company to retrieve model airplanes or balls that land inside the fence of a substation.

Use appliances only as designed and directed by the manufacturer.

Always disconnect appliances before inserting a tool or object or before cleaning.

Replace frayed cords.

Report downed trees that are near or on fallen power lines.

Stay away from swimming areas during an electrical storm.

Get indoors or in a car during an electrical storm.

Dust outlet covers or remove them to wash.

Carefully remove wall-switch covers when papering or painting.

Cover unused outlets with plastic outlet covers.

Replace burnt-out fuses or circuit breakers.

Keep electrical appliances in good repair.

Unplug computers and televisions during electrical storms.

Turn off appliances when not in use.

Don'ts

Don't fly a kite near power lines.

Don't climb a tree, ladder, or pole near a power line.

Don't climb the fence of a substation.

Don't use an appliance near a tub, shower, or pool.

Don't use a metal knife or fork to lift toast out of a toaster unless the toaster is unplugged.

Don't use an appliance with a frayed cord.

Don't touch a tree that is downed near power lines. It may be covering dangerous live wires.

Don't swim, play in an open field, or stand under a tree during an electrical storm.

Don't use an umbrella with metal ribs, a golf club, or shoes with metal cleats during an electrical storm.

Don't use liquids or spray cleaners on outlets or wall switches.

Don't paint or wallpaper over wall switch covers or outlets.

Don't put anything other than a plug or safety cover in an outlet.

Don't repair burnt out fuses.

Don't use frayed cords.

Don't use telephones during electrical storms.

Don't run cords under carpets.

(Continued)

LIST 5–10. (Continued)

Buy extension cords that are correctly rated for the specific appliances with which you are using them.

Don't use an extension cord that is not correctly rated for the appliance you are plugging into it.

The Science Teacher's Book of Lists, © 1993 by Prentice Hall

LIST 5–11. THE QUARK THEORY

The atom is the smallest particle of an element retaining the properties of that element. In the 1930s physicists were aware of four subatomic particles:

- **Electrons**—negatively charged particles orbiting the nucleus of an atom; the lightest massive elementary particle.
- **Protons**—positively charged particles, located in the nucleus of an atom.
- **Neutrons**—uncharged particles located in the nucleus of an atom.
- **Photon**—quantum of light energy.

Today physicists recognize more than two hundred subatomic particles. Large electron-positron colliders (LEP) are huge particle accelerators in which the collision of accelerated particles releases enormous amounts of energy, which condense into particles. LEPs have been built to investigate the nature of matter, the internal structure of the atom, and the forces that effect the component parts. They are providing information about subatomic particles and supportive data for the Quark Theory, which states that particles of matter can be grouped into two groups: hadrons and leptons.

A Classification of the Particles of Matter According to the Quark Theory

HADRONS	*LEPTONS*
• Term is from the Greek for bulky	• Term is from the Greek for lightweight, thin
• Heavy	• Light
• Feel the strong nuclear force	• Feel the weak nuclear force
• Are not elementary particles	• Are elementary particles
• Examples, two subspecies:	• Examples:

BARYONS	*MESONS*	*CHARGED*	*NOT CHARGED*
neutrons	pions	electron	corresponding neutrino
protons	kaons	muon	corresponding neutrino
		tau	corresponding neutrino

Other particles which feel the strong force

- Are made up of quarks, which are treated as elementary particles
- Can only exist in triples (called baryons) or in pairs (called mesons)
- Gluons are the particles responsible for binding quarks together
- Proton charge is the basic unit of electrical charge

Other particles which feel the weak force

(Continued)

LIST 5-11. (Continued)

The Fundamental Particles of Matter Are Quarks and Leptons

QUARKS			*LEPTONS*	
Charge is a fraction of a proton's	$\frac{2}{3}$	$-\frac{1}{3}$	-1	0
Spin	$\frac{1}{2}$		Varies	
Flavor, symbol	up, u	down, d	electron, e	its neutrino, ν_e
	charm, c	strange, s	muon, μ	its neutrino, ν_μ
	top, (t)	bottom, b	tau, τ	its neutrino, ν_t

Each of these particles has an antiparticle, which has the same mass and spin but opposite charge.

Particle Concepts

- Matter is made of atoms.

- Atoms are made of electrons orbiting about a nucleus composed of protons and neutrons, which are made up of smaller particles, quarks and leptons.

- Electrons are the lightest massive elementary particle and are responsible for electricity and chemical reactions. Each has a charge of -1.

- The nucleus of an atom is the core of the atom and is made mostly of neutrons and protons.

- Neutrons are uncharged particles that make up the nucleus of an atom along with protons. They are believed to be made up of three quarks. They take part in weak nuclear interactions.

- Protons are stable, positively charged particles that make up the nucleus of an atom along with neutrons. They are believed to be made up of three quarks. Each proton has a charge of $+1$. They take part in strong nuclear interactions.

- Quarks are a group of elementary particles. Protons and neutrons are each made up of three quarks. Quarks received their name from Dr. Murray Gell-Mann who won the Nobel prize in physics in 1969 for his investigations of subatomic particles.

- There are different types of quarks.

- Physicists think there are at least six "flavors" or types of quarks:

      Up   Down
      Charm   Strange
      Top (Truth)   Bottom (Bottom)

(Continued)

LIST 5–11. (Continued)

- Each flavor is thought to come in three "colors":

  Red

  Green

  Blue

- Leptons are a class of particles that can travel on their own and do not participate in strong interactions. They have a spin of $\frac{1}{2}$. Types of leptons are:

Electron	Electron neutrino
Muon	Muon neutrino
Tau	Tau neutrino

- In 1979, Steven Weinberg, Sheldon Glashow, and Abdus Salam shared the Nobel Prize for discovering the link between electromagnetism and the weak force of radioactive decay.

- In 1984, Carlo Rubbia and Simon van de Meer shared the Nobel Prize for discovering W and Z particles which had been predicted by Weinberg and Glashow.

- In 1988, Leon Lederman, Melvin Schwartz, and Jack Steinberger shared the Nobel Prize for work which led to a better understanding of elementary particles and force.

- In 1989, Norman Ramsey, Hans Dehmelt, and Wolfgang Paul shared the Nobel Prize for developing methods to isolate atoms and subatomic particles.

- In 1990, Richard Taylor, Jerome Frieman, and Henry Kendall shared the Nobel Prize for confirming the existence of quarks.

LIST 5–12. SUBATOMIC PARTICLE TERMINOLOGY

alpha—the nucleus of a helium atom consisting of two neutrons and two protons; given off by some radioactive substances

antiparticle—for every particle there is a counterpart consisting of the same mass and spin and with opposite electrical charge, baryon number, lepton number, etc.

baryons—a group of strongly interacting nuclear particles built from three quarks which includes protons, neutrons, and hyperons (unstable hadrons)

baryon number—the total number of baryons in a system minus the total number of antibaryons; a quantity assigned to elementary particles; quarks are assigned a baryon number $\frac{1}{3}$, and antiquarks $-\frac{1}{3}$

beta decay—there are two types of beta decay recognized: the transformation of the neutron into a proton, electron, and antineutrino; and the transformation of a nucleus in which the atomic number changes by 1 with the emission of an electron or positron

boson—particles that have integral spin or rotation; examples are meson, photon, and W boson

bubble chamber—a vessel filled with heated fluid to detect particles. Charged particles are shot through the chamber causing the fluid to boil along the paths of particles, producing bubble paths which can be photographed

charm—a quantum number equal to the number of charm quarks in a particle minus the number of anticharm quarks; one of the quark flavors

charmonium—a system consisting of a charm quark and an anticharm quark

color—a property possessed by quarks and gluons; a type of charge believed to be the source of the strong force between quarks. This usage has no relation to visible color

deuterium—an isotope of hydrogen in which the nucleus contains one proton and one neutron

deuteron—the nucleus of deuterium, which consists of one proton and one neutron

elementary particle—a particle that cannot be subdivided; the building blocks of matter

Fermi constant—the parameter that fixes the strength with which the weak force couples to particles of matter

fermion—the generic term for all particles having spin which is an odd multiple of $\frac{1}{2}$; all known elementary particles

The Science Teacher's Book of Lists, © 1993 by Prentice Hall

(Continued)

LIST 5–12. (Continued)

flavor—the name given to the quality that distinguishes quarks and leptons; the flavors of quarks are up and down, strange and charmed, top (truth) and bottom (beauty)

glueball—a neutral meson made up of a collection of gluons

gluon—messenger or carrier of the interquark force; electrically neutral, intermediary agent between quarks, having spin 1, having color, and existing in collections whose colors must add up to white

hadrons—objects made up of quarks and/or anti quarks, such as, protons, neutrons, antiprotons, and pions

hyperons—unstable hadrons

mesons—a class of strongly interacting particles made up of combinations of quarks and antiquarks, which are unstable because matter and antimatter can annihilate each other

muon—unstable lepton with a negative charge, 207 times heavier than an electron

neutrino—means "tiny neutron." A massless, electrically neutral lepton, given off during the neutron decay process. Discovered in the 1950s through nuclear reactors

nucleon—generic term for protons and neutrons

pions or π meson—the lightest meson, a class of strongly interacting particles. There are charged pions and neutral pions

particle physics—the scientific study of elementary particles, the building blocks of matter

photon—quantum particle of the electromagnetic field

proton—positively charged component of the nucleus of an atom; consists of three quarks

psi/J or J/psi—particle discovered in 1974 by Richter who named it "psi" and also discovered by Ting who named it "J," which provided evidence that quarks, the fundamental building blocks of matter, exist

spin—proton, electrons, and neutrons have an intrinsic angular movement known as spin; the spin of a particle tells what the particle looks like from different directions. A particle with a spin of 0 looks like a dot, the same from all directions. Particles do not spin on their axis.

strong force (interaction)—the dominant force which acts between hadrons, such as the force which holds neutrons and protons in the nucleus of an atom

superconductivity—the phenomenon in some substances in which their resistance drops to or close to zero, when their temperature is lowered to extremely low temperatures

(Continued)

LIST 5–12. (Continued)

synchrotron—a particle accelerator

tau lepton—a negatively charged lepton

top quark—thought to be the heaviest of all atomic particles with a mass at least 90 times that of a proton

upsilon—massive meson built from a bottom quark and a bottom antiquark

weak force (interaction)—one of the fundamental forces of nature; it is involved in beta-decay and radioactive decay of the nuclei, and neutrino interactions

Z boson—a neutral heavy boson; a particle that is similar to a photon except mass; It transmits part of the weak force between hadrons and leptons; its existence was predicted by Glashow, Salam, and Weinberg in the theory of the amalgamated weak-electromagnetic force.

LIST 5–13. NUCLEAR ENERGY: A RELATIONSHIP BETWEEN MATTER AND ENERGY

Albert Einstein was the first physicist to predict a relationship between matter and energy. One way that he expressed this relationship was in his formula:

$E = mc^2$
Energy = mass times the speed of light squared

(the speed of light multiplied by itself or
186,000 miles/second $\times$ 186,000 miles/second
also expressed 3×10^8 m/s $\times$ 3×10^8 m/s)

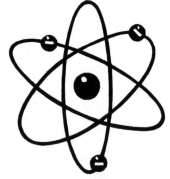

This formula ($E = mc^2$) illustrates that even a small mass multiplied by $186,000^2$ will result in a large number and thus a large amount of energy. Consequently, physicists have been working to develop ways of releasing the energy in the mass of atoms. The two routes to release nuclear energy that scientists have been investigating are fission and fusion.

LIST 5–14. A COMPARISON OF FISSION AND FUSION

FISSION	*FUSION*
• Splitting the nucleus of an atom releases energy.	• Fusing or joining nuclei of atoms releases energy.
• Most of the energy released is heat.	• Takes place at high temperatures.
• Heavy atoms are used.	• Light atoms are used.
• Uranium-235, is used most often.	• Hydrogen (the deuterium isotope) is frequently used. Two such hydrogen atoms, each containing one proton and one neutron, are fused into one helium atom and release energy.
• The power of present-day nuclear power plants that generate electricity.	• Not yet developed to generate electricity on large scale in power plants.
• Takes place in a reactor.	• Take place in a "tokamak," reactor, Russian for "doughnut-shaped."
• The power of the atomic bomb.	• The trigger reaction of the hydrogen bomb.
• Produces radioactive wastes.	• In a reactor, does not produce radioactive wastes.
• Scientists are investigating ways to make energy using fission that are less costly and safer.	• Scientists are investigating ways to make energy using fusion on a large scale.

LIST 5–15. THE ELECTROMAGNETIC SPECTRUM AND SOME USES

The electromagnetic spectrum consists of visible and invisible colors, waves, and rays. The component parts are radio waves, infrared light, visible light, ultraviolet light, X rays, gamma rays, and cosmic rays. These component parts have different wavelengths and frequencies. Only the colors of the visible spectrum can be seen by humans.

The colors of the visible spectrum, which can be observed in a rainbow or white light diffracted by a prism, are:

Red **O**range **Y**ellow   **G**reen   **B**lue **I**ndigo **V**iolet

(A helpful memory device is "Roy G. Biv")

Uses of the Electromagnetic Spectrum

COMPONENT	MODERN USES
Radio waves	Radio and television broadcasting, radar; attempts at communication with life beyond Earth; radio telescopes
Infrared light	Heat lamps
Visible light	Lighting homes, businesses, schools; photography; laser beams for surgery; guidance of missiles and other weapons
Ultraviolet light	Suntan lamps, fluorescent lamps, kill germs
X rays	Internal medical observations, expecially of bones and teeth: (air travel) security by inspecting closed packages; treating diseases; inspecting metals for internal defects
Gamma rays	Treating cancer patients
Cosmic rays	Atomic research

The Science Teacher's Book of Lists, © 1993 by Prentice Hall

LIST 5–16. BANDS OF THE
ELECTROMAGNETIC RADIATION SPECTRUM

BAND NAME	WAVELENGTH (METERS)	FREQUENCY CYCLES/SEC (HERTZ)	SOURCES
Cosmic photons (rays)	3×10^{-15}	10^{23}	Astronomical
Gamma rays	3×10^{-14}	10^{22}	Radioactive nuclei
Gamma rays/X rays	3×10^{-13}	10^{21}	
X rays	3×10^{-12}	10^{20}	Atomic inner shell
Soft X rays	3×10^{-11}	10^{19}	Electron impact on a solid
Ultraviolet light/X rays	3×10^{-10}	10^{18}	
Ultraviolet light	$3 \times 10^{-8 \text{ to } -9}$	10^{17}	Sunlight, electric arcs
Visible light	3×10^{-7}	$10^{15 \text{ to } 16}$	Sun, electric lights
Infrared	$3 \times 10^{-5 \text{ to } -6}$	$10^{13 \text{ to } 14}$	Hot bodies, molecules
Far infrared	3×10^{-4}	10^{12}	Hot bodies, molecules
Microwaves	3×10^{-3}	10^{11}	Electronic devices
Microwaves, radar	3×10^{-2}	10^{10}	Electronic devices
Radar, interstellar hydrogen	3×10^{-1}	10^{9}	Electronic devices
Television, FM radio	3	10^{8}	Electronic devices
Short-wave radio	30	10^{7}	Electronic devices
AM radio	300	10^{6}	Electronic devices
Long-wave radio	3000	10^{5}	Electronic devices
Induction heating	3×10^{4}	10^{4}	Electronic devices
Electric power (AC)	$3 \times 10^{6 \text{ to } 7}$	$10–100$	Generators
Direct current	Infinity	0	Batteries

Note: Some of the bands are determined by natural conditions, such as visible light; others are designated by people, for example, radio bands and microwaves. Because of the great difference in wave lengths over the whole spectrum, different units of length are commonly used for some of the bands.

LIST 5–17. FORMS AND EXAMPLES OF ENERGY

Energy is the ability to do work. There are seven forms of energy.

Forms and Examples of Energy

FORM	EXAMPLE
Atomic energy is the energy stored in nucleus of atoms, also called nuclear energy	Atomic bombs, nuclear weapons, nuclear power plants
Chemical energy is the energy stored in chemicals, fossil fuels, and substances that can burn or take part in chemical changes.	Add vinegar to baking soda, chemical energy is released with the fizz of carbon dioxide bubbles. Chemical reactions release energy such as heat and light.
Electrical energy is the energy of moving electrons.	Television, telephone, computer, household appliances.
Heat energy is the energy of moving molecules.	Friction caused by two objects moving over each other, as in rubbing two hands together or the electrical resistance in a stove element. Electrical and chemical energy can be used to produce heat.
Light energy is the energy of visible light.	Stars produce light. Electrical energy can be used to produce light.
Mechanical energy is the energy of moving objects.	Any moving object, falling water, meteor (shooting star).
Sound energy is the energy of vibrating objects in a medium of air, water, or solids.	Playing any musical instruments, using vocal chords, sound of television. There is no sound in the vacuum of outer space.

One form of energy can be transformed into another form of energy but cannot be created or destroyed. For example, electrical energy is frequently used to produce heat and light. Nuclear energy can be used to produce electricity through heat, steam, turbines, and generation.

In the production of one kind of energy, another form of energy can be given off. For example, mechanical energy frequently causes friction, giving off heat. During many chemical reactions, heat is given off.

> A helpful device for remembering the kinds of energy:
>
> ## A. C. Helms =
> **Atomic, chemical, heat, electrical, light, mechanical, and sound.**

The Science Teacher's Book of Lists, © 1993 by Prentice Hall

LIST 5–18. A CLASSIFICATION OF ENERGY

Examples of Potential and Kinetic Energy

POTENTIAL	*KINETIC*
Energy stored in stationary things.	Energy in moving things.

Examples

A match has potential chemical energy stored in the match head and the stick.	As a match is struck (using mechanical energy), the potential energy is released. The match gives off heat and light, the light flickers, ashes fall.
Uranium 235 has potential nuclear energy.	When U 235 undergoes fission, nuclear energy is released in the forms of heat, light, and sound. The heat can be used to change water to steam that can turn turbines to generate electricity.
Water at the top of a waterfall has potential energy of position.	As the water cascades over a waterfall it releases energy that can be used to turn a water wheel attached to a coil of wire near a magnet and cause electrons to flow in the wire, producing electricity.
A stretched guitar string has potential mechanical energy	When someone plucks a guitar string, kinetic energy results and is transferred into sound as the string vibrates.

LIST 5–19. LIGHT AND SOUND WAVES

Light and sound are two forms of energy that travel in waves.

Properties of Light and Sound Waves

LIGHT WAVES	*SOUND WAVES*
Transverse waves ripple like water waves.	Longitudinal waves ripple like a Slinky™ toy spring.
Travel at 300,000 km/sec. or 186,000 mi./sec.	Travel at 337.6 meters/sec. or 1108 ft/sec. in air.
Top of each wave is the crest.	Top of each wave is the crest.
The wavelength is the distance from the crest of one wave to the crest of the next wave.	The wavelength is the distance from the crest of one wave to the crest of the next wave.
The frequency is the number of waves that pass a point each second.	The frequency is the number of waves that pass a point each second.
The amplitude is a measure of the height of the wave at the crest.	The amplitude is the measure of the height of the wave at the crest.
The larger the amplitude, the brighter the light.	The larger the amplitude, the louder the sound.
Does not travel in an opaque solid; travels through some clear glass, some plastics, etc.	Does not travel in a vacuum. Thus, there is no sound in space. Travels in solids, liquids, and gases at differing speeds.
Is transmitted, reflected, absorbed, and refracted	Is transmitted, reflected, absorbed, and refracted
Intensity: bright or dim	Intensity: loud or soft
Color: visible spectrum only	Pitch: the higher the frequency, the higher the pitch

Examples

Lightning	Thunder
Sunlight, artificial light, televisions, lasers	Music, records, compact disks, voice, noise radio, ultrasonic sound, sonar
Energy that we sense through seeing	Energy that we sense through hearing.
The absence of light is darkness.	The absence of sound is silence.
Ultraviolet light is not received by human eyes.	Ultrasound is not received by human ears.
Excessive ultraviolet light can damage skin and eyes.	Excessive loudness can damage ears, causing deafness and physical distress.

The Science Teacher's Book of Lists, © 1993 by Prentice Hall

LIST 5-20. THREE BASIC TYPES OF LENSES

Lenses are curved pieces of glass or other transparent material, usually circular, that are used to bend light in special ways.

The Three Basic Types of Lenses

CONVEX	*CONCAVE*	*CONVEX-CONCAVE*
	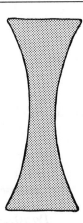	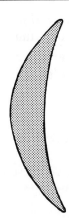
Curved outward.	Curved inward.	Curved outward on one side and inward on the other side.
Magnifies objects nearby. Used in microscopes, cameras, glasses for farsighted people. Can project images on a screen. Can focus the rays of the sun on a piece of a paper; the paper will burn. Human eye has convex lens.	Forms real images. Used in glasses for nearsighted people.	Forms real images. Used in some eyeglasses to help magnify and focus.

LIST 5–21. ABOUT HEAT

Heat is a form of energy.

Energy can move things: a pinwheel placed over a glowing lamp or a beaker of boiling water will turn.

Heat is a form of energy that we can feel.

The higher the heat energy, the faster molecules move.

The lower the heat energy, the slower molecules move.

Heat Travels in Two Ways

CONDUCTION	*CONVECTION*
Heat travels through solids by conduction.	Heat travels through air and water by convection.
To observe:	***To observe:***
Place drops of melted wax along a strip of copper. Hold one end with a clamp; place the other end in a flame. The wax near the flame melts first, then the next drop, etc.	Place sawdust in a beaker of water. Heat the water. The sawdust will float from the bottom to the top in the spiral of the convection current.
Explanation:	***Explanation:***
The copper molecules in the flame get hot first, move faster, bump into those around them, causing other molecules to move faster, transferring heat along the strip.	Cold water/air is heavier than warm water/air. Cold water/air falls. Warm water/air rises, taking the heat with it.
Everyday uses:	***Everyday uses:***
Metal pans for cooking Buildings insulated to keep warm in winter and cool in summer Coolers and thermos bottles	Convection ovens Chimneys Ocean currents Solar heating

The Science Teacher's Book of Lists, © 1993 by Prentice Hall

(Continued)

LIST 5–21.   (Continued)

Conductors of Heat

GOOD CONDUCTORS	POOR CONDUCTORS (INSULATORS)	
Copper	Air	Wax
Aluminum	Glass	Paper
Iron	Polystyrene	Fiberglass
	Wood	

Generalizations

- Most good conductors of heat are good conductors of electricity.
- Most poor conductors of heat are poor conductors of electricity.
- Metals are good conductors of heat and electricity and nonmetals are poor conductors of heat and electricity.

LIST 5–22. SOME LAWS OF SCIENCE

Avogadro's law—equal volumes of gases at the same temperature and pressure contain equal numbers of molecules.

Boyle's law—the volume of a gas is inversely proportional to its pressure if the temperature is held constant.

Charles' law—a volume of a gas is proportional to its absolute temperature if the pressure is held constant.

Dalton's law—the total pressure of a gas mixture is equal to the sum of the partial pressures of its components.

Coulomb's law—the force between two electric charges is directly proportional to the product of their charges and inversely proportional to the square of the distance between them.

Graham's law—the rate of effusion of a gas is inversely proportional to the square root of its molar mass.

Henry's law—the solubility of a gas in a liquid is directly proportional to its partial pressure.

Hubble's law—galaxies recede from each other with a velocity proportional to their distance.

Hund's rule—ordinarily, electrons will not pair in an orbital until all orbitals of equal energy contain one electron.

Ideal gas law—the relationships between pressure, volume, temperature, and amount for any gas at moderate pressure: $PV = nRT$.

law of momentum—When moving things interact with one another, the sum of all of their momenta never changes.

LeChatelier's principle—when a system at equilibrium is disturbed, it responds in such a way as to counteract the change.

Newton's universal law of gravitation—every body attracts every other body in the universe with a force depending on the mass of the bodies and the inverse square of the distance between them.

Ohm's law—the electric current (I) through conductors is equal to the potential difference across the conductor, (v) divided by the resistance (R), or $I = v/R$.

Pauli exclusion principle—in an atom no two electrons can have the same set of four quantum numbers.

perfect gas law (combined gas law)—the product of pressure and volume is proportional to temperature.

the inverse square law—force depends upon the reciprocal of the distance squared.

the first law of motion—A body in motion or at rest remains so unless acted upon by an outside force.

(Continued)

LIST 5–22. (Continued)

the second law of motion—The acceleration produced on a body by a force is inversely proportional to its mass.

the third law of motion—forces always exist in pairs; the mutual forces between two bodies are equal and opposite, or for every action there is an equal and opposite reaction.

the first law of thermodynamics—law of conservation of energy: energy can neither be created nor destroyed. This has been amended: In non-nuclear events, energy can neither be created nor destroyed; the change in energy (ΔE) of a system is the sum of the heat flow into the system (q) and the work (w) done upon the system: $\Delta E = q + w$.

the second law of thermodynamics—The negentropy (a measure of the disorder involved in changing from one form of energy to another) of the universe is always decreasing. Energy runs downhill from higher to lower grades.

LIST 5–23. CHAOS THEORY

Throughout history, the study of physics has been investigating and quantifying systems and events so that predictions and explanations could be based on data gathered. When data were not available from which one could make predictions, it was believed that with more information and technological improvements, predictions and/or explanations could be made.

Now many scientists believe that some systems are not predictable no matter what the data or technological advances. For example, a great deal of money and time have been invested in long-term weather forecasts. For those who accept Chaos, long-term weather forecasts are unpredictable, now and in the future regardless of technological advances because of the various factors which cause weather to be a disparate system. The Chaos Theory is an attempt to build mathematical (theoretical) models of the system like weather, flowing fluids, population, etc.

Scientists now believe there is more order in chaos than originally thought and believe that the chaotic behavior of some systems is deterministic and can be coupled with differential equations to produce reliable short-term predictions, even for weather systems. Thus, some short-term nonperiodic behaviors can be predicted but many long-term nonperiodic behaviors caused by the inherent nonlinear nature of a system are unpredictable resulting from the random nature of the driving forces that affect the system.

Chaos: A Glossary*

attractor—The geometrical object toward which a system's trajectory—represented as a curve in *phase space*—converges in the course of time. In other words, the attractor "attracts" all trajectories whose initial conditions were within a certain range, called a *basin of attraction*. When a system is slightly disturbed its trajectory eventually returns to the attractor. If an attractor is a closed curve, it is called a *limit-cycle attractor* and describes periodic oscillations. An attractor consisting of a single point in phase space is called a *fixed-point attractor* and describes stationary states. Limit cycles and fixed points are nonchaotic attractors. A chaotic attractor is also known as a *strange attractor*.

basin of attraction—The set of all initial conditions of a system for which trajectories representing that system in phase space will asymptotically approach a particular attractor.

bifurcation—The appearance of qualitatively different solutions to non-linear equation as a parameter is varied. The new solution may be time dependent, or even chaotic. Bifurcations also provide a mathematical description of pattern formation.

(Continued)

*Used with permission: "Chaos: A Glossary," Phillip F. Schewe and Jerry Gollub, American Institute of Physics, New York, 1985.

LIST 5–23. (Continued)

chaos—Nonperiodic (irregular) behavior caused by the inherent nonlinear nature of a system, as opposed to *noise*, which is the nonperiodic behavior of a system resulting from a stochastic (random) driving force. Many scientists now believe that chaotic behavior can often be characterized by deterministic coupled nonlinear differential equations and that these equations may in certain cases be applicable to such disparate systems as the weather, fluid flow, Josephson junctions, and fibrillating hearts. Short-term temporal evolution of such systems can be accurately predicted. Long-term behavior, however, is unpredictable because nearby trajectories on the strange attractor in phase space separate (exponentially) rapidly as time evolves. Thus, even though the system is deterministic—that is, described by deterministic differential equations—long-term predictability would be possible only if the initial conditions were known to infinite precision. Chaos pertains to the (nonperiodic) evolution in time of physical systems; it does not provide an adequate description of *turbulence*, which also requires spatial complexity.

chaotic—The property of a system that behaves in a very complicated but deterministic way. In practice the behavior of a chaotic system can only be predicted in the near future.

differential equation—A mathematical expression of the dynamics of a system in which the important variables and their rates of change appear. If both time and space are involved, the expression is a partial differential equation; if only time appears, it is said to be an ordinary differential equation.

equilibrium—The state of a system that remains unchanged so long as no additional external force is applied. If following a slight disturbance the system returns to an equilibrium state, this state is called a stable equilibrium. An unstable equilibrium is a state in which a slight disturbance causes the system to depart irrevocably from its equilibrium state.

fractal—A mathematical structure or curve whose dimensionality is not an integer. Fractals also exhibit self-similarity. Strange attractors are fractal in nature.

instability—The property of a state whose behavior radically changes when slightly perturbed. For example, a balanced pencil is unstable because any small perturbation will cause it to fall. Instabilities are common in many types of nonlinear systems, including fluid systems (where they often precede turbulence), growing crystals, and electronic circuits.

linear—The property of a system whose response to a change in some input variable is proportional to the variable.

noise—Nonperiodic behavior of a system resulting from a stochastic (random) driving force, such as thermal agitation; as opposed to chaos, which

(Continued)

LIST 5–23. (Continued)

is nonperiodic behavior of a deterministic system caused by its inherent nonlinear nature.

nonequilibrium system—A system through which energy (or matter) is being transported, such as a turbulent fluid or a growing crystal. The subjects of thermodynamics and statistical mechanics provide physicists with well-developed tools for treating systems at or near equilibrium, but nonequilibrium systems are much more difficult to analyze.

nonlinear—The property of a system whose response to a change in some input variable is not proportional to the variable. Many systems are nonlinear in nature, systems such as certain electrical circuits, the weather, turbulent fluid flow, plasmas, oscillating chemical reactions, and population biology.

period doubling—One of the routes to chaos in which the period (repeat time) of an oscillating system (for example, a convecting fluid) doubles repeatedly as a parameter (say, the temperature gradient) is increased. It is believed that all systems that become chaotic by the period-doubling process do so in the same universal way. See bifurcation.

phase space—An abstract space used to describe the behavior of a system. The number of coordinates needed equals the number of degrees of freedom of the system. In order to describe a system of n particles, for example, the phase space would have $6n$ dimensions, one each for three spatial coordinates and three momentum components of all the particles. The status of the system can be denoted by a point moving about in the multidimensional phase space. Many systems can be well described by a phase space containing a small number of degrees of freedom (collective coordinates), even though they are made up of a very large number of particles.

renormalization transformation—A transformation of a mathematical function that involves a change of scale. The repetitive use of such a transformation was the key to the discovery of the universal properties of several routes to chaos.

self-similarity—The property by which an object (or mathematical function) preserves its structure when magnified by a certain scale factor. Fractals are examples of self-similar objects.

stochastic process—A process characterized by random effects. The thermal agitation of atoms in a solid is an example of a stochastic process.

strange attractor—The geometrical object or shape toward which the trajectory of a chaotic system—represented as a curve in phase space—tends in the course of time. Strange attractors are fractals, objects of noninteger dimension, and consist of an infinite number of closely spaced layers. Nearby trajectories diverge from each other by an amount that

(Continued)

The Science Teacher's Book of Lists, © 1993 by Prentice Hall

LIST 5–23. (Continued)

that is exponential in time (and not simply proportional to time), while remaining on the attractor.

transition to chaos—The process by which a system—such as a flowing fluid or an insect population—evolves toward nonperiodic time dependence as one or more parameters are varied. Some periodic systems become chaotic by a process called *period doubling* in which the time it takes the system to repeat itself (its period) doubles and doubles again (and so on, until the period is essentially infinitely long) as a parameter—the velocity of a fluid, say—is increased.

turbulence—Fluid motion composed of eddies or vortices of many different sizes. At a single location, the time evolution of the motion is chaotic. The mathematical description of chaos—that is, the study of a chaotic system's temporal behavior—does not characterize the spatial complexity of the turbulence at any one time. Thus, chaos has to do with complexity of time, turbulence with complexity in space and time.

EARTH SCIENCE

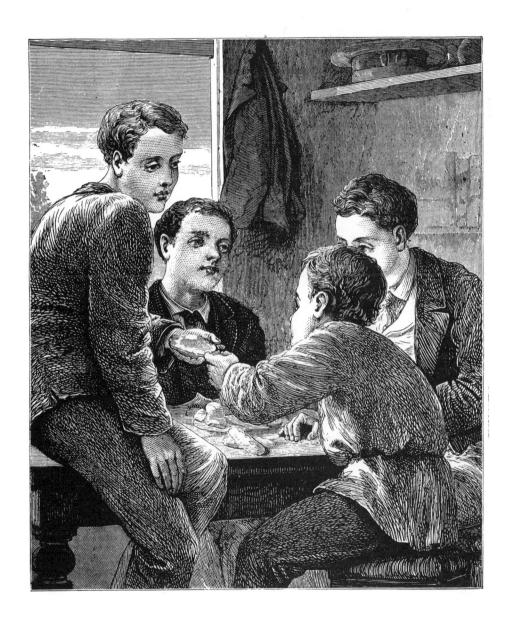

LIST 6–1. EARTH SCIENCE VOCABULARY

aeolian—(sediments) deposited by wind

alluvial fan—a fan-shaped bank of sediment deposited by a river

alluvium—sediment deposited by running water

amber—a fossil gum from the sap of ancient plants; may contain trapped and preserved insects and spiders

arenaceous—sediments containing lots of sand

anticline—an upfold in layers of rocks

atom—smallest part of an element

authigenic—formation of minerals during or after deposition

basic—an igneous rock with less than 10 percent free quartz and with 45 to 55 percent silica; consists mainly of plagioclase feldspar and pyroxene

batholith—a large mass of intrusive igneous rocks of unknown depth

benthic—on the ocean floor

bio-micrite—limestone consisting of organic matter in a matrix of calcite

calcrete—gravels cemented by tufa, the calcareous and siliceous rock deposits of springs, ponds, or ground water

caldera—the giant summit depression of a volcano

cinder cone—steep-sided volcano formed from cinders and ash

cleavage—the tendency of some minerals to break along different planes

compound—a chemical substance containing more than one element in fixed amounts

compression—force that decreases the volume of a substance

conchoidal—a curved fracture which is characteristic of some rocks and minerals such as in quartz

concretion—a mass of rock usually rounded in shape; fossils are frequently contained in these rounded masses

conglomerate—also known as pudding stone; a sedimentary rock composed of pebbles and gravel embedded in loosely cemented material

conservation—preservation and protection of natural resources through wise, planned use

continental drift—theoretical shift of continents due to weakness in the suboceanic crust

convection—transfer of heat by fluid motion

core—the layer of the earth beneath the mantle, at the center of the earth

crevasse—a fissure or chasm-like opening in a glacier

crust—the outer layer of the Earth's surface

cryptocrystalline—extremely fine crystalline mass; not a glass

(Continued)

LIST 6–1. (Continued)

crystals—naturally occurring solids in which the atoms are arranged in repeating patterns, causing the surface of the solid to be made of symmetrical planes; examples: calcite, halite, galena, and quartz

crystallize—to separate from a solution or melt as a solid

crystallography—the study of crystals

decomposition—a chemical reaction in which compounds break down into simpler substances

delta—triangular-shaped deposit at the mouth of a stream

density—mass of a body divided by its volume; the density of a rock determines how heavy it feels. A piece of granite has a greater density than a piece of pumice with an equal volume.

diagenesis—the chemical and physical processes which transform soft sediment into consolidated rock; these take place near the Earth's surface at low temperatures and pressures

diastrophism—movement of the Earth's crust, creating mountains, oceans and ocean basins

dike—an intrusion of igneous rock in older rocks with a high angle of dip

druse—a cavity in a rock or mineral vein where well-formed, minute crystals project

drumlin—glacial hill

dunes—hills of loose sand created by the wind

earthquake—a series of elastic waves in the Earth's crust caused by sudden relaxation of strains along faults and by volcanic action

elastic—the property of returning to original shape after bending or stretching

element—a basic unit of matter that cannot be changed into any simpler form of matter by ordinary means; a substance whose atoms are all chemically the same

epicenter—the part of Earth's surface that is directly above the origin of an earthquake

epoch—a division in geologic time smaller than a period, such as Pliocene

equigranular—a sample where all of the grains are the same size

erosion—gradual wearing away of the Earth's surface by wind, water, and ice

escarpment—the face or slope of a cliff

euhedral—well-formed crystals

exfoliation—the cracking or peeling of rocks on the surface

extrusive—molten, volcanic rocks which have cooled on the surface of the Earth

(Continued)

The Science Teacher's Book of Lists, © 1993 by Prentice Hall

LIST 6-1. (Continued)

fault—a break or fracture in Earth's crust

fault-block mountain—a mountain formed when a block of rock is raised along a fault

fissure—a crack in the Earth's interior through which lava flows

flotation—the process by which ore is separated from its rocky impurities; in a soapy emulsion of oil and water, the oil concentrates at the surface where it can be skimmed

fold—a bend in the rock strata

foliation—consisting of thin parallel layers, as in mica

foraminifera—small, shell-forming protozoans that lived in ocean waters during the Mississippian period; used by geologists as indicators for the presence of oil-bearing strata

fossil—a mold, cast, or impression of all or part of ancient organisms that has been preserved in Earth's crust; the best known are dinosaur fossils

fossil fuel—fuels made from carbon-fossil residues: gas, oil, and coal

fracture—a crack or break in a rock other than along a plane; the way a mineral breaks

geology—study of the origin, history, and structure of the Earth

geothermal energy—energy from the heat within Earth's crust

geyser—natural hot spring that intermittently ejects water and steam into the air

glacier—a large body of slow moving ice and snow formed in areas where the rate of snowfall exceeds the rate of snowmelt; it slowly moves down a slope, changing the land forms, until it melts or breaks away

hardness—resistance of a rock or mineral to being scratched

heat—the form of energy which flows between two objects because of their difference in temperature

hopper crystals—crystals with hollowed faces, such as cubes of halite

hydrocarbon—organic compounds containing only hydrogen and carbon; provide natural resources such as fossil fuels: coal, oil, and natural gas

hydrology—study of the effects of water on the Earth's surface, soil, underlying rocks, and atmosphere

igneous rocks—rocks formed when molten material in or on Earth's surface cools and hardens

intrusive—igneous material formed among pre-existing rocks below the surface

isostasy—state of balance of the Earth's crust; any equilibrium resulting from an equalization of pressure or forces

(Continued)

LIST 6–1. (Continued)

joint—a crack in a rock mass that occurs as pressure decreases on that rock mass because the overlying rock is eroded away permitting the rock mass to expand

kettle—depression in a glacier deposit formed by the melting of a covered block of ice

lava—molten rock that reaches Earth's surface

lithosphere—the Earth's rocky crust plus the rigid upper part of the mantle

lodestone—a naturally occurring magnet; a form of magnetite

loess—wind deposits of silt and dust-size particles

luster—the shiny, reflecting quality and brilliance of the surface of minerals

magma—molten rock mixed with gases within the Earth from which igneous rock is formed

magnetism—the ability to attract metals; occurs in iron, nickel, magnetite, and cobalt

mantle—the layer of Earth just beneath the crust

mass—the measurement of the quantity or amount of material in an object

matter—anything that takes up space and has mass

meander—to wander; riverbeds wander and widen as each flows through the path of least resistance, frequently giving a snake-like path

metals—elements that are solid (except for mercury) having characteristic luster, malleability, and high electrical and heat conductivity

metamorphic rocks—rocks that are formed when existing rocks undergo pressure and heat for extended periods of time

metasomatism—a change in a rock due to the addition of a new material, often by the fluids circulating in the crust

mineral—naturally occurring, inorganic nongaseous substances with limited chemical variability and distinctive internal crystalline structure

mixture—two or more substances combined in any amounts so that each retains its chemical identity

mineralogist—a scientist who studies minerals and rocks

molecule—a group of atoms that share electrons

moraine—glacial deposits of gravel, sand, and boulders

nodule—a small lump of mineral found on the ocean floor or elsewhere

nonmetals—elements that do not possess the properties of metals

ore—a natural mineral deposit from which a metal can be extracted

orogeny—the long-term processes that lead to the development of a mountain range

paleontologist—a scientist who studies ancient life in fossil form

(Continued)

The Science Teacher's Book of Lists, © 1993 by Prentice Hall

LIST 6–1. (Continued)

pelitic—muddy sediment

petrographic microscope—optic instrument used to study rock features

physical properties—characteristics that help identify a substance; these characteristics can be observed and/or measured

pinacoid—a pair of parallel crystal faces

plates—huge blocks of rocks that make up the Earth's crust

plucking—results when a glacier picks up large blocks of bedrock and moves them away

poles—the ends of the axis of a planet; the ends of a magnet

pressure—force per unit of area

radon—a radioactive, gaseous chemical element formed by the decay of uranium in rocks and soil

rift zone—a network of fissures, or cracks through which lava flows

roasting—a metallurgical process in which a sulfide ore is heated in air

rock—matter formed in Earth's crust usually made up of a mixture of solid minerals; some are made up of only a single mineral as in limestone; generally the minerals cannot be recognized visually because of their microscopic particle size

saccharoidal—the sugary rock texture observed in marbles and quartzites

schillerization—coloration in certain minerals due to minute, rod-like inclusions of voids, iron ore, and other minerals

schist—medium to coarse metamorphic rocks composed of parallel layers such as mica and talc

sedimentary rocks—rocks formed by consolidation of sediments; examples: limestone, sandstone, and shale

seismograph—an instrument that measures and records the direction, intensity, and time of an earthquake

seismologists—scientists who study Earth movements

shearing—results when forces cause two adjacent parts of a solid to slide past one another in directions that are parallel to the plane of contact

silicate—most abundant group of minerals found in Earth's crust

silt—solid particles larger than clay particles but smaller than sand grains

slag—a by-product, resulting from a metallurgical process, which floats on molten metal

soil—loose mineral material, usually with some organic material, on Earth's surface that supports plant and animal life; the word *dirt* is not a proper name for soil

specific gravity—the ratio of the weight of an object to the weight of an equal volume of water

(Continued)

LIST 6–1. (Continued)

spur—a lateral ridge projecting from a mountain

strata—distinct layers of sedimentary rocks

streak—(1) a vein of a mineral; (2) a line made by drawing a mineral along a smooth surface leaving color and texture which help identify the mineral; (3) the color of a thin layer of finely powdered mineral

streak plate—an unglazed tile upon which a mineral is drawn to leave a line of color and texture to help identify the mineral

subsoil—the soil just below the topsoil

syncline—a fold in rock strata in which the layers lean together from opposite sides; opposite of anticline; downfolded rock layers

talus—fragmentary rock found at the base of a steep mountain or slope

tectonics—geology of Earth's structural deformation

tenacity—the ability of a mineral to hold together

thrust—a strong forward motion causing a horizontal movement of Earth's crust

topsoil—the uppermost layer of soil

ultra-basic—group of igneous rocks with less than 45 percent silica

vapor—a condensable gas

vent—an opening in Earth's surface permitting the escape of gases, liquids, fumes, etc.; the main lava chamber in the neck of a volcano

volcano—a vent in Earth's crust through which rock, ash, dust, gases, and/ or magma are expelled

volcanic mountain—a cone-shaped mountain formed by layers of volcanic lava and ash deposited around a volcanic vent

volume—the amount of space occupied by matter

weathering—the processes that physically and chemically break apart and change rocks

weight—the gravitational force that Earth (or other body) exerts on an object

zeolite—a silicate mineral used to soften water

The Science Teacher's Book of Lists, © 1993 by Prentice Hall

LIST 6–2. MINERALS AND ROCKS

Minerals—are chemicals found naturally in the Earth. Except for elemental mercury (a liquid), they are solid. They crystallize from melted rock or are deposited from a solution.

Rocks—are usually made up of a mixture of minerals. Some are made up of only a single mineral, as in limestone. Generally the minerals cannot be recognized visually in rocks because the particles are microscopic. There are three types of rocks. Each is formed by a different process.

The Three Types of Rocks

TYPE OF ROCK	FORMATION	COMMENTS
1. Igneous	Formed when melted rock rises to or near the earth's surface and cools.	Melted rock is called magma. When magma reaches the Earth's surface through a volcano, it is called lava.
2. Sedimentary	Formed when air and water deposit particles. Particles may develop from erosion and weathering. Under heat and pressure these particles merge to form sedimentary rocks.	Examples of sedimentary rock: sandstone, shale mudstone, and conglomerates.
3. Metamorphic	Formed when existing rocks undergo heat and pressure for a long time.	Examples: Shale → slate Limestone → marble Sandstone → quartzite

> **Mnemonic: Mr. Sim (Minerals, rocks, sedimentary, igneous, metamorphic)**

LIST 6–3. EXAMPLES OF THE THREE TYPES OF ROCKS

Igneous	*Metamorphic*	*Sedimentary*
Basalt	Slate	Boulder clay (till)
Greisen	Phyllite	Conglomerate
Granite	Marble	Iron-rich conglomerate
Granodiorite	Mica schist	Black shale
Diorite	Garnet mica schist	Red sandstone
Intermediate lavas	Amphibolite	Rock salt
Andesitic pumice	Eclogite	Freshwater limestone
Pegmatite	Hornfels	Chalk
Dolerite	Metaquartzite	Coral limestone
Spilite	Serpentinite	Lignite
Troctolite	Mylonite	Flint
Obsidian	"Sugary" marble	Amber
Microgranite	Granulite	Chert
Porphyritic microgranite	Augen gneiss	Ironstone
Quartz porphyry	Biotite schist	Calcareous breccia
Pitchstone	Hornblende schist	Breccia
Porphyritic pitchstone	Garnet mica schist	Polygenetic conglomerate
Granophyre	Kyanite schist	Stalactite
Rhyolite tuff	Gneiss	Orthoquartzite
Banded rhyolite	Chiastolite slate	Arkose
Larvikite	Grey marble	Grit
Syenite		Micaceous sandstone
Porphyritic micro-syenite		Ripple-marked sandstone
Porphyritec		Coquina
Andesite		Greensand
Trachyte		Greywacke
Trachytic agglomerate		Mudstone
Gabbro		Gypsum rock
Olivine gabbro		Marl with gypsum
Tuff		Green marl
Ropy lava		Red marl
Pumice		Potash ore
Volcanic bomb		

The Science Teacher's Book of Lists, © 1993 by Prentice Hall

LIST 6–4. SOME NAMES OF MINERALS

Adamite
Agate
Alabaster
Amazonstone
Amethyst
Andalusite
Andradite
Antigorite
Antimony
Apatite
Apophyllite
Aquamarine
Aragonite
Arsenic
Arsenopyrite
Artinite
Augite
Azurite
Barite
Barytocalcite
Bauxite
Beryl
Biotite
Bismuth
Borax
Bornite
Bournonite
Calcite
Campyllite
Carnallite
Cassiterite
Celestine
Cerussite
Chabazite
Chalcedony

Chalcosine
Chalcocite
Chalybite
Chessylite
Chlorite
Chromite
Chrysocolla
Chrysolite
Cinnabar
Citrine
Cobaltite
Copper
Corundum
Cryolite
Cuprite
Daisy gypsum
Desert rose
Diamond
Dolomite
Emerald
Enargite
Enstatite
Fluorite
Fluorspar
Franklinite
Gahnite
Galena
Garnet
Goethite
Gold
Gossan
Graphite
Gypsum
Halite
Heliodor

Hermatite
Hornblende
Iceland spar
Ilmenite
Iron pyrites
Jasper
Kaolin
Lazurite
Limonite
Magnesite
Magnetite
Manganite
Milky quartz
Moss agate
Neptunite
Niccolite
Nickeline
Olivine
Opal
Orpiment
Orthoclase
Peacock ore
Pectolite
Pyrite
Pyrope
Pyrophyllite
Quartz
Rhodochrosite
Rock crystal
Rose quartz
Ruby
Rutile
Sapphire
Satin spar
Serpentine

Gold chalice

Copper kettle

(Continued)

LIST 6–4. (Continued)

Silver	Thulite	Vanadinite
Smithsonite	Tiger's eye	Vesuvianite
Smoky quartz	Topaz	Wad
Soapstone	Tourmaline	Wavellite
Spinel	Tremolite	Witherite
Stalactite	Trevorite	Wolframite
Sulphur	Turquoise	Wulfenite
Talc	Ulexite	Zincite
Tennantite	Uvarovite	Zircon

NOTE: To locate photographs of these minerals consult: *Rocks, Minerals and Fossils of the World,* Chris Pellant with Roger Phillips, Little, Brown and Co., Boston, 1990.

Silverware

The Science Teacher's Book of Lists, © 1993 by Prentice Hall

LIST 6–5. SOME INTERESTING FACTS ABOUT ROCKS AND MINERALS

In the descriptions listed, five carats equals one gram. A similar word, *Karat*, is used to describe gold: pure gold is 24 Karat.

iron pyrite—(iron sulfide) has a golden color and metallic luster which has caused many to mistake it for gold; it is therefore called "fool's gold."

calcite—in clear rhombic cleavage shapes (Iceland spar) exhibits double refraction, making lines viewed through it appear double.

gold—is found in small quantities in many parts of the United States.

Cape May diamonds—clear quartz pebbles found at Cape May, New Jersey, are called Cape May diamonds; likewise, quartz crystals from near Herkimer, New York, are called Herkimer diamonds.

granulated quartz and garnet—are used to make abrasive papers.

manganese oxide nodules—found on some ocean floors are a source of manganese.

obsidian—black volcanic glass nodules, found in the western states, are sometimes called Apache tears.

mica—or muscovite, in clear colorless sheets, was used for windows in stoves and lanterns and is still used in electrical devices and appliances, such as toasters and flatirons.

geodes—are hollow nodules lined with crystal or agate

hematite—is the ore found at one of the world's largest iron-producing ore bodies, which is located at the western end of Lake Superior on the Canadian-United States border. The form of hematite can be tabular (flat shape with broad faces) or rhombohedral crystals

fairy stones—are twinned crystals of staurolite. They occur at 60° and 90° crosses. Many of those for sale as jewelry have been carved and oiled to improve their appearance.

flint—many forms produce sparks when struck with steel. Before matches, flint and steel were used with tinder to start fires. Flint and steel were also used to fire flintlock rifles.

fluorescence—many minerals when viewed under ultraviolet light show different colors, called fluorescence.

identification of minerals—can be done with X rays because minerals diffract or bend X rays to give characteristic patterns on photographic film.

largest uncut diamond—254 carats; on exhibition at the Smithsonian Institution.

the Black Star—largest sapphire, found in Australia. A bust of President Eisenhower was carved out of it and given to him.

(Continued)

The Science Teacher's Book of Lists, © 1993 by Prentice Hall

LIST 6–5. (Continued)

the Cullinan diamond—found in South Africa in 1905. Before it was cut it was as big as a man's fist and weighed 21 ounces. Yielded the Star of Africa, 530.2 carats, which was placed in the King of England's Scepter, and other large stones.

the Hope diamond—45.5 carats, blue color, on display at the Smithsonian Institution.

the Kohinoor diamond—108.9 carats in its present cut form. Legend traced it back 5000 years.

the Star of Asia—is a 330-carat sapphire housed at the Smithsonian Institution.

the Star of India—is a 536-carat sapphire, housed at the American Museum of Natural History.

largest hole (mine) dug by humans—Bingham open-pit copper mine near Salt Lake City, Utah; 805 m deep (close to half a mile deep); largest producer of copper.

largest geode—from Rio Grande do Sul; 33 × 16.5 × 10 feet; estimated to weigh 70,000 pounds; lined with amethyst crystals. A 400-pound section is at the Smithsonian Institution.

Unique samples of:

- **gold**—one of the finest crystallized specimens was found at the Red Ledge Mine in California. It is housed at the Cranbrook Institute.

- **stibnite**—crystal groups up to two feet long have been found in Japan. One of the best samples is housed at Bryn Mawr College, Pennsylvania.

- **proustite**—is a complex silver salt which is ruby red in color. An unusual group of crystals are housed at Harvard University Mineralogical Museum.

- **halite**—common salt; clear, cubic crystals that are three and four feet on the edges are housed at the Vienna Natural History Museum.

- **jade**—a 500-pound sample is exhibited at the Los Angeles County Museum.

- **tiger eye quartz**—is found only in Zaire; export is now controlled by the government.

- **rose beryl**—a 250-carat cut gem from Madagascar is housed at the Paris Natural History Museum.

- **blue topaz**—a 377-carat cut gem from Siberia is housed at the Paris Museum of Natural History.

- **alexandrite**—is green in daylight and red in artificial light; the largest cut stone weighs 66 carats, is housed at the Smithsonian Institution.

The Science Teacher's Book of Lists, © 1993 by Prentice Hall

LIST 6–6. INTRODUCTION TO MOHS' SCALE OF MINERAL HARDNESS

Frederick Mohs (1773–1839) was a German mineralogist who developed Mohs' Scale of Mineral Hardness. This scale is used to determine a mineral's hardness or resistance to scratching and to identify unknown samples by comparing their hardness with known samples.

On the scale, the hardness increases with each number. Thus, number 1, talc, is the softest mineral and number 10, diamond, is the hardest mineral. Hardness differences between numbers are not equal. In the scale, each mineral can scratch the previous one and is scratched by the one following. Minerals are tested by scratching the unknown with test samples and by the objects in the last column.

Mohs' Scale of Mineral Hardness

HARDNESS SCALE	MINERAL	COMMON TESTS
1	Talc	Scratched by fingernail
2	Gypsum	Scratched by fingernail
3	Calcite	Scratched by copper coin and brass pin
4	Fluorite	Scratched by glass
5	Apatite	Scratched by glass, scratches Steel nail
6	Feldspar or Orthoclase	Scratched by steel file Scratches glass
7	Quartz	Scratches glass
8	Topaz	Scratches glass
9	Corundum	Scratches glass
10	Diamond	Scratches all common materials

LIST 6–7. MOHS' SCALE OF HARDNESS WITH CHEMICAL COMPOSITION AND FORMULAS

Friedrich Mohs (1773–1839) was a German mineralogist. On Mohs' Scale of Mineral Hardness, hardness increases with number. Hardness differences between numbers are not equal. In the scale, each mineral can scratch the previous one and is scratched by the following one. Minerals are tested by scratching the unknown with samples and by the objects in the last column.

Mohs' Hardness Scale With Chemical Composition and Formulas

SCALE	MINERAL	COMPOSITION	FORMULA	SCRATCH TEST
1	Talc	Hydrous magnesium silicate	$Mg_3Si_4O_{10}(OH)_2$	Scratched by fingernail
2	Gypsum	Calcium sulfate hydrate	$CaSO_4.2H_2O$	Thumb nail, 2+
3	Calcite	Calcium carbonate	$CaCO_3$	Copper coin, 3 Brass pin, 3+
4	Fluorite	Calcium fluoride	CaF_2	
5	Apatite	Calcium phosphate chloride/fluoride	$Ca_5(PO_4)_3(F,Cl,OH)$	Pocket knife, 5.5 Window glass, 5.5
6	Orthoclase	Potassium aluminum silicate	$KAlSi_3O_8$	Steel file, 6.5
7	Quartz	Silicon dioxide	SiO_2	
8	Topaz	Hydrous aluminum silicate	$Al_2SiO_4(OH,F)_2$	
9	Corundum	Aluminum oxide	Al_2O_3	
10	Diamond	Carbon	C	

LIST 6–8. NAMING AND CLASSIFYING MINERALS

The naming and classification of minerals is different from that of plants and animals. There are only about 3000 different recognized minerals. Minerals are named in a rather nonsystematic way. Such a name may be derived in some way from the name of the discoverer, a location where it was first found, a person or place selected to be honored, some property which it exhibits, and so on. Many mineral names end with the suffix, "ite," which means stone. At the present time a new mineral and its proposed name must undergo a strict analysis, with identification and the data approved by an international committee established by the community of mineral chemists.

Minerals are classified in three principal ways: chemical composition, crystalline form, and mode of origin. Other properties also may be used to characterize and distinguish a mineral, such as hardness, specific gravity, optical properties, and X-ray diffraction. Classification of substances by crystal form is provided in List 6–11, Introduction to the Six Systems of Mineral Crystals and in List 6–12, Crystal Forms.

MINERAL NAMES	COMMENTS
Azurite	A dark blue copper carbonate; $CuCO_3$
Magnetite	A magnetic or magnetizable iron oxide; Fe_3O_4
Fluorite	Calcium fluoride; CaF_2
Calcite	Calcium carbonate; $CaCO_3$
Franklinite	An oxide of iron, manganese, and zinc; $(Fe,Mn,Zn)(FeO_2)_2$ found in Franklin, New Jersey
Aragonite	A calcium carbonate found in Aragon, Spain
Goethite	An iron oxide named for the poet and scientist Johann von Goethe
Smithsonite	Zinc carbonate; $ZnCO_3$; named for James Smithson (1754–1829), founder of the Smithsonian Institution
Brucite	Magnesium hydroxide; $Mg(OH)_2$; named for Archibald Bruce (1717–1818), American mineralogist who first described the mineral
Adamite	A hydroxy zinc arsenate; $Zn_2AsO_4(OH)_2$; named for Gilbert-Joseph Adam, who supplied the first specimen

LIST 6–9. CLASSIFYING MINERALS BY CHEMICAL COMPOSITION

Minerals are the natural, inorganic, nongaseous substances of Earth and other planets, which have a specific chemical composition. The word "rock" is often used loosely to describe any natural, inorganic, solid substance; but more specifically it means a solid comprised of a mixture of minerals.

A mineral may be an element or a compound. Some elements that occur in nature are copper, silver, gold, sulfur, and carbon (graphite and diamond). Two minerals that occur as liquids are mercury and water (solid mineral is ice). Minerals are commonly divided by chemical composition, into eight to ten groups.

Classifying Minerals by Chemical Composition

GROUP	EXAMPLE	CHEMICAL NAME	FORMULA
Element	Gold	Gold	Au
	Silver	Silver	Ag
Oxides; hydroxides	Quartz	Silicon dioxide	SiO_2
Sulfides	Pyrite	Iron sulfide	FeS_2
Halides	Halite (salt)	Sodium chloride	$NaCl$
Carbonates; nitrates; borates	Calcite	Calcium carbonate	$CaCO_3$
Sulfates; chromates; molybdates; tungstates	Gypsum	Calcium sulfate hydrate	$CaSO_4.2H_2O$
Phosphates; arsenates; vanadates	Turquoise	Hydrated copper aluminum phosphate	$H_5[Al(OH)_2]_6Cu(OH)(PO_4)_4$
	Pyromorphite	Lead phosphate arsenate chloride	$Pb_5(PO_4,AsO_4)_3Cl$
	Vanadinite	Lead vanadate chloride	$Pb_5(VO_4)_3Cl$
Silicates*	Orthoclase (a feldspar)	Potassium aluminum silicate	$KAlSi_3O_8$
	Muscovite (a mica)	Hydrous potassium aluminum silicate	$KAlSi_3O_{10}(OH)_2$

---

*The silicates have several subdivisions.

LIST 6–10. SOME MINERALS AND THEIR CHEMICAL SYMBOL OR FORMULA

Metallic Minerals		Nonmetallic Minerals	
NAME	*SYMBOL OR FORMULA*	*NAME*	*SYMBOL OR FORMULA*
Copper	Cu	Sulfur	S
Chalcocite	Cu_2S	Quartz	SiO_2
Cuprite	Cu_2O	Ice	H_2O
Lead	Pb	Graphite	C
Gold	Au		
Galena	PbS		
Cerussite	$PbCO_3$		
Anglesite	$PbSO_4$		
Sylvanite	$(Au,Ag)Te_2$		
Silver	Ag		
Mercury	Hg		
Cinnabar	HgS		
Iron	Fe		
Magnetite	Fe_3O_4		
Hematite	Fe_2O_3		
Pyrite	FeS_2		
Nickel	Ni		
Niccolite	NiAs		
Millerite	NiS		
Cobaltite	CoAsS		
Tin	Sn		
Zincblende (Sphalerite)	ZnS		
Zincite	ZnO		
Smithsonite	$ZnCO_3$		
Zinc	Zn		
Kyanite	Al_2SiO_5		
Chromite	$FeCr_2O_4$		
Manganite	MnO(OH)		
Uraninite	UO_2		
Cassiterite	SnO_2		

Generalization: Most minerals contain metallic elements.

LIST 6–11. INTRODUCTION TO THE SIX SYSTEMS OF MINERAL CRYSTALS

Minerals have different crystal forms. Mineralogists can identify minerals and make inferences about their development by observing the crystal form.

Six Systems of Crystals

SYSTEM	DESCRIPTION	EXAMPLES
Cubic (Isometric)	The axes are of equal length and are at right angles to one another.	Cubes of halite and pyrite
Tetragonal	Two axes are of equal length; a third is not equal; all three axes are at right angles to each other.	Cassiterite, rutile, and zircon.
Hexagonal	Three equal axes at 120° angles arranged in one plane with at least one more axis of a different length.	Calcite, cinnabar and quartz.
Orthorhombic	Three axes of different lengths but all at right angles to each other.	Barite, celestite, and sulfur.
Monoclinic	Three unequal axes, two of which are at right angles. The third forms an angle (not a right angle) with the plane of the others.	Augite, gypsum, and micas.
Triclinic	Three unequal axes none of which forms right angles to any other.	Amazonite, turquoise, plagioclase feldspars.

LIST 6–12. CRYSTAL FORMS

A common meaning of the word *crystal* is a natural or synthetic solid with regular flat faces. The solid substance may be transparent or opaque. Gemstones are cut into various shapes with flat faces, but these shapes are not the natural crystal form. The external regularity of a crystal indicates a regular arrangement of the atoms or molecules in the solid. This internal arrangement may be determined by X-ray examination. Perfect crystals have elements of symmetry, which are imaginary lines, planes, or a point. This geometrical symmetry may not be the same as the molecular symmetry.

Classification

Crystals are classified into six principal systems with 32 sub-classes. The systems and examples are given below.

Classification of Crystals into Six Systems with Examples

SYSTEM	GEOMETRICAL FORMS FOR SELECTED SUB-CLASSES	SUBSTANCES THAT CRYSTALLIZE IN THE SYSTEM
Isometric	Cube	Common salt
	Octahedron	Diamond, gold
Hexagonal	Hexagonal prism	Quartz, tourmaline, graphite
Tetragonal	Tetragonal dipyramid	Zircon
Orthorhombic	Rhombic prism	Sulfur, topaz
Monoclinic	Prism pinacoid	Gypsum, mica, borax, talc, chrisotile asbestos
Triclinic	Pinacoid	Amazonite, turquoise

LIST 6–13. CRYSTAL GROWING

Crystals may be grown in several ways. Any of the procedures can be done on a very small scale.

Growing Crystals

PROCEDURE	EXAMPLES
Cooling a melted material	Sulfur
Sublimation (cooling vapor from a heated solid)	Sulfur, iodine, moth balls (naphthalene)
Evaporation of a solvent	Water solution of salt
Cooling a saturated solution	Alum in water, sugar in water
Chemical reaction to produce insoluble crystalline product	Silver nitrate and salt (sodium chloride) in water yield microscopic crystals of silver chloride and soluble sodium nitrate.

LIST 6–14. AN INTRODUCTION TO GEM MINERALS

There are different types of gem minerals. They are prized for their physical properties of luster, transparency, color, and hardness. Transparency, lack of flaws, brilliance of color, and size enhance the value of individual gems.

Gems

TRANSPARENT	*QUARTZ*	*OPAQUE, NON-QUARTZ*
Diamond	Rose quartz	Amazonite
Emerald	Smoky quartz	Rhodochrosite
Ruby	Amethyst	Hematite
Sapphire	Jasper	Jet (a form of coal)
Aquamarine crystal	Agate	Turquoise
Topaz	Carnelian	Malachite
Garnet	Rock crystal	Obsidian
Spodumene	Bloodstone	Rhodonite
Zircon	Black opal	Lapis-lazuli
Tourmaline	Fire opal	Moonstone
Spinel	Precious opal	Jade
Chrysoberyl	Sard	Nephrite
	White chalcedony	Jadeite
	Chrysoprase	

LIST 6–15. SYNTHETIC GEMS

The hardness of gems make them highly suitable for some tools and mechanical parts such as drills and mechanical watches. The high cost of gems has prompted research in the development of synthetic gems. In the 1900s considerable progress was made in developing synthetic gems. In 1902, a process for fusing alumina (Al_2O_3), in a hot flame was developed. By adding mineral pigments, synthetic gems can be made, such as synthetic rubies and sapphires. Synthetic gems can be dyed and have their color changed by heat, chemical changes, or radioactivity. In 1957, borazon, a synthetic diamond, was developed. Its hardness is close to that of diamond and it is able to withstand higher temperatures. Today synthetic diamonds are made for use as abrasives and cutting tools. Synthetic gems are also used in watches and for making copies of expensive jewelry, and costume jewelry.

Examples of Synthetic Gems

Ruby	Topaz	Sapphire	Tourmaline	Blue zircon
Emerald	Spinel	Diamond	Alexandrite	Zircon

LIST 6–16. CALCULATING THE SPECIFIC GRAVITY OF A MINERAL

Calculating the specific gravity of a sample of a mineral can be useful in helping to identify a mineral, if one has a list or reference for the specific gravity of minerals.

Equal-sized samples of different minerals will have different weights. Specific gravity (SG) is a way of measuring this difference by comparing the weight of the sample with a standard, usually water. The specific gravity of a mineral can be determined by dividing the weight of the sample by the volume of water displaced by that sample, or by the apparent loss in weight while suspended in water. The formula for calculating specific gravity is:

$$\text{Specific Gravity} = \frac{\text{Mineral Weight}}{\text{The volume of water displaced by the mineral}}$$

Since the volume of displacement is equivalent to the apparent loss in weight of the mineral while suspended in water, the formula can be rewritten as:

$$\text{SG} = \frac{\text{Dry Mineral Weight}}{\text{Dry Mineral Weight} - \text{Wet Mineral Weight}}$$

Dry mineral weight

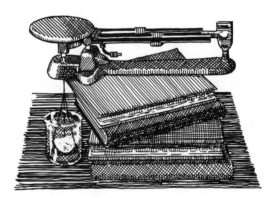

Wet mineral weight

(Continued)

LIST 6–16. (Continued)

Steps to Calculate the Specific Gravity of a Mineral

Steps to Calculate the SG of a Mineral

1.   Use a balance to weigh the mineral.

2.   Suspend the mineral from the balance tray in water and weigh again.

3.   Dry weight minus wet weight = loss due to buoyancy by water

4. $SG = \dfrac{\text{weight of mineral in g}}{\text{vol. of displaced water in cc}}$

Example Using a Sample of Corundum

1.   The dry sample weighs 57 g.

2.   The sample in water weighs 43 g.

3.   57 g − 43 g = 14 g
     (equivalent to a volume of 14 cc)*

4. $SG = \dfrac{57\ g}{14\ cc} = 4.0714$ or 4.1 g/cc

NOTE: The volume of displacement can also be determined by pouring water into a graduated cylinder, noting the number of milliliters; adding the mineral sample to the water, noting the number of milliliters of water displaced. This is not as accurate as weighing the sample.

In addition, if one has a scale that moves freely and returns to the same point after tilting, paper clips, small nails or tacks of uniform size can be used for weights. In this case:

$$SG = \frac{\text{weight (\#) in paper clips (etc.)}}{\text{\# of paper clips removed when sample is hung in water}}$$

$$\frac{20\ \text{paper clips}}{5\ \text{paper clips}} = 4\text{g/cc}$$

---

*One gram of water has a volume of one cubic centimeter.

LIST 6–17. SPECIFIC GRAVITY OF SOME MINERALS

SPECIFIC GRAVITY G/CC	MINERAL	SPECIFIC GRAVITY G/CC	MINERAL
1.6	Carnallite	4.8–5.2	Pyrite (Iron Pyrites)
1.9–2.5	Opal	4.5–5.0	Ilmenite
2.1	Sulfur	5.9–6.0	Crocoite
2.2	Graphite	6.5–7.1	Pyromorphite
2.3	Gypsum	7.0	Wulfenite
2.5	Serpentine	7.5	Galena
2.65	Quartz	7.6	Wolframite
2.7	Calcite	7.8	Niccolite
2.8	Talc	8.0	Cinnabar
3.5	Diamond	8.9	Copper
3.9–4.1	Corundum (Blue—sapphire red–ruby)	9.5	Uraninite
		9.6–11*	Silver
		9.7–9.8	Bismuth
4.5	Barite	15.5–19.3*	Gold
4.7	Zircon		

*Variations usually due to alloying with other metals.

A recommended reference that provides the specific gravity of minerals along with descriptions of physical properties and colored photographs: *Rocks, Minerals & Fossils of the World* by Chris Pellant with Roger Phillips, Little, Brown and Company, Boston, 1990.

LIST 6–18. SETTING UP A ROCK AND/OR FOSSIL COLLECTION

Setting up a collection enables one to observe, compare, classify, analyze, and identify specimens and can lead to an enjoyable hobby or career. Frequently, people want to know the name of a sample, but once they learn the name they can think of nothing to do with the sample. Actually, identifying the name might be the last thing that you learn about a sample because you may need to perform many tests and/or consult books to determine the name. Earlier lists in this section provide information for using Mohs' Scale of Hardness, specific gravity, and systems of classification.

Items that are recommended for getting started with a rock or fossil collection:

1. Work gloves for picking up samples.
2. A canvas bag in which to place samples while in the field.
3. A notebook and pencil to jot down notes about a sample as you find it, especially the location where the sample is found.
4. A magnifying lens.
5. Many samples can be picked up from the ground, but if you decide to dig for some you will need a geologist's hammer, cold chisel, and safety glasses.
6. Old newspapers and a paint brush to clean your samples.
7. Something in which to store and/or display your samples. Consider a box with cotton on the bottom and a clear glass or plastic cover. Such boxes can be bought from supplier or made by the collector.
8. A quick-drying nontoxic paint and India ink for numbering specimens.
9. A field guide to help identify specimens.
10. Tables of data for recording information about each specimen. Tables of data can be stored in a notebook or in a computer, or one can use a system of file cards.

Collections Data Table

NO. OF SPECIMEN	LOCATION	DATE	COLLECTOR	PHYSICAL PROPERTIES	NAME OF SPECIMEN

The Science Teacher's Book of Lists, © 1993 by Prentice Hall

LIST 6-19. SOME MUSEUMS AND EXHIBITS OF ROCKS AND MINERALS IN THE U.S.

AZ—Petrified Forest National Monument Museum
    University of Arizona, Tucson

CA—San Diego Natural History Museum
    California State Division of Mines Museums

DC—Smithsonian Institution, Washington, D.C.

DE—University of Delaware, Penny Hall, Geology Department, Newark

CO—Denver Museum of Natural History

MA—Peabody Museum of Natural History, New Haven

GA—Georgia State Museum, Atlanta

IL—Chicago Natural History Museum

IN—Indiana State Museum, Indianapolis

KA—University of Kansas, Lawrence

MA—Harvard University Mineralogical Museum, Cambridge

MI—University of Michigan Mineralogy Museum, Ann Arbor

MS—Missouri Resources Museum, University of Missouri, Jefferson City

MT—Montana School of Mines, Butte

NJ—New Jersey State Museum, Trenton

NM—New Mexico—New Mexico Institute of Mining and Technology,
    Socorro

NY—American Museum of Natural History, New York City
    Bear Mountain State Park (permanent exhibits)

OH—Cleveland Museum of Natural History

PA—Philadelphia Academy of Natural Sciences
    Franklin Institute, Philadelphia
    Carnegie Museum, Pittsburgh

SD—South Dakota School of Mines and Technology, Rapid City

NOTE: There are many smaller collections in state capitals and universities.

LIST 6–20. EARTH ZONES

Although the shells of the earth are commonly pictured as sharply bounded layers, they probably grade from one to another and there is movement of material from layer to layer. With the exceptions of mines and oil drilling in the crust, the earth's layers and composition cannot be observed directly. They are inferred from data gathered from seismic waves produced by earthquakes, volcanoes, and explosions. The earth's outer surface temperature varies a great deal with location and season. The earth's inner zone temperatures also vary.

EARTH ZONES OR SHELLS	TYPICAL COMPOSITION	DEPTH MILES	TEMPERATURE °C	SPECIFIC GRAVITY G/CC
Upper crust	granite	12–15	~13–730	2.8
Subcrust	basalt	25		3.2
Mantle	peridotite and other minerals	900	800–1100	3
	pyroxene-olivine	~450	870	6
	nickel-iron-olivine other minerals: magnesium iron silicates silicon aluminum iron	450	2,200	8
Outer core, hot liquid	nickel-iron	1,400	2,200–5,000	10
Inner core, solid	nickel-iron	1,600	8,000–10,000	10

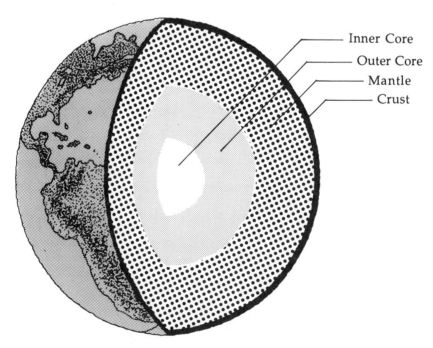

Inner Core
Outer Core
Mantle
Crust

The Science Teacher's Book of Lists, © 1993 by Prentice Hall

LIST 6–21. CONCENTRATION OF METALLIC ELEMENTS IN PRINCIPAL ZONES IN THE EARTH

ZONE:	WHOLE EARTH	MANTLE	OCEANIC CRUST	CONTINENTAL CRUST	UPPER CONTINENTAL CRUST
Rock type:	Chondrites[1]	Ultra-[2] mafics	Oceanic[3] Basalts	Andesites[4]	High Calcium[5] Granites
Silicon	17.8	20.5	23.2	27.8	31.4
Aluminum	1.3	2.0	8.1	9.1	8.2
Iron	25.1	9.4	8.5	4.7	3.0
Calcium	1.4	2.5	8.1	5.0	2.5
Sodium	0.7	0.02	2.1	2.7	2.8
Potassium	0.1	0.01	0.2	1.3	2.5
Magnesium	14.4	20.4	4.7	2.1	0.9
Titanium	0.1	0.03	0.08	0.4	0.3

Note: Based on the analysis of the rock types thought to approximate the composition of a given zone. The core of the earth is thought to be composed principally of iron with about 6 percent nickel. Each zone does not consist of one type of rock.

[1] Stony meteorites
[2] Rich in iron and magnesium minerals
[3] Of oceanic volcanic origin
[4] Extrusive, consisting of oligoclase and other minerals
[5] Igneous, with calcium minerals

LIST 6–22. MOST COMMON ELEMENTS OF THE EARTH'S CRUST

POSITION	ELEMENT	PERCENT	POSITION	ELEMENT	PERCENT
1	Oxygen	46.17	9	Titanium	*Note:* The sum
2	Silicon	27.69	10	Phosphorous	of 9–15 is
3	Aluminum	8.07	11	Carbon	1.17%
4	Iron	5.05	12	Hydrogen	
5	Calcium	3.65	13	Manganese	
6	Sodium	2.75	14	Sulfur	
7	Potassium	2.58	15	Chlorine	
8	Magnesium	2.08			

Note: Derived from the analysis of many rocks and minerals and estimates of their prevalence.

LIST 6–23. A GEOLOGICAL TIME SCALE

Time	Years[a]	Era	Yrs.[b]	Period		
	Recent		Yrs.[c]	Quaternary		
		Cenozoic Interval of modern life known as the Age of Mammals	64.8	Tertiary		
	65 million					
Phanerozoic		Mesozoic Interval of middle life known as the Age of Dinosaurs	77.6	Cretaceous		
			64	Jurassic		
			37	Triassic		
	245 million					
		Paleozoic Interval of old life	41	Permian		
			70	Carboniferous	30	Pennsylvanian
					40	Mississippian
			52	Devonian		
			30	Silurian		
			67	Ordovician		
			65	Cambrian		
	570 million					
Precambrian	5 billion					

[a]years ago
[b]approximate duration in millions of years
[c]recent time, 10,000 years to the present

NOTE: Geological time scales are derived from analysis of rocks and fossils, from radioactive isotopes of elements, such as uranium, potassium-40, and carbon-14, from magnetic polarity of iron constituents of rocks, and from the locations of rock strata in relation to one another. Time

(Continued)

LIST 6–23. (Continued)

Yrs.[b]	Epoch	Some Life Appearances and Occurrences
10,000	Holocene	Modern life
1.6	Pleistocene	Huge mammals such as mammoths, American bison
3.7	Pliocene	Human family appears, modern apes appear
18.4	Miocene	Apelike Dryopithecidae and Ramapithecidae appear
12.9	Oligocene	Monkeys appear, Indrichotherium[d]
21.2	Eocene	Whales appear, mammals flourish
8.6	Paleocene	Adaptive radiation of mammals[e] begins
		Extinction of dinosaurs and swimming reptiles Diatoms appear, angiosperm (flowering plants) expand Teleost fish appear
		Dinosaurs flourish, cycads flourish, first birds appear
		Ferns become abundant but gymnosperms remain dominate; small mammals and pterosaurs appear Reptiles replace amphibians as dominant land animal
		Gymnosperms become dominant plant form
		Coal swamps flourish, insects with foldable wings appear Early reptiles
		Insects with fixed wings abundant Coal swamps develop, adaptive radiation of crinoids
		First forests, first insects, amphibians invade the land
		Jawed fish, early land plants
		Jawless fish, general marine adaptive radiation
		Trilobites appear Fossils become abundant
		Marine invertebrates appear Multicell organisms appear Bacteria appear Blue-green algae appear

[d]formerly "Baluchitherium," the largest known land animal

[e]adaptive radiation—the rapid development of species from one ancestral group

intervals are divided into eons, eras, periods and epochs covering five billion years. There are further divisions and subdivisions.

Naming and classification change as knowledge advances, so one may find disagreement in different sources especially with dates and duration but there is general agreement on the sequence of eras, periods, and epochs.

LIST 6–24. A GEOLOGICAL EVENT FACILITATING ANIMAL IMMIGRATION

Fossil evidence indicates that the Isthmus of Panama was formed during the Pliocene Epoch building a land bridge between North and South America. This geological event provided a natural bridge enabling many animals to immigrate to areas that had previously been unavailable to them. More North American animals immigrated to South America than vice versa.

Examples of North American Animal Families that Immigrated to South America:

bear	pig
camel	rabbit
cat	rat
deer	rhino
dog	skunk
elephant	squirrel
horse	tapir

Examples of South American Animal Families that Immigrated to North America:

anteaters

armadillos

monkeys

opossums

porcupines

sloths

LIST 6–25. ONGOING CHANGES IN THE EARTH'S SURFACE

The Earth's surface is undergoing changes continuously. New formations are continuously being built up, old formations are continuously being eroded or worn away, and their eroded particles are deposited or recycled to build new formations. Thus, these changes in the earth's surface can be classified into two basic types: building up and wearing down.

Changes in Earth's Surface

BUILDING UP	WEARING DOWN
Plates, huge blocks of the rocky crusts, move, causing:	Weathering, changing of the crust, by chemical and physical changes:
1. Earthquakes to occur	1. Chemical weathering—changes the chemical make up of some minerals; caused by pressure, heat, acids, oxygen, and some plants and animals
2. Mountains to form 3. Volcanoes to erupt Sediment deposited by: a. Ice/glaciers b. Water c. Wind	2. Physical weathering—changes the physical properties of the rocks and minerals by eroding the crust resulting in movement of rock and soil by: a. Ice/glaciers, water freezing in rock crevasses b. Water moving (rain, rivers, etc.) c. Wind

LIST 6–26. THE THEORY OF PLATE TECTONICS

The theory of plate tectonics proposes that the lithosphere (the Earth's crust plus the rigid upper part of the mantle) is composed of plates (large areas of land mass and ocean bed), which are gradually moving over the face of the earth. The velocity of plate movement varies from plate to plate and within plates, being in the range of 2 cm to 20 cm per year. The idea is supported in part by the possible close fit of some coast lines with one another, for example, eastern South America and western Africa, and the coincidence of rock formations and fossil finds at the proposed points of contact. At many of the plate boundaries there are oceanic ridges formed by plate separation and influx of new volcanic material from below. The lithosphere is made up of 25 plates. The names of the major plates are listed below.

Major Tectonic Plates

NO.	PLATE	NO.	PLATE
1	Eurasian	7	Nazca
2	Indo-Australian	8	North American
3	Antarctic	9	South American
4	Pacific	10	Caribbean
5	Philippine	11	African
6	Cocos	12	Arabian

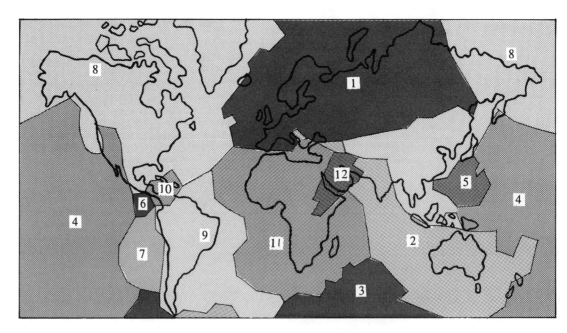

The Science Teacher's Book of Lists, © 1993 by Prentice Hall

LIST 6–27. ESTIMATED DISTRIBUTION OF WATER IN THE EARTH ENVIRONMENT

LOCATION	WATER VOLUME CUBIC MILES	PERCENTAGE OF TOTAL WATER
Salty and Brackish Waters		
Oceans and seas	321,000,000	96.5
Groundwater (saline water zone)	3,088,000	0.93
Saltwater lakes	20,500	0.006
Fresh and Slightly Mineralized Water		
Glaciers and permanent snow cover	5,772,000	1.7
Groundwater (fresh water zone)	2,526,000	0.75
Ground ice (permafrost strata)	70,000	0.02
Fresh water lakes	22,000	0.006
Soil moisture	3,960	0.001
Atmospheric water	3,100	0.001
Marsh water	2,760	0.001
Rivers	500	0.0002
Biological water (plants/animals)	260	0.0001
Grand totals	**332,500,000**	**99.92%**

The Science Teacher's Book of Lists, © 1993 by Prentice Hall

NOTE: This information represents a best estimate. If one were to calculate the percentages to three or more places, the total would add up to 100%. In using the data above, round off 99.92% to 100%.

LIST 6–28. SIZE OF AN EARTHQUAKE*

The size of an earthquake can be measured qualitatively by the degree of ground shaking at a particular location, as indicated by the effects or damage caused (intensity). More commonly, however, earthquake size is determined quantitatively by the displacement (or amplitude) of the ground motions as they are recorded by the signal on a seismograph (which is translated to a number of magnitude). This concept was introduced in 1935, by the noted seismologist, Charles F. Richter.

To cover the huge size range of earthquakes, the Richter Scale is made logarithmic. That is, each time the amplitude of the measured earthquake waves increases 10 times, the magnitude increases by 1 unit. For example, a magnitude-6 earthquake has an amplitude 10 times greater than a magnitude-5 event at the same location. The magnitude scale is open ended. Small earthquakes occur much more frequently than large earthquakes; every day 9,000 earthquakes having a magnitude greater than 1.0 occur worldwide.

Earthquakes

MAGNITUDE	AVERAGE OCCURRENCE PER YEAR	SEISMIC ENERGY RELEASE EQUIVALENT TO
3	49,000	Smallest earthquakes commonly felt
4	6,000	Detonation of 1,000 tons of explosives
5	800	Atomic bomb tests in the South Pacific in 1946
6	120	Energy to launch 2 million NASA Space Shuttles
7	18	Energy generated by Niagara Falls (Canada–U.S.A.) in 4 months
8	1	1906 San Francisco earthquake, or energy to form Meteor Crater, Arizona

*SOURCE: "This Dynamic Planet: World Map of Volcanoes, Earthquakes, and Plate Tectonics," compiled by Tom Simkin, Robert I. Tilling, James N. Taggart, William J. Jones, and Henry Spall, Smithsonian Institution and the U.S. Geological Survey, 1989.

LIST 6–29. POINTING TO THE NORTH POLE

The north pole is the northern location of the earth's rotational axis. From this point every direction is south. The earth is a giant magnet and the northern focal point of its magnetic field is not at the geographic north pole but at a point about 1200 miles to the south in northern Canada. Magnetic compasses point toward the north magnetic pole. Therefore, to know the true north direction with a compass a correction must be made which varies with one's position in the country.

Directions are expressed by thirty-two names such as north, east, south, and west. In order to indicate more directions, the circular compass face is divided into 360 sections called degrees which are marked clockwise. Thus, north is 0°, east is 90°, south is 180°, west is 270°, and so on. That brings us back to the correction of compass readings to true north. The table shows approximate corrections for the United States. More corrections are given on topographic maps of the U.S. Geological Survey.

The deviation in a compass reading from true north is known as *declination*. Some pocket compasses have a built in means of making the correction for declination. To go from a compass reading in the field and orient a map to true north, subtract a west declination and add an east declination.

Approximate Compass Corrections for the Contiguous United States*

EAST DECLINATION IN DEGREES (ADD)					WEST DECLINATION IN DEGREES (SUBTRACT)			
20	15	10	5	0	5	10	15	20
MT;W	MT;E	ND;E	MN;E	WS;E	MI;E	NY;W	VT	ME;NE
ID;N	WY;C	SD;C	IO;E	IN;C	OH;E	PA;E	NH;W	
WA	UT	NB	MO;E	KY;C	WVA	NJ	MA;E	
OR	NV;S	KA	AK;C	TN;E	VA;C	DE	RI	
CA;S	OK;W	MS	GA;C	NC;C	MD			
AZ	TX;W	LA	FL;C					

*State abbreviations followed by W, western; E, eastern; N, northern; S, southern; C, central; and NE, northeastern. If a state has been omitted, that area falls between the zones for adjacent states.

(Continued)

The Science Teacher's Book of Lists, © 1993 by Prentice Hall

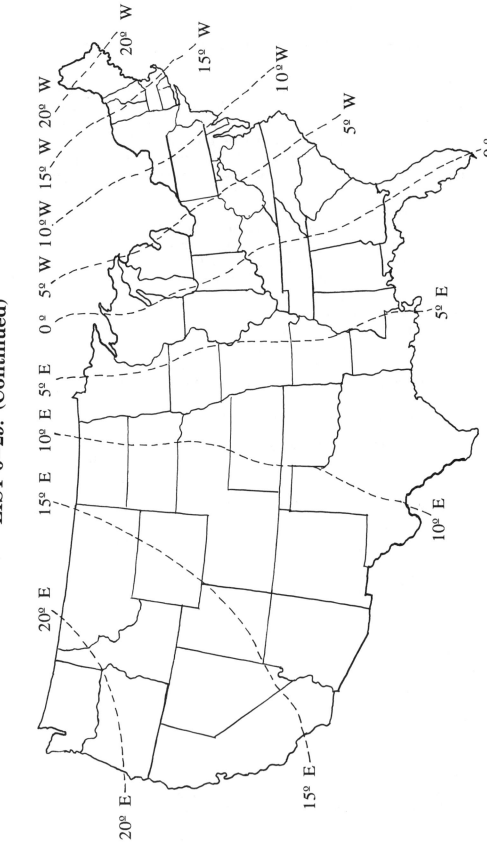

20º W

15º W

10º W

5º W

0º

20º W
15º W
10º W
5º W
0º
5º E
10º E
15º E
20º E

5º E

10º E

15º E

20º E

LIST 6–30. NATURAL WONDER SUPERLATIVES: LARGEST, SMALLEST, HIGHEST, ETC.

largest desert—the Sahara. Its sands cross the borders of many countries: Algeria, Chad, Egypt, Libya, Mali, Mauritania, Morocco, Niger, Sudan, and Tunisia. Other large deserts are: the Australian Desert, Arabian Desert, and the Gobi Desert.

highest mountain range—the Himalayas, which contain the 200 highest mountains in the world.

highest mountain—Mount Everest; 8,848 m (29,028 ft) into the clouds over Nepal and Tibet

longest mountain range—the Andes, which are 7,200 km (4,475 mi) long and meander through Venezuela, Colombia, Ecuador, Peru, Bolivia, Argentina, and Chile.

greatest of all mountain ranges—the undersea range of Indian-East Pacific Oceans Cordillera; it extends 30,720 km (49,428.4 miles) from the Gulf of Aden to the Gulf of California. It rises from the sea between Australia and Antarctica with an average height of its peaks at 2400 m (8000 ft).

largest mountain measured from its submarine base to its peak—Mauna Kea; a volcanic mountain on Hawaii; 10,043 m (33,476 ft) high, rising 4139 m (13,769 ft) above the sea.

largest fresh-water lake—Lake Superior 82,680 sq. km (31,830 sq. mi.). It borders Canada and the United States.

largest inland sea—the Caspian Sea has an area of 373,230 sq. km. (143,500 sq. mi.)

deepest lake—Lake Baikal in Siberia, 1.62 miles deep, (8,533 ft).

longest river—the Nile 6,632 km (4,150 mi) long.

shortest river—the D River in Oregon; connects Devil's Lake to the Pacific Ocean, 132 m (440 ft) long at low tide.

largest ocean—the Pacific Ocean: 165,880,000 sq. km (63,800,000 sq. miles), represents about 46 percent of the world's oceans.

longest coastline—Canada; has more than 250,000 km (155,376 mi) of coastline.

largest island—Greenland has an area of about 2,184,000 sq. km (840,000 sq. miles).

largest archipelago (group of islands)—Indonesia; more than 13,000 islands.

deepest spot—the Marianas Trench in the Pacific Ocean, 10,912 m (35,800 feet) below the ocean's surface.

(Continued)

LIST 6–30. (Continued)

lowest spot on earth—Dead Sea, Israel and Jordon, 397 m (1,302 ft) below sea level.

largest tropical coral reef—Australia's Great Barrier Reef; over 1,300 miles long and 80,900 square miles.

highest waterfall—Angel Falls in Venezuela on a branch of the Carrao River, a 963.6 m (3,212 ft) vertical drop.

largest continent—Eurasia; 54,737,800 sq. km. (21,053,000 sq. miles) of area, including islands.

smallest continent—Australia; 7,644,000 sq. km. (2,940,000 sq. miles)

largest glacier—Lambert Glacier, Antarctica; 640 km (400 miles) long.

highest average temperatures—the hot, desert countries of Mali, Upper Volta, and Niger in Africa.

sunniest place—the Sahara Desert in the Sudan.

driest country—Egypt, with 55.8 mm (2.2 in) of rain per year.

coldest place—Antarctica; average temperature is $-60°C$ ($-76°F$).

coldest natural temperature ever recorded—$-88°C$ ($-127°F$) at Vostok, Antarctica in 1960.

wettest country—Colombia; receives 4,099 mm (161.4 in.) of rain a year.

wettest place—Mount Waialeale on the Hawaiian island of Kauai. It rains almost every day.

LIST 6–31. CLASSIFICATION, PRONUNCIATION, AND LENGTH OF SELECTED DINOSAUR GENERA

Dinosaurs are a group of extinct, four-legged animals that ruled the earth from 150 million years ago to about 60 million years ago. Fossil evidence indicates that they ranged in length from ten cars parked end to end, to the size of a chicken. There are about 150 known [species] of dinosaurs, and some species have more than one common name. Paleontologists, scientists who study prehistoric forms of life through fossil evidence, group dinosaurs for the purposes of identification and study into two groups or orders:

(1) Saurischia (or lizard hip)
(2) Ornithischia (or bird hip)

Name, Pronunciation, and Length of Some Dinosaur Genera

SELECTED SAURISCHIA		SELECTED ORNITHISCHIA	
Name Pronunciation	Length ft/m	Name Pronunciation	Length ft/m
Albertosaurus al-BERT-oh-SAW-rus	26 ft. 8 m	Ankylosaurus an-KY-low-SAW-rus	35 ft. 10.7 m
Allosaurus AL-oh-SAW-rus	35 ft. 11 m	Bagaceratops BAG-a-SER-a-tops	3.3 ft. 1 m
Apatosaurus (Brontosaurus) a-PAT-oh-SAW-rus	70 ft. 21 m	Camptosaurus KAMP-toe-SAW-rus	23 ft. 7 m
Brachiosaurus BRACK-ee-oh-SAW-rus	75 ft. 23 m	Corythosaurus ko-RITH-oh-SAW-rus	33 ft. 10 m
Compsognathus KOMP-sog-NAY-thus	2 ft. 60 cm	Dryosaurus DRY-oh-SAW-rus	13 ft. 4 m
Diplodocus dip-LOD-oh-kus or dip-low-DOE-kus	90 ft. 27 m	Fabrosaurus FAB-roe-SAW-rus	3.3 ft. 1 m
Elaphrosaurus ee-LAF-roe-SAW-rus	10 ft. 3 m.	Geranosaurus jer-AN-oh-SAW-rus	4 ft. 1.2 m
Euhelopus yoo-HEL-oh-pus	50 ft. 15 m	Hadrosaurus HAD-roe-SAW-rus	33 ft. 10 m
Lufengosaurus loo-FENG-oh-SAW-rus	20 ft. 6 m.	Hylaeosaurus, an ankylosaur HY-lee-oh-SAW-rus	20 ft. 6 m
Ornitholestes or-NITH-oh-LESS-teez	6.5 ft. 2 m	Iguanodon i-GAW-no-DON	30 ft. 9 m
Ornithomimus or-NITH-oh-MIME-us	13 ft. 4 m	Kentrosaurus, a stegosaur KEN-tro-SAW-rus	16.5 ft. 5 m
Oviraptor OVE-ih-RAP-tor	6 ft. 1.8 m	Lambeosaurus LAM-bee-oh-SAW-rus	50 ft. 15 m

(Continued)

LIST 6–31. (Continued)

SELECTED SAURISCHIA		SELECTED ORNITHISCHIA	
Name Pronunciation	**Length ft/m**	**Name Pronunciation**	**Length ft/m**
Plateosaurus	26 ft.	Lexovisaurus, a stegosaur	16.5 ft.
PLAT-ee-oh-SAW-rus	8 m	lex-OVE-ih-SAW-rus	5 m
Procompsognathus	3.3 ft.	Lycorhinus	4 ft.
pro-COMP-sow-NAY-thus	1 m	LIE-koe-RINE-us	1.2 cm
Saltopus	2 ft.	Monoclonius	20 ft.
SALT-oh-pus	60 cm	MON-oh-KLONE-ee-us	6 m
Segnosaurus	30 ft.	Muttaburrasaurus	23 ft.
SEG-no-SAW-rus	9 m	MUT-a-BUR-a-SAW-rus	7 m
Supersaurus	100 ft.	Ouranosaurus	23 ft.
super-SAW-rus	30 m	oo-RAN-oh-SAW-rus	7 m
Tyrannosaurus	50 ft.	Pentaceratops	20 ft.
tie-RAN-oh-SAW-rus	15 m	PEN-ta-SER-a-tops	6 m
Ultrasaurus	92 ft.	Pinacosaurus, an ankylosaur	18 ft.
UL-tra-SAW-rus	30.5 m	pin-AK-oh-SAW-rus	5.5 m
Velociraptor	6 ft.	Protoceratops	6 ft.
vel-OS-i-RAP-tor	1.8 m	pro-toe-SER-a-tops	1.8 m
		Stegosaurus	29 ft.
		STEG-oh-SAW-rus	9 m
		Styracosaurus	18 ft.
		STY-rak-oh-SAW-rus	5.5 m
		Triceratops	30 ft.
		try-SER-a-tops	9 m

Adapted from: Benton, Michael, *The Dinosaur Encyclopedia*, Wanderer Books, Simon & Schuster, Inc., New York, 1984.

Stegosaurus

LIST 6–32. SOME MUSEUMS THAT DISPLAY DINOSAUR FOSSILS

Hooded dinosaur

In Canada

- Dinosaur Provincial Park, Patricia, Alberta
- National Museum of Canada, Ottawa, Ontario
- Provincial Museum of Alberta, Edmonton, Alberta
- Royal Ontario Museum, Toronto, Ontario
- Tyrell Museum of Paleontology, Drumheller, Alberta
- Zoological Gardens, Calgary, Alberta

In the United States

- Academy of Natural Science, Philadelphia, Pennsylvania
- American Museum of Natural History, New York, New York
- Brigham Young University, Provo, Utah
- California Academy of Science, San Francisco, California
- Carnegie Museum of Natural History, Pittsburgh, Pennsylvania
- Carter County Museum, Ekalaka, Montana
- Cleveland Museum of Natural History, Cleveland, Ohio
- Denver Museum of Natural History, Denver, Colorado
- Dinosaur National Monument, Jensen, Utah
- Field Museum, Chicago, Illinois
- Geology Museum at the University of California at Berkeley, California
- Los Angeles County Museum of Natural History, Los Angeles, California
- Museum of Comparative Zoology, Cambridge, Massachusetts
- Museum of Natural History, Princeton University, Princeton, New Jersey
- Peabody Museum of Natural History, Yale University, New Haven, Connecticut
- Utah Museum of Natural History, Salt Lake City, Utah

Outside of North America

- Argentine Museum of Natural Science, Buenos Aires, Argentina
- Beijing Natural History Museum, China
- Belgian Royal Museum of Natural History, Brussels, Belgium
- British Museum (Natural History), London, England

(Continued)

LIST 6–32. (Continued)

- Geology Museum, Calcutta, India
- Humboldt University, Berlin, Germany
- Institute of Natural History, Berlin, Germany
- Museum of La Plata, Argentina
- National Museum of Natural History, Paris, France
- National Science Museum, Tokyo, Japan
- Paleontological Institute of the Academy of Science, Moscow, Russia
- Senckenberg Museum, Frankfurt, Germany
- University of Tübingen, Germany
- University of Uppsala, Sweden
- University of Zürich, Switzerland

section 7
METEOROLOGY

LIST 7–1. METEOROLOGY VOCABULARY

air—a mixture of gases (on Earth, mostly nitrogen and oxygen)

air mass—a large body of air that has about the same temperature and moisture content throughout

air pressure—the force of the air pressing on the earth's surface, equal to 14.7 pounds per square inch at mean sea level; varies with humidity; frequently stated as 15 pounds of pressure per square inch

Alberta Clipper—a low-pressure system that develops in or near the province of Alberta in winter and moves rapidly east or southeast through Canada and/or the United States laying a swath of light snow (2″ to 4″)

anemometer—instrument used to measure wind speed

anticyclone—large area of high pressure around which winds blow clockwise in the northern hemisphere

altitude—distance above sea level

atmosphere—the layer of gases, water, and particles surrounding the Earth; the layer of gases surrounding a planet

back-door cold front—a cold front that approaches from the northeast rather than the northwest

brief—of short duration

Celsius scale—temperature scale developed by Celsius in which water boils at 100 degrees and freezes at 0 degrees

chance—scattered; a 30% to 50% probability of measurable precipitation

cirrus—high clouds (usually above 16,000 feet) composed of ice crystals

climate—the average daily or seasonal weather patterns of a region

clear—opaque cloud cover less than 10 percent

cloud seeding—releasing small, solid particles of carbon dioxide or silver iodide into cool clouds that are heavy with moisture. Moisture may form around the particles causing rain or snow

condensation—the change in state of water from gas to a liquid

convection—the movement of heat through liquids and gases by currents

cumulonimbus cloud—a massive, vertically developed cloud frequently accompanied by heavy rains, lightning, hail and gusty winds; also known as an "anvilhead"

cumulus cloud—a cloud in the shape of individually detached white fluffy domes (cauliflower-like tops) with a flat base; also known as fair-weather clouds

dew—moisture that has condensed on objects near the ground

dew point—the temperature at which water vapor in the air condenses to a liquid

(Continued)

LIST 7–1. (Continued)

Doppler radar—radar that determines whether the direction of precipitation and smaller airborne particles is towards or away from the radar set and thus identifies windflow such as strong thunderstorms and tornadic winds

downburst—a strong localized downdraft of rain-cooled air in or near a thunderstorm

dust devil—small rapidly rotating wind vortex made visible by dust and debris

El Niño—a warming of the tropical Pacific Ocean surface waters producing warm currents along the coasts of Central and South America, which sometimes are associated with significant changes in the circulation over the northern hemisphere

evaporation—the change in state (of water) from a liquid to a gas

fair—less than 40 percent opaque cloud cover, no precipitation, no extremes in temperature or wind

Fahrenheit—the temperature scale developed by Fahrenheit in which water boils at 212 degrees and freezes at 32 degrees

fog—a cloud with its base at Earth's surface

freezing point—the temperature at which a liquid changes to a solid or vice versa; the temperature at which solid and liquid phases can coexist at equilibrium

front—the area of contact and transition between two air masses usually of different temperatures; cold front if cold air is advancing, warm if cold air is retreating, stationary if boundary is not moving

frost—small, thin ice crystals that develop when a layer of air cools to condensation by contact with a cold surface whose temperature is below freezing

frost action—the breaking down of rocks by repeated freezing and melting of water

gas—the state of matter that has no definite shape or volume

geostationary satellite—a satellite that revolves at the same rate as the Earth spins causing it to remain over the same geographic location

global winds—bands of winds circling the Earth

GOES—Geostationary Operational Environment Satellite

greenhouse effect—the trapping and building up of heat by some gases in the atmosphere

ground fog—fog caused on land by the cooling of the lower atmosphere; also known as radiation fog

gust—a brief sudden increase in wind speed

The Science Teacher's Book of Lists, © 1993 by Prentice Hall

(Continued)

LIST 7–1. (Continued)

haze—fine dry or wet particles in the air that reduce visibility

heat—a form of energy that a body possesses because of motion of its molecules; moves from warmer matter to cooler matter

high—whirling mass of air of high pressure, an anticyclone; generally brings fair weather; winds blow clockwise around highs in the Northern hemisphere

high tide—the time at which the ocean water level reaches its highest point on land

high wind—winds of 40 mph and/or gusts of 58 mph

humidity—the amount of water vapor in the atmosphere

Indian summer—a period of summerlike weather in autumn which follows a period of cool weather that has been accompanied by the first frost

intermittent—occurring at frequent intervals

inversion—temperature increases with altitude; contrary to the normal situation of temperature decreasing with altitude

isobar—a line on a weather map that connects points of equal sea-level barometric pressure

jet stream—a core of strong winds in the atmosphere

knot—a unit of measure for speed of water or wind; one nautical mile per hour equals 1.15 mph

La Niña—a cooling of the tropical Pacific surface waters (opposite of El Niño); sometimes associated with weather of the northern hemisphere

land breeze—wind that blows from the land toward the water

lightning—an electrical discharge due to a build up of electrons usually during a thunderstorm

likely—in probability of precipitation statements; the equivalent of a 60% to 70% chance of precipitation

liquid—the state of matter that has a definite volume but no definite shape

low—an area of low pressure; a cyclone; winds blow counterclockwise around lows in the Northern Hemisphere

low tide—the time at which the ocean water level is at its lowest point on land

meteorology—the science that investigates the atmosphere, its interactions, and its processes

microburst—a strong localized downdraft from a convective cloud, often from a thunderstorm; usually associated with wind shear and turbulence

millibar—a unit of atmospheric pressure; normal sea-level surface pressure is 1013.4 millibars or 29.92 inches (760 mm) of mercury or 14.7 lbs./in.^{2}

(Continued)

LIST 7–1. (Continued)

NMC—National Meteorological Center

NOAA—National Oceanic and Atmospheric Administration; the National Weather Service is a part of NOAA, which is part of the U.S. Department of Commerce

NOAA Weather Radio—24-hour continuous VHF broadcasts of weather forecasts and observations from the National Weather Service offices

NOAA Weather Wire—a communication system for the transmitting of National Weather Service products to the electronic and print media

overcast—90% or more of the sky is covered by opaque clouds

ozone—a form of oxygen composed of three atoms per molecule; in the upper atmosphere it filters much of the harmful ultraviolet radiation from the sun; in the lower atmosphere it is a pollutant created by a chemical reaction of sunlight with auto emissions

ozone layer—the thin layer of ozone gas in the upper atmosphere that blocks most of the sun's ultraviolet radiation

partly cloudy—30% to 70% of the sky is covered by opaque clouds

POP—*Probability of* measurable *p*recipitation (.01 inch or greater) expressed as a percentage

precipitation—water, in liquid or solid form, that falls from the atmosphere to the ground

pressure—the weight of the atmosphere; the force caused by the effect of gravity on the atmosphere

relative humidity—the amount of water vapor in the air compared with the total amount of water vapor that the air can hold at that temperature, if it were saturated; expressed as a percentage

ridge—an elongated (stretched) area of high pressure

sea breeze—wind that blows from the water toward the land

seasons—quarterly divisions of the Earth's year caused by the Earth's revolution: winter, spring, summer, and fall

smog—a mixture of smoke and fog in the atmosphere; can restrict visibility and be harmful to health

solar energy—energy from the sun

stationary front—a transition zone between air masses of two different temperatures that are moving slowly or not at all

temperature—degree of hotness or coldness measured on a definite scale

thunder—the sound caused by lightning discharge as it heats the air rapidly and causes it to expand

tides—the regular rise and fall of Earth's surface water caused by gravitational attraction by the moon

(Continued)

LIST 7–1. (Continued)

trough—elongated (stretched) area of low pressure

valley fog—fog formed in valleys and other low areas as a result of cooling in the lower airmass

virga—precipitation falling that evaporates before hitting a surface

visibility—the horizontal distance one can see and identify a prominent object

water vapor—water in the form of mist in the air when below the boiling point (rather than steam in the air from boiling water)

warning—a public announcement that a hazard is either occurring or about to occur

weather—atmospheric conditions at a given time

weather forecast—a prediction of future weather conditions

weathering—the processes of breaking up or changing the chemical composition of objects because of exposure to the elements

wind—moving air

wind direction—the direction from which the wind is blowing

W. M. O. Code—World Meteorology Organization Code is a system of meteorological symbols consisting of one or two numbers and/or letters used as an international shorthand for data transmission

World Meteorology Organization—weather organization of the United Nations

The Science Teacher's Book of Lists, © 1993 by Prentice Hall

LIST 7–2. TYPES OF PRECIPITATION

NAME	SYMBOL	DESCRIPTION
Drizzle	L	Composed of fine drops (less than .02 inch or .5 mm in diameter) very close together, which appear to float while following air currents; unlike fog droplets, drizzle falls to the ground. Too small to appreciably disturb puddles of water
Freezing drizzle	ZL	Drizzle which freezes on contact with the ground or objects
Rain	R	Liquid water particles ranging from 0.02 inch (0.5 mm) or larger; in contrast to drizzle, the rain drops are widely separated
Freezing rain	ZR	Rain that freezes on contact with the ground or objects
Hail	A	Concentric layered spheres or lumps of ice
Sleet	IP	Transparent or translucent ice pellets having a diameter of 0.2 inch (5 mm) or less; the ice pellets are round or irregular, usually rebound when striking the ground or hard surface, and make a sound on impact
Snow	S	Ice particles in complex hexagonal patterns; usually occurs when the surface temperature is near or below 35°F

LIST 7–3. STORMS

NAME	DESCRIPTION
Blizzard	Storm in which there is considerable falling snow and/or blowing snow with visibility less than ¼ mile and winds of 35 mph or more.
Cyclone	An area of low pressure around which winds blow in a counterclockwise direction in the northern hemisphere; usually accompanied with clouds and precipitation.
Extratropical	A nontropical low-pressure system.
Flash flood	A flood that occurs within a few hours of heavy rain, dam failure, or ice jam release.
Funnel cloud	A rotating, cone-shaped column of air extending downward from the base of the clouds; when it touches the ground it is called a tornado.
Gale	Winds with speeds of 39 mph to 54 mph (34 kn to 47 kn).
Hurricane	A widespread, intense low-pressure area originating in the tropics, producing a storm with high winds of 74 mph or more and heavy rains.
Monsoon	Persistent seasonal wind usually associated with warm season over continents; often leads to regular rainfall patterns.
Nor'easter	A storm moving along the east coast producing northeast surface winds capable of producing strong winds, heavy rain, and snow; occurring most often during winter.
Storm	A weather condition caused by unsettled atmospheric conditions; for mariners, sustained winds of at least 48 knots.
Thunderstorm	A local storm with tall clouds, heavy rains, and thunder and lightning.
Tornado	A column of air violently rotating in the shape of a funnel that extends from the base of a cumulonimbus cloud to the ground.
Tropical storm	A low-pressure system originating in the tropics with wind speeds of 39 mph to 73 mph.
Typhoon	A hurricane that occurs in the western Pacific Ocean.

LIST 7–4. WATCHES, WARNINGS, AND ADVISORIES FOR NON-ROUTINE WEATHER*

The United States Weather Department is charged with alerting the public about potential weather hazards. Alerts are broadcast over television and radio.

1. *Warnings* are the most immediate and warn of *imminent* life- /or/ property-threatening weather.

2. *Watches* refer to weather events of *potential* danger to the public, but with a lower probability of occurrence than a warning.

3. *Advisories* refer to an immediate weather hazard but usually one of less potential danger than a watch or warning.

TERM	ISSUED
Blizzard warning	When winds are expected to be 35 mph or more accompanied with falling and drifting snow frequently reducing visibility to less than $\frac{1}{4}$ mile
Blowing and drifting snow advisory	When visibility is intermittently or steadily below $\frac{1}{4}$ mile
Coastal flood watch	12–36 hours before the possibility of coastal flooding from an extratropical or nontropical storm
Coastal flood warning	For widespread major coastal flooding occurring or expected to occur within the next 12 hours
Dense fog advisory	When widespread visibility is at or below $\frac{1}{4}$ mile for several hours
Flash flood warning	For specific locations when flash flooding is imminent or in progress
Flood watch	When flooding is possible, usually within 12 to 24 hours
Flood warning	When flooding of a water system in a normally dry area is expected. It differs from a flash flood warning in that the flood usually has a longer lead time and a longer duration
Freeze warning	When surface temperature is expected to drop below 32°F during the growing season
Freezing rain/drizzle advisory	When an accumulation of ice makes surfaces and power lines hazardous
Frost warning	When widespread and heavy frost is expected during the growing season
High wind watch	When high winds (of 40 mph or more and/or gusts to 58 mph or more) are expected to last for one hour or more within the next 12 hours

(Continued)

Adapted from: "Guide to National Weather Service Office and Products in Southern New England," prepared by the Weather Service Forecast Office, Boston, Massachusetts, revised 1991.

LIST 7–4. (Continued)

TERM	*ISSUED*
High wind warning	When sustained winds (of 40 mph or more and/or gusts to 58 mph or more) are expected to last for one hour or more within the next 12 hours
Hurricane watch	24–36 hours before the possibility of hurricane conditions
Hurricane warning	When hurricane conditions (winds of 74 mph and/or dangerously high tides) are expected in 24 hours or less
Severe thunderstorm and tornado watches	When severe thunderstorms or tornadoes are possible in a given area within the next six hours
Severe thunderstorm warning	When a thunderstorm with winds of at least 58 mph or accompanied by hail of at least $\frac{3}{4}$ inch in diameter is likely during the next hour, or is occurring
Snow advisory	When snow accumulation is expected between 2 and 6 inches during a 12-hour period
Tornado warning	When a tornado has been reported by a reliable observer, seen on radar, or when conditions are likely for a tornado to form within the next hour
Wind chill advisory	When a combination of winds and low temperatures are expected to produce an equivalent temperature of less than $-30°F$ or $-35°F$
Winter storm watch	When heavy snow, heavy rain, sleet, or a combination of snow and strong winds is anticipated within the next 36 hours. The probability of occurrence is less for a watch than a warning, and the potential snow accumulation is the same.
Winter storm warning	When heavy snow, freezing rain, sleet, damaging ice, or a combination of snow and strong winds, is anticipated within the next 12 hours
Winter weather advisory	In lieu of two or more specific advisories for winter-type events

LIST 7–5. MARINE WARNINGS
AND ADVISORIES*

The term *knot* is used with marine warnings and advisories. One knot is equal to 1.15 miles (or one nautical mile per hour). Winds of 4 to 6 knots are described on the Beaufort Scale as a slight breeze. Winds of 64 to 71 knots are identified as a hurricane.

TERM	ISSUED
Gale warning	When winds reach 34 knots or more (extratropical system)
Hurricane warning	For sustained winds of 64 knots or more in conjunction with a tropical cyclone
Small craft advisory	For coastal zones where winds sustain a speed of 25 knots or more; or when the sea is rough
Special marine warning	When winds are expected to reach 34 knots or more for up to two hours as might occur with thunderstorms
Storm warnings	For sustained winds of 48 knots or more (extratropical system)
Tropical storm warnings	For sustained winds of 34 to 63 knots in conjunction with a tropical cyclone

LIST 7–6. SKY CONDITION TERMS
USED IN PUBLIC FORECASTS*

TERM	PERCENTAGE OF SKY COVERED WITH OPAQUE CLOUDS
Clear or sunny	Less than 10
Mostly sunny	10–30
Partly cloudy or partly sunny	30–70
Mostly cloudy	70–90
Cloudy	90–100
Variable cloudiness	Varies, 20–90

The Science Teacher's Book of Lists, © 1993 by Prentice Hall

Adapted from: "Guide to National Weather Service Office and Products in Southern New England," prepared by the Weather Service Forecast Office, Boston, Massachusetts, revised 1991.

LIST 7–7. PROBABILITY, UNCERTAINTY, AND QUALIFIERS IN FORECASTS*

PROBABILITY OF MEASURABLE PRECIPITATION (POP) (PERCENTAGE)	EXPRESSION OF UNCERTAINTY	AREA QUALIFYING
0	None	None
10	Slight chance	Isolated or few
20	Slight chance	Widely scattered
30–50	Chance	Scattered
60–70	Likely	Numerous
80–100	Near certain, referred to as "categorical forecast"	Near certain, categorical forecast

*Adapted from: "Guide to National Weather Service Office and Products in Southern New England," prepared by the Weather Service Forecast Office, Boston, Massachusetts, revised 1991.

LIST 7–8. WEATHER INSTRUMENTS

Meteorologists use a variety of instruments to assist them in observing and recording data about the weather. They interpret this data to make predictions or weather forecasts.

anemometer—wind gauge; an instrument for measuring wind speed; it is made of four cups on a crossbar that spin about a post as the wind blows

barometer—an instrument for measuring air pressure; a drop in pressure can help predict unsettled weather; a rise in the barometer can help predict settled weather

hygrometer—an instrument for measuring the relative humidity in the air; if the humidity is 15 percent then the air is dry

radar—an instrument used to detect precipitation by measuring the strength of the signal transmitted and received

radiosonde—a radio transmitter with weather instruments, attached to a weather balloon, which measures and transmits pressure, humidity, temperature, and winds as the balloon ascends

rain gauge—an instrument for measuring the amount of rain in an area, usually in inches

thermometer—an instrument for measuring temperature in degrees; the two common thermometers are the Fahrenheit and the Celsius

weather satellites—devices orbiting the earth, carrying cameras and transmitters, which photograph cloud patterns and transmit the pictures to Earth

wind vane—an instrument that points in the direction from which the wind is blowing; we say, "The wind is out of the north," or "It's a north wind."

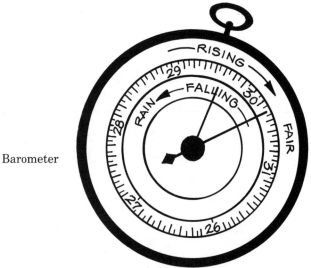

Barometer

LIST 7–9. STEPS FOR DETERMINING THE PERCENT OF RELATIVE HUMIDITY

1. Use or make a hygrometer, consisting of two Celsius or two Fahrenheit thermometers, one of which has a wet cloth wrapped around its bulb. As the water evaporates it will reduce the temperature.

2. Make sure the two thermometers register the same temperature before applying a wet cloth to one of the thermometers.

3. Place a wet cloth around the bulb of one thermometer.

4. Observe both thermometers.

5. As the water evaporates from the cloth, the temperature of the thermometer wrapped in the cloth will decrease.

6. Record the readings from the dry-bulb and wet-bulb thermometers.

7. Subtract the wet-bulb reading from the dry-bulb, and refer the difference to the Relative Humidity Chart listed below. This example uses the Celsius scale.

Dry-bulb reading	30 °C	Find 30° in the dry-bulb column and 10° in the difference column. The intersection of these two provides the relative humidity in percent. In this case, the relative humidity is 36 percent.
Wet-bulb reading	20 °C	
(Difference)	10°	

Percentage of Relative Humidity

TEMPERATURE OF DRY BULB (°C)	DIFFERENCE: DRY-BULB READING – WET-BULB READING (°C)												
	1	2	3	4	5	6	7	8	9	10	12	14	16
45	94	88	83	78	73	68	63	59	55	51	42	35	28
40	93	88	82	77	71	65	61	56	52	47	38	31	23
35	93	87	80	75	68	62	57	52	47	42	33	24	16
30	92	86	78	72	65	59	53	47	41	36	26	16	8
25	91	84	76	69	61	54	47	41	35	29	17	6	
20	90	81	73	64	56	47	40	32	26	18	5		
15	89	79	68	59	49	39	30	21	12	4			

LIST 7–10. CLOUDS

More than one hundred years ago, Luke Howard, an English scientist, investigated clouds. He observed, identified, and later named four basic types of clouds. In keeping with the tradition in the scientific community at the time, he used Latin terms to name the clouds.

The Four Types of Clouds

NAME	*LATIN FOR*	*DESCRIPTION*
1. Cumulus	"heap" or "pile"	Appear as fluffy "heaps" of white cotton "piled" atop a relatively flat bottom. These clouds are low-altitude clouds: 1,500 ft. to 10,000 ft.

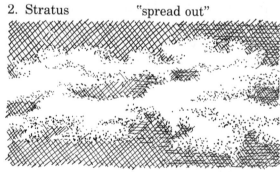

2. Stratus	"spread out"	Are flat on the top and bottom; they are "spread out" over great distances and produce cloudy days. These clouds are low-altitude clouds: near the surface to 3,000 ft.

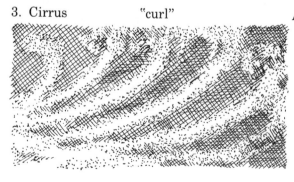

3. Cirrus	"curl"	Appear as if someone spread "curls" of cotton across the sky. These "curls" are sometimes referred to as "mare's tails," and consist of ice crystals. These clouds are high-altitude clouds: 16,500 ft. to 45,000 ft.

(Continued)

LIST 7–10. (Continued)

4. Nimbus   "rainstorm"   Storm clouds. Combination clouds, cumulo-nimbus, are the towering thunderhead clouds with dark bottoms that bring thunderstorms and hail.

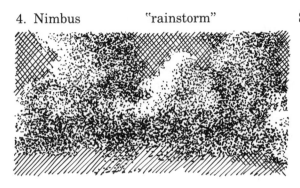

"Combination" Clouds

Altocumulus	"high" + "heaps"	Are high-altitude heaps of white or gray clouds; usually light intermittent rain or snow; usually bring light, continuous precipitation
Cirrocumulus	"heaps of curls"	Are high, thin clouds looking like small heaps of cotton; fair weather clouds
Cirrostratus	"curl" + "spread out"	Are spread-out, curls of white; can produce a halo around the moon or sun; often a sign of approaching bad weather
Cumulonimbus	"heap" + "storm"	Are frequently accompanied by heavy showers, lightning, gusty winds, and sometimes hail
Fractocumulus	"broken up" + "heaps"	Are broken up or torn (tattered) heaps of white fluff
Nimbostratus	"spread-out rain"	Are dark gray clouds spread across the sky; caused by precipitation; often accompanied by restricted visibility

LIST 7–11. WEATHER SYMBOLS

Weather symbols are plotted on maps and the information is used by the meteorologist to forecast the weather. With the development of computers and telecommunications, weather symbols have been coded for transmission by telecommunications and decoding on maps. Modern-day meteorologists are spared the chore of plotting all of the symbols and are able to invest their time in interpreting the data to predict the weather and issue any warnings, watches, or advisories necessary.

Some of these symbols can be seen on weather maps displayed on weather reports given over television and published in newspapers.

SYMBOL	*DESCRIPTION*	*SYMBOL*	*DESCRIPTION*
∞	Haze	☰	Fog
⧖	Well-developed dust devils	☰	Fog, patches
⌐↓	Thunderstorms	⧖↓	Heavy thunderstorms with hail
▽	Squall(s)	)(	Funnel cloud(s)
•▽	Rain showers	••	Light rain
•••∴	Moderate rain	∴•	Heavy rain
ꜛ ꜛ	Drizzle	◐∿	Freezing rain
∿	Freezing drizzle	△	Ice pellets, sleet
✳▽	Snow flurries	✳ ✳	Light snow

(Continued)

LIST 7–11. (Continued)

SYMBOL	DESCRIPTION	SYMBOL	DESCRIPTION
✳ ✳ ✳	Moderate snow	✳ ✳✳ ✳	Heavy snow
←——→	Ice needles	↑→	Drifting snow
(L)	Low-pressure center	(H)	High-pressure center
▲▲▲▲	Cold front (surface)	⌒⌒⌒	Warm front (surface)
△△△△	Cold front (aloft)	⌒⌒⌒⌒	Warm front (aloft)
▼●▼●	Stationary front (surface)	●●▲●	Occluded front (surface)

LIST 7–12. THE STATION MODEL AND EXPLANATION*

Computers and/or meteorologists at central weather stations receive weather data which are charted on one of two basic types of weather maps: surface charts and upper air charts. Surface charts include: wind speed and direction, amount of clouds, temperature, visibility, present weather, dew point, cloud type, height of cloud base, pressure, pressure change in the last three hours, pressure tendency, amounts of cloud, inches of precipitation in the last three hours. All of this information is charted on a weather map in a space no larger than a dime, for each sending station. A meteorologist then draws isobars, marks positions of fronts, and analyzes all of the data to forecast the weather.

The Station Model

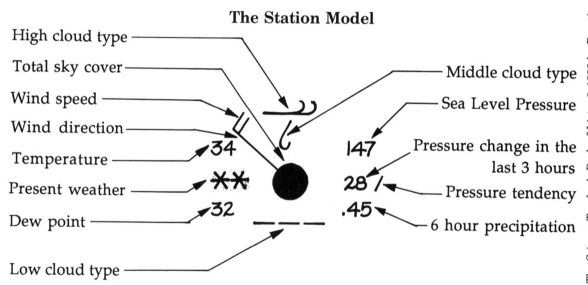

The Science Teacher's Book of Lists, © 1993 by Prentice Hall

(Continued)

*Source: Aviation Weather Services AC 00-45C, U.S. Department of Transportation, Federal Aviation Administration, Office of Flight Operations and U.S. Department of Commerce, NOAA, National Weather Service, Washington, D.C., revised 1985.

LIST 7–12. (Continued)

Explanation of the Station Model

1. Total sky cover: overcast
2. Temperature: 34°F, dew point: 32°F
3. Wind: blowing **from** the northwest at 20 knots relative to true north. Wind speeds are in knots and are indicated as:

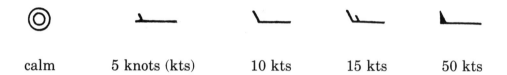

| calm | 5 knots (kts) | 10 kts | 15 kts | 50 kts |

A circle around the station means calm. A half-flag has a value of 5 knots, a full-flag 10 knots, and a pennant 50 knots. These are used in an appropriate combination to represent wind speed; e.g. two pennants indicated wind speed of 100 knots. Wind direction stated is the direction **from which the wind is blowing.** For example:

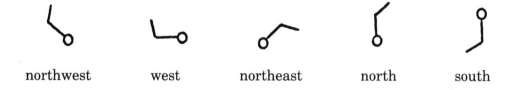

| northwest | west | northeast | north | south |

4. Present weather: continuous light snow
5. Predominant low, mid, high cloud report: fractostratus or fractocumulus of bad weather, altocumulus in patches, dense cirrus
6. Sea level pressure: 1013.4 millibars (mb). Always shown as three digits to the nearest tenth of a millibar. For 1000 mb or greater, prefix a 10 to the three digits. For less than 1000 mb prefix a 9 to the three digits.

    | 108 = 1010.8 mb | 888 = 988.8 mb |
    | 225 = 1022.5 mb | 961 = 996.1 mb |

7. Pressure change in the past 3 hours: increased steadily or unsteadily by 2.8 mb. Actual change is in tenths of a millibar
8. 6-hour precipitation: 45 hundreds of an inch. Amount is given to the nearest hundredth of an inch

LIST 7–13. SKY COVER SYMBOLS

SYMBOL	*TOTAL SKY COVER*
○	No clouds, clear sky
◔	Less than $\frac{1}{10}$ or $\frac{1}{10}$
◔	$\frac{2}{10}$ or $\frac{3}{10}$
◕	$\frac{4}{10}$
◑	$\frac{5}{10}$
⊖	$\frac{6}{10}$
◕	$\frac{7}{10}$ to $\frac{8}{10}$ inclusive
⬤	$\frac{9}{10}$ or overcast with openings
⬤	Completely overcast
⊗	Sky obscured

LIST 7–14. CODES FOR WEATHER SYMBOLS
AND OBSTRUCTION TO VISION*

CODE	WEATHER	CODE	OBSTRUCTION TO VISION
T	Thunderstorm	BD	Blowing Dust
T+	Severe Thunderstorm	BN	Blowing Sand
A	Hail	BS	Blowing Snow
IC	Ice Crystals	BY	Blowing Spray
IP(W)	Ice Pellets (Showers)	K	Smoke
L	Drizzle	H	Haze
R	Rain	D	Dust
R W	Rain Showers	F	Fog
S	Snow	GF	Ground Fog
SG	Snow Grains	IF	Ice Fog
SP	Snow Pellets		
S W	Snow Showers		
ZL	Freezing Drizzle		
ZR	Freezing Rain		

*Source: Decoding Surface Weather Observations, U.S. Department of Commerce, National Oceanic and Atmospheric Administration, National Weather Service, WS Form TAB-0-1, revised 8-82.

The Science Teacher's Book of Lists, © 1993 by Prentice Hall

LIST 7–15. POETIC WEATHER PREDICTIONS

Fishermen, farmers, and sailors all need to know the weather. Before modern technology aided meteorologists, those who watched the weather noted patterns. Setting these patterns to sayings and poems made them easier to remember and useful for predictions. Here are some weather sayings:

Evening red, morning gray
Sets the traveler on his way;
Evening gray, morning red,
Brings down rain upon his head.

Red sky at morning,
Sailors take warning;
Red sky at night,
Sailor's delight.

Mares' tails and mackerel scales,
Make lofty ships carry low sails.

A ring around the sun or moon,
Brings rain or snow upon us soon.

When the wind veers toward the sun,
Trust it not for back 'twill run.

A cow with its tail to the west,
Makes the weather best.

When the glass falls low,
Prepare for a blow;
When it rises high,
Let all your kites fly.

When dew is on the grass,
Rain will never come to pass.

When the mist creeps up the hill,
Fisher, out and try your skill;
When the mist begins to nod,
Fisher then put up your rod.

Year of snow,
Crops will grow.

When the days begin to lengthen,
The cold begins to strengthen.

When the snow falls dry it means to
  lie;
But flakes light and soft bring rain oft.

Snow flakes increasing in size,
Expect a thaw soon.

If the robin sings in the bush
Then the weather will be coarse;
If the robin sings on the barn,
Then the weather will be warm.

When spiders weave their webs by
  noon,
Fine weather is coming soon.

If bees stay at home, rain will soon
  come;
If they fly away, fine will be the day.

Swallows fly high; clear blue sky;
Swallows fly low: rain we shall know.

When a squirrel eats nuts in a tree
Weather as warm as warm can be.

A rainbow in the morning
Is the shepherd's warning;
A rainbow at night
Is the shepherd's delight.

The higher the cloud,
the finer the weather.

Clouds look as if scratched by a hen,
Be ready to reef your top sails in.

If wooly fleeces spread the heavenly
  way,
Be sure no rain disturbs the summer's
  day.

When clouds appear like rocks and
  towers,
The earth's refreshed with frequent
  showers.

Wind in the west,
Weather at its best.

Clear moon,
Frost soon.

(Continued)

LIST 7–15. (Continued)

Red moon doth blow;
White moon neither rain nor snow.

Year of snow,
Fruit will grow.

When a cow endeavors to scratch its ear,
It means a shower is very near.
When it thumps its ribs and tail,
Look out for thunder, lightning, hail.

LIST 7–16. WEATHER SAYINGS

The locust sings when it is to be hot and clear.

As long as the sun shines one does not ask for the moon. (*Russian proverb*)

The sky is the daily bread of our lives. (*Emerson*)

The sky is the same color wherever you go. (*Russian proverb*)

A man should learn to sail in all winds. (*Italian proverb*)

The morning steals upon the night, melting the darkness. (*Shakespeare*)

If you walk on snow, you cannot hide your footprints. (*Chinese proverb*)

When it rains, it rains on all alike.

Winter comes fast on the lazy. (*Irish proverb*)

Wide black bands on "wooly bear" caterpillars mean a hard winter is upon us.

The busier the squirrels, the harder the winter.

A storm is coming when winter birds are seen to be unusually busy feeding.

Some people are weather-wise, some are otherwise. (*Poore Richard's Almanack*)

What would have become of us had it pleased Providence to make the weather unchangeable? (*Sidney Smith*)

Lightning never strikes twice in the same place. (*Not true, incidentally!*)

Everybody talks about the weather, but nobody does anything about it.

April showers bring May flowers.

It never rains but it pours.

It's raining cats and dogs (or buckets).

Carry an umbrella and keep the rain away.

A little rain never hurt anybody.

A fair weather friend.

Every cloud engenders not a storm. (*Shakespeare*)

Sometime hath the brightest day a cloud. (*Shakespeare*)

Every cloud has a silver lining.

It's an ill wind that blows nobody good.

Time and tide wait for no man.

The Science Teacher's Book of Lists, © 1993 by Prentice Hall

AVIATION AND SPACE SCIENCE

LIST 8–1. FREQUENTLY USED
AIR AND SPACE TERMS

absolute magnitude—the magnitude a star would have if viewed from 10 parsecs, 32.6 light years

air pressure—the weight of air pushing against the earth's surface; this weight exerts a force of about 14.7 pounds per square inch (760 torr) at sea level; varies with humidity and altitude

albedo—the reflectivity or brightness of a celestial object such as a planet or moon

aperture—the unobstructed diameter of the mirror or objective in a telescope or in a pair of binoculars

apparent magnitude—the apparent visual brightness of a celestial body

artificial satellite—man-made object that is placed in orbit about a natural object in space

asteroids—chunks of rock, metal, and ice that orbit our sun, found mostly between Mars and Jupiter, varying in size from boulders to small moons; also called planetesimals or minor planets

astronaut—a space explorer

astronomical unit—unit for measuring distances in space, based on the distance from the earth to the sun, equal to 93 million miles (149.6 million km); abbreviated AU

astronomy—the study of the universe beyond Earth's atmosphere

aurora—the shifting, glowing lights seen over the polar regions caused when energized particles from the sun react with the particles in the Earth's upper atmosphere; the energized particles come from solar flares

axis—imaginary line about which an object spins

atmosphere—layer of gas that surrounds a celestial body

barometer—weather instrument that measures atmospheric pressure

binary star—a pair of stars that orbits about a common center of gravity; also called double stars

black dwarf—massive white dwarf star that has consumed its fuel and no longer gives off any light

black hole—a region of highly warped space-time, around a collapsed massive star, in which the gravitational field is so strong that not even light can escape

comet—an object made of ice, dust, and gas which orbits the sun with its tail of dust pointing away from the sun

conjunction—occurs when two or more planets appear close together in the sky

(Continued)

LIST 8–1. (Continued)

constellation—a group of stars that gives the appearance of a pattern when viewed from Earth; there are at least 88 named constellations

crater—a concave indentation in the surface of a planet or moon caused by the impact of a meteoroid

crust—the outermost layer of soil on a planet or moon

declination—the angular distance between a celestial object and the celestial equator

density—the proportion of mass to volume

eclipse—when one celestial body blocks the view of another, such as when the moon blocks our view of the sun during a solar eclipse

elliptical galaxy—a large group of stars that appears in the shape of an ellipse

first-quarter moon—the phase of the moon when it is one quarter of its orbit about the earth, resulting in only one half of its lighted surface facing the earth; See List 8–20, The Phases of the Moon

fission—a nuclear reaction in which nuclei are split, releasing enormous amounts of energy; fission and fusion reactions alternate on stars until all of their fuel is consumed

fusion—a nuclear reaction in which nuclei join together to form a larger nucleus; fission and fusion reactions alternate on stars until all of their fuel is consumed

full moon—the phase of the moon when all of the lighted half of the moon is facing the earth

galaxy—an assemblage of millions to hundreds of billions of stars, nebulae, gas, and dust; galaxies rotate around their centers and have been observed in shapes of spirals, spheres, and ellipsoids; galaxy clusters seem to be the largest-known structures in the universe

Galilean satellites—Jupiter's first four moon's discovered, by Galileo: Io, Europa, Ganymede, and Callisto

gravity—the force of attraction between objects

Hubble classification—a system of grouping galaxies according to their shape, developed by Edwin Hubble

inner planets—the four planets closest to the sun: Mercury, Venus, Earth, and Mars

last-quarter moon—phase of the moon when it is three-quarters of its orbit about the earth and only one half of its lighted surface faces the earth; See List 8–20, The Phases of the Moon

lens—clear, curved glass that bends light; used in optical telescopes and binoculars to magnify distant heavenly objects

(Continued)

LIST 8–1. (Continued)

light—visible form of electromagnetic radiation

light year—the distance light travels in a vacuum in one year; about 10^{13} km or 6 trillion miles; the standard unit of distance used by astronomers

lunar eclipse—when the sun, earth, and moon are aligned in such away that the moon is blocked from view on Earth by Earth's shadow

lunar phases—the apparent changing shapes of the moon that can be viewed from Earth (caused by the amount of the lighted half of the moon that is visible from Earth); see List 8–20, The Phases of the Moon

magnetic field—the lines of magnetic force around a planet or moon caused by magnetic deposits on the planet or moon

mass—the measure of the amount of matter in an object

matter—anything that has mass and takes up space

moon—natural satellites that orbit planets

meteor—a streak of light seen in the sky caused by the fiery, atmospheric friction from entry of a meteoroid through Earth's atmosphere; commonly called a shooting star or fireball

meteorite—the portion of a meteoroid that has survived the atmospheric friction and crashed into Earth's surface

meteoroid—small particles of interplanetary objects in space

Milky Way—light from thousands of stars that are located along the main plane of our galaxy

nebula—an enormous cloud of interstellar dust and gases

neutron star—small dense star that resulted from a massive star which exploded as a supernova

new moon—the beginning of the moon's monthly orbit around the earth when the dark side of the moon faces the earth; see List 8–20, The Phases of the Moon

nonmetal—element having properties opposite of a metal

nova—a star which suddenly flares up to 100,000 times its brilliance before fading away over a period of months or years

observatories—places that house optical and radio telescopes used by astronomers for scientific observations and research of space

objective—the main lens or lenses of a telescope or binoculars

orbit—the elliptical, closed path that one celestial body travels about another

outer planets—the five planets farthest from the sun: Jupiter, Saturn, Uranus, Neptune, and Pluto

planet—large, heavenly, nonluminous body which revolves about a star

(Continued)

The Science Teacher's Book of Lists, © 1993 by Prentice Hall

LIST 8-1. (Continued)

planetariums—places that house equipment that simulates the movements of the universe

planetesimal—synonym for asteroid

pulsar—rapidly-spinning neutron star which gives off regular bursts of radiation

quasar—(from *quasi*-stell*ar*) distant and luminous object probably about the size of a large star, which gives off energy equal to that of thousands of galaxies, believed to be at the core of active galaxies

radiation—movement of energy in the form of rays and waves

radio telescope—large dish-like instrument that gathers radio waves from distant objects in space

rays—lines of impact emanating from a crater; also thin beams of radiation coming from a source

red giant—after about 10 million years, a yellow star enlarges and cools down, forming a red giant star; thus, red stars are older, larger, and cooler than yellow stars

revolution—the movement of one body, in an elliptical path, around another

rocket—engine for propelling spacecraft; capable of exiting the earth's gravitational pull and maneuvering in space

rotation—the spin of an object about its center line, the axis; celestial bodies spin on their axes

satellite—any small body orbiting a larger one

shooting star—popular term for a meteor

solar eclipse—when the earth, sun, and moon are aligned in such a way that the moon blocks all or most of the sun from view on part of the earth

solar flare—an eruption on the surface of the sun

solar system—a system of planets, comets, satellites, and debris that orbits about a star

solar wind—the stream of energized particles given off by the sun

sound—a form of energy which can travel through solids, liquids, and gases, producing vibrations that can be heard; it cannot travel through a vacuum (and therefore cannot be heard in space)

space probe—a spacecraft, without humans, which gathers data about objects in space

space shuttle—a spacecraft capable of carrying people and equipment into space and returning to Earth

(Continued)

LIST 8–1. (Continued)

space station—a spacecraft that stays in space for long periods of time, orbiting Earth or other heavenly body

spectroscope—instrument used for viewing the spectrum of a light source directly

spectroscopy—the study of the spectra

spectrum—the bands of colors or wavelengths obtained when light passes through a prism or drop of moisture

spiral galaxy—galaxy that extends "arms" from a central region as it spins about its axis

star—celestial object composed mostly of hydrogen and helium that shines by producing its own light through nuclear conversion of hydrogen to helium and back to hydrogen; a self-luminous sphere of gas

sunspot—magnetic storm on the sun; it appears as a dark region on the sun because it is cooler than the surrounding area

supernova—the explosion of a high-mass star

telescope—optical instrument composed of lenses, which makes objects appear closer and brighter, used for observing celestial bodies

terminator—the division between the light and dark sides of a planet or satellite

theory—an idea that is supported by scientific evidence

temperature—a measure, in degrees, of the intensity of heat

thermometer—instrument for measuring the intensity of heat

universe—everything that exists: matter, radiation, and space

white dwarf—an old, dense star that results after a red giant star consumes its fuel over a long period of time

zenith—the point in the sky directly above the observer

zodiacal light—a faint glow of light caused by dust in the plane of the Earth's orbit

LIST 8–2. SELECTED EVENTS IN BALLOON TRAVEL

YEAR **EVENT**

1783   *October 15:* F.P. de Rosier ascended to 84 ft. in a tethered hot-air balloon built by Montgolfier brothers, France.

       November 21: de Rosier and Marquis d'Arlandes in a similar balloon made a free flight at Chateau La Muette, Bois de Boulogne; 25 minutes, $5\frac{1}{2}$ miles.

1784   Madame Thible, first woman in free flight, with Monsieur Fleurant at Lyon, France. Montgolfier balloon reached height of 8500 feet.

1836   *November 7–8:* First long-distance flight. Hydrogen balloon from Vauxhall Gardens, London, England to near Weilberg in Duchy of Nassau, Germany, 480 miles; by Charles Green, Robert Holland, and Monck Mason.

1859   *July 2:* First long flight in the United States: St. Louis, Missouri to Henderson, New York; 1120 miles, by J. C. Wise, J. La Mountain, and O. A. Gager.

1861   *October 1:* Army of the Potomac (USA) had five balloons (two more in 1862) for use in reconnaissance and to direct artillery fire. Thaddeus S. C. Lowe was chief aeronaut. Their use was abandoned in 1863.

1870   Balloons were used in the Franco-Prussian war, 1870–71.

1906   *September 30:* First international balloon race for the Gordon Bennett Trophy. Sixteen balloons started from Tuileries, France. Won by Lt. Frank P. Lahm, U.S. Army, who landed near Whitby, Yorkshire, England; 402 miles.

1961   *May 4:* World record for altitude in a manned free balloon is by M. D. Ross and V. A. Prather over Gulf of Mexico; 113,739.9 ft.

1978   First crossing of the Atlantic ocean by a gas balloon was by B. L. Abruzzo, M. L. Anderson, and L. M. Newman; 3107.62 miles in 137 hr. 5 min., 50 sec.

1980   World altitude record for manned hot-air balloon is by B. J. Notton at Longmont, Colorado; 55,135 ft.

1987   Largest hot-air balloon ever flown was the *Virgin Atlantic Flyer* with a volume of 2.13 million cu. ft.; diameter, 166 ft.; height, 180 ft. 5 in. This balloon made the first trans-Atlantic crossing by hot-air balloon on July 2–3, 1987 from Sugarloaf, Maine, to Limavardy, Northern Ireland; crew was Richard Branson and Per Lindstrand

LIST 8–3. SELECTED EVENTS
IN AIRSHIP TRAVEL

Airships, or dirigibles, are gas-filled, sausage-shaped balloons which were designed to provide control of direction and speed of flight. They may be nonrigid or have an internal rigid framework. The gases most commonly used were hydrogen and helium.

YEAR	*EVENT*
1852	*September 24:* The first powered, manned flight in an airship was by Henry Gifford from the Paris Hippodrome to Trappes, powered by a steam engine; 17 miles; average speed 5 mph.
1884	*August 9:* The first fully controlled powered flight was in a ship, *La France*, driven by an electric powered propeller, on a circular, 5-mile course from Chalais-Meudon, France, by C. Renard and A. Krebs, French Corps of Engineers; 23 min., maximum speed 14.5 mph.
1900	*July 2:* First Zeppelin flight was by Count F. von Zeppelin with five passengers from Lake Constance, Germany; 20 min; ship was 420 ft. by 38 ft., powered by two Daimler engines of 16 hp each.
1903	*November 12:* First fully controlled air journey in history was by ship designed and flown by Lebaudy brothers; 37 miles from Moisson to Champ-de-Mars, Paris.
1909	*October 16:* First commercial airline begun by Zeppelin in Germany in 1910–1913; carried over 34,000 passengers between major German cities.
1914–18	Dirigibles were used for military operations in World War I by Germany, Britain, and the USA.
1919	First two-way crossing of the Atlantic by any aircraft was by the British ship R-34, commanded by G. H. Scott with a crew of 30. July 2–4 westward, July 9–13 eastward; East Fortune, Scotland to New York; return to Pullham, Norfolk, England; 6330 miles in 183 hr. and 8 min.
1921	*December 1:* First airship to use helium was the Goodyear C-7 of the United States.
1937	*May 6:* Major airship disaster was the loss of the German *Hindenberg* by fire as it approached the moorings at Lakehurst, New Jersey, after a flight from Frankfurt, Germany; 35 of 97 occupants were killed. This tragedy marked the end of the commercial dirigible industry.

The Science Teacher's Book of Lists, © 1993 by Prentice Hall

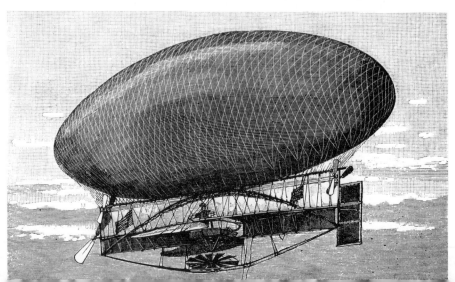

LIST 8–4. GLIDERS AND KITES

Various kites and gliders were the subjects of experiments in the nineteenth and twentieth centuries.

YEAR	EVENT
1853	George Cayley, an English engineer, built the first craft that was constructed to glide with the wind and lift with updrafts, later called a glider. It flew a distance of 500 yards.
1891–96	O. Lilienthal of Germany built and flew successfully a craft of the hang-glider type near Berlin, and P. S. Pilcher in Great Britain flew related gliders of his own construction.
1900–02	Orville and Wilbur Wright in the U.S. flew gliders which formed the basis of later work on powered flight.
1944	Large numbers of gliders were used to transport men and equipment across enemy lines in World War II.
1972	*April 25:* The greatest straight line distance in a single-seat glider was made by H. Grosse of West Germany: 907 miles.
1983	*April 25:* The greatest goal-and-return distance in a single-seat glider was made by Thomas Knauff of the U.S. in the *Nimbus III*: 1023 miles.
1986	*June 2:* The greatest distance for an unpowered hang-glider was made by R. Haney of the U.S.; 199.75 miles.

The Science Teacher's Book of Lists, © 1993 by Prentice Hall

LIST 8–5. POWERED AIRCRAFT

Before the Wright brothers, several airplanes were flown but for some the records are not fully documented. The Wright brothers were the first to perform sustained, powered flight with directional control. Control was by wing-warping.

YEAR	EVENT
1903	*December 17:* Orville Wright flew an engine-powered plane at Kitty Hawk, North Carolina for 120 ft. On the same day another flight of 852 ft. was made.
1908	*May 14:* First passenger in a powered airplane was C. W. Furnas with Wilbur Wright as pilot; 2.5 miles.
1908	*June 20:* The first American other than the Wright brothers to fly was Glenn H. Curtiss in his *June Bug*; 1266 ft. On July 4 he flew 5090 ft.
1908	*September 21:* Most important endurance flight to this date was by Wilbur Wright for $41\frac{1}{3}$ miles.
1909	*July 25:* First person to fly the English Channel was Louis Bleriot from Les Baraques to Dover Castle in his Bleriot XI monoplane.
1909	From 1909 on, plane building and flights in many countries took place with increasing distances and times. Mail and passenger services were begun in several locations.
1911	*September 17–November 5:* C. P. Rodgers flew from New York to Pasadena, California, in a series of hops in a Burgess-Wright biplane.
1914–18	Fighter planes played an important role in combat during World War I.
1923	*May 2–3:* The first nonstop crossing of the United States was by O. G. Kelly and M. J. Macready in a Fokker T-2 from Long Island, New York to San Diego, California; 2516 miles in 26 hrs., 50 min.
1924	*April 6–September 28:* First round-the-world flight. Four Douglas DWCs set out and two made the trip from Seattle, Washington. Crew of the *Chicago* was L. H. Smith and L. P. Arnold; crew of the *New Orleans* was E. Nelson and J. Harding, Jr.; 27,553 miles in 175 days; flying time 371 hrs., 11 min.
1926	*May 9:* First flight over the North Pole was by R. E. Bird and F. Bennett in a Fokker FVIIA-3m; 1600 miles.
1927	*May 20–21:* Nonstop solo flight over the North Atlantic from Long Island, New York to Paris, France by Charles Lindbergh in monoplane, *Spirit of St. Louis*; 3610 miles; 33 hrs., 39 min.
1931	*June 23–July 1:* Record round-the-world flight in 8 days, 15 hrs., 51 min. by Wiley Post and Harold Gatty in a Lockheed Vega from New York.
1932	*May 20–21:* First solo flight over the North Atlantic by a woman was by Amelia Earhart from Harbor Grace, Newfoundland, to Londonderry, Northern Ireland in a Lockheed Vega monoplane; 15 hrs., 18 min.
1933	*July 15–22:* First solo around-the-world airplane flight was made by Wiley Post; 7 days, 18 hrs., 49 min.
1934–	During World War II there was extensive development and use of fighter planes, transport planes, bombers, and surveillance planes for military purposes. This period is the subject of numerous specialized books.

(Continued)

LIST 8–5. (Continued)

YEAR	*EVENT*
1940	*May 21:* First successful flight of a single-rotor helicopter was by Igor Sikorsky at Stratford, Connecticut.
1942	*October 1:* First jet airplane built in USA by Bell Aircraft Co., flown by R. M. Stanley at Muroc Dry Lake, California.
1947	*October 17:* First supersonic flight was by C. E. Yeager of the U.S. Air Force in a rocket-powered Bell X-I.
1952	*May 2:* First turbojet airliner to enter regular passenger service was the deHaviland Comet I (G-ALYP) by British Overseas Airways between London and Johannesburg, South Africa.
1953	*November 20:* First flight at twice the speed of sound (1327 mph) made by S. Crossfield in a Douglass D-558-2 Skyrocket.
1959	*October:* First round-the-world passenger service begun by Pan American Airways with the Boeing 707, *Clipper Windward.*
1970–72	Jumbo jets joined the commercial air fleets: Boeing 747 in 1970; Douglas DC-10 in 1971; Lockheed L-1011 in 1972.
1969–76	World's first supersonic commercial transport for regular passenger services were the British Aircraft Corp./Aerospatiale Concorde, which on March 2 and April 9, 1969 began extensive flight testing. First passenger services were operated on January 2, 1976; BAC from London to Bahrain, and Concorde from Paris to Rio de Janeiro.

LIST 8–6. THE NINE KNOWN PLANETS IN OUR SOLAR SYSTEM

Physical Description of the Nine Known Planets in Our Solar System

NAME OF PLANET	DISTANCE FROM SUN (MILLIONS OF KM)	DIAMETER (IN KM)	NO. OF MOONS	HAS RINGS	MAIN GASES IN ATMOSPHERE
Mercury	58	4,878	0	No	Helium, hydrogen, oxygen
Venus	108	12,100	0	No	Carbon dioxide, nitrogen
Earth	150	12,756	1	No	Nitrogen, oxygen
Mars	228	6,787	2	No	Carbon dioxide, nitrogen
Jupiter	778	142,800	16	Yes	Hydrogen, helium, ammonia
Saturn	1,427	120,000	18	Yes	Hydrogen, helium, ammonia
Uranus	2,897	51,200	15	Yes	Hydrogen, helium, methane
Neptune	4,520	48,600	8	Yes	Hydrogen, helium, methane
Pluto	5,900	2,300	1	No	Methane

(Continued)

LIST 8–6. (Continued)

TILT OF AXIS	MAGNETIC FIELD	SURFACE MATERIAL	FAMOUS FEATURE	DISCOVERED
Near 0°	Weak	Rock and dust of basalt	About size of Earth's moon	Pre-history
3°	None	Rock of granite	Second brightest object in our night sky	Pre-history
23° 27′	Yes	Water and soil containing granite	Home to plant and animal life	Pre-history
25° 12′	None	Rock and dust of basalt	The red planet "canals"	Pre-history
3° 5′	Yes 15 × Earth's	Gaseous	Giant Red Spot	Pre-history
26° 44′	Yes 70% of Earth's	Gaseous	Rings	Pre-history
97° 55′	Yes 55° from spin axis	Gaseous	Rotates on its side compared to Earth	1781
28° 48′	Yes 50° from spin axis	Gaseous	Great Dark Spot	1846
?	?	Frozen methane	Orbit overlaps Neptune's	1930

LIST 8–7. PLANETARY TIME: ROTATION AND REVOLUTION

The time that it takes a planet to turn or rotate once on its axis is called a day. Earth takes about 24 hours to turn once or rotate on its axis.

The time that it takes a planet to revolve or orbit its sun is called a year. It takes Earth about 365 days to orbit the sun. Thus, one year on Earth takes about 365 days.

Planetary Time

PLANET	ROTATION LENGTH IN EARTH TIME	REVOLUTION LENGTH IN EARTH TIME
Mercury	58.7 days	88.0 days
Venus	243.0 days	224.7 days
Earth	23.9 hours	365.3 days
Mars	24.6 hours	687.0 days
Jupiter	9.9 hours	11.9 years
Saturn	10.7 hours	29.5 years
Uranus	17.2 hours	84.0 years
Neptune	17.0 hours	164.8 years
Pluto	6.4 days	248.5 years

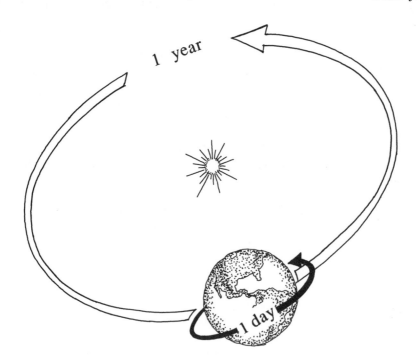

LIST 8–8. MASS, VOLUME, DENSITY, SURFACE GRAVITY, ESCAPE VELOCITY, AND ALBEDO OF THE NINE PLANETS IN OUR SOLAR SYSTEM

PLANET	MASS EARTH = 1	VOLUME EARTH = 1	DENSITY WATER = 1	SURFACE GRAVITY EARTH g = 1	ESCAPE VELOCITY MILES/SEC.	ALBEDO*
Mercury	0.06	0.06	5.43	0.37	2.2	.06
Venus	0.81	0.86	0.89	0.88	6.3	.76
Earth	1.00	1.00	5.52	1.00	7.0	.36
Mars	0.12	0.15	3.93	0.38	3.1	.16
Jupiter	317.8	1,323.00	1.33	2.51	37.7	.73
Saturn	95.16	752	0.71	1.07	22.4	.76
Uranus	14.55	64	1.31	0.93	13.1	.93
Neptune	17.23	54	1.77	1.23	14.3	.84
Pluto	0.002	0.01	1.1	0.04	1.9	.14

*Albedo is the reflectivity of an object. It is expressed as a ratio between the amount of light reflected from an object compared to the amount of light that falls on it. Thus, Mercury reflects 6% of the light that falls on it and Earth reflects 36%.

LIST 8–9. ABOUT THE NINE PLANETS IN OUR SOLAR SYSTEM

Mercury

- Has an ancient, heavily cratered surface, resembling that of our moon.
- Has huge cliffs, 2 km (1 mi.) high and 1500 km (932 mi.) long, crisscrossing the planet's surface.
- Has a crater, Caloris Basin, that is wider than the distance between New York City and San Francisco.
- Has temperatures on the sunlit side to 510°C (950°F) and on the dark side to −210°C (−346°F).
- Takes 59 Earth days to make one rotation on its axis.
- Spins at a rate of about 10 km (about 6 mi.) per hour.
- Appears to have a crust of light silicate rock, similar to that of Earth.

Venus

- Resembles Earth in size and density more than any other planet.
- Has surface temperatures that reach 482°C (900°F, hot enough to melt lead).
- Has evidence of two active volcanic areas.
- Has a mountain higher than Mount Everest, Earth's highest mountain.
- Has clouds composed of sulfuric acid.
- Cloud circulation is from east to west and reaches speeds of 362 km or (225 mi.) per hour.
- Has many electrical storms.

Earth

- Has an intense radiation zone, the Van Allen radiation belts, surrounding it.
- Has an upper atmosphere, which expands during the day and contracts at night and is affected by changes in solar activity, all of which affect the weather.
- Is the only planet known to have life in any form.
- Its rapid spin and molten nickel-iron core produce an extensive magnetic field, which, coupled with the atmosphere, protects us from harmful radiation coming from nearby stars including our sun.

(Continued)

The Science Teacher's Book of Lists, © 1993 by Prentice Hall

LIST 8–9. (Continued)

Mars

- Has a red landscape.
- Has temperatures of $-21°C$ $(-6°F)$ in summer and $-124°C$ $(-191°F)$, during winter.
- Possesses an atmosphere that is primarily made up of carbon dioxide with small percentages of nitrogen, oxygen, and argon, with trace amounts of krypton and xenon.
- Possesses about 0.0001 as much water in its atmosphere as Earth does, which can condense and form clouds that swirl about the upper atmosphere and form fog in valleys.
- Has towering volcanoes.
- Has two irregularly shaped moons with cratered surfaces.

Jupiter

- Is a whirling ball of liquid hydrogen, topped with a colorful atmosphere of mostly hydrogen and helium with small percentages of methane, ammonia, ethane, acetylene, phosphine, germanium tetrahydride, and possibly hydrogen cyanide.
- Has a giant red spot, which is a tremendous atmospheric storm, rotating counterclockwise, similar to a hurricane on Earth.
- Is the largest planet in the solar system.
- Rotates once every 9 hours, 55 minutes.
- Requires almost 12 Earth years to complete one revolution around the sun.
- Has rings; sixteen moons and many other moons suspected.

Saturn

- Is composed mostly of hydrogen.
- Has thousands of ringlets circling it.
- Has countless rings made up of low-density particles, which orbit the equator. These particles vary in size from dust particles to boulders and are composed of ice and frosted rocks.
- Has at least eighteen moons with many more suspected.

Uranus

- Has a summer and winter that each last 21 Earth years.
- Requires 42 Earth years to spin once on its axis.

(Continued)

LIST 8–9. (Continued)

- Has an atmosphere that contains methane, which gives it its greenish color.
- Has a system of rings discovered in 1977.
- Has fifteen moons.

Neptune

- Has roughly the same mass and diameter as Uranus.
- Has an atmosphere that contains methane, which gives it its greenish color.
- Has atmosphere composed of hydrogen and helium.
- Requires 165 Earth years to complete one revolution around the sun.
- Has a system of rings and at least eight moons with many more suspected.

Pluto

- Orbits the sun in such a way that it travels farther from the sun than any of the planets (making it the ninth planet) and periodically orbits inside Neptune's orbit (making it the eighth planet).
- Travels in an orbit that is at times well above and below the plane of the orbits of the other eight planets.
- Has been calculated to have a diameter of about 3,000 km (1,864 mi.), which is roughly that of our moon.
- Appears to have a surface covered with solid methane.
- Is thought, by some scientists, to have been a moon of Neptune.
- Has at least one moon.

LIST 8–10. MANY MOONS

There are many moons, or natural satellites, in our solar system. Earth has one moon revolving around it. On evenings when there is a full moon, moonlight shimmers on bodies of water and reflects off snow covered meadows, treating viewers to wondrous sights. Earth's moon, like all moons, is a heavenly body that revolves around a planet reflecting starlight. Moons do not produce and give off light; rather they reflect light from a star. Earth's moon reflects light from the sun.

Some planets have no moon, some have one or more moons, and some have moonlets, very small moons. What a sight a moonlit night must be on a multiple-moon planet! Scientists number moons as they are discovered and give them interesting names after their discovery is confirmed. The official name is approved by the International Astronomical Union. As new probes view planets from different angles, new moons and moonlets may be discovered.

NAME OF PLANET	NUMBER OF MOONS	NAME OF MOONS
Mercury	0	
Venus	0	
Earth	1	Moon
Mars	2	Phobos, Deimos
Jupiter	16	Metis, Adrastea, Amalthea, Thebe, Io, Europa, Ganymede, Callisto, Leda, Himalia, Lysithea, Elara, Ananke, Carme, Pasiphae, Sinope, others suspected
Saturn	18	Atlas, 1980S27, 1980S26, Janus, Epimetheus, Mimas, Enceladus, Tethys, Telesto, Calypso, Dione, Dione B, Rhea, Titan, Hyperion, Iapetus, Phoebe, 1981S13, others suspected
Uranus	15	Miranda, Ariel, Umbriel, Titania, Oberon, Puck, Belinda, Cressida, Portia, Rosalind, Desdemona, Juliet, Bianca, Ophelia, Cordelia
Neptune	8	Triton, Nereid, 1989N1, 1989N2, 1989N3, 1989N4, 1989N5, 1989N6, many others suspected
Pluto	1	Charon

LIST 8–11. THE CONSTELLATIONS[a]

Northern

NAME	FIGURE	NAME	FIGURE
Andromeda	chained lady	Lacerta	lizard
Aquila	eagle	Leo minor	lion cub
Auriga	charioteer	Lynx	lynx
Boötes	herdsman	Lyra	harp or lyre
Camelopardalis	giraffe	Ophiuchus	man holding serpent
Canes venatici	hunting dogs		
Cassiopeia	lady in the chair	Pegasus	winged horse
Cepheus	Ethiopian king	Perseus	Perseus holding the head of Medusa
Coma berenices	Berenice's hair		
Corona borealis	northern crown	Sagitta	arrow
Cygnus	swan	Serpens	serpent borne by Ophiuchus
Delphinus	dolphin		
Draco	dragon	Triangulum	triangle
Equuleus	colt	Ursa major[b]	great bear
Hercules	kneeling man; Hercules	Ursa minor[c]	little bear
		Vulpecula	little fox

Zodiacal[d]

NAME	FIGURE	NAME	FIGURE
Aquarius (Oct.)	water carrier	Libra (June)	balance
Aries (Dec.)	ram	Pisces (Nov.)	fish
Cancer (Mar.)	crab	Sagittarius (Aug.)	archer
Capricornus (Sept.)	goat	Scorpius (July)	scorpion
Gemini (Feb.)	twins	Taurus (Jan.)	bull
Leo (Apr.)	lion	Virgo (June)	virgin

[a]Constellations are groups of stars that appear to be closely associated in the sky but which may be at greatly varying distances from the observer. Since ancient times they have been imagined to depict various forms and have been assigned names, many of mythological origin. Names in modern usage are given in the table.

[b]The Great Bear is also known as the Big Dipper or the Drinking Gourd. The two stars on the lip side of the dipper form an imaginary line which leads to the *north polar star*, Polaris.

[c]The Little Bear is also known as the Little Dipper. The outermost star in its handle is Polaris.

[d]The zodiacal constellations appear in the ecliptic, a zone in the sky within which lie the paths of the moon, sun and principal planets. In the table are given the months within which the constellations appear at the meridian (an imaginary line overhead from north to south) at 9:00 P.M. Because of the gradual shift in the angle of the earth's axis of rotation with respect to the plane of its orbit (precession), the position of the constellations and the Signs of the Zodiac now differ by about one month (30° of arc in 2150 years) from their original observed positions. For example, Aries and its sign were assigned to the period of March and arose on the horizon with the sun at that time. Today, Aries is still retained in astrology (a pseudo science) as the constellation for March, even though it rises in April and the constellation actually arising with the sun in March is Pisces. There has been a corresponding shift of all the other Zodiacal constellations. There will be another shift of one month (30°) in the next 2150 years.

(Continued)

LIST 8–11. (Continued)

Southern

NAME	FIGURE	NAME	FIGURE
Antlia	pump (for ship)	Lupus	wolf held by hand of centaurus
Apus	bird of paradise		
Ara	altar	Mensa	table mountain; mesa
Caelum	graving tool		
Canis major	great dog	Microscopium	microscope
Canis minor	little dog	Monoceros	unicorn
Carina	keel (of ship)	Musca	the fly
Centaurus	centaur	Norma	square (figure)
Cetus	whale (sea monster)	Octans	octant
Chamaeleon	chameleon	Orion	hunter
Circinus	drawing compasses	Pavo	peacock
Columbia	dove	Phoenix	a phoenix
Corona austrina	Southern crown	Pictor	painter's easel
Corvus	crow; raven	Piscis austrinus	Southern fish
Crater	cup	Puppis	stern (of ship)
Crux	Southern cross	Pyxis	mariner's compass
Dorado	swordfish	Reticulum	rhomboidal net
Eridanus	river	Sculptor	sculptor's workshop
Fornax	chemical furnace	Scutum	a shield
Grus	crane (a bird)	Sextans	sextant
Horologium	clock	Telescopium	telescope
Hydra	water serpent (f.)	Triangulum Australe	Southern triangle
Hydrus	water serpent (m.)	Tucana	toucan (a bird)
Indus	the Indian	Vela	sails (of ships)
Lepus	hare	Volans	flying fish

LIST 8–12. CLASSIFICATION OF STARS BY COLOR AND TEMPERATURE

Most stars are classified into one of seven groups according to their color spectrum, which is caused by the temperatures in the star's atmosphere. Type "O" stars are the hottest and type "M" stars are the coolest.

Classification of Stars

CLASS	APPROX. TEMP. IN °C	APPROX. TEMP. IN °F	COLOR	EXAMPLE
O	35,000–40,000	63,000–90,000	Blue	Alnilam, Iota Orionis
B	11,000–35,000	20,000–63,000	Blue	Rigel, Spica
A	7,500–11,000	13,500–20,000	White	Sirius, Vega, Castor
F	6,000–7,500	11,000–13,500	Yellowish white	Procyon, Canopis
G	5,100–6,000	9,200–11,000	Yellow	Sun, Capella
K	3,600–5,100	6,500–9,200	Orange	Arcturus, Albebanan
M	2,000–3,600	3,000–6,500	Red	Betelgeuse, Antares, Benard's star

Mnemonic for the seven star groups: "O, Be A Fine Girl Kiss Me."

LIST 8–13. LIFE CYCLES OF TWO TYPES OF STARS

Scientists theorize that stars develop and disappear through a process consisting of stages. Despite the fact that stars are not living organisms, scientists use terms such as *life cycle*, *birth*, and *death*. These terms are descriptive analogies, not scientific biological description.

Stages of an Average-mass Star

1. Nebula
2. Contraction of gases
3. Birth of star
4. Yellow star
5. Red giant
6. White dwarf

Stages of a High-mass Star

1. Nebula
2. Contraction of gases
3. Birth of star
4. Blue giant
5. Red giant
6. Nova or supernova
7. Neutron star or pulsar

Note: Depending on mass or other conditions, a high-mass star may evolve to a supergiant. Most stars eventually contract to white dwarfs. However, some explode as supernovas producing neutron stars called pulsars.

The Science Teacher's Book of Lists, © 1993 by Prentice Hall

LIST 8–14. SOME UNMANNED SPACE PROBES

NAME	*COUNTRY*	*DATE*	*COMMENTS*
Sputnik 1	USSR	10/04/57	First earth satellite; gathered data about air density, temperature, cosmic radiation, meteoroids
Explorer 1	USA	1/31/58	The first American satellite; discovered radiation belts surrounding the Earth, which were later named the Van Allen radiation belts after James Van Allen, whose Geiger-counter equipment aboard the satellite discovered them
Luna 2	USSR	9/12/58	First probe to investigate the moon; gathered data about magnetic field, cosmic and solar radiation
Pioneer 5	USA	3/11/60	Transmitted information from 22.5 million miles; mapped interplanetary magnetic field and interaction of Earth's magnetic field with solar wind
Mariner 2	USA	12/14/61	Venus probe passed within 22,000 miles of Venus and relayed information that Venus has high surface temperature and no magnetic field
Ranger 7	USA	7/28/64	Mission to photograph the moon; produced over 4000 photographs
Pegasus 1	USA	2/16/65	Satellite for meteoroid detection
Ranger 8	USA	2/17/65	Produced over 7000 photographs of the moon
Surveyor 3	USSR	4/17/67	Tested lunar soil
Mariner 9	USA	11/13/71	Mars probe (launched 5/30); orbited Mars, took photographs, returned data for months, mapped the entire planet; revealed hundreds of channels (which suggest Mars experienced a different climate in the past), immense volcanoes, layered ice caps, colossal canyon systems
Luna 20	USSR	2/14/72	Landed on moon and brought back samples
Pioneer 10	USA	3/02/72	Encountered Jupiter in a "flyby"; sent data to Earth
Venera 8	USSR	3/27/72	Reached Venus on 7/22 and landed instruments
Viking 1	USA	7/20/76	Soft-landed on Mars and sent data and photographs to Earth
Viking 2	USA	9/03/76	Soft-landed on Mars and sent data and photographs to Earth
Voyager 1	USA	3/05/79	Closest approach to Jupiter; relayed photographs; 11/12/80 closest approach to Saturn; relayed photographs and data on newly discovered rings and moons

(Continued)

LIST 8–14. (Continued)

NAME	COUNTRY	DATE	COMMENTS
Pioneer 11	USA	9/01/79	Closest approach to Saturn; photographs and data relayed to Earth
Vega 1	USSR	12/15/84	Launched mission to fly by Venus on 6/85
Vega 2	USSR	12/21/84	Left landers on Venus and continued on toward Halley's Comet
Voyager 2	USA	1/24/86	Made its closest approach to Uranus; returned pictures of planet and five major satellites
Magellan	USA	5/04/89	Spacecraft launched from shuttle to map surface of Venus
Galileo	USA	10/18/89	Spacecraft launched from shuttle for 6-year journey to Jupiter

The Science Teacher's Book of Lists, © 1993 by Prentice Hall

LIST 8–15. SELECTED MANNED SPACE FLIGHTS

NAME	COUNTRY	DATE	DURATION	ASTRONAUTS/ COSMONAUTS	NOTES
Vostok 1	USSR	4/12/61	1.8 hrs.	Yuri Gagarin	First human in space
Mercury-Redstone 3	USA	5/05/61	15 min.	Alan B. Shepard, Jr.	First American in space
Mercury-Atlas 6	USA	2/20/62	4.9 hrs.	John H. Glenn, Jr.	First manned orbital flight
Vostok 3	USSR	8/11–8/15/62	94.3 hrs.	Andrian G. Nikolayev	Part of first Soviet "group flight"
Voskhod 1	USSR	10/12–10/13/64	24.3 hrs.	Boris Yegorov Konstantin Feoktistov Vladimir Komarov	First three-man crew
Gemini 3	USA	3/23/65	4.9 hrs.	Virgil Grissom John Young	First US two-man crew
Gemini 4	USA	7/3–7/7/65	97.9 hrs.	James McDivitt Edward H. White	White spent 21 min. outside spacecraft
Gemini 8	USA	3/16/66	10.7 hrs.	David R. Scott Neil Armstrong	Docked with unmanned vehicle; mission aborted due to malfunction
Apollo 7	USA	10/11–10/22/68	260.1 hrs.	Walter Schirra Jr. Donn F. Eisele R. Walter Cunningham	Three-man module
Apollo 8	USA	12/21–12/27/68	147 hrs.	Frank Borman James Lovell, Jr. William Anders	Flight around moon
Apollo 11	USA	7/16–7/24/69	195 hrs.	Neil Armstrong Edwin E. Aldrin, Jr. Michael Collins	First manned moon landing
Apollo 12	USA	11/14–11/24/69	244.6 hrs.	Charles Conrad, Jr. Richard Gordon, Jr. Alan Bean	Second manned moon landing

(Continued)

LIST 8–15. (Continued)

NAME	COUNTRY	DATE	DURATION	ASTRONAUTS/ COSMONAUTS	NOTES
Soyuz 9	USSR	6/2–6/19/70	425 hrs.	Andrian Nikolayev Vitaly Sevastyamov	Duration flight
Apollo 15	USA	7/26–7/28/71	295 hrs.	David Scott James Irvin Alfred Worden	Fourth manned moon landing
Skylab 11	USA	7/28–9/26/73	1427 hrs.	Alan Bean Jack Lousma Owen Garriott	Record endurance test in space
Apollo-Soyuz-19	USA/USSR	7/15–7/24/75	9 days	Thomas Stafford Donald Slayton Vance Brand	Apollo-Soyuz cooperative docking
		7/15–7/21/75	6 days	Aleksel Leonov Valery Kubasov	
Soyuz T-10	USSR	2/8–4/11/84	63 days	Leonid Kizim Oleg Atkov Vladimir Solovyev	Ferried crew to Salyut 7 space station
Soyuz T-12	USSR	7/17–7/29/84	12 days	V. Dzhanibekov Svetlana Savitskaya Igor Volk	Ferried crew to Salyut 7; first woman to walk in space, S. Savitskaya

The Science Teacher's Book of Lists, © 1993 by Prentice Hall

LIST 8-16. SOME SPACE SHUTTLE FLIGHTS

SPACECRAFT	DATE	ASTRONAUTS	NOTES
Columbia 1	4/12–4/14/81	John W. Young Robert L. Crippen	First reusable shuttle
Columbia	3/22–3/30/82	Jack Lousma C. Gordon Fullerton	Science instruments and experiments
Columbia	6/27–7/4/82	Thomas Mattingly, 2d Henry Hartsfield, Jr.	Science experiments
Columbia	11/11–11/16/82	Vance Brand Robert Overmyer Joseph Allen William Lenoir	Deployed commercial satellites
Challenger	6/18–6/24/83	Robert L. Crippen Sally K. Ride Norman Thagard John Fabian Frederick Hauck	Deployed retrievable satellite; first American woman in space
Challenger	8/30–9/5/83	Guion Bluford Richard Truly Daniel Brandenstein William Thornton Dale Gardner	First African-American in space; night launch; heavy lift robot arm
Columbia	11/28–12/8/83	John Young Brewster Shaw, Jr. Robert Parker Owen Garriott Byron Lichtenberg Ulf Merbold	Full Spacelab; 71 experiments
Challenger	2/3–2/11/84	Robert Stewart Bruce McCandless 2d Vance Brand Robert Gibson Ronald McNair	Untethered space walk
Challenger	4/6–4/13/84	Robert L. Crippen Francis R. Scobee George D. Nelson Terry J. Hart James D. Van Hoften	First repair of a satellite by another spacecraft
Challenger	10/5–10/13/84	Kathryn Sullivan Robert L. Crippen Jon A. McBride Sally K. Ride Marc Garneau David C. Leestma Paul D. Scully-Power	Sullivan and another did space walk to operate model refueling station; Garneau was the first Canadian in space

(Continued)

LIST 8-16. (Continued)

SPACECRAFT	DATE	ASTRONAUTS	NOTES
Discovery	4/12–4/19/85	Sen. Jake Garn Karol Bobko Donald Williams Charles Walker Jeffrey Hoffman S. David Griggs M. Rhea Seddon	Launched satellites, spacewalk
Challenger	1/28/86	Francis R. Scobee Michael J. Smith Judith A. Resnick Ellison S. Onizuka Ronald E. McNair Gregory B. Jarvis Christa McAuliffe	Fuel tank exploded after takeoff; lost craft and crew, including C. McAuliffe, the first teacher selected for a space mission
Atlantis	5/4–5/8/89	David Walker Ronald Grabe Mary L. Cleave Norman E. Thagard Mark C. Lee	Launched spacecraft *Magellan* to map Venus
Atlantis	10/18–10/23/89	Donald E. Williams Michael McCulley Shannon Lucid Ellen S. Baker Franklin Chang-Diaz	Launched spacecraft *Galileo* to Jupiter
Discovery	4/24–4/29/90	Bruce McCandless 2d Kathryn D. Sullivan Loren J. Shriver Charles F. Bolden Jr. Steven A. Hawley	Launch of Hubble telescope in orbit around Earth (returned pictures of Jupiter on 10/21/91)

LIST 8–17. OBSERVATORIES

Observatories are sites where huge optical and radio telescopes are used to observe the universe by professional astronomers. Some observatories permit amateur astronomers, educators, classes, and other interested persons to make appointments. Some of these are listed below:

- Allegheny Observatory, Pittsburgh, Pennsylvania
- Kitt Peak National Observatory, Tucson, Arizona
- Mt. Cuba Astronomical Observatory, Greenville, Delaware
- Mt. Wilson Observatory, Los Angeles, California
- National Radio Astronomy Observatory, Greenbank, West Virginia
- U.S. Naval Observatory, Washington, D.C.

LIST 8–18. PLANETARIUMS

Planetariums are places that provide simulations of the universe and explain concepts about astronomy. In addition to putting on specific shows for school classes, planetariums usually have regular shows for the public, which are listed in newspapers and other media. Some planetariums are:

- Adler Planetarium, Chicago, Illinois
- Albert Einstein Planetarium, National Air and Space Museum, Washington, D.C.
- Buhl Planetarium, Pittsburgh, Pennsylvania
- Charles Hayden Planetarium, Boston, Massachusetts
- Davis Planetarium, Baltimore, Maryland
- Fairbanks Museum, St. Johnsbury, Vermont
- Fels Planetarium, Philadelphia, Pennsylvania
- Fernbank Planetarium, Atlanta, Georgia
- Griffith Planetarium, Los Angeles, California
- Hayden Planetarium, New York, New York
- Morrison Planetarium, San Francisco, California

LIST 8–19. SOLAR TERMS

chromosphere—the middle layer of the sun's atmosphere between the photosphere and the corona, made up of large cells of rising gas where fiery eruptions called spicules, flares, and prominences occur

convection zone—the layer of the sun in which bubbling gases keep energy constantly moving toward the surface; extends to within 100 miles from the surface

core—the center of the sun, composed mostly of hydrogen and small amounts of helium and other gases, which fuels continuous fission and fusion reactions, releasing enormous amounts of energy

corona—the outermost layer of the sun's atmosphere, composed mostly of hydrogen and small amounts of helium and other gases; extends a few million miles into space

flare—a fiery eruption in the chromosphere of the sun, can disturb radio transmission on Earth

photosphere—the semitransparent inner layer of the sun's atmosphere, made up of columns of rising gas called granular cells, forms the visible surface

prominence—great clouds of gas, in the chromosphere of the sun, that form loops that extend for miles above the sun's surface

radiation zone—the most dense zone, located between the core and the convection zone

solar wind—a stream of energized particles that escapes from the sun's corona and "blows" outward into space

spicules—fiery eruption in the chromosphere of the sun

sunspots—appear as dark spots on the sun's photosphere, where the temperature of the gases (about 8,000°F) are cooler than those in the rest of the sun's surface (about 11,000°F); are thought to be magnetic storms on the sun's surface

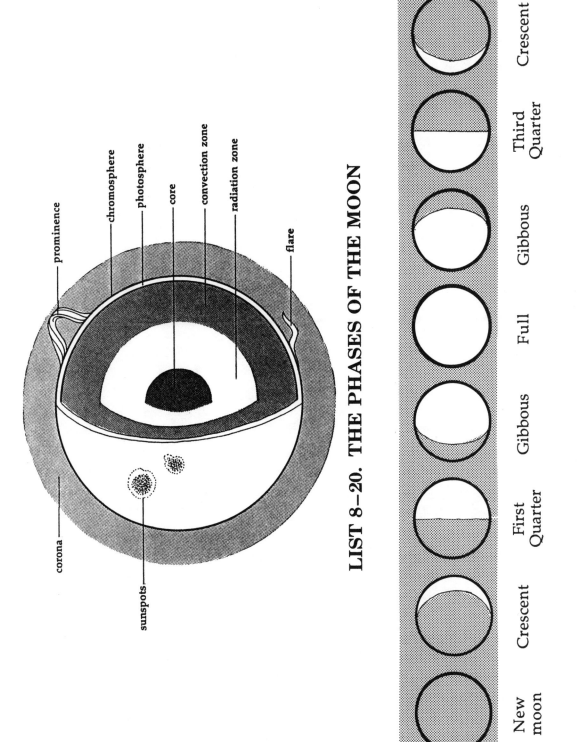

The Science Teacher's Book of Lists, © 1993 by Prentice Hall

LIST 8–20. THE PHASES OF THE MOON

prominence

chromosphere

photosphere

core

convection zone

radiation zone

flare

corona

sunspots

New moon

Crescent

First Quarter

Gibbous

Full

Gibbous

Third Quarter

Crescent

MEASUREMENTS
AND NUMBERS

LIST 9–1. METRIC EQUIVALENTS

Mass Measure

10 milligrams	=	1 centigram
10 centigrams	=	1 decigram
10 decigrams	=	1 **gram**
10 grams	=	1 decagram
10 decagrams	=	1 hectogram
10 hectograms	=	1 kilogram
100 kilograms	=	1 quintal
10 quintals	=	1 metric ton

Liquid Measure

10 milliliters	=	1 centiliter
10 centiliters	=	1 deciliter
10 deciliters	=	1 **liter**
10 liters	=	1 decaliter
10 decaliters	=	1 hectoliter
10 hectoliters	=	1 kiloliter

Linear Measure

10 millimeters	=	1 centimeter
10 centimeters	=	1 decimeter
10 decimeters	=	1 **meter**
10 meters	=	1 decameter
10 decameters	=	1 hectometers
10 hectometers	=	1 kilometer

Square Measure

100 sq. millimeters	=	1 sq. centimeter
100 sq. centimeters	=	1 sq. decimeter
100 sq. decimeters	=	1 **sq. meter**
100 sq. meters	=	1 sq. decameter
100 sq. decameters	=	1 sq. hectometer
100 sq. hectometers	=	1 sq. kilometer

Cubic Measure

1000 cu. millimeters	=	1 cu. centimeter
1000 cu. centimeters	=	1 cu. decimeter
1000 cu. decimeters	=	1 **cu. meter**
1000 cu. meters	=	1 cu. decameter
1000 cu. decameters	=	1 cu. hectometer
1000 cu. hectometers	=	1 cu. kilometer

Note:

1 cubic centimeter = 1 milliliter
1 cubic decimeter = 1 liter
The prefix *deca* is also spelled *deka*.

LIST 9–2. STANDARD METRIC UNITS

METRIC UNIT	*NAME*	*ABBREVIATION*
Standard unit of mass	gram	g
Standard unit of length	meter	m
Standard unit of volume	liter	l

Metric/English Conversions

TO CONVERT FROM	*TO*	*MULTIPLY BY*
inches	centimeters	2.54
feet	centimeters	30.5
centimeters	inches	0.39
millimeters	inches	0.039

Temperature Conversion

TEMPERATURE	*SOME EQUIVALENTS*

$$°C = \frac{(°F - 32)}{9} \times 5$$

$$0°C = 32°F$$
$$1°C = 1.8°F$$
$$10°C = 18°F$$

or

$$C = (°F - 32) \div 1.8$$

$$°F = \frac{°C \times 9}{5} + 32$$

$$16°C = 61°F$$
$$37°C = 98.6°F$$
$$100°C = 212°F$$

or

$$°F = (°C \times 1.8) + 32$$

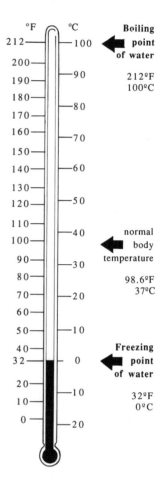

Boiling point of water
212°F
100°C

normal body temperature
98.6°F
37°C

Freezing point of water
32°F
0°C

LIST 9–3. METRIC PREFIXES, SYMBOLS, AND EXAMPLES

PREFIX	MEANING	SYMBOL	EXAMPLE	
tera	trillion	T	1 teragram	= 1,000,000,000,000 g
giga	billion	G	1 gigagram	= 1,000,000,000 g
mega	million	M	1 megagram	= 1,000,000 g
kilo	thousand	k	1 kilogram	= 1,000 g
hecto	hundred	h	1 hectogram	= 100 g
deca/deka	ten	da	1 decagram	= 10 g
		g	**gram**	
deci	one tenth	d	1 decigram	= 0.1 gram
centi	one hundredth	c	1 centigram	= 0.01 g
milli	one thousandth	m	1 milligram	= 0.001 g
micro	one millionth	μ	1 microgram	= 0.000,001 g
nano	one billionth	n	1 nanogram	= 0.000,000,001 g
pico	one trillionth	p	1 picogram	= 0.000,000,000,001 g
femto	one quadrillionth	f	1 femtogram	= 0.000,000,000,000,001 g
atto	one quintillionth	a	1 attogram	= 0.000,000,000,000,000,001 g

The Science Teacher's Book of Lists, © 1993 by Prentice Hall

LIST 9–4. SOME COMMON METRIC ABBREVIATIONS AND APPROXIMATE U.S. EQUIVALENTS

Mass/Weight

UNIT	ABBR.	EQUIVALENT
milligram	mg	0.015 grain
centigram	cg	0.154 grain
decigram	dg	1.543 grains
gram	**g**	0.035 ounce[a]
decagram	dag	0.353 ounce
hectogram	hg	3.527 ounces
kilogram	kg	2.2046 pounds
quintal	q	220.46 pounds
metric ton	MT	2,204.61 pounds

[a]avoirdupois.

Volume/Capacity

UNIT	ABBR.	EQUIVALENT
milliliter	ml	0.27 fluid dram
centiliter	cl	0.34 fluid ounce
deciliter	dl	0.21 pint
liter	**l**	1.057 quarts
decaliter	dal	2.64 gallons
hectoliter	hl	2.84 bushels
kiloliter	kl	1.31 cubic yards

Length

UNIT	ABBR.	EQUIVALENT	
millimeter	mm	0.04 inch	(1 in = 25.4 mm)
centimeter	cm	0.394 inch	
decimeter	dm	3.94 inches	
meter	**m**	39.37 inches	
decameter	dam	32.81 feet	
hectometer	hm	109.36 yards	
kilometer	km	0.62 mile	(1 mile = 1.609 km)

Approximate Measurements: One millimeter is about the thickness of a thumb nail. One centimeter is about the width of the little finger. Five grams is close to the weight of a nickel. One teaspoon holds 5 ml. One tablespoon is about 15 ml.

NOTE: 1 grain = 0.0648 gram

LIST 9–5. SOME U.S. MEASUREMENTS AND METRIC EQUIVALENTS

Liquid Measure

U.S. UNIT	U.S. EQUIVALENTS	METRIC EQUIVALENTS
1 fluid ounce	8 fluid drams	29.574 milliliters
1 pint	16 fluid ounces	0.4732 liter
2 pints	1 quart	0.9463 liters
4 quarts	1 gallon	3.7853 liters

Dry Measure

U.S. UNIT	U.S. EQUIVALENTS	METRIC EQUIVALENTS
1 pint	$\frac{1}{2}$ quart	0.551 liter
1 quart	2 pints	1.101 liters
1 peck	8 quarts	8.809 liters
1 bushel	4 pecks	35.239 liters

Weight

U.S. UNIT*	U.S. EQUIVALENTS		METRIC EQUIVALENTS
1 grain	0.036 dram	0.002285 ounce	64.79891 milligrams
1 dram	27.344 grains	0.0625 ounces	1.772 grams
1 ounce	16 drams	437.5 grains	28.350 grams
1 pound	16 ounces	7,000 grains	453.5924 grams
1 ton (short)	2,000 pounds		907.18 kilograms
1 ton (long)	1.12 short tons	2,240 pounds	1016.0 kilograms

*Also known as Avoirdupois Units

Length

U.S. UNIT	U.S. EQUIVALENTS		METRIC EQUIVALENTS
1 inch	0.083 foot		2.54 centimeters
1 foot	$\frac{1}{3}$ yard	12 inches	0.3048 meter
1 yard	3 feet	36 inches	0.9144 meter
1 rod	$5\frac{1}{2}$ yards	$16\frac{1}{2}$ feet	5.0292 meters
1 statute mile[a]	1,760 yards	5,280 feet	1,609 kilometers
1 nautical mile[b]	2,025 yards	6,076 feet	1.852 kilometers

[a]land
[b]international

(Continued)

The Science Teacher's Book of Lists, © 1993 by Prentice Hall

LIST 9–5. (Continued)

Area

U.S. UNIT	U.S. EQUIVALENTS	METRIC EQUIVALENTS
1 square inch	0.007 square foot	6.4516 square centimeters
1 square foot	144 square inches	929.030 square centimeters
1 square yard	9 square feet	0.836 square meters
1 acre	4,840 square yards	4,047 square meters
1 square mile	640 acres	2,590 square kilometers

Volume

U.S. UNIT	U.S. EQUIVALENTS	METRIC EQUIVALENTS
1 cubic inch	0.00058 cubic foot	16.387 cubic centimeters
1 cubic foot	1.728 cubic inches	0.028 cubic meter
1 cubic yard	27 cubic feet	0.765 cubic meter

Angular Measurement

UNIT	EQUIVALENTS
1 minute	60 seconds
1 degree (°)	60 minutes
1 quadrant or 1 right angle	90 degrees
1 circle	4 quadrants or 360° degrees

Apothecaries' Weight

APOTHECARY WEIGHT UNIT =	U.S. EQUIVALENTS	METRIC EQUIVALENTS
1 scruple	20 grains	1.296 grams
1 dram	60 grains	3.888 grams
1 ounce	480 grains	31.1035 grams
1 pound	5,760 grains	373.242 grams

NOTE: One grain = 0.0648 gram

The Science Teacher's Book of Lists, © 1993 by Prentice Hall

LIST 9–6. COMPARISONS BETWEEN METRIC AND ENGLISH SYSTEMS OF MEASURING WEIGHT, VOLUME, AND LENGTH

Metric   **English**

Weight

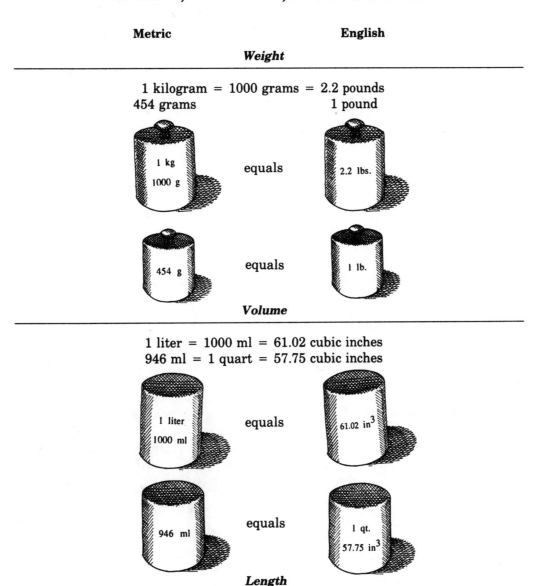

1 kilogram = 1000 grams = 2.2 pounds
454 grams   1 pound

1 kg
1000 g   equals   2.2 lbs.

454 g   equals   1 lb.

Volume

1 liter = 1000 ml = 61.02 cubic inches
946 ml = 1 quart = 57.75 cubic inches

1 liter
1000 ml   equals   61.02 in^3

946 ml   equals   1 qt.
57.75 in^3

Length

1 centimeter = 0.394 inch
2.54 centimeters = 1 inch

The Science Teacher's Book of Lists, © 1993 by Prentice Hall

LIST 9–7. METRIC CONVERSIONS

TO CHANGE	TO	MULTIPLY BY
inches	millimeters	25.4
inches	centimeters	2.54
feet	meters	0.3048
yards	meters	0.9144
miles	kilometers	1.6093
quarts (liquid)	liters	0.946
pints (liquid)	liters	0.4732
pounds	grams	453.6
ounces (fluid)	milliliters	29.57
ounces (avoirdupois)	grams	28.35
tons (short	kilograms	907.185
tons (short)	metric tons	0.9072
tons (long)	metric tons	1.0160
cubic yards	cubic meters	0.765
cubic inches	milliliters	16.387
cubic feet	liters	28.32

Examples:

1 ounce = 0.06 lb = 28.35 g
1 pound = 453.59 g
1 fluid ounce = 29.573 ml
1 quart = 0.946 l ml
1 gal = 3.785 l ml
1 ml = 0.034 fluid ounces
1 l = 1.057 quarts
1 l = 0.264 gallons

The Science Teacher's Book of Lists, © 1993 by Prentice Hall

LIST 9–8. ROMAN NUMERALS

The Roman system of numbering is still sometimes used in present-day writing to number chapters and subsections, for tables of data, and dates of book publication. It provides a means of distinguishing a series of items of one type from those of another designated by Arabic numerals. Roman numerals also are often used on clock faces and monuments.

The system is quite simple and is based on use of the following letters:

ROMAN NUMERAL	ARABIC NUMERAL	ROMAN NUMERAL	ARABIC NUMERAL
I	1	C	100
V	5	D	500
X	10	M	1000
L	50		

Intermediate and larger numbers are formed by addition and subtraction according to these rules: (1) Roman numerals of equal value or a smaller numeral following a larger one are added; (2) a small numeral preceding a larger one is subtracted. Up to four like symbols may be used in sequence, although the usual number is three. Sometimes there is more than one way to represent a value. Some examples are given below.

ROMAN NUMERAL	ARABIC NUMERAL	ROMAN NUMERAL	ARABIC NUMERAL
III	3	LXXX	80
IV	4	XC	90
VIII	8	IC	99
IX	9	MCCC	1300
XV	15	MCD	1400
XIX	19	MM	2000
IL	49	MCML	1950
LXII	62	MCMLXXXIX	1989

To represent large numbers, a period has sometimes been used to signify multiplication: M.IV = 4000; M.V = 5000; M.M. = 1,000,000. There is no zero in the Roman numeral system. In the Arabic System, the zero is invaluable. It represents "none" and acts as a place holder. For example:

	ARABIC		ROMAN
No ones	0		—
One—one	1	I	One
One—ten	10	X	Ten
One—hundred	100	C	One hundred
One—thousand	1000	M	One thousand

LIST 9–9. SOME EARLY NUMBER SYSTEMS

One of the easiest ways to keep numerical track of points is a tally system. Think of someone, living before paper and pencil were available, trying to keep track of the sheep he trades for other animals and/or items. He probably would have used some type of tally system. He could have made marks in the dirt or for a more permanent record could have cut notches on a stick. Here are a few examples of early number systems, influenced by tallies.

Chinese:

一	二	三	四	五	六	七	八	九	十	百	千
1	2	3	4	5	6	7	8	9	10	100	1,000

Egyptian:

1	2	3	4	5	6	7	8	9	10	100	1,000

Mayan:

1	2	3	4	5	6	7	8	9	10

20	40	60	80	100

(Maya ⬭ made a number 20 times larger.)

LIST 9–10. BASE TWO

The base two, or binary, system uses two symbols. It is used in electronic calculators and computers because the two symbols are easily translated into "on" and "off" electronic switches. The written symbols are 1 and 0.

- Columns in the base ten system increase (from right to left) by a multiple of ten; for example:
  1000's   100's   10's   1's
- Columns in the base two system increase (from right to left) by a multiple of 2; for example:
  128's   64's   32's   16's   8's   4's   2's   1's
- Base ten: 117
  100's   10's   1's
  1   1   7   = 117
  (100 + 10   + 7   = 117 base ten)
- Base two: the equivalent of 117 in the base ten system
  128's 64's   32's   16's   8's   4's   2's   1's
      1   1   1   0   1   0   1 = 1110101 base two
      (64 + 32   + 16 + 0   + 4   + 0   + 1 = 117 base ten)
- Base two: the equivalent of 170 in the base ten system
  1   0   1   0   1   0   1   0 = 10101010 base two
  (128 + 0 + 32 + 0 + 8 + 0 + 2 + 0 = 170 base ten)

LIST 9–11. USEFUL FORMULAS

To investigate the physical world, scientists have developed and utilize many mathematical formulas. Some of the most useful formulas are:

Area of a circle

$A = \pi r^2$

Area of a circle equals π or 3.1416 times the radius squared

Area of a rectangle

$A = lw$

Area of a rectangle equals its length times its width

Area of trapezoid

$A = \frac{1}{2}h$ (base 1 + base 2)

Area of a trapezoid equals $\frac{1}{2}$ times the height, times the sum of the two bases

Area of a triangle

$A = \frac{1}{2}bh$

Area equals $\frac{1}{2}$ times the base times the height

Avogadro's number

The number of molecules in 1 mole of a molecular substance = 6.0238×10^{23}

Applying Avogadro's number

Mass of a molecule or atom =
$$\frac{\text{gram molecular weight}}{6.02 \times 10^{23}}$$

Density

$D = M/V$

Density equals mass divided by volume

Effort

Effort = R/M.A.

Effort equals resistance divided by mechanical advantage

Energy

$E = mc^2$

Energy equals mass times the speed of light squared (c^2)

Force

$F = MA$

Force equals mass times acceleration

Ohm's Law

$I = E/R$

Amperes (I) equal volts (E) divided by resistance (R)

Mean

$$\bar{x} = \frac{\Sigma x}{n}$$

Mean or average ($\bar{x}$) = the sum of individual figures (Σx) divided by the total number (n) of those figures

The Science Teacher's Book of Lists, © 1993 by Prentice Hall

(Continued)

LIST 9–11. (Continued)

M.A. of a lever	M.A. = L of effort arm/L of resistance arm Mechanical Advantage equals length of effort arm divided by length of resistance arm
M.A. of a ramp	M.A. = L/H Mechanical advantage equals the length of the ramp divided by the height of the ramp
Mole	Mole = sum of atomic weights expressed in grams
Pressure	P = F/A Pressure equals force divided by area
Speed	S = D/T Speed equals a unit of distance traveled divided by a unit of time traveled
Temperature conversions	$°C = \frac{5}{9}(°F - 32)$; $°F = \frac{9}{5}C + 32$; $°K = C + 273.15$
Velocity	$V = \frac{1}{2}at^2$ Velocity equals one half of the acceleration multiplied by the time squared
Volume of a cone	$V = \frac{1}{3}\pi r^2 h$ Volume of a cone equals $\frac{1}{3}$ times π or 3.1416, times the radius squared, times the Height
Volume of a cylinder	$V = \pi r^2 h$ Volume of a cylinder equals 3.14 times the radius squared, times the height
Volume of a rectangular prism	V = lwh Volume equals length times width times height
Volume of a sphere	$V = \frac{4}{3}\pi r^3$ Volume of a sphere equals $\frac{4}{3}$ times π or 3.1416, times the radius cubed
Work	W = FD Work equals force times distance

NOTE:

a) π—pronounced "pie," is equal to 3.14159265+, which is frequently rounded off to 3.1416

b) squared—to multiply a number by itself; for example $5^2 = 5 \times 5 = 25$

c) cubed—to multiply a number times itself three times; for example $5^3 = 5 \times 5 \times 5 = 125$

LIST 9–12. HOW MUCH WOULD YOU WEIGH ON OTHER PLANETS?

> Your weight on a planet =
> your Earth weight times the surface gravity of that planet.

Thus, if you wish to know what your weight would be on Pluto, you need to multiply your Earth weight by the surface gravity of Pluto. Use the chart to find the surface gravity of Pluto.

Example: How much does a person who weighs 130 pounds on Earth weigh on Pluto?

Earth weight times surface gravity of planet = weight on that planet
130 lbs   ×   0.05   =   6.55 pounds

Did this person lose weight? Not really. The body mass stays the same. The numbers appearing on a scale (not a balance) would show between 6 and 7 pounds, and clothes would fit the same. But the numbers appearing on a balance would be 130 pounds, because the weights are affected to the same degree as the person.

Surface Gravity of the Planets in Our Solar System and Our Moon

PLANET	SURFACE GRAVITY COMPARED TO EARTH'S
Mercury	0.37
Venus	0.88
Earth	1.00
Mars	0.38
Jupiter	2.51
Saturn	1.07
Uranus	0.93
Neptune	1.23
Pluto	0.04
Earth's moon	0.17

LIST 9–13. ENORMOUS DISTANCES: ASTRONOMICAL UNITS AND LIGHT YEARS

Distances in our solar system are so tremendous that units of measurements such as miles, meters, and kilometers are too small to be helpful. Thus, scientists have developed a unit of measurement based on the distance between Earth and the sun, the astronomical unit (AU). The average distance between Earth and the sun is 93 million miles or 149,600,000 km. Thus, 1 AU equals 93 million miles or 149,600,000 km.

PLANET	DISTANCE FROM THE SUN IN ASTRONOMICAL UNITS (AU)
Mercury	0.387
Venus	0.723
Earth	1.000
Mars	1.524
Jupiter	5.203
Saturn	9.539
Uranus	19.182
Neptune	30.214
Pluto	39.439

Outside our solar system, distances between objects in space are even greater than the distances within our solar system. Thus, scientists have developed a unit of measurement to deal with these enormous distances, the light year. A light-year is the distance that light travels in one year. Light travels a distance of about 9.5 trillion kilometers or about 6 trillion miles in one year. Thus, it is much simpler to write about a distance of 1 light year as opposed to 9.5 trillion kilometers. Remember, light year refers to distance not time.

Distance from Earth in Light Years to:

Sirius, the Dog Star	8.8 light years away
Cygnus, a star in Cygnus, the swan	10.6 light years away
Altair, a star in Aquila, the eagle	16 light years away
Arcturus, a star in Boötes, the herdsman	36 light years away
Regulus, a star in Leo, the lion	86 light years away
Spica, a star in Virgo, the virgin	230 light years away
Antares, a star in Scorpio, the scorpion	410 light years away
Polaris, the Pole Star in the Little Dipper	782 light years away
Orion Nebula	1,625 light years away
Messier 31, the nearest spiral galaxy	2 million light years away

LIST 9–14. EXPRESSING LARGE AND SMALL NUMBERS

Everyone knows a million, a billion, perhaps a trillion. But what do you do if the numbers get larger? Someone foresaw the really big numbers coming and there are names for them. The names below are for the U.S. system. Each name is for a number one thousand times the one before except for googol and googolplex.

NUMBER	NUMBER OF ZEROS	POWERS OF TEN
thousand	3	10^3
million	6	10^6
billion	9	10^9
trillion	12	10^{12}
quadrillion	15	10^{15}
quintillion	18	10^{18}
sextillion	21	10^{21}
septillion	24	10^{24}
octillion	27	10^{27}
nonillion	30	10^{30}
decillion	33	10^{33}
undecillion	36	10^{36}
duodecillion	39	10^{39}
tredecillion	42	10^{42}
quattuordecillion	45	10^{45}
quindecillion	48	10^{48}
sexdecillion	51	10^{51}
septendecillion	54	10^{54}
octodecillion	57	10^{57}
novemdecillion	60	10^{60}
vigintillion	63	10^{63}
googol	100	10^{100}
googolplex	101	10^{101}

The Science Teacher's Book of Lists, © 1993 by Prentice Hall

You may not have much use for the names except in the pursuit of trivia—or to write a check. However, the numbers in the right column are very handy and often used. The raised number is called the *exponent* and tells the number of times that ten is multiplied by itself to obtain the number expressed. You will find numbers expressed in this way in the lists on Geological and Fossil Ages and in the list of Properties of Light and Other Electromagnetic Waves.

Exponents can be used to express multiplication of numbers (other than 10) by themselves; for example, $2^2 = 4$; $2^3 = 8$.

Now, how does one express very small or fractional numbers by this system? For the decimal system, one uses a negative exponent for the number of zeros to the right of the decimal point plus one; that is, 0.01 equals 10^{-2}, 0.001 equals 10^{-3}, and so on.

LIST 9–15. PREFIXES FOR METRIC QUANTITIES

A group of prefixes has been selected for designating large and small quantities of standard units. These are given in the table.

Multiples and Submultiples of Metric Units

FACTOR	PREFIX	SYMBOL	FACTOR	PREFIX	SYMBOL
10^{12}	tera	T	10^{-2}	centi	c
10^{9}	giga	G	10^{-3}	milli	m
10^{6}	mega	M	10^{-6}	micro	μ
10^{3}	kilo	k	10^{-9}	nano	n
10^{2}	hecto	h	10^{-12}	pico	p
10	deca	da	10^{-15}	femto	f
10^{-1}	deci	d	10^{-18}	atto	a

Hence, there are words megaton (Mton), kilowatt (kW), the slang "megabucks (M\$)," nanosecond (nsec), and picoCurie (pCi). For other numbers, such as two million two hundred thousand or five and one half billion, one writes 2.2×10^{6} and 5.5×10^{9}, respectively. These are read as two point two times ten to the sixth (power) or 2.2 mega units and five point five times ten to the ninth (power) or 5.5 giga units.

LIST 9–16. PARTS PER MILLION

Parts per million (ppm) and parts per billion (ppb) are used in reporting very low concentrations of materials such as toxic substances in air or water. These phrases should mean that out of a million or a billion units of a substrate, there are present the reported number of units of the foreign material. These units of measure should be the same unless expressly stated to be otherwise. The usage of the terms is sometimes ambiguous.

Examples of Laboratory and Workplace Exposure Limits for Air Contaminants

These exposure limits were prescribed by OSHA (Occupational Safety and Health Administration) in 1989, and may change as more is learned about health hazards. The values are time-weighted averages for an eight hour-work period.

SUBSTANCE	PERMISSIBLE EXPOSURE LIMIT	
	ppm	mg/m³
Acetic acid	10	25
Acetone	1000	2400
Ammonia	50	35
Benzene	10	
Chlorine	0.5	1.5
Para-dichlorobenzene	75	450
Ethyl acetate	400	1400
Formaldehyde	3	
Gasoline	300	900
Graphite dust		15[a]
Malathion dust		15
Marble dust		15
Methyl alcohol	200	260
Naphthalene	10	50
Ozone	0.1	0.2
Phenol	5	19
Propane	1000	1800
Sulfur dioxide	5	13

---

[a]Or 15 million particles/ft.³

LIST 9–17. SIMPLE STATISTICS: MODE, MEDIAN, MEAN, AND RANGE

Mode, median, mean, and range are examples of simple statistics that enable one to analyze data and are especially helpful in answering questions having more than one correct answer, such as:

- How many drops of water are in one milliliter?
- How long does it take for one stick of sugarless gum to lose its flavor?
- How long does it take an ice cube to melt at room temperature?
- What's the flavor of ice cream most frequently sold at ice cream shops?
- How many days of school are missed by the students in your class?

To answer these and similar questions, one must identify a way to control all the variables possible, actually gather the data, and then analyze that data. To analyze the data, one calculates the:

mode—the number that occurs most frequently in a series of observations.

median—the middle number in a series of numbers arranged in order of value. To calculate the median, list the numbers in order of value. Cross out the top and bottom numbers until the middle number is identified. Circle the middle number.

mean—the value that is commonly called an "average." To calculate the mean add all of the numbers in the series. Divide the sum by the quantity of numbers.

range—the difference between the highest and the lowest numbers in a series. In questions where one can expect observations to be similar, the lower the difference, the more confidence one can place in the results. The higher the difference, the less confidence one can place in the data.

(Continued)

LIST 9–17. (Continued)

Example for introducing students to determining an answer when there is more than one numerical value:

How Many Drops of Water in One Milliliter, When Using One Eyedropper?

TRIAL	NO. OF DROPS	MODE	MEDIAN	MEAN	RANGE
1	29	29	29	29	R = H − L
2	30	30	30	30	R = 32 − 29 = 3
3	31	31	30	31	
4	30	30	(30)	30	
5	30	30	31	30	
6	32	32	31	32	
7	31	31	32	31	
		30	30	213/7 = 30.42 or 30	3

To go beyond an introduction to basic statistics and conduct such an investigation, students need to gather the raw data from a number of trials and in this case a number of eye droppers. The more trials and the lower the range, the higher the degree of confidence the investigator can place in the results.

LIST 9–18. A FREQUENCY DISTRIBUTION TABLE

A frequency distribution table shows the frequency with which each value in a set of data occurs. This provides the observer with another way to analyze the data gathered. When deciding which items to restock after taking inventory, it is particularly helpful to transpose that data to a frequency distribution table. For example, a clerk in a small men's shoe store listed the sizes of bedroom slippers in stock for Brand X Slippers: 7, 8, 6, 8, 10, 11, 12, 13, 7, 8, 12.

To set up a Frequency Distribution Table:

1. Use a ruler to draw two columns.
2. Write the headings; see table.
3. List scores/sizes from the highest to the lowest; see table.
4. Record the frequency of each score/size.

FREQUENCY DISTRIBUTION OF SLIPPERS	
SCORES (χ)	FREQUENCY (F)
13.........................	1
12.........................	2
12	
11.........................	1
10.........................	1
8.........................	3
8	
8	
7.........................	2
7	
6.........................	1

LIST 9–19. CHECKLIST FOR GRAPHING CONVENTIONS

Graphs provide a way of looking at and analyzing data. Here is a checklist to help you set up a bar or line graph which can be used to analyze the data gathered.

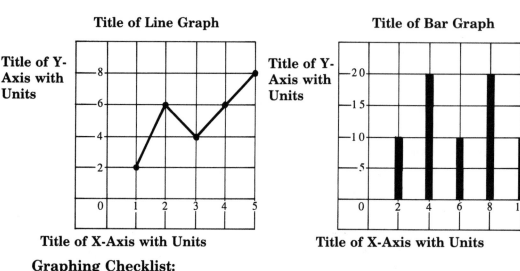

The Science Teacher's Book of Lists, © 1993 by Prentice Hall

Graphing Checklist:

___ 1. Use a ruler to construct each axis and later to connect coordinates on line graphs or to construct bars on bar graphs.

___ 2. Write a zero at the intersection of the two axes.

___ 3. Remember that the intersection of the x- and y-axes is zero (not 1) and is the starting point of the x and y number lines.

___ 4. Label each axis to describe what was observed.

___ 5. Label the horizontal (x-axis) with the manipulated variable of the investigation. (Identify what you manipulate in an investigation, such as number of days, number of cubic centimeters of fertilizer, hours of light. Write this on the "manipulative" or horizontal axis. That which is a result of the manipulation is written on the "responding" or vertical axis.)

___ 6. Label the vertical (y-axis) with the responding variable of the investigation.

___ 7. Label the units of measurements on each axis.

___ 8. Number the x and y axes by writing the numerals at even intervals on the vertical and horizontal lines of each axis.

___ 9. Write a title that explains what the graph shows. To do this, use words from the labels of both axes and your investigation.

___ 10. Plot your data on the graph.

(Continued)

LIST 9–19. (Continued)

__ 11. Observe the completed graph to look for patterns, predictions, and interpretations.

__ 12. Look at the plotted coordinates, and when possible make interpretations that can be made based on the data that fall inside the plotted coordinates. These "internal" inferences are called "interpolations." For example, look at the line graph. No data have been plotted on the x axis at 1.5, but one can interpolate that 4 responds on the y axis.

__ 13. Observe the plotted coordinates for patterns. If possible, make inferences or predictions that fall outside of or exit the data. These "exit" inferences are called "extrapolations." For example, look at the bar graph. No data have been plotted on the x axis at 12, but one can extrapolate that 20 responds on the y axis.

LIST 9–20. SOME INTERESTING NUMBERS

Prime Numbers

Prime numbers are those numbers, which can be divided evenly by no other whole number than itself or 1. Examples:

1, 3, 5, 7, 11, 13, 17, 23, 29, 31, 37, 41, 43, 47, 51, 53, 59, 61, 67, 71, 73, 79, etc. π (pi) is a prime number.

Upside-Down Numbers

Upside-down numbers are ones that read as numbers when viewed upside down; examples: 1991 reads 1661. Some more interesting upside-down numbers read the same when observed upside down. Look at these numbers. Then turn the page upside down and observe the numbers. These numbers read the same right-side up and upside-down when written by hand:

101	986	1001	1111	1691	1881	1961
10001	11011	18081	19061	111111	100001	

For example: 1961   1961

The Nifty Nines

The sum of the digits in the products in the nine times table equals 9 or is 9.

$9 \times 1 = 9$

$9 \times 2 = 18 \ (1 + 8 = 9)$

$9 \times 3 = 27 \ (2 + 7 = 9)$

$9 \times 4 = 36 \ (3 + 6 = 9)$

$9 \times 5 = 45 \ (4 + 5 = 9)$

$9 \times 6 = 54 \ (5 + 4 = 9)$

$9 \times 7 = 63 \ (6 + 3 = 9)$

$9 \times 8 = 72 \ (7 + 2 = 9)$

$9 \times 9 = 81 \ (8 + 1 = 9)$

$9 \times 10 = 90 \ (9 + 0 = 9)$

$9 \times 11 = 99$ (two 9s)

$9 \times 12 = 108 \ (1 + 0 + 8 = 9)$

LIST 9–21. CALCULATING THE VOLUME FRACTION OF A FLOATING ICEBERG ABOVE THE WATER LINE

Formula for calculating the volume of ice floating above water:

$$\frac{\text{(Density of water minus density of ice)}}{\text{Density of water}} \times 100 = \% \text{ volume of ice above water}$$

Example in fresh water:

$$\frac{1.00 \text{ g/cc} - 0.92 \text{ g/cc} \times 100}{1.00 \text{ g/cc}} = 8\%$$

A 100 cc chunk of ice in fresh water would have 8% or 8 cc above water.

Example in salt water:

$$\frac{1.040 \text{ g/cc} - 0.92 \text{ g/cc} \times 100}{1.040 \text{ g/cc}} = 11.5\%$$

A 100 cc chunk of ice in salt water would have 11.5% or 11.5 cc above the water.

This will work for any liquid and any solid lighter than the liquid. It does not tell how high an iceberg is because that depends on the shape above and below the surface of the water. Salt water may vary in density with location.

Reminder: Density equals mass per volume; the density of water is 1 gram per cc; since the density of ice is less than that of water, ice floats in water.

Objects float higher and people float more "easily" in salt water than in fresh water.

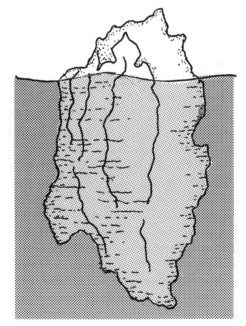

A large percentage of an iceberg is underwater.

LIST 9–22. QUANTITIES, UNITS, AND SYMBOLS COMMONLY USED IN SCIENCE

QUANTITY	NAME OF SI UNIT*	SYMBOL OF SI UNIT*
acceleration	meter per second squared	m/s^2
amount of substance	mole	mol
temperature	degree Celsius	°C
density	kilogram per cubic meter	kg/m^3
electric capacitance	farad	F
electric charge	coulomb	C
electric conductance	siemens	S
electric current	ampere	A
electric field strength	volt per meter	V/m
electric resistance	ohm	Ω
energy, quantity	joule	J
flux of light	lumen	lm
force	newton	N
frequency	hertz	Hz
illumination	lux	lx
length	meter	m
luminance	candela per square meter	cd/m^2
magnetic field strength	ampere per meter	A/m
magnetic flux	weber	Wb
magnetic flux density	tesla	T
mass	kilogram	kg
plane angle	radian	rad
power	watt	W
pressure	newton per square meter	N/m^2
pressure/stress	pascal	Pa
solid angle	steradian	sr
thermodynamic temperature	kelvin	K
time	second	s
velocity	meter per second	m/s
voltage	volt	V

The Science Teacher's Book of Lists, © 1993 by Prentice Hall

*"SI Unit"—stands for the International System of Units.

LIST 9–23. SYMBOLS AND SIGNS FREQUENTLY USED IN SCIENCE AND MATH

SYMBOL	USAGE OR MEANING	SYMBOL	USAGE OR MEANING
+	plus	&	and
−	minus	%	per cent
±	plus or minus	™	trade mark
×	multiplied by	©	copyright
÷	divided by	Σ	sum
=	equal to	[ ]	brackets
≠	not equal to	( )	parentheses
>	greater than	Ω	ohm
<	less than or angle	μΩ	microhm
:	ratio	MΩ	megohm
⊥	perpendicular	∪	logical sum
‖	parallel	∞	infinity
°	degrees	π	pi
′	minute	Δ	triangle, increment
″	second	√	Radical; root; square root
∴	therefore	↓	precipitate
∵	because	↑	gas
→	approaches the limit (math) yields or produces (chemistry) direction of flow (physics)		
← ⇄	reversible reaction (chemistry) electric current		

SELECTED SCIENTISTS AND THEIR CONTRIBUTIONS

LIST 10–1. WORDS OF SCIENCE AND TECHNOLOGY DERIVED FROM PEOPLE'S NAMES

WORD AND SYMBOL	MEANING[a]	DERIVATION
Electricity and Magnetism		
volt, V	unit of electrical potential	Alessandro Volta, 1745–1827, Italian physicist
ampere, A	unit of electrical flow	Andre M. Ampere, 1775–1836, French mathematician and physicist
watt, W	unit of electrical power	James Watt, 1736–1819, Scottish engineer and inventor
ohm, Ω (V/A)	unit of electrical resistance	Georg S. Ohm, 1787–1854, German physicist
mho (A/V)	unit of electrical conductivity	Inverse of Ohm, German physicist
farad, F	unit of electrical capacitance	Michael Faraday, 1791–1867, English chemist and physicist
coulomb, C	unit of electric charge	Charles A. Coulomb, 1736–1806, French physicist
maxwell, Mx	unit of magnetic flux	James C. Maxwell, 1831–1879, Scottish physicist
hertz, Hz	frequency of electro-magnetic waves	Heinrich R. Hertz, 1857–1894, German physicist
weber, Wb	unit of magnetic flux	Wilhelm E. Weber, 1804–1891, German physicist
tesla, T	magnetic flux density	Nikola Tesla, 1856–1943, Yugoslavian-born, American electrical inventor
henry, H	unit of inductance	Joseph Henry, 1797–1878, American physicist and inventor
gauss, G	unit of magnetic field intensity	Karl F. Gauss, 1777–1855, German mathematician
Radiation		
curie, Ci	unit of radium radiation	Pierre Curie, 1859–1906, Marie Curie, 1867–1934, French physicists
roentgen, R	unit of radiation	Wilhelm K. Roentgen, 1845–1923, German physicist
oersted, Oe	unit of magnetic intensity	Hans C. Oersted, 1777–1851, Danish physicist

(Continued)

LIST 10–1. (Continued)

WORD AND SYMBOL	MEANING[a]	DERIVATION
Force, Pressure, and Energy		
newton, N	unit of force	Sir Isaac Newton, 1642–1727, English natural philosopher
pascal, Pa	unit of force or pressure	Blaise Pascal, 1623–1662, French natural philosopher and mathematician
torr	unit of atmospheric pressure	Evangelista Torricelli, 1608–1647, Italian physicist and mathematician
joule, J	unit of energy	James P. Joule, 1818–1889, English physicist
Dimensions		
angstrom, Å	unit of length, equal to 10^{-8} centimeter, to specify radiation wavelengths	Anders J. Angstrom, 1814–1874, Swedish physicist
Baumé, Bé	scale of liquid densities	Antoine Baumé, 1728–1804, French pharmacist
Temperature		
Fahrenheit, F	unit of temperature	Gabriel D. Fahrenheit, 1686–1744, German physicist
Celsius, C	unit of temperature	Anders Celsius, 1701–1744, Swedish astronomer
Kelvin, K	unit of temperature	William Thomson, Lord Kelvin, 1824–1907, British physicist
Elements		
fermium, Fm	atomic number 100	Enrico Fermi, 1901–1954, Italian physicist
curium, Cm	atomic number 96	See Curie above
einsteinium, E	atomic number 99	Albert Einstein, 1879–1955, German-born American physicist
mendelevium, Mv	atomic number 101	Dmitri I. Mendeleev, 1834–1907, Russian chemist
nobelium, No	atomic number 102	Alfred B. Nobel, 1833–1896, Swedish inventor
Minerals[b]		
danalite	cobaltian arsenopyrite	J. Freeman Dana, 1793–1827, American mineralogist
frondelite	a manganese-iron phosphate	Clifford Frondel, 1907– American mineralogist

(Continued)

LIST 10-1. (Continued)

WORD AND SYMBOL	MEANING[a]	DERIVATION
goethite	a hydrous iron oxide	Johann von Goethe, 1749–1832, German poet and naturalist
kunzite	a gem variety of spodumene	G. E. Kunz, 1856–1932, American mineralogist
liebigite	calcium uranium carbonate hydrate	Justus von Liebig, 1803–1873, German chemist
morganite	variety of beryl	J. P. Morgan, 1837–1913, American financier
scheelite	calcium tungstate	Karl W. Scheele, 1742–1786, Swedish chemist
Technology		
macadam	road surfacing	John L. McAdam, 1756–1836, Scottish inventor
pasteurize	process of sterilization	Louis Pasteur, 1822–1895, French chemist
galvanize	process of coating with zinc	Luigi Galvani, 1737–1798, Italian physiologist
mercerize	process of treating cotton with alkali to improve strength and luster	John Mercer, 1791–1866, English inventor
daguerreotype	photographic process and product	Louis J. M. Daguerre, 1789–1851, French scenic painter/physicist
bakelite™	synthetic resin	Leo H. Baekeland, 1863–1904, American chemist

[a]More exact definition of units will be found under the specific subject lists.

[b]A great many minerals are named for people. The names often were chosen by or refer to the discoverer.

LIST 10–2. ABOUT THE NOBEL PRIZE AND WINNERS IN PHYSICS

Nobel
Medal

The Nobel Prize consists of a gold medal, a diploma, and a gift of money. It is awarded annually to reward those who have made significant contributions to humanity in physics, chemistry, medicine-physiology, literature, and peace. An award in economics was awarded in 1969. The initial fund of $9,200,000 was bequeathed by Alfred Bernhard Nobel, the inventor of dynamite, and is administered by the Central Bank of Sweden. Decisions to recognize contributions in physics and chemistry are made by the Swedish Academy of Science in Stockholm, and for medicine or physiology by the Caroline Institute in Stockholm. The awards are usually presented in Stockholm on December 10, the anniversary of Nobel's death. The value of the prize was worth approximately $470,000 in 1989, $710,000 in 1990, and $985,000 to $1 million in 1991.

Nobel Prize Winners in Physics

YEAR	NAME	RECOGNIZED FOR
1901	Roentgen, Wilhelm K.	Discovering X rays
1902	Lorentz, Hendrik A.	Investigating effects of magnetism on radiation
	Zeeman, Pieter	Displacement of spectrum lines by magnetic field
1903	Becquerel, Antoine Henri	Discovering radioactivity
	Curie, Marie S.	Research in radioactivity
	Curie, Pierre	
1904	Rayleigh, Lord	Discovering argon
1905	von Lenard, Philipp	Discovering penetrating power of cathode rays
1906	Thomson, Joseph J.	Investigating electrical properties of gases
1907	Michelson, Albert A.	Determining the velocity of light
1908	Lippmann, Gabriel	Developing a method for color photography
1909	Marconi, Guglielmo	Inventing radiotelegraphy
	Braun, Carl F.	Improvements in radio transmission
1910	van der Waals, Johannes	Law of continuity of liquids and gaseous states
1911	Wien, Wilhelm	Investigation of black body radiation
1912	Dalen, Nils Gustaf	Inventing an automatic regulator for gas lamps
1913	Onnes, Heike K.	Liquefaction of helium at temperature near absolute zero
1914	von Laue, Max	Proof of regular arrangement of atoms in crystals
1915	Bragg, William H.	Explanation of atomic structure of crystals
	Bragg, William L.	

(Continued)

LIST 10–2. (Continued)

YEAR	NAME	RECOGNIZED FOR
1917	Barkla, Charles G.	Discovery of characteristic radiations of elements
1918	Planck, Max	Formulating the quantum theory
1919	Stark, Johannes	Decomposition of spectrum lines by an electric field
1920	Guillaume, Charles E.	Production of invar, a nickel-iron alloy used in surveyor's tapes and chronometer balance wheels
1921	Einstein, Albert	Developing theory of relativity, discovering law of photoelectric effect
1922	Bohr, Niels H. D.	Developing the theory of atomic structure, which explained that electrons move in orbits
1923	Millikan, Robert	Proving the electrical nature of electrons
1924	Siegbahn, Karl M. G.	Establishing a unit of measure for short-wave radiations
1925	Franck, James Hertz, Gustav	Laws governing impact of electrons upon the atom
1926	Perrin, Jean Baptiste	Explaining the Brownian movement in liquids
1927	Compton, Arthur, H.	Proving wave-length alternation of X rays
	Wilson, Charles T. R.	Showing paths of ionized atoms in a cloud chamber
1928	Richardson, Owen W.	Investigation of electricity emission from hot bodies
1929	de Broglie, Louis V. (Prince de Broglie)	Proving matter consists of waves in addition to corpuscles
1930	Raman, Chandrasekhara V.	Investigation of infrared absorption bands of transparent substances
1932	Heisenberg, Werner	Developing the principle of uncertainty for electrons
1933	Schrodinger, Erwin	Developing the theory that an atom is composed of a positive nucleus surrounded by a field of negative electricity
	Dirac, Paul M. A.	Developing the theory that there is one kind of fundamental particle in nature
1935	Chadwick, James	Discovering the neutron
1936	Anderson, Carl D.	Discovering the positron
	Hess, Victor Franz	Investigation of the origin of cosmic radiation
1937	Davisson, Clinton J.	Interference in electronic bombardment of crystals
	Thomson, George P.	Investigation of thin metallic surfaces
1938	Fermi, Enrico	Transmutation of atoms by adding neutrons to the nucleus
1939	Lawrence, Ernest O.	Inventing the cyclotron
1943	Stern, Otto	Discovering the magnetic moment of the proton, and contributing to atomic ray method
1944	Rabi, Isidor I.	Developing resonance method of recording the magnetic properties of atomic nuclei

(Continued)

LIST 10–2. (Continued)

YEAR	NAME	RECOGNIZED FOR
1945	Pauli, Wolfgang	Developing Pauli's exclusion principle
1946	Bridgman, Percy W.	Research in atmospheric pressure
1947	Appleton, Edward V.	Discovering Appleton layer in the atmosphere, which reflects radio shortwaves
1948	Blackett, Patrick, M. S.	Developing Wilson method to study courses of radioactive particles, and discoveries in cosmic radiation
1949	Yukawa, Hideki	Mathematical prediction of the meson 14 years before its discovery
1950	Powell, Cecil F.	Investigating cosmic rays
1951	Cockroft, John D. Walton, Ernest T. S.	Investigations in transmutation of atomic nuclei by accelerating atomic particles
1952	Bloch, Felix Purcell, Edward Mills	Measuring magnetic fields in atomic nuclei
1953	Zernike, Frits	Developing special microscope
1954	Born, Max Bothe, Walter	Investigations leading to the foundations of modern nuclear physics
1955	Lamb, Willis E.	Discoveries of the hydrogen spectrum
	Kusch, Polykarp	Discovering the magnetic moment of the electron
1956	Bardeen, John Brattain, Walter H. Shockley, William B.	Developing an electric transistor
1957	Lee, Tsung Dao Yang, Chen Ning	Proving that the principle of conservation of parity does not apply in nuclear reactions
1958	Cherenkov, Pavel Frank, Ilya M. Tamm, Igor Y.	Joint discovery of Cherenkov effect
1959	Segre, Emilio Chamberlain, Owen	Discovery of the antiproton
1960	Glaser, Donald	Inventing the bubble chamber to photograph the smashing of atoms
1961	Hofstadter, Robert Mossbauer, Rudolf L.	Study of atomic nucleus, neutrons and protons
1962	Landau, Lev D.	Developing theories for condensed matter
1963	Wigner, Eugene P.	Developing atomic theory
	Jensen, J. Hans Mayer, Maria Goeppert	Discoveries about nuclear shell structure
1964	Townes, Charles H. Basov, Nikolai G. Prochorov, Aleksander	Investigations in quantum electronics which led to oscillators and amplifiers based on maser-laser principle
1965	Tomonaga, Shinichiro Schwinger, Julian Feynman, Richard F.	Research in quantum electrodynamics

The Science Teacher's Book of Lists, © 1993 by Prentice Hall

(Continued)

LIST 10–2. (Continued)

YEAR	NAME	RECOGNIZED FOR
1966	Kastler, Alfred	Work that led to the invention of the laser
1967	Bethe, Hans A.	Energy production of stars
1968	Alvarez, Luis	Discovery of resonance particles
1969	Gell-Mann, Murray	Classification of elementary particles
1970	Alfven, Hannes	Research in plasma physics
	Neel, Louis	Work in antiferromagnetism
1971	Gabor, Dennis	Invention of holography
1972	Schrieffer, John R.	Theory of superconductivity without electrical
	Cooper, Leon N.	resistance at absolute zero
	Bardeen, John	
1973	Giaever, Ivan	Theories on super conductors and semiconductors
	Esaki, Leo	important to microelectronics
	Josephson, Brian D.	
1974	Ryle, Martin	Improvements in radiotelescopy
	Hewish, Antony	Discovery of pulsars
1975	Rainwater, James	Studies proving the asymmetrical structure of
	Mottelson, Ben	the atomic nucleus
	Bohr, Aage	
1976	Richter, Burton	Discovery of the subatomic particle that
	Ting, Samuel C. C.	establishes the existence of charm
1977	Van Vleck, John H.	Study of the magnetic properties of atoms
	Anderson, Philip	Amorphous semiconductors
	Mott, Nevill F.	
1978	Kapitsa, Pyotr	Discovery of microwave radiation from the Big Bang, and research in low-temperature physics
	Penzias, Arno A.	Discovery of microwave radiation from the Big
	Wilson, Robert	Bang
1979	Weinberg, Steven	Discovering the link between electromagnetism
	Salam, Abdus	and the weak force of radioactive decay
	Glashow, Sheldon L.	
1980	Cronin, James W.	Showing that charge parity and time symmetry
	Fitch, Val L.	could be violated
1981	Bloembergen, Nicolass	Improvements in lasers applied to the study of
	Siegbahn, Kai M.	matter
	Schaalow, Arthur	
1982	Wilson, Kenneth G.	Theory of phase transitions
1983	Chandrasekhar, Subrahmanyan	Investigations in the aging and collapse of stars
	Fowler, William A.	
1984	Rubbia, Carlo	Discovery of W and Z particles
	van der Meere, Simon	
1985	von Klitzing, Klaus	Discovery of the quantized Hall effect
1986	Ruska, Ernst	Designing the first electron microscope
	Binnig, Gerd W.	Designing the scanning tunneling microscope
	Rohrer, Heinrich	*(Continued)*

LIST 10–2. (Continued)

YEAR	NAME	RECOGNIZED FOR
1987	Muller, K. Alex Bednorz, Georg J.	Discovery of superconductivity at a higher temperature than ever known
1988	Lederman, Leon M. Schwartz, Melvin Steinberger, Jack	Work that improved the understanding of elementary particles and force
1989	Ramsey, Norman, F.	Work that led to the development of the atomic clock
	Dehmelt, Hans G. Paul, Wolfgang	Developed methods to isolate atoms and subatomic particles
1990	Taylor, Richard E. Kendall, Henry W. Friedman, Jerome I.	Confirming the reality of quarks
1991	de Gennes, Pierre-Gilles	Discoveries about ordering of molecules in
1992	George Charpak	Inventions of particle detectors
1993	Joseph H. Taylor Russell A. Hulse	Discovery of a binary pulsar
1994	Clifford G. Shull Bertram N. Brockhouse	Adapting beams of neutrons as probes to explore the atomic structure of matter
1995	Martin L. Perl Frederick Reines	Discoveries of "two of nature's most remarkable subatomic particles"—the tau and the neutrino
1996	David M. Lee Douglas D. Osheroff Robert C. Richardson	Discovery that helium-3, a rare form of the element, flows without resistance at very low temperatures

The Science Teacher's Book of Lists, © 1993 by Prentice Hall

LIST 10–3. NOBEL PRIZE WINNERS IN MEDICINE & PHYSIOLOGY

YEAR	NAME	RECOGNIZED FOR
1901	von Behring, Emil A.	Discovering diphtheria antitoxin
1902	Ross, Ronald	Explaining the life cycle of the malaria parasite
1903	Finsen, Niels, R.	Identifying the curative effects of ultraviolet rays
1904	Pavlov, Ivan P.	Investigating conditioned stimulus response behavior in animals
1905	Koch, Robert	Discovering the bacilli that cause tuberculosis and cholera
1906	Golgi, Camillo	Discovering that nerves form interlacement
	Ramon y Cajal, Santiago	Investigating the structure of the brain and nerves
1907	Laveran, Charles L. A.	Identifying the parasite that causes malaria
1908	Ehrlich, Paul	Discovering salvarsan, specific for syphilis
	Metchnikoff, Elie	Study of immunity in infectious diseases
1909	Kocher, Emil Theodor	Surgery of the thyroid gland
1910	Kossel, Albrecht	Study of the chemical composition of body cells
1911	Gullstrand, Allvar	Research in the mechanics of vision
1912	Carrel, Alexis	Transplanting living tissue
1913	Richet, Charles	Research in anaphylaxis and serum therapy
1914	Barany, Robert	Developing methods of diagnosis for disorders of the inner ear
1919	Bordet, Jules	Research in antitoxic action; serum for whooping cough
1920	Krogh, August	Discovery of element regulating action of capillaries
1922	Hill, Archibald V.	Research into heat produced by muscular activity
	Meyerhof, Otto	Investigating the chemical changes that accompany muscular contractions
1923	Banting, Frederick Macleod, J. J. R.	Developing the insulin method for treating diabetes
1924	Einthoven, William	Inventing cardiometer for measuring heart action
1926	Fibiger, Johannes	Experimental production of cancer
1927	Wagner-Jauregg, Julius	Malarial cure for general paralysis
1928	Nicolle, Charles	Discovery of typhus vaccine

(Continued)

The Science Teacher's Book of Lists, © 1993 by Prentice Hall

LIST 10–3. (Continued)

YEAR	NAME	RECOGNIZED FOR
1929	Eijkman, Christiaan	Discovery of vitamin B
	Hopkins, Frederick G.	Discovery of vitamin A
1930	Landsteiner, Karl	Classification of individuals by blood groups
1931	Warburg, Otto H.	Research in cancer
1932	Sherrington, Charles S.	Explanation of how the nervous system integrates bodily functions
	Adrian, Edgar D.	Explanation of physiology of sensations
1933	Morgan, Thomas H.	Discovery of the gene
1934	Minot, George R.	Discovery of cure for pernicious anemia
	Murphy, William P.	
	Whipple, George H.	
1935	Spemann, Hans	Discoveries in embryonic evolution
1936	Dale, Henry H.	Discovery of cure for anemia
	Loewi, Otto	
1937	von Szent-Gyorgyi, Albert	Investigating metabolism and the effects of vitamins A and C
1938	Heymans, Corneille	Demonstrated link between blood changes and breathing
1939	Domagk, Gerhard	Discovering prontosil
1943	Dam, Henrik	Discovery of vitamin K
	Doisy, Edward A.	
1944	Erlanger, Joseph	Discovery of different functions of single nerve fibers
	Gasser, Herbert S.	
1945	Fleming, Alexander	Discovery of penicillin
	Florey, Howard W.	
	Chain, Ernst B.	
1946	Muller, Hermann J.	Genetic influence of X rays
1947	Cori, Carl F.	Explaining enzymatic synthesis of animal starch
	Cori, Gerty T.	
	Houssay, Bernardo A.	Discovery of the role of the hormones produced by the pituitary gland
1948	Muller, Paul	Development of DDT
1949	Hess, Walter Rudolph	Discoveries in brain function
	Moniz, Antonio	Developed prefrontal lobotomy (brain surgery)
1950	Kendall, Edward C.	Research in hormones, which included the discovery of cortisone
	Hench, Philip S.	
	Reichstein, Tadeus	
1951	Theiler, Max	Discovering a vaccine for yellow fever
1952	Waksman, Selman A.	Research in the discovery of streptomycin
1953	Lipmann, Fritz A.	Discoveries about living human cells
	Krebs, Hans A.	
1954	Enders, John F.	Discovery that poliomyelitis virus can grow in cultures of different tissues
	Weller, Thomas	
	Robbins, Frederick C.	

(Continued)

The Science Teacher's Book of Lists, © 1993 by Prentice Hall

LIST 10–3. (Continued)

YEAR	*NAME*	*RECOGNIZED FOR*
1955	Theorell, Alex H. T.	Discoveries about oxidation enzymes
1956	Richards, Jr., Dickinson	Richards and Cournand used Forssmann's
	Cournand, Andre F.	technique (1929) of working a catheter into a
	Forssmann, Werner	heart chamber from a vein to test heart function
1957	Bovet, Daniel	Drugs that relieve allergies
1958	Beadle, George W.	Discovery that genes regulate chemical events
	Tatum, Edward Lawrie	
	Lederberg, Joshua	Genetic recombinations
1959	Ochoa, Severo	Discovery of the mechanisms in the biological
	Kornberg, Arthur	synthesis of ribonucleic and deoxyribonucleic acids (RNA and DNA)
1960	Medawar, Peter B.	Joint discovery of acquired immunological
	Burnet, MacFarlane	tolerance
1961	von Bekesey, Georg	Discoveries in workings of the inner ear
1962	Watson, James Dewey	Discoveries of molecular structure of nucleic acids
	Crick, Francis H. C.	
	Wilkins, Maurice H. F.	
1963	Hodgkin, Alan L.	Research in nerve cells
	Huxley, Andrew F.	
	Eccles, John C.	
1964	Bloch, Konrad E.	Discoveries of mechanism and regulation of
	Lynen, Theodor	cholesterol and fatty acid metabolism
1965	Jacob, Francois	Discoveries of genetic control of enzyme and virus
	Lwoff, Andre	synthesis
	Monod, Jacques	
1966	Huggins, Charles B.	Cancer research
	Rous, Francis Peyton	
1967	Granit, Ragnar A.	Discoveries in the structure and chemical
	Wald, George	workings of the human eye
	Hartline, Haldan K.	
1968	Holley, Robert W.	Breaking the genetic code that determines cell
	Khorana, Hans Gobind	function
	Nirenberg, Marshall W.	
1969	Delbruck, Max	Discoveries about the functions and reproduction
	Hershey, Alfred D.	of viruses
	Luria, Salvador E.	
1970	Axelrod, Julius	Discoveries about the chemical transmissions of
	Katz, Bernard	nerve impulses
	Von Euler, Ulf	
1971	Sutherland, Earl W.	Discovery of cyclic AMP
1972	Edelman, Gerald and	Identifying the chemical structure of antibodies
	Porter, Rodney R.	

The Science Teacher's Book of Lists, © 1993 by Prentice Hall

(Continued)

LIST 10–3. (Continued)

YEAR	NAME	RECOGNIZED FOR
1973	von Frisch, Karl Lorenz, Konrad Tinbergen, Nikolaas	Research about individual and social behavior of animal species
1974	De Duve, Christian R. Claude, Albert Palade, George Emil	Furthering electron microscopy and knowledge of the structure of cells
1975	Baltimore, David Temin, Howard M.	Discovery of reverse transcriptase, an enzyme that catalyzes the formation of DNA on an RNA template
	Dulbecco, Renato	Discovery of the interaction between host cells and viruses
1976	Blumberg, Baruch Gajdusek, D. Carleton	Identification of hepatitis antigen and slow viruses
1977	Yalow, Rosalyn S. Schally, Andrew Guillemin, Roger C. L.	Improvements in the snythesis and measurement of hormones
1978	Nathans, Daniel Smith, Hamilton O. Arber, Werner	Discovery and use of restriction enzymes for DNA
1979	Cormack, Alain M. Hounsfield, Geoffrey N.	Invention of computed axial tomography (CAT scan), special X-ray picture taking techniques
1980	Benacerraf, Baruj Snell, George D. Dausset, Jean	Discovery of the role of antigens in organ transplants
1981	Hubel, David H. Sperry, Roger W. Wiesel, Tosten, N.	Research about the organization and function of brain areas
1982	Bergstrom, Sune Karl Samuelsson, Bengt Vane, John Robert	Research about formation and function of prostaglandins, hormonelike substances that fight diseases
1983	McClintock, Barbara	Discovery of mobile genes in corn chromosomes
1984	Jerne, Niels K.	Research on the immune system
	Milstein, Cesar Koehler, Georges J. F.	Research on monoclonal antibodies
1985	Brown, Michael S. Goldstein, Joseph L.	Research on the regulation of cholesterol metabolism
1986	Cohen, Stanley Levi-Montalcini, Rita	Studies of the mechanisms of cell and organ growth
1987	Tonegawa, Susumu	Research about antibodies and the immune system
1988	Elion, Gertrude B. Black, James Hitchings, George H.	Discoveries of important principles that have been applied to drug treatments

(Continued)

The Science Teacher's Book of Lists, © 1993 by Prentice Hall

LIST 10-3. (Continued)

YEAR	NAME	RECOGNIZED FOR
1989	Bishop, Michael J. Varmus, Harold E.	Developed a unifying theory of cancer development
1990	Murray, Joseph E.	First kidney transplants
	Thomas, E. Donnall	Transplanted bone marrow from one person to another
1991	Neher, Edwin Sakmann, Bert	Discoveries in cell function which are illuminating causes of diseases and may lead to specific drugs
1992	Edmond H. Fischer Edwin G. Kerbs	Discovery of a regulatory mechanism affecting almost all cells
1993	Phillip A. Sharp Richard J. Roberts	Discovery of "split genes"
1994	Alfred G. Gilman Martin Rodbell	Discovery of G-proteins that help cells respond to outside signals
1995	Edward B. Lewis Eric F. Wieschaus Christiane Nusslein-Volhard	Studies of the fruit fly that will help explain congenital malformations
1996	Peter C. Doherty Rolf M. Zinkernagel	Discovery of how the immune system identifies cells infected with viruses

LIST 10–4. NOBEL PRIZE
WINNERS IN CHEMISTRY

YEAR	NAME	RECOGNIZED FOR
1901	van't Hoff, Jacobus, H.	Founded the science of sterochemistry; investigations in osmotic pressure
1902	Fischer, Emil H.	Developed synthetic production of sugar
1903	Arrhenius, Svante A.	Developed theory of ionization in electrolysis of liquids
1904	Ramsay, William	Discovered argon and neon
1905	von Baeyer, Adolf	Analysis of indigo; development synthetic dyes
1906	Moissan, Henri	Electric furnace, synthetic diamond, isolation of fluorine
1907	Buchner, Eduard	Discovering cell-less fermentation
1908	Rutherford, Ernest	Proving that atoms consist of protons and electrons
1909	Ostwald, Wilhelm	Making nitrogen explosives from ammonia
1910	Wallach, Otto	Synthesis of essential oils, perfumes, and gums
1911	Curie, Marie S.	Discovery of polonium and radium
1912	Grignard, Victor	Synthesis of hydrocarbons, alcohols, and aldehydes
	Sabatier, Paul	Hydrogenation by catalytic agents
1913	Werner, Alfred	Coordination theory of valence
1914	Richards, Theodore	Precise determination of atomic weights
1915	Willstätter, Richard	Research in the coloring agents in plants
1918	Haber, Fritz	Synthetic production of ammonia from nitrogen
1920	Nernst, Walter	Inventing electric lamp and reversible galvanic cells
1921	Soddy, Frederick	Developed the theory of isotopes
1922	Aston, Francis W.	Study of isotopes by mass spectrograph
1923	Pregl, Fritz	Microchemical analysis; antiseptic iodine solution
1925	Zsigmondy, Richard	Ultramicroscope; discovery of nature of colloids
1926	Svedberg, Theodor	Study of colloids
1927	Wieland, Heinrich	Research of fermentation in the digestive process
1928	Windaus, Adolf O. R.	Discovery and isolation of vitamin D
1929	Harden, Arthur von Euler-Chelpin, Hans	Study of enzyme action in sugar fermentation
1930	Fischer, Hans	Synthesis of hemin, blood constituent
1931	Bergius, Friedrich	Producing gasoline by liquefaction of coal
	Bosch, Karl	Developing a commercial production of ammonia from nitrogen derived from the atmosphere
1932	Langmuir, Irving	Gas-filled tungsten lamp; atomic hydrogen produced
1934	Urey, Harold Clayton	Discovering heavy water
1935	Joliot, Frederic Joliot, Irene Curie	Transmuting elements by displacement or addition of component parts of atoms

(Continued)

The Science Teacher's Book of Lists, © 1993 by Prentice Hall

LIST 10–4. (Continued)

YEAR	*NAME*	*RECOGNIZED FOR*
1936	Debye, Peter J. W.	Investigations in atomic structure of molecules
1937	Haworth, Walter N.	Study of vitamin C
	Karrer, Paul	Studies of vitamins A and G, and vegetable coloring
1938	Kuhn, Richard	Research on carotenoids and vitamins
1939	Butenandt, Adolf F. J.	Isolation of the male sex hormone, androsterone
	Ruzicka, Leopold	Synthesis of male sex hormone, androsterone
1943	de Hevesy, Georg	Studying chemical processes by using isotopes as indicators
1944	Hahn, Otto	Investigations on splitting the uranium atom
1945	Virtanen, Artturi L.	Work in agricultural biochemistry
1946	Sumner, James B.	Work in enzyme research
	Northrop, John H.	Work in virus research
	Stanley, Wendell M.	
1947	Robinson, Robert	Investigations of biologically important plant products
1948	Tiselius, Arne W. K.	Biochemical investigation of proteins and enzymes
1949	Giauque, William	Study of substances at low temperatures
1950	Alder, Kurt	Discovery of diene synthesis, by which odors and chemical compounds can be artificially reproduced
	Diels, Otto, Paul H.	
1951	Seaborg, Glenn T.	Discovering plutonium
	McMillan, Edwin M.	
1952	Martin, Archer	Developing chromatographic analysis for identifying and separating chemical elements
	Synge, Richard, L. M.	
1953	Staudinger, Hermann	Investigation of giant molecules
1954	Pauling, Linus Carl	Discoveries of forces that hold molecules together
1955	du Vigneaud, Vincent	First synthesis of a polypeptide hormone
1956	Semenov, Nikolai	Work on chemical reaction kinetics to improve the internal combustion engine and plastics
	Hinshelwood, Cyril N.	
1957	Todd, Alexander R.	Research in proteins, nucleotides, and nucleotic enzymes
1958	Sanger, Frederick	Investigated structure of proteins, especially insulin
1959	Heyrovsky, Jaroslav	Discovery and development of polarographic analysis
1960	Libby, Willard F.	Developing carbon 14 dating
1961	Calvin, Melvin	Identified sequence of chemical reactions in photosynthesis
1962	Perutz, Max F.	Mapping protein molecules using X rays
	Kendrew, John C.	
1963	Ziegler, Karl	Producing large molecular substances by uniting simple hydrocarbons
	Natta, Giulio	

(Continued)

LIST 10–4. (Continued)

YEAR	NAME	RECOGNIZED FOR
1964	Hodgkin, Dorothy	Identifying the structure of biochemical compounds needed in combating pernicious anemia
1965	Woodward, Robert B.	Contributions in organic synthesis
1966	Mulliken, Robert S.	Investigations of electronic structure of molecules
1967	Eigen, Manfred Norrish, Ronald G. Porter, George	Study of high-speed chemical reactions
1968	Onsager, Lars	Contributions to the theoretical basis of diffusion of isotopes
1969	Hassel, Odd Barton, Derek H. R.	Determination of the three-dimensional shape of organic compounds
1970	Leloir, Luis F.	Discovery of sugar nucleotides and their biosynthesis of carbohydrates
1971	Herzberg, Gerhard	Investigation of the geometry of molecules in gases
1972	Anfinsen, Christian B. Moore, Stanford Stein, William H.	Research in enzyme chemistry
1973	Fischer, Ernst Otto Wilkinson, Geoffrey	Research in the chemistry of ferrocene
1974	Flory, Paul J.	Study of long-chain molecules
1975	Cornforth, John W. Prelog, Vladimir	Investigation of enzyme-substrate combinations Investigation of asymmetric compounds
1976	Lipscomb, William N.	Investigation of bonding in boranes
1977	Prigogine, Ilya	Nonequilibrium theories in thermodynamics
1978	Mitchell, Peter	Work on biological energy transfer
1979	Brown, Herbert C. Wittig, George	Study of boron-containing organic compounds Study of phosphorus-containing organic compounds
1980	Berg, Paul Gilbert, Walter Sanger, Frederick	Development of recombinant DNA Development of methods to map the structure of DNA
1981	Fukui, Kenichi Hoffman, Roald	Application of the laws of quantum mechanics to chemical reactions
1982	Klug, Aaron S.	Developments in the electron microscope and the study of acid-protein complexes
1983	Taube, Henry	Discoveries in the mechanics of chemical reactions
1984	Merrifield, R. Bruce	Discovery of a method of creating peptides and proteins
1985	Karle, Jerome Hauptman, Herbert A.	Equations to determine the structure of molecules

The Science Teacher's Book of Lists, © 1993 by Prentice Hall

(Continued)

LIST 10–4. (Continued)

YEAR	NAME	RECOGNIZED FOR
1986	Lee, Yuan T. Herschbach, Dudley R. Polanyi, John C.	Invention of the crossed-beam molecular technique Invention of chemiluminescence to study the emission of light as a result of chemical reactions
1987	Cram, Donald J. Pedersen, Charles Lehn, Jean-Marie	Work on "crown ethers," or macrocyllic polyethers; making complicated molecules that perform the same functions as natural proteins
1988	Deisenhofer, Johann Huber, Robert Michel, Hartmut	Unraveled the structure of proteins that play a crucial part in understanding energy-converting mechanisms of photosynthesis
1989	Cech, Thomas R. Altman, Sidney	Independently discovered that RNA could actively aid chemical reactions in cells
1990	Corey, Elias James	Developing new ways to synthesize complex molecules
1991	Ernst, Richard R.	Refinements in nuclear magnetic resonance spectroscopy, a new technique of chemical analysis
1992	Rudolph A. Marcus	Mathematical analysis of how the overall energy in a system of interacting molecules changes and induces an electron to jump from one molecule to another
1993	Kary B. Mullis Michael Smith	Contributions to the science of genetics
1994	George A. Olah	Research opening up new ways to break apart and rebuild compounds of carbon and hydrogen
1995	F. Sherwood Rowland Mario Molina Paul Crutzen	Pioneering work in explaining the chemical processes that deplete the earth's ozone shield
1996	Harold W. Kroto Robert F. Curl, Jr. Richard E. Smalley	Discovery of a new class of carbon molecules

LIST 10–5. ENRICO FERMI AWARD WINNERS

This award, in the amount of $100,000, is presented by the United States Department of Energy to recognize exceptional scientific or technological achievements related to the development of nuclear energy. It is not presented every year.

1954	Enrico Fermi		1981	W. Bennett Lewis
1956	John von Newman		1982	Herbert Anderson Seth Neddermeyer
1957	Ernest O. Lawrence		1983	Alexander Hollaender John Lawrence
1958	Eugene P. Wigner			
1959	Glenn T. Seaborg		1984	Robert R. Wilson George Vendryes
1961	Hans A. Bethe			
1962	Edward Teller		1985	Norman C. Rasmussen Marshall N. Rosenblath
1963	J. Robert Oppenheimer			
1964	Hyman G. Rickover		1986	Ernest D. Courant M. Stanley Livingston
1966	Otto Hahn Lise Meitner Fritz Strassman		1987	Luis W. Alvarez Gerald F. Tape
1968	John A. Wheeler		1988	Richard B. Setlow Victor F. Weisskopf
1969	Walter H. Zinn			
1970	Norris E. Bradbury		1990	George A. Cowan Robley D. Evans
1971	Shields Warren Stafford L. Warren		1992	Leon M. Lederman Harold Brown John S. Foster, Jr.
1972	Mason Benedict			
1976	William L. Russell			
1978	Harold M. Agnew Wolfgang K. H. Panofsky		1993	Freeman J. Dyson Liane B. Russell
1980	Alvin M. Weinberg Rudolf E. Peirls		1995	Ugo Fano Martin Kamen

The Science Teacher's Book of Lists, © 1993 by Prentice Hall

LIST 10–6. BARNARD MEDAL

This is awarded by Columbia University on the recommendation of the National Academy of Science for a notable discovery in physical or astronomical science or a novel application of science to purposes beneficial to the human race. It is not awarded every year.

1920	Albert Einstein	1965	William A. Fowler
1935	Edwin P. Hubble	1975	Louis P. Hammett
1950	Enrico Fermi	1980	Andre Weil
1955	Isidor I. Rabi	1985	Benoit Mandelbrot

LIST 10–7. EINSTEIN MEDAL AND AWARD

This award, in the amount of $100,000, is presented by the United States Department of Energy to recognize exceptional scientific or technological achievements related to the development of nuclear energy. It is not presented every year.

1951	Julian Schwinger	1961	Luis W. Alvarez
1951	Kurt Gödel	1962	Shields Warren
1954	Richard P. Feynman	1965	John A. Wheeler
1958	Edward Teller	1967	Marshall N. Rosenbluth
1959	Willard F. Libby	1972	Eugene P. Wigner
1960	Leo Szilard		

LIST 10–8. SOME INVENTIONS AND DISCOVERIES

DATE	NAME AND LIFE SPAN	INVENTION OR DISCOVERY
1450	Johan Gutenberg (1398–1468)	Printing from movable type
1676	Anton van Leeuwenhoek (1632–1723)	Used lenses to observe, draw, and describe bacteria
1679	Denis Papen	Pressure cooker
1764	James Hargreaves (?–1778)	Spinning jenny perfected, 1766
1765	James Watt (1736–1819)	Steam engine
1775	Richard Arkwright (1732–1792)	Water frame for cotton yarn making
1777	Antoine L. Lavoisier (1743–1794)	Explained combustion; known as the father of modern chemistry
1784	William Murdock (1754–1839)	Locomotive; 1792, gas lighting
1784	James Rumsey (1743–1792)	Steamboat
1787	Oliver Evans (1755–1819)	Automatic flour mill
1790	Samuel Hopkins	Potash process (first U.S. patent)
1794	Eli Whitney (1765–1825)	Spinning machines
1807	John C. Stevens (1749–1838)	Propeller driven steamboat
1807	Robert Fulton (1765–1815)	Steamboat
1830	Robert L. Stevens (1787–1859)	Railroad track and spike
1831	Michael Faraday (1791–1867)	Induction of electric currents
1834	Cyrus McCormick (1809–1884)	Grain reaper
1836	Samuel Morse (1791–1872)	Telegraph
1839	Jacques M. Daguerre (1779–1851)	Photographic process
1844	Henry D. Thoreau (1817–1862)	Improved lead pencils
1846	Elias Howe (1819–1867)	Sewing machines
1865	Henry Bessemer (1813–1898)	Steel making process
1867	Joseph Lister (1827–1912)	Antiseptic surgery
1868	Christopher L. Sholes (1819–1890)	Remington typewriter
1869	John W. Hyatt (1837–1920)	Celluloid
1876	Alexander G. Bell (1847–1922)	Telephone
1885	Jan Matzeliger (1852–1889)	Shoe lasting machine
	Alfred B. Nobel (1833–1896)	Dynamite, synthetic rubber and leather, artificial silk
	Louis Pasteur (1822–1895)	Anti-rabies treatment
1886	Charles M. Hall (1863–1914)	Process for producing aluminum
1888	Nikola Tesla (1856–1943)	Induction motor
		Electric power transmission
1889	Thomas Edison (1847–1931)	Electric light
1896	Gugliemo Marconi (1874–1937)	Wireless telegraph

The Science Teacher's Book of Lists, © 1993 by Prentice Hall

(Continued)

LIST 10–8. (Continued)

DATE	NAME AND LIFE SPAN	INVENTION OR DISCOVERY
1903	Orville Wright (1871–1948)	Airplane
	Wilbur Wright (1867–1912)	
	Leo Baekeland (1863–1944)	Bakelite™, a group of plastics
1906	Lee De Forest (1873–1961)	Vacuum tube amplifier
1911	Elmer A. Sperry (1860–1930)	Gyroscopic compass
1924	David Mannes (1899–1964)	Kodachrome™ color film
	Leopold Godowsky, Jr. (1900–1983)	
1926	Roy Chapman Andrews (1884–1960)	Discovered fossilized dinosaur eggs
1928	Alexander Fleming (1881–1955)	Penicillin
1930	Wallace H. Carothers (1896–1937)	Neoprene rubber; 1934, nylon
1937	Niels Christensen (1865–1952)	O-rings
1938	Chester Carlson (1906–1968)	Xerography
1947	Edwin H. Land (1909–1991)	Polaroid photographic film and camera
	John Bardeen (1908–1991)	Transistor
	Walter Brattain (1902–1987)	
	William Shockley (1910–1989)	
1955	Jonas Salk (1914–)	Polio vaccine
1965	Paul Morgan (1911–1992)	One of the inventors of Kevlar® and other high-strength fibers
1972	William Higinbotham (1910–)	First video game
1973	Stanley H. Cohen	Fragments of DNA can be inserted into bacteria cells where they could be reproduced; beginning of genetic engineering
	Herbert W. Boyer	
1974	Martin L. Perl	Named a variety of leptons: *tau electron* or *tauon*
1974	Charles T. Kowall (1940–)	Thirteenth moon of Jupiter, numerous supernovas, and Chiron, later determined to be the largest known comet
1977	Donald Johanson (1943–)	Parts of hominid fossil believed to be 4 million years old, leg and thighbones indicated it was a bipedal female
1989	Henry A. Erlich and coworkers	Method to identify a person or rule out a person from the DNA in one hair

NOTE: The date is that of a patent, patent application, notebook record, public demonstration or announcement. Many inventors made other important discoveries. Unfortunately, not all birth and death dates are readily available.

LIST 10–9. DISCOVERERS OF CHEMICAL ELEMENTS

DATE	SCIENTIST	NAME OF ELEMENT
1450	Valentine	Antimony
1669	Brand	Phosphorus
1735	Brandt	Cobalt
1735	Ulloa	Platinum
1751	Cronstedt	Nickel
1766	Cavendish	Hydrogen
1771	Scheele	Fluorine
1772	Rutherford	Nitrogen
1774	Priestly, Scheele	Oxygen
1774	Gahn	Manganese
1774	Scheele	Chlorine
1782	Hjeim	Molybdenum
1782	Von Reichenstein	Tellurium
1783	d'Elhujar	Tungsten
1789	Klaproth	Uranium
1789	Klaproth	Zirconium
1790	Crawford	Strontium
1791	Gregor	Titanium
1794	Gadolin	Yttrium
1797	Vauquelin	Chromium
1798	Vauquelin	Beryllium
1801	Hatchett	Niobium
1803	Klaproth	Cerium
1803	Wollaston	Palladium
1803	Wollaston	Rhodium
1804	Tennant	Iridium
1804	Tennant	Osmium
1807	Davy	Potassium
1808	Davy	Barium
1808	Davy	Calcium
1808	Gay-Lussac, Thenard	Boron
1811	Courtois	Iodine
1817	Arfvedson	Lithium
1817	Stromeyer	Cadmium
1817	Berzelius	Selenium
1823	Berzelius	Silicon
1825	Oersted	Aluminum
1826	Balard	Bromine
1829	Bussy	Magnesium
1839	Mosander	Lanthanum
1843	Mosander	Erbium
1845	Klaus	Ruthenium
1860	Bunsen, Kirchhoff	Cesium

(Continued)

The Science Teacher's Book of Lists, © 1993 by Prentice Hall

LIST 10–9. (Continued)

DATE	SCIENTIST	NAME OF ELEMENT
1863	Reich, Richter	Indium
1868	Janssen, Lockyer	Helium
1875	Boisbaudran	Gallium
1878	Soret, Delafontaine	Holmium
1885	Welsbach	Neodymium
1885	Welsbach	Praseodymium
1886	Marignac	Gadolinium
1886	Winkler	Germanium
1886	Boisbaudran	Dysprosium
1894	Rayleigh, Ramsay	Argon
1898	Ramsay, Travers	Krypton
1898	Ramsay, Travers	Neon
1898	Ramsay, Travers	Xenon
1898	Curie, Marie and Pierre	Polonium
1898	Curie, Marie and Pierre, and Bemont	Radium
1899	Debierne	Actinium
1900	Dorn	Radon
1907	Welsbach, Urbain	Lutetium
1940	McMillan, Abeison	Neptunium
1940	Corson and others	Astatine
1940	Seaborg and others	Plutonium
1944	Seaborg and others	Americium
1945	Glendenin, Marinsky, and Coryell	Promethium
1949	Thompson, Ghiorso, and Seaborg	Berkelium
1950	Thompson and others	Californium
1955	Ghiorso and others	Mendelevium
1958	Ghiorso and others	Nobelium
1969	Ghiorso and others	Rutherfordium

LIST 10–10. SOME NOTED WOMEN SCIENTISTS

DATES	NAME	CONTRIBUTION
1716–1774	Anna M. Manzolini	Anatomist, discovered the termination of the oblique muscle of the eye; constructed anatomical models, which were used for study throughout Europe
1799–1847	Mary Anning	Made important paleontological find including first complete ichthyosaur skeleton (1811), a plesiosaur, and a pterodactyl; no formal training
1821–1910	Elizabeth Blackwell	Pioneer in opening medical profession to women; founder and physician to New York Infirmary for Women and Children
1858–1947	Rosa Smith Eigenmann	Ichthyologist, author, worked on the taxonomy of fishes
1862–1945	Florence Bascom	Geologist, first woman to serve as geologist for U.S. Geological Survey, first woman elected to Geological Society of America; worked on mapping formations in Pennsylvania, Maryland, and New Jersey
1863–1948	Florence Merrian Bailey	Naturalist specializing in ornithology, wrote about birds; first woman to be made a fellow of the American Ornithologists Union
1863–1941	Annie Jump Cannon	Astronomer and writer; simplified methodology for studying stellar spectra
1863–1951	Margaret Clay Ferguson	Botanist; directed the modernization of Wellesley's botany department; research in spores, pine forests, and genetics in petunias; first woman president of the Botanical Society of America
1867–1949	Mary Orr Evershad	Astronomer and writer; wrote about solar prominences; concluded forces other than gravity and eruptive forces affected the sun's surface
1867–1934	Marie Sklodowska Curie	Physicist and chemist; won 1903 Nobel Prize in Physics for research in radioactivity; shared 1991 Nobel Prize in Chemistry with husband, Pierre, for discoveries of radium and polonium
1874–1938	Charlotta Joaquina Maury	Paleontologist; served as research paleontologist and leader for expeditions to Venezuela (1910–11), other Latin American countries, official paleontologist to Brazil (1914–38), specialized in Antillean, Venezuelan and Brazilian strategraphy and fossil faunas

(Continued)

LIST 10–10. (Continued)

DATES	NAME	CONTRIBUTION
1883–1955	Alice Middleton Boring	Cytologist, geneticist, zoologist; made contributions to literature on the taxonomy of Chinese amphibians and reptiles
1896–1957	Gertrude T. Cori	Shared the 1948 Nobel Prize in Physiology and Medicine for work in explaining enzymatic synthesis of animal starch
1897–1956	Irene Curie Joliot	Shared the 1935 Nobel Prize in Chemistry with her husband for their discovery that stable atoms can be made to be radioactive by bombarding them with neutrons
1900–	Honor Bridget Fell	Cell biologist; investigated cell reproduction
1901–1977	Margaret Mead	Anthropologist, educator, and author; curator of ethnology at American Museum of Natural History; innovations in recording and presenting ethnological data
1902–	Barbara McClintock	Geneticist, educator; won many awards including the 1983 Nobel Prize in Medicine and Physiology for discovering mobile gene in corn chromosomes
1906–1972	Marie Goeppert Mayer	Nuclear physicist; shared the 1963 Nobel Prize in Physics with Hans J. Jensen for discoveries about nuclear shell structure
1907–1964	Rachel L. Carson	Naturalist; writer of books which informed the public about the possible effects of pesticides and other pollutants on the environment
1909–	Rita Levi-Montalcini	Shared the Nobel Prize in Physiology and Medicine in 1986 for work in the study of the mechanisms of cell and organ growth
1910–1982	Dorothy C. Hodgkin	Won 1964 Nobel Prize in Chemistry for determination of the structure of vitamin B_{12}, cholesterol iodide, and penicillin
1913–	Birgit Vennesland	Biochemist; worked on the use of carbon isotope tracers; 1964 ACS Garvan Medal
1918–	Joan Maie Freeman	Physicist; investigated sub-atomic particles

(Continued)

LIST 10–10. (Continued)

DATES	NAME	CONTRIBUTION
1918–	Gertrude B. Elion	Shared the 1988 Nobel Prize in Medicine and Physiology for discoveries of principles that have led to drug treatments for leukemia, septic shock and tissue rejection; 1968 American Chemical Society's Garvan Medal; first woman named to National Inventors Hall of Fame
1921–	Rosalyn S. Yalow	Shared the 1977 Nobel Prize in Physiology and Medicine for improvements in the synthesis and measurement of hormones
1923–	Stephanie Kwolek	First chemist to prepare a liquid crystalline solution of an aromatic polyamide; precursor to Kevlar® fibers
1931–	Mary L. Good	Chemist, educator, research executive, author; won numerous awards including 1973 American Chemical Society's Garvan Award
1932–1985	Dian Fossey	Zoologist; studied Rwanda's rare mountain gorillas for 18 years; founded the Karisoke Research Institute to study gorillas in the wild; author, educator
1934–	Jane Goodall	Anthropologist; founded the Gombe Stream Research Center in 1965 where students could observe chimpanzees and baboons under her direction; author and educator
1940–	Kathleen M. Nauss	Investigating effects of dietary factors on cancer and immune functions and health effects of auto emissions
1942–	Muhao S. Wang	Research in environmental management; industrial, solid, and hazardous wastes
1942–	Manjula K. Gupta	Research in mechanisms by which hormones initiate cancer and alter immune response
1946–	Biruté Galdikas	Primatologist; studies orangutans in the wild in Borneo; educator, author; seen on National Geographic specials about orangutans
1949–	Karen Ann Carlberg	Research in effects of exercise training on female reproductive function; endocrine, metabolic and cardiovascular responses to stress

(Continued)

The Science Teacher's Book of Lists, © 1993 by Prentice Hall

LIST 10–10. (Continued)

DATES	NAME	CONTRIBUTION
1950–	Judith Totman Parrish	Investigating ancient marine high-productivity systems; paleoclimate of supercontinent Pangaea
1951–	Margaret Anne Cascieri	Research in the interaction and regulation of secretions, importance in diseases such as diabetes
1951–	Sally K. Ride	Physicist, educator, writer, former astronaut; in 1983 became the first American woman in space
1952–	Jacqueline K. Barton	Chemist, awarded the American Chemical Society Award in Pure Chemistry in 1988

NOTE: Unfortunately, not all birth and death dates are readily available.

LIST 10–11. GARVAN MEDAL RECIPIENTS

The Garvan Medal was established in 1936 as an American Chemical Society award. Set up through funding by Mr. Francis P. Garvan, the medal is awarded in recognition of significant achievements by women chemists in America. It consists of an inscribed gold medal, a replica of the medal, and an honorarium.

DATE	CHEMIST	CONTRIBUTION/PLACE OF RESEARCH
1937	Emma Perry Carr	Hydrocarbon structure by far UV Mt. Holyoke College
1940	Mary Engle Pennington	Food chemistry Private consultant
1942	Florence B. Seibert	Chemistry of tuberculosis University of Pennsylvania
1946	Icie Macy-Hoobler	Nutrition chemistry Children's Fund of Michigan
1947	Mary Lura Sherrill	Molecular structure Mt. Holyoke College
1948	Gerty T. Cori	Enzymatic synthesis and reactions Washington School of Medicine
1949	Agnes Fay Morgan	Chemistry of vitamins University of California at Berkeley
1950	Pauline Beery Mack	Calcium chemistry of bone Pennsylvania State University
1951	Katherine Blodgett	Monomolecular films General Electric Research Laboratory
1952	Gladys Emerson	Chemistry of vitamin E Merck Institute for Therapeutic Research
1953	Leonora Neuffer Bilger	Asymmetric nitrogen compounds University of Hawaii
1954	Betty Sullivan	Cereal chemistry Russell-Miller Milling Co.
1955	Grace Medes	Discovery and study of tyrosinosis Lankenau Hospital Research Institute
1956	Allene R. Jeanes	Fundamental research on dextran Northern Utilization Research Branch, USDA
1957	Lucy W. Pickett	Vacuum ultraviolet spectroscopy Mt. Holyoke College
1958	Arda A. Green	Purification of enzymes Johns Hopkins University
1959	Dorothy V. Nightingale	Organic synthetic reactions University of Missouri
1960	Mary L. Caldwell	Crystalline enzyme preparation Columbia University
1961	Sarah Ratner	Protein production controlling enzymes Public Health Research Institute, New York

(Continued)

The Science Teacher's Book of Lists, © 1993 by Prentice Hall

LIST 10–11. (Continued)

DATE	CHEMIST	CONTRIBUTION/PLACE OF RESEARCH
1962	Helen M. Dyer	Experimental carcinogenesis mechanisms National Cancer Institute
1963	Mildred Cohn	Oxygen-18 enzyme mechanism studies University of Pennsylvania
1964	Briget Vennesland	Enzymic hydrogen transfer studies University of Chicago
1965	Gertrude E. Perlmann	Studies of protein structure Rockefeller Institute
1966	Mary L. Peterman	Cellular chemistry Sloan-Kettering Institute of Cancer Research
1967	Marjorie J. Vold	Theoretical models of colloids University of Southern California
1968	Gertrude B. Elion	Drugs for chemotherapy Burroughs-Wellcome and Co.
1969	Sofia Simmonds	Bacteria amino acid metabolism Yale University
1970	Ruth R. Benerito	Studies on cellulose properties Southern Utilization R & D Division, USDA
1971	Mary Fieser	Chemical literature Harvard University
1972	Jean'ne M. Shreeve	Inorganic fluorine compounds University of Idaho
1973	Mary L. Good	Mossbauer spectroscopy Louisiana State University
1974	Joyce J. Kaufman	Quantum calculations of drug action Johns Hopkins University
1975	Marjorie C. Caserio	Physical organic chemistry University of California at Irvine
1976	Isabella L. Karle	Crystallography Naval Research Laboratory, Washington, DC
1977	Marjorie G. Horning	Neonatal toxicology Baylor College of Medicine
1978	Madeleine M. Joullie	Heterocyclic and medicinal chemistry University of Pennsylvania
1979	Jenny P. Glusker	Biochemical reaction mechanisms Institute for Cancer Research, Philadelphia
1980	Helen M. Free	Clinical test systems Miles Laboratories, Inc.
1981	Elizabeth K. Weisburger	Metabolic activation of carcinogens National Cancer Institute
1982	Sara Jane Rhoads	Organic reaction mechanisms University of Wyoming
1983	Ines Mandl	Biomedical chemical research Columbia University

(Continued)

LIST 10–11. (Continued)

DATE	CHEMIST	CONTRIBUTION/PLACE OF RESEARCH
1984	Martha L. Ludwig	X-ray crystallography of proteins University of Michigan
1985	Catherine C. Fenselau	Mass spectrometry of biochemicals Johns Hopkins University
1986	Jeanette G. Grasselli	Spectroscopy for industrial applications Standard Oil Company, Ohio
1987	Janet U. Osteryoung	Electrochemistry State University of New York at Buffalo
1988	Marye Anne Fox	Photoelectrochemistry University of Texas, Austin
1989	Kathleen C. Taylor	Catalysis and surface chemistry General Motors Research Laboratories
1990	Darleane C. Hoffman	Nuclear chemistry University of California at Berkeley
1991	Cynthia M. Friend	Mechanics of surface reactions Harvard University
1992	Jacqueline K. Barton	Designing transition-metal complexes that recognize specific sights on DNA and RNA California Institute of Technology
1993	Edith Flanigen	Silicate chemistry Universal Oil Products
1994	Barbara J. Garrison	Computational models that shed new light on surface chemical properties Pennsylvania State University
1995	Angelica M. Stacy	New process for transition of metal oxides University of California-Berkeley
1996	Geraldine L. Richmond	Application of nonlinear optical techniques to surfaces University of Oregon
1997	Karen W. Morse	Chemistry of boron compounds Western Washington University

The Science Teacher's Book of Lists, © 1993 by Prentice Hall

SCIENCE AND SCIENCE EDUCATION RESOURCES

LIST 11–1. PROFESSIONAL ORGANIZATIONS WITH PUBLICATIONS FOR SCIENCE TEACHERS

The address for association-education publications is frequently the college address of the editor, who is a member of the association and a professor. Thus, as the editorship is changed, the address of the publication is changed. To identify the current address and/or editors for publications not provided, locate a current copy of the periodical in a library and check the front matter.

ORGANIZATION	PUBLICATION
American Association for the Advancement of Science (AAAS) 1333 H Street, N.W. Washington, D.C. 20005	*Science Books and Films* (Newsletter: Reviews of science books and films.) *Science Education News* *Science*
American Association of Physics Teachers (AAPT) 57 East 55th Street New York, New York 10022	*The Physics Teacher* *The American Journal of Physics*
American Chemical Society (ACS) 1155 16th Street, N.W. Washington, D.C. 20036	*Chemical and Engineering News* *Journal of Chemical Education* *ChemMatters* (High school) *WonderScience* (Elementary)
American Forestry Association 919 17th Street, N.W. Washington, D.C. 20036	*American Forests*
American Geological Institute 1515 Massachusetts Avenue, N.W. Washington, D.C. 20036	*Geotimes*
American Institute of Physics 335 East 45th Street New York, New York 10017	*Physics Today*
American Meteorological Society 3 Joy Street Boston, Massachusetts 02108	*Weatherwise*
American Museum of Natural History 79th Street and Central Park West New York, New York 10024	*Natural History*
American Nature Association 1214 15th Street, N.W. Washington, D.C. 20036	*Nature Magazine*
Central Association of Science and Mathematics Teachers P.O. Box 48 Oak Park, Illinois 60305	*School Science and Mathematics*

(Continued)

LIST 11–1. (Continued)

ORGANIZATION	*PUBLICATION*
National Audubon Society 1130 Fifth Avenue New York, New York 10028	*Audubon Magazine* *Outdoors Illustrated*
National Association of Biology Teachers (NABT) 11250 Roger Bacon Drive, #19 Reston, Virginia 22090	*The American Biology Teacher* *News and Views* (Newsletter) NABT/NSTA Standardized Biology Test AIDS Education Software Careers in Biology: An Introduction A Source Book of Biotechnology Activities
National Association for Research in Science Teaching (NARST) John Wiley & Sons 605 Third Avenue New York, New York 10016	*Journal of Research in Science Teaching*
National Association of Geology Teachers (NAGT)	*Journal of Geological Education*
National Science Teachers Association (NSTA) 1742 Connecticut Avenue, N.W. Washington, D.C. 20009-1171	*Journal of College Science Teaching* *The Science Teacher* (High school) *Scope* (Middle School) *Science and Children* (Elementary)
Woods Hole Oceanographic Institute Woods Hole, Massachusetts 02543	*Readers Guide to Oceanography*

LIST 11–2. SCIENCE AND SCIENCE EDUCATION ORGANIZATIONS

American Academy of Arts and
   Sciences
136 Irving Street
Cambridge, Virginia 23235

American Academy of Forensic
   Sciences
225 South Academy Boulevard
Colorado Springs, Colorado 80910

American Academy of Optometry
School of Optometry
University of Alabama
Birmingham, Alabama 35294

American Anthropological Association
1703 New Hampshire Avenue, N.W.
Washington, D.C. 20009

American Association of Colleges of
   Pharmacy
1426 Prince Street
Alexandria, Virginia 22314

American Astronomical Society
P.O. Box 3818, University Station
Charlottesville, Virginia 22903

American Dairy Science Association
Pennsylvania State University
225 Borland
University Park, Pennsylvania 16802

American Dental Association
211 East Chicago Avenue
Chicago, Illinois 60611

American Dietetic Association
Division of Education and Research
430 North Michigan Avenue
Chicago, Illinois 60611

American Geographical Society
156 Fifth Avenue, #600
New York, New York 10010

American Geological Institute
4200 King Street
Alexandria, Virginia 22302

American Institute of Biological
   Sciences
1401 Wilson Boulevard
Arlington, Virginia 22209

American Institute of Chemical
   Engineers
345 East 47th Street
New York, New York 10017

American Institute of Chemists
Northeast Missouri State University
Kirksville, Missouri 63501

American Institute of Physics
335 East 45th Street
New York, New York 10017

American Institute of Professional
   Geologists
7828 Vance Drive, #103
Arvada, Colorado 80003

American Medical Association
535 North Dearborn Street
Chicago, Illinois 60610

American Meteorological Society
University of Wisconsin
Madison, Wisconsin 53706

American Pharmaceutical Association
2215 Constitution Avenue, N.W.
Washington, D.C. 20037

American Physical Society
335 East 45th Street
New York, New York 10017

American Public Health Association
1015 15th Street, N.W.
Washington, D.C. 20005

American Society of Ichthyologists and
   Herpetologists
Florida State Museum
University of Florida
Gainesville, Florida 32611

(Continued)

LIST 11–2. (Continued)

American Society of Zoologists
Department of Biology
University of California
Riverside, California 92521

Botanical Society of America
1223 West 22nd Street
Cedar Falls, Iowa 50613

History of Science Society
Education Committee
504 Third Street
Washington, D.C. 20003

National Geographic Society
17th & M Streets, N.W.
Washington, D.C. 20036
(202)775-6701

National Institute of Science
P.O. Box 2784
Prairie View, Texas 77446

National Science Foundation
1800 G Street, N.W.
Washington, D.C. 20550

Union of Concerned Scientists
1384 Massachusetts Avenue
Cambridge, Massachusetts 02238

Wildlife Management Institute
1101 14th Street, N.W., #725
Washington, D.C. 20005

LIST 11–3. ORGANIZATIONS WITH A HUMANE AND/OR CONSERVATION MISSION

American Nature Study Society
Pocono Environmental Education
  Center
R.D. 1, Box 268
Dingham's Ferry, Pennsylvania 18328

Animal Legal Defense Fund
1363 Lincoln Avenue
San Rafael, California 94901
(415) 459-0885

Animal Legal Defense Fund (ALDF)
Dissection Hotline
1363 Lincoln Avenue, #7
San Rafael, California 94901
800-922-FROG [3764]

Animal Protection Institute
P.O. Box 22505
5894 Southland Park Drive
Sacramento, California 95882

Bat Conservation International
P.O. Box 162603
Austin, Texas 78716
(512) 327-9721
(800) 538-BATS

Center for Marine Conservation
1725 DeSales Street, N.W.
Washington, D.C. 20036

Conservation Trees
The National Arbor Day Foundation
100 Arbor Avenue
Nebraska City, Nebraska 68410

Cousteau Society
930 West 21st Street
Norfolk, Virginia 23517
also:
777 Third Avenue
New York, New York 10017

Dian Fossey Gorilla Fund
45 Inverness Drive, East; Suite A
Englewood, Colorado 80112-5480
(303) 790-2349

Ecological Society of America
Environmental Sciences Division
Oak Ridge National Laboratory
Oak Ridge, Tennessee 37831

Environmental Defense Fund
1616 P Street, N.W.
Suite 150
Washington, D.C. 20036

Friends of the Earth
529 Commercial Street
San Francisco, California 94111

Friends of Washoe
Central Washington University
Psychology Building
Ellensburg, Washington 98926

Funds for Animals
40 West 57th Street
New York, New York 10019

Gorilla Foundation
Box 620-530
Woodside, California 94062

Greenpeace
USA Headquarters
1436 U Street, N.W.
Washington, D.C. 20009   *(Continued)*

LIST 11–3. (Continued)

Humane Society of the United States
2100 L Street, N.W.
Washington, D.C. 20037
(202) 452-1100, (800) 4 HUMANE

International Primate Protection
League (IPPL)
P.O. Box 766
Summerville, South Carolina 29484
(803) 871-2280

Jane Goodall Institute
P.O. Box 41720
Tucson, Arizona 85717

Loon Preservation Committee
High Street
Humiston Building
RR #4, Box 240-E
Meredith, New Hampshire 03253

National Advancement of Humane
Education (NAAHE)
Box 362
East Haddam, Connecticut 06423

National Audubon Society
950 Third Avenue
New York, New York 10022

Nature Conservatory
Suite 800
1800 North Kent Street
Arlington, Virginia 22209

National Wildlife Federation
1400 16th Street, N.W.
Washington, D.C. 20036-2266
(800) 432-6564

People for the Ethical Treatment of
Animals (PETA)
P.O. Box 42516
Washington, D.C. 20077-4865
(301) 770-7444

Sierra Club
730 Polk Street
San Francisco, California 94109

Whale Adoption Project
International Wildlife Coalition
634 North Falmouth Highway
P.O. Box 388
North Falmouth, Massachusetts 02556
(508) 564-9980

Wilderness Society
1901 Pennsylvania Avenue, N.W.
Washington, D.C. 20006

World Wildlife Fund (WWF)
The Conservation Foundation
1250 24th Street, N.W.
Washington, D.C. 20037
(202) 778-9542

LIST 11–4. CONSERVATION ORGANIZATIONS INTERESTED IN RAIN FORESTS

Conservation Foundation
1250 24th Street, N.W.
Suite 500
Washington, D.C. 20037

Conservational International
1015 18th St., N.W., Suite 1002
Washington, D.C. 20005

Friends of the Earth (International)
530 7th Street, S.E.
Washington, D.C. 20003

Natural Resources Defense Council
1350 New York Avenue, N.W.
Washington, D.C. 20005

Nature Conservancy
1815 North Lynn Street
Arlington, Virginia 22209

Rainforest Action Network
300 Broadway, Suite 28
San Francisco, California 94009

Rainforest Alliance
295 Madison Avenue, Suite 1804
New York, New York 10017

SITES/Smithsonian Institute
110 Jefferson Avenue, S.W.
Washington, D.C. 20560

Tropical Ecosystem Research and
    Rescue Alliance
Terra International
Washington, D.C. 20036

World Resources Institute
1735 New York Avenue, N.W.
Washington, D.C. 20006

For information on McDonald's
    rainforest policy:
McDonald's Environmental Affairs
McDonald's Corporation, Oak Brook,
    Illinois 60521

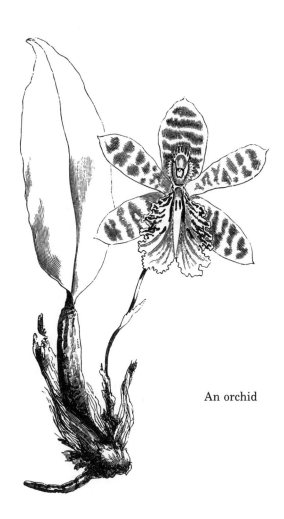

An orchid

LIST 11–5. EXPERIENTIAL, INQUIRY SCIENCE EDUCATION PROGRAMS

Beginning in the late 1950s and through the 1960s, a number of effective, hands-on, inquiry science programs were developed. Each had its own emphasis on particular content areas and skills. Each required teacher training and specific materials to be effective in the classroom. Many have not become a part of schools' science curricula mostly due to districts and publishers not addressing the need to provide for continued teacher training and replenishment of consumable supplies upon which the activities depend.

Many of the original publishers no longer publish these hands-on science programs. Nevertheless, some of these programs still exist and have been updated. They still require teacher training, involvement, and a means for the teacher to replenish broken and consumable supplies. The most lasting contributions these inquiry programs have made may be that they have influenced those who write and publish science textbooks in such a way that science books now contain more ideas for investigations and application of process skills as well as content; and those who train teachers now include an excellent blend of process skills and conceptual development.

Because these programs have been made available by different publishers at different times, we recommended contacting the American Association for the Advancement of Science (See List 11–1) to determine which publisher or supplier offers a particular program.

Examples of Science Inquiry Programs

PROGRAM	COMMENTS
Adapting Science Materials for the Blind (ASMB). Developed at Lawrence Hall of Science, University of California Berkeley, California 94720.	For students in grades 1–6 who are visually impaired; a version of SCIS, Science Curriculum Improvement Study, with modified equipment that enables visually impaired and sighted students to work together.
Biological Sciences Curriculum Study (BSCS); developed at University of Colorado. Green version, 7th Edition Kendall/Hunt 4050 Westmark Drive P.O. Box 1840 Dubuque, Iowa 52004–1840 (800) 258-5622	For high school students; consists of three courses based on molecular, cellular, and ecological approaches.

The Science Teacher's Book of Lists, © 1993 by Prentice Hall

(Continued)

LIST 11–5. (Continued)

PROGRAM	COMMENTS
BUZ, a Hands-on Electrical Energy Program Call or write: Mr. Martin F. Duffy, Manager Consumer and Community Relations Delmarva Power 800 King Street Wilmington, Delaware 19899 (302) 429-3607	For grades 4–8; contents: static and current, wise and safe use of electricity; teacher training, student materials and supplies; available to teachers in the Delmarva service territory, in Vermont, and to a power company and/or business education partnership which will provide teacher training and supplies.
ChemCom, Chemistry in the Community, a project of the American Chemical Society. Available from: Kendall/Hunt 4050 Westmark Drive P.O. Box 1840 Dubuque, Iowa 52004-1840 (800) 258-5622	For high school students; emphasis on the role of chemistry in everyone's life; uses activities to make students aware of chemistry-related issues in their community and their potential contributions to those issues. Students discover real-world applications.
Conceptually Oriented Program in Elementary Science (COPES) Developed at New York University 4 Washington Place New York, New York 10003	For elementary students; provides hands-on explorations in five conceptual areas, spirally constructed.
Contemporary Physics Education Project (CPEP) Science Kit & Boreal Laboratories® 777 East Park Drive Tonawanda, New York 14150 (800) 828-7777	For high school and college, New Edition of the Fundamental Particle Chart and software package provide description of subatomic particles and outlines their interaction.
Elementary School Science (ESS) Developed at Educational Development Center 55 Chapel Street Newton, Massachusetts 02160	For students in grades K–9; Over fifty units in physical sciences, provide hands-on discovery investigations. Available from Delta Education, Inc. P.O. Box 915, Hudson, NH 03051 (800) 258-1302.
Foundational Approaches in Science Teaching (FAST); Developed by: Curriculum Research & Development Group, University of Hawaii.	For students in grades 6–10; provides a multidisciplinary, integrated inquiry program that develops lab skills, thinking skills and concepts. Three levels available from: FAST Program, EMC-University of Hawaii, 1436 Spring Valley Drive, Roseville, California 95661 (916) 782-3773

(Continued)

LIST 11–5. (Continued)

PROGRAM	COMMENTS
Full Option Science System (FOSS) Developed at: Lawrence Hall of Science Berkeley, California 94720	For students in grades 3–6; sequential, multisensory, hands-on, laboratory curriculum; 16 modules available from: Britannica Encyclopaedia Britannica Educational Corporation (800) 554-9862, Ext. 6554
The GrowLab™ Indoor Garden National Gardening Association 180 Flynn Avenue Burlington, Vermont 05401 (802) 863-1308	For teachers in grades K–8; over 40 lesson plans, over 200 activities that provide opportunities to master concepts and skills in an interdisciplinary approach; funded by National Science Foundation.
Harvard Project Physics Developed at Harvard University, supported by Carnegie Corp., Ford Foundation, Alfred P. Sloan Foundation, U.S. Office of Education and Harvard.	For average high school students. Basic philosophy: physics is for everyone.
Interdisciplinary Approaches to Chemistry (IAC)	For high school; modular approach. Emphasis on making chemistry relevant and on student success.
Middle School Life Science Kendall/Hunt 4050 Westmark Drive P.O. Box 184 Dubuque, Iowa 52004-1840 (800) 258-5622	For middle school students; developed by teachers in the Jefferson County Public Schools with funding from the National Science Foundation.
Outdoor Biological Instructional Strategies (OBIS). Developed by Lawrence Hall of Science University of California Berkeley, California 94720	For elementary through high school. Available from Delta Education, Inc.
Physical Science Study Committee (PSSC) Developed by a group of physicists at Cambridge, Massachusetts during the late 1950s. PSCS 7th Edition Kendall/Hunt Publishing Co. (800) 258-5622	For high school; textbook, lab guide, teacher's guide, supplies, and films. Fewer topics covered at greater depth, emphasis on lab work, required higher level thinking skills. Excellent results documented in a variety of studies.

The Science Teacher's Book of Lists, © 1993 by Prentice Hall

(Continued)

LIST 11–5. (Continued)

PROGRAM	*COMMENTS*
Science, a Process Approach (SAPA). Updated version known as SAPA II. Also known as AAAS because it was developed by the American Association for the Advancement for Science. 1776 Massachusetts Avenue, N.W. Washington, D.C. 20036	For elementary school; can be extended into middle school. Provides over 100 modules structured around the process skills of science. Available from Delta Education, Inc.
Science Education Alternative Series (SEAS) Serin House Publishers 5905-D, Suite 160 Paradise, California 95969	Seas-1, Science: A Way of Learning Seas-2, Science: The Changing Earth Seas-3, Science: Ecology & The Changing Environment* Seas-4, Science: Interactions in Life Science* For middle school students
Science for Life and Living Developed by Biological Science Curriculum Study, BSCS. Supported in part by the National Science Foundation	For elementary students; available from: Kendall/Hunt Publishing Company 4050 Westmark Drive P.O. Box 184 Dubuque, Iowa 52004-1840 (800) 258-5622
Science & Technology: Investigating Human Dimensions Developed by Biological Science Curriculum Study, BSCS. Supported in part by the National Science Foundation	For middle school students; available: Kendall/Hunt Publishing Company
Science Improvement Curriculum Study (SCIS). Updated version known as SCIS 3, pronounced "skiss three." Developed at Lawrence Hall of Science University of California Berkeley, California 94720	For elementary students; laboratory approach to investigating life and physical sciences; sequential program. Available from Delta Education Inc.
University of Illinois Astronomy Program U. of I. Department of Astronomy Urbana, Illinois 61801	For elementary and middle age students in grades 5–8; a sequential series of modules introducing basic astronomy.

---

*Formerly Interaction of Man and the Biosphere (IMB)

LIST 11–6. SOME SOURCES FOR SCIENTIFIC EQUIPMENT & SUPPLIES

Apple Computer, Inc.
20525 Mariani Avenue
Cupertino, California 95014
(408) 996-1010

American Science and Surplus
601 Linden Place
Evanston, Illinois 60202
(708) 475-8440

Brock Optical Inc.
220 Live Oak Boulevard
Casselberry, Florida 32707
(800) 780-9111

Carolina Biological Supply Co.
2700 York Road
Burlington, North Carolina 27215
(800) 334-5551

Connecticut Valley Biological Supply
Co., Inc.
82 Valley Rd.
Southhampton, Massachusetts 01073
(800) 628-7748

Coronet/MIT Film & Video
The Discovery Channel's® Interactive
Library™
108 Wilmot Road
Deerfield, Illinois 60015
(800) 621-2131

Delta Education, Inc.
P.O. Box 915
Hudson, New Hampshire 03051
(800) 258-1302

Edmund Scientific Co.
Dept. 11A1, E715 Edscorp Bldg.
Barrington, New Jersey 08007
(609) 573-6250

Educational Activities, Inc.
P.O. Box 392
Freeport, New York 11520
(800) 645-3739

Fisher Scientific Co.
Educational Division
4901 W. Le Moyne Street
Chicago, Illinois 60651
(800) 955-1177

FWJ Optical Systems, Inc.
FIND-R-SCOPE® Infrared Viewer
629 S. Vermont Street
Palatine, Illinois 60067-6949
(708) 358-2500

Genesis (Genesis Owl Pellet Pak)
P.O. Box 2242
Mount Vernon, Washington 98273
(206) 428-6764

Herbach and Rademan Inc.
18 Canal Street
Bristol, Pennsylvania 19007
(215) 426-1700

Hubbard Scientific
1120 Halbibe Street
P.O. Box 760
Chippewa Falls, WI 54729
(800) 323-8368

Junior Engineering Technical Society
(JETS)
1420 King Street
Suite 405
Alexandria, Virginia 22314-2715

Ken-a-vision® Manufacturing Co., Inc.
5615 Raytown Road
Kansas City, Missouri 64133
(816) 353-4787

Knowledge Revolution
15 Brush Place
San Francisco, California 94103
(800) 766-6615

Learning Technologies, Inc.
STARLAB Planetarium Systems
59 Walden Street
Cambridge, Massachusetts 02140
(800) 537-8703

The Science Teacher's Book of Lists, © 1993 by Prentice Hall

(Continued)

LIST 11–6. (Continued)

Learning Spectrum
Science on a Shoestring
1390 Westridge Drive
Portola Valley, California 94028
(800) USE-SOS-2

Leica Inc.
ZOOM 2000™ Microscope
111 Deerlake Road
Deerfield, Illinois 60015
(800) 248-0123

Meiji Techno America
Microscopes
2186 Bering Drive
San Jose, California 95131
(800) 832-0060

Merlan Scientific LTD.
CHAMP II Laboratory Interface
247 Armstrong Avenue
Georgetown, Ontario
L7G 4X6
Canada
(800) 387-2474

NASCO
P.O. Box 901–0901
Fort Atkinson, Wisconsin 53538-0901
(800) 558-9595

National Science Teachers Association
  (NSTA)
Publications and Awards Programs
1742 Connecticut Avenue, N.W.
Washington, D.C. 20009-1171
(202) 328-5800

Ohaus Scale Corporation
29 Hanover Road
P.O. Box 900
Florham Park, New Jersey 07932
(800) 672-7722

Orbis Scientific, Inc.
P.O. Box 3890
Milton, Florida 32572
(904) 626-0708

Pellets
3004 Pinewood
Bellingham, Washington 98225
(206) 733-3012

LaMotte Co.
(The Outdoor Classroom)
P.O. Box 329
Chestertown, Maryland 21620
(800) 344-3100

TOPS Learning Systems
10970 S. Mulino Road
Canby, Oregon 97013

Sargent-Welch Scientific Co.
P.O. Box 1026
Skokie, Illinois 60077
(800)-SARGENT

Skulls Unlimited
P.O. Box 6741
Moore, Oklahoma 73153
(800) 659-SKUL

SWIFT Instruments, Inc.
P.O. Box 562
San Jose, California 95106
(800) 523-4544

Vernier Software
(Macintosh®, IBM®, Apple II®)
2920 S.W. 89th Street
Portland, Oregon 97225
(503) 297-5317

Videodiscovery
1700 Westlake Avenue, N., Suite 600
Seattle, Washington 98109-3012
(800) 548-3472

Ward's Natural Science Establishment
5100 Henritt Road
Henritt, New York 14467
(716) 359-2505, (800) 962-2660

NOTE: Addresses and phone numbers may change. A recommendation for identifying current toll-free phone numbers is to call 800 information: 1 800 555-1212.

POTPOURRI

LIST 12–1. STATES' OFFICIAL BIRD, TREE, AND FLOWER

STATE	BIRD	TREE	FLOWER
Alabama	Yellowhammer	Southern Pine	Camellia
Alaska	Willow Ptarmigan	Sitka Spruce	Forget-me-not
Arizona	Cactus Wren	Paloverde	Saguaro Cactus
Arkansas	Mockingbird	Pine	Apple Blossom
California	Valley Quail	Redwood	Golden Poppy
Colorado	Lark Bunting	Blue Spruce	Rocky Mountain Columbine
Connecticut	Robin	White Oak	Mountain Laurel
Delaware	Blue Hen Chicken	American Holly	Peach Blossom
Florida	Mockingbird	Sabal Palm	Orange Blossom
Georgia	Brown Thrasher	Live Oak	Cherokee Rose
Hawaii	Nene (Hawaiian Goose)	Kukui	Hibiscus
Idaho	Mountain Bluebird	White Pine	Syringa
Illinois	Cardinal	White Oak	Native Violet
Indiana	Cardinal	Tulip Tree	Peony
Iowa	American Goldfinch	Oak	Wild Rose
Kansas	Western Meadowlark	Cottonwood	Sunflower
Kentucky	Cardinal	Kentucky Coffee Tree	Goldenrod
Louisiana	Eastern Brown Pelican	Bald Cypress	Magnolia
Maine	Chickadee	White Pine	Pine Cone & Tassel
Maryland	Baltimore Oriole	White Oak	Black-eyed Susan
Massachusetts	Chickadee	American Elm	Mayflower
Michigan	Robin	White Pine	Apple Blossom
Minnesota	Common Loon	Red Pine	Lady's Slipper
Mississippi	Mockingbird	Magnolia	Magnolia Blossom

(Continued)

LIST 12–1. (Continued)

STATE	BIRD	TREE	FLOWER
Missouri	Bluebird	Dogwood	Hawthorn
Montana	Western Meadowlark	Ponderosa Pine	Bitterroot
Nebraska	Western Meadowlark	Cottonwood	Goldenrod
Nevada	Mountain Buebird	Bristlecone Pine and Single-leaf Piñon	Sagebrush
New Hampshire	Purple Finch	White Birch	Purple Lilac
New Jersey	American Goldfinch	Red Oak	Purple Violet
New Mexico	Roadrunner	Piñon	Yucca Flower
New York	Eastern Bluebird	Sugar Maple	Rose
North Carolina	Cardinal	Pine	Dogwood
North Dakota	Western Meadowlark	American Elm	Wild Prairie Rose
Ohio	Cardinal	Buckeye	Scarlet Carnation
Oklahoma	Scissor-tailed Flycatcher	Redbud	Mistletoe
Oregon	Western Meadowlark	Douglas Fir	Oregon Grape
Pennsylvania	Ruffed Grouse	Hemlock	Mountain Laurel
Rhode Island	Rhode Island Red Chicken	Red Maple	Violet
South Carolina	Carolina Wren	Palmetto	Yellow Jessamine
South Dakota	Ring-necked Pheasant	Black Hills Spruce	Pasqueflower
Tennessee	Mockingbird	Tulip Poplar	Iris
Texas	Mockingbird	Pecan	Bluebonnet
Utah	Sea Gull	Blue Spruce	Sego Lily
Vermont	Hermit Thrush	Sugar Maple	Red Clover
Virginia	Cardinal	Dogwood	Dogwood
Washington	Willow Goldfinch	Western Hemlock	Rhododendron
West Virginia	Cardinal	Sugar Maple	Big Rhododendron
Wisconsin	Robin	Sugar Maple	Wood Violet
Wyoming	Western Meadowlark	Cottonwood	Indian Paintbrush

The Science Teacher's Book of Lists, © 1993 by Prentice Hall

LIST 12–2. SOME FIELDS OF SCIENCE AND MEDICINE

anthropogeography—study of the geographical distribution of people and their relationship to the environment

anthropography—branch of anthropology that investigates the distribution of people according to their physical characteristics, languages, and customs

anthropology—study of mankind; physical, mental, social characteristics of humans in groups; often restricted to primitive peoples

archaeology—study of life and culture of ancient people through excavation of cities and artifacts

astrophysics—study of physical properties and phenomena of stars, planets, and other heavenly bodies

astronomy—study of stars, planets, and all other heavenly bodies

audiology—study of hearing

bacteriology—study of bacteria, one-celled microorganisms

biology—study of the origin and physical characteristics of living organisms

biochemistry—the branch of chemistry that investigates the chemical processes of living organisms

bionomics—the branch of biology that investigates the adaptation of living organisms to their environment

bionomy—study of the natural laws that control life processes

biophysics—branch of physics that investigates living matter

botany—study and classification of plant life

cardiology—study of the heart, its functions, and diseases

chronology—study of measuring time, dating events in order of occurrence

chemistry—study of the composition, properties, and reactions of matter

cosmology—study of the universe

criminology—study of crime

cryptology—study of codes and cyphers

cytology—study of cells

dermatology—branch of medicine studying the skin, its functions, and diseases

embryology—branch of medicine investigating the formation and development of embryos

(Continued)

LIST 12–2. (Continued)

endocrinology—branch of medicine concerned with the functions of the endocrine glands and the internal secretions of the body

ethology—naturalistic study of animal behavior through observation and gathering of data rather than direct experimentation and dissection

entomology—branch of zoology that investigates insects

epidemiology—branch of medicine that investigates the causes and control of epidemics and spreading of diseases

gastroenterology—branch of medicine concerned with the function and diseases of the digestive system

geology—study of the history and physical nature of the earth; also known as earth science

gynecology—branch of medicine that is concerned with the study and treatment of women's diseases, especially of the genitourinary tract

hematology—study of the blood and its diseases

herpetology—branch of zoology that investigates reptiles and amphibians

histology—branch of biology that is concerned with the microscopic study of the structure of organs

hydrology—the study of properties, laws, and distribution of water

ichthyology—branch of zoology that investigates fish

immunology—the branch of medicine that investigates immunity to diseases and the functions of the immune system

kinetics—the study of motion of mass in relation to the forces acting upon them

laryngology—branch of medicine that investigates and treats the larynx and adjacent parts

lichenology—study of lichen, the large group of mosslike organisms made up of an alga and a fungus

limnology—study of the biological, chemical, geographical, and physical features of bodies of fresh water

lithology—study of rocks

malacology—branch of zoology investigating mollusks

mammalogy—branch of zoology that investigates mammals

meteorology—study of the atmosphere, including weather and climate

microbiology—the branch of biology that is concerned with microorganisms

mineralogy—study of minerals

The Science Teacher's Book of Lists, © 1993 by Prentice Hall

(Continued)

LIST 12–2. (Continued)

morphology—study of the structure of plants and animals

mycology—branch of botany that investigates fungi

myrmecology—branch of entomology that investigates ants

nephology—branch of meteorology that investigates clouds

neurology—study of the nervous system

oceanography—study of the ocean

oncology—branch of medicine that investigates tumors

ophthalmology—study of the eye

organology—study of animal organs

ornithology—branch of zoology that studies birds

orthopedics—branch of medicine concerned with the treatment of diseases and injuries to joints and bones

osteology—study of bones

otolaryngology—branch of medicine combining the fields of laryngology and otology

otology—branch of medicine concerned with the ear and its diseases

paleontology—branch of geology and biology that investigates prehistoric life forms through study of fossils

parasitology—the study of parasites and the conditions and diseases they cause

pathology—the study of disease

pharmacology—study of preparation, amounts, uses, and effects of drugs

photochemistry—branch of chemistry that investigates the effects of light in producing chemical actions

phycology—branch of botany that investigates algae

physics—study of matter and energy

physiology—branch of biology that deals with vital processes of living organisms

phytology—study of plants

phytopathology—study of plant diseases and their control

psychiatry—branch of medicine concerned with understanding and treating mind disorders

psychobiology—branch of biology concerned with the inner workings of the mental and biological processes of an individual

psychology—study of animal and human mental processes

psychopathology—study of the abnormalities and diseases of the mind

(Continued)

LIST 12–2. (Continued)

pteridology—study of ferns

radiology—study of radiant energy, X rays, etc

rheumatology—branch of medicine concerned with deformity and disease of joints

rhinology—branch of medicine that deals with the nose

seismology—study of earthquakes and related matters

serology—study of the use and properties of serums (animal fluids)

sexology—study of human sexual behavior

spectrology—study of spectra: light and other radiant energy

splanchnology—branch of medicine that investigates the internal organs

stoichiology—study of the make up of animal tissue

thermodynamics—study of relationship of heat and mechanical energy and the conversion of one to the other

urology—branch of medicine that deals with the urinogenital system

volcanology—study of volcanoes

zoogeography—branch of zoology that describes the distribution of animals and their habits

zoology—the study and classification of animals

zymology—the study of fermentation

The Science Teacher's Book of Lists, © 1993 by Prentice Hall

LIST 12–3. ROOT WORDS: AIDS IN UNDERSTANDING SCIENTIFIC TERMS

Many science terms contain root words that have their origin in Greek or Latin. Knowing the meaning of these root words helps with analyzing new terms to understand and to remember them. Here are some root words commonly used in the sciences.

abscis—cut off; the *abscission* of leaves from a tree in autumn

aero—air; *aero*bic exercises, *aero*nautics

agri—field; *agri*culture

alt—high; *alto* clouds are high in the atmosphere, *alt*itude

ang—bend; *ang*les can be considered as "bent lines"

angi—vessel; *angio*sperms are plants that produce seeds in their "vessel," the fruit

anthr—human; *anthr*opology is the study of humans

apic—tip; *apic*al dominance in plants means the dominate growth is at the tips of buds, roots and stems

aqua—water; an *aqua*rium holds water and water organisms

aud—hear; *aud*ible

archae—ancient; *archae*ology is the study of ancient people

arthr—joint; *arthr*opods are invertebrates with jointed bodies and legs

astr—star; *astr*onomy, *astr*onaut

aux—grow; *aux*in is a growth hormone in plants

bar—weight; *bar*ometer measures the "weight" of air pressure

bio—life; *bio*logy is the study of life

blast—a formative cell; osteo*blast* forms bone cells

brachi—arm; *brachi*al artery supplies blood to the arm

bry—grow; an em*bry*o is a growing, developing organism

cal—hot; a *cal*orie is a unit of heat

cand—glow; a lighted *cand*le glows

cardi—heart; *cardi*ology is the study of the heart; *cardi*ac, *cardi*ogram

carot—carrot; *carot*ene is the name of the red, yellow, and orange pigment in plants

centr—center; *centr*ifugal force is an inward pull to the center of the system

cephal—head; *cephal*opods are animals that are composed of a head and foot, such as octopus, squid, and nautilus

(Continued)

LIST 12-3. (Continued)

cerebr—brain; the *cerebr*um is a part of the brain; *cerebr*al pertains to the brain

cervic, cervix—neck; *cervic*al spine is the part of the spine located in the neck

chlor—green; *chlor*ophyll is the green pigment in plants necessary for photosynthesis

chrom—color; *chrom*osomes are deeply staining bodies in the nucleus that contain genes

chron—time; the *chron*ology of events is the order of time in which they occurred

cide, cise—kill, cut; sui*cide* is to kill oneself; in*cis*or is a tooth designed for cutting food

cili—small hair; small hairlike *cili*a line the insides of air sacs "sweeping" out pollutants

cline—lean; an in*cline*d plane

con—together or combine; *con*cept, *con*crete

corp—body; *corp*uscle

cran—skull; *cran*ial pertaining to the skull

cosmo—universe; *cosmo*logy is the study of the universe; a *cosmo*naut travels the universe

crat—rule; aristo*crat* is one who rules; demo*crac*y is rule by the people

cycl—circle; the water *cycl*e demonstrates how rain falls to earth, evaporates, and returns to the clouds

cyt—cell; *cyt*ology is the study of cells

decid—to fall off; *decid*uous plants shed their leaves at the end of their growing season

dehis—split; *dehis*cent fruit splits open when ripened

dent—tooth; *dent*al

derm—skin; epi*derm*is is the outer layer of skin

dont—tooth; an ortho*dont*ist works on teeth

ecol—house; *ecol*ogy is the study of an organism in its habitat

evol—to unroll; *evol*ution, complex organisms "unroll" from simpler ones

fil—a thread; Edison experimented with many fine thread-like *fil*aments to develop the light bulb

frac—break; *frac*ture, *frag*ment

fric—rub; *fric*tion is produced by rubbing two items together

The Science Teacher's Book of Lists, © 1993 by Prentice Hall

(Continued)

LIST 12–3. (Continued)

gam—marriage; mono*gam*y, married to one person; bi*gam*y, married to two people at the same time

gamet—wife or husband; the *gamet*angium is the part of a plant that produces reproductive cells, *gamet*es

gastr—stomach; *gastr*ointestinal tract, *gastr*ic juices

gen—birth, race; *gen*eration, *gen*ocide

geo—earth; *geo*logy

gon—angle; penta*gon*, octa*gon*

gon—seed; *gon*ads

grad—step; increments on a *grad*uated cylinder

gram—written, letter; tele*gram*, mono*gram*

graph—write; tele*graph*

gyn—women; *gyn*ecologist

gymn—naked; *gymn*osperms are plants that produce "naked" seeds, seeds without fruits

hab—hold; *hab*it

hem—blood; *hem*oglobin, the pigment in red blood cells

hepat—liver; *hepat*itis, an inflammation of the liver

hist—tissue; *hist*ology, the study of tissues

hom—man; *hom*icide, *Hom*o sapiens

homo—same; *homo*zygous, identical members of a gene pair

hydr—water; *hydr*oelectric is electricity that is generated by water

imag—likeness; *imag*e

integ—whole; *integ*ral

ject—throw; e*ject*

lab—work; *lab*or, *lab*oratory

lat—side; objects with bi*lat*eral symmetry can be cut in half to produce matching halves

leuk—white; *leuk*ocytes are white blood cells

luc—light; trans*luc*ent

lum—light; *lum*inous objects give off light

luna—moon; *luna*r

lust—shine; *lust*er

mar—sea; *mar*ine

max—greatest; the speed of light is the *max*imum speed

(Continued)

LIST 12–3. (Continued)

menin—membrane; *menin*gitis is an inflammation of any of the membranes enclosing the brain

miss—send; *miss*iles

morph—shape, form; insects change shape during meta*morph*osis

mut—change; a *mut*ation is a genetic change

myo—muscle; *myo*logy is the study of the muscles; *myo*sin is the most common protein in muscle

neur, nerv—nerve; *nerv*ous system, *neur*on

ocu—eye; *ocu*list studies the eye, bin*ocu*lars enhance vision

ost—bone; *ost*eology is the study of the bones

paleo—old; *paleo*ntology is the study of fossils

path—disease; *path*ology is the study of diseases

ped, pod—foot; snails glide upon a pseudo*pod*, a false foot, and are gas-tro*pod*s

phloe—bark; *phlo*em, the food-conducting tissue in vascular plants

photo—light; *photo*synthesis is the process by which green plants make their food in the presence of light

phys—nature; *phys*ical sciences investigate the physical workings of the universe

plankt—wandering; *plankt*on are microscopic organisms that wander about the sea

put—think; com*put*er

rad—ray, spoke; *rad*ius

rect—straight; *rect*angle

rhiz—root; *rhiz*omes are underground stems that resemble roots

san—health; *san*itary

scend—climb; a*scend*, de*scend*

sci—know; *sci*ence is the search for knowledge

sect—cut; dis*sect*

sens—feel; *sens*ation

serv—save; con*serv*e, pre*serv*ation

som—body; chromo*som*e

son—sound; *son*ar, *son*ic

stell—star; con*stell*ation, *stell*ar

sum—highest; *sum*mit

ten—stretch; *ten*dons

(Continued)

LIST 12–3. (Continued)

terr—land; *terr*estrial, extra*terr*estrial

tort—twist; con*tort*

trib—give; *trib*utary, con*trib*ute

tropi—turn; many plants are photo*tropi*c and geo*tropi*c, that is, their leaves turn towards light and their roots turn towards the ground

vac—empty; *vac*uum

ver—truth; *ver*ify

void—empty; de*void*, *void*ed

volv—roll; planets re*volv*e around their sun

vor—eat; carni*vor*es eat meat; herbi*vor*es eat plants; omni*vor*es eat plants and meat

xanth—yellow; *xanth*ophyll the yellow pigment found in plants

xyl—wood; *xyl*em is the water conducting tissues in the woody part of plants

zoo—animal; *zoo*logy is the study of animals

LIST 12–4. PREFIXES USED
IN SCIENCE TERMINOLOGY

A prefix is a group of letters added before a root word, which changes the meaning of that word. A prefix can change the meaning completely as in adding the prefix *a* to *symmetrical*, which forms *asymmetrical*, meaning not symmetrical. Or it can expand the meaning as in adding *tri* to *angle* to form *triangle*. Knowing the meanings of prefixes and root words is helpful in learning, remembering, and spelling scientific terms.

PREFIX	*MEANING*	*EXAMPLE*
a, ab	away, from	abduct, abnormal
a, an	not, without	asymmetrical, amoral
ad (af, ag, an, ap)	to, toward	adapt, adduct
ambi	both sides	ambidextrous
andro	a man	androecium (male part of a flower)
ante	before, forward	antecedent, anteflexion
anti	against	antibody
as	to	ascend, aspire
auto	self	autotrophic (organisms that produce their own food)
bi	two	bicycle, biennial
by	near, aside	bypass, bystander
bio	life	biology, biochemistry
circ, circu, circum	around	circumference, circumcision
co, con	with	congenital (with birth)
contra	against	contraception
cyt	cell	cytology
di	two	disaccharide (a compound made of two sugar molecules)
dia	across	diagonal, diameter
dis	apart	dissect
e	out	eject, erupt
ecto	outside	ectoplasm
em	in	embalm, embed
en	in	enclose, envelop
epi	upon	epicenter, epidermis
equ	equal	equidistant, equation
ex	out	exhaust, exit
extra	outside	extrapolate, extraterrestrial
gravi	heavy	gravity, gravitropism
hemi	half	hemisphere
hetero	different	heterosexual, heterozygous
homo, hom	same	homosexual, homozygous
hyper	excessive	hyperactive, hypersecretion
hypo	under	hypodermic, hypothesis

(Continued)

The Science Teacher's Book of Lists, © 1993 by Prentice Hall

LIST 12–4. (Continued)

PREFIX	MEANING	EXAMPLE
im/in	into	implant, import, incision
in/im	not	incomplete, immoral
inter	between	interstitial
intra	within	intracellular, intravenous
iso	equal	isometric, isosceles
macro	large	macrobiotic, macronucleus
mal	bad	malfunction, malnutrition
mega	large	megacycle, megahertz
meso	middle	mesoderm, mesophytes
meta	after	metaphase, metamorphosis
micro	small	microscopic, microchip
mono	one	monocot, monosaccharide
multi	many	multicolored, multiply
oligo	small	oligopoly, oligogene
omni	all	omnifarious, omnivorous
oo	egg	oocyte, oogamy
pan	all	panacea, panorama
para	near, beside	parachute, parallel
peri	all around	perimeter, periscope
photo	light	photosynthesis, phototropism
pre	before	prefix, prenatal
pro	forward	progress, project
poly	many	polyester, polygamous, polysaccharide
post	after	postnatal, posterior
pseudo	false	pseudoscience, pseudopod
re	back	recall, retract
retro	back	retrograde, retrorocket
semi	half	semicircular, semilunar
sub	under	submerge, subterranean
super	more than	superfine, supernova
super, supra	over	superimpose, supraorbital
sym/syn	with, together	symbiosis, symmetrical, synthesis
trans	across	transfer, transport
ultra	beyond	ultramicroscopic, ultrasound
under	below	underground, understand
under	less than	undertone, underweight
with	back	withdrawal, withhold

LIST 12–5. SUFFIXES USED
IN SCIENCE TERMINOLOGY

A suffix is a group of letters added to the end root word. A suffix usually adds additional meaning to the root word. For example, *science + ist = scientist.* A suffix can also change a meaning from singular to plural, such as *eruption + s = eruptions*, and change tense such as, *dissect + ed = dissected.* Knowing the meanings and functions of suffixes and root words is helpful in learning, remembering, and spelling scientific terms.

SUFFIX	*MEANING OR FUNCTION*	*EXAMPLE*
a	plural	data, criteria
able	able	viable
ad	forms adverbs of direction	cephalad (toward the head)
ae	plural, feminine	algae, larvae
ant	one who	assistant, immigrant
arium	place for	aquarium, planetarium
ary	place for	library, mortuary
asis, asia, esis	condition	hemostasis, psychogenesis, aphasia
cide	kill	biocide, homicide, suicide
cle	small	icicle, particle
cule	small	miniscule, molecule
ectomy	surgical removal	appendectomy, tonsillectomy
emia	condition of blood	anemia
en	made of	golden, wooden
gen	produces	pathogens
gram	write	electrocardiogram, telegram
graph	write	electrocardiograph, telegraph
i	plural	alumni, termini
ic	pertaining to	hemophiliac, metallic
id	state of	acid, solid
ide	use in chemical compounds	carbon dioxide, sodium chloride
ine	use in elements and compounds; associated with halogens	chlorine, fluorine, iodine
ist	one who practices	chemist, physicist
ite	rock or mineral	bauxite, granite
itis	inflammation	appendicitis, bronchitis, hepatitis
let	small	leaflet, owlet
like	relating to	childlike, lifelike
ment	action or process	encirclement, development
ment	product	instrument, fragment
oid	like, in the form of	platinoid, thyroid, asteroid, humanoid
ol	alcohol	ethanol, methanol
ology	study of	biology, zoology

(Continued)

The Science Teacher's Book of Lists, © 1993 by Prentice Hall

LIST 12–5. (Continued)

SUFFIX	MEANING OR FUNCTION	EXAMPLE
oma	tumor	carcinoma
ose	common ending for carbohydrates, especially sugars	glucose, sucrose, cellulose
osis	action, process	psychosis, osmosis, meiosis
ory	place for	laboratory, conservatory
pathy	disease	dermopathy, psychopathy
phobia	fear of	brontophobia, claustrophobia
phyll	leaf	chlorophyll, mesophyll
ry	occupation	dentistry, forestry
scope	instrument	microscope, telescope
ular	relating to	cellular, granular
ure	action or process	enclosure, exposure
ward	direction	backward, upward
y	quality of	cloudy, fruity

LIST 12-6. SCIENCE PROCESS SKILLS AND DEFINITIONS

Science process skills are those skills that scientists use to help them conduct investigations and reach conclusions. Their findings may range from "there are insufficient data to reach a conclusion" to the development of a generalization or new theory. During the 1960s, inquiry science curricula introduced educators and young students to incorporating science process skills in lessons along with content and concepts so that students could discover and understand concepts as they worked like scientists by using science process skills. During the 1990s most science educators agree that the most effective method for teaching science includes the inquiry method in which students apply process skills to make discoveries and to develop concepts.

Prior to the introduction of science process skills in inquiry science programs, science texts frequently referred to "the scientific method." This attempt at providing students with an organized approach to solving problems frequently led to the misconception that there is one and only one scientific method. Scientists have applied process skills in different approaches to investigate problems. The science process skills are classified into two groups: basic and integrated process skills.

Science Process Terms and Definitions

I. The Basic Process Skills are the fundamentals of investigating.

observing—using as many of the five senses as are safe to use along with any needed equipment to gather information about the properties of a given object or event

inferring—explaining what one thinks about an object or event based on one's observations

classifying—grouping or sorting objects and having a rationale for that grouping based on observable properties. For instance binomial classifications group objects by twos: those with a physical characteristic and those without that characteristic.

predicting—stating what one thinks will happen based on the information that one has. As the information becomes more sophisticated, so do the predictions. Predictions should be discussed as "being supported by the data" or "not supported by the data" rather than as right or wrong.

using space/time relationships—describing objects in relation to other objects in regard to spatial orientation, symmetry, and motion

measuring—using instruments to quantify physical properties of an object

recording data—writing information in an organized manner usually on a table or chart rather than in sentences or outlines

(Continued)

The Science Teacher's Book of Lists, © 1993 by Prentice Hall

LIST 12–6. (Continued)

communicating with graphs—using line and bar graphs to quantify and display data gathered. Graphs provide the investigator with another way to look for patterns and relationships. See List 9–19, Checklists for Graphing Conventions

analyzing data—reviewing findings; using statistics to determine the reliability and significance of the findings

interpreting data—organizing information gathered to look for patterns and relationships; reporting the findings and conclusions

interpolating from the data—making predictions based on the findings by staying within the actual findings; such as using a graph to look for patterns and predictions that fall "inside" the plotted data

extrapolating from the data—making predictions based on the findings by going beyond the actual findings; such as using a graph to look for patterns and predictions that continue beyond (or "exit") the graph

basing conclusions on the data—formulating ideas and conclusions based on the information gathered rather than on desires, superstition, or guesses

investigating—careful gathering of information, which may include any combination of the basic processes. It differs from experimenting in that it lacks a control, a variable, and a hypothesis.

II. The Integrated Process Skills build upon the basic process skills to enable the investigator to design and conduct an experiment with a hypothesis, controlled variables, and experimental variables and to analyze and interpret the data to reach conclusions.

formulating a hypothesis—stating formally what one predicts will be the outcome/s in a given experiment before beginning the experiment

designing an experiment—preparing a well thought out plan to research a topic by formulating a hypothesis and identifying controlled and experimental variables

controlling the variables—attempting to control all of the variables possible within an experiment

recording the data—writing the information, including observations, and measurements, in an organized chart, table of data, or journal

analyzing data—reviewing findings; using statistics to determine the reliability and significance of the findings

interpreting the data—analyzing the findings to make interpolations and extrapolations and when appropriate to make conclusions and recommendations

(Continued)

The Science Teacher's Book of Lists, © 1993 by Prentice Hall

LIST 12–6. (Continued)

experimenting—conducting a carefully controlled search for truth about a topic, which includes controlled and experimental variables and a hypothesis

calculating experimental error—calculating the limitations in an experiment

verifying the hypothesis—stating that the findings demonstrate the predicted outcomes for a specific experiment occurred

nullifying the hypothesis—stating that the findings demonstrate the predicted outcomes for a specific experiment did not occur

providing a control—providing a standard of comparison to check the findings in an experiment

providing variables—providing the experimental or altered objects and conditions, which are compared to the control in an experiment

LIST 12–7. PIAGETIAN GLOSSARY

Jean Piaget and his colleagues at the University of Geneva, Switzerland, investigated how children learn. They theorize that children move through four different stages of mental development.

Piaget's Four Stages of Mental Development

1. The Sensorimotor Stage (0–2 years).
A baby squeezing a rubber toy that makes noise or watching a mobile move.

2. The Preoperational Stages (2–7 years).
A child who can use simple phrases to describe or request; such as saying "cold," after taking a bit of ice cream.

3. The Concrete-operational Stage (7–11 years).
Child with 5 apples subtracts or removes 2 apples to explain that 3 apples are left.

4. The Formal-operational Stage (11–14 plus years).
Preadolescent or adolescent using the formula $A = L\,W$ to calculate the area of a square.

(Continued)

LIST 12–7. (Continued)

Science educators have been attempting to apply the findings of Piaget and his associates to improve the teaching of science particularly at the preschool and elementary levels. The following terms have been used by Piaget, his associates, and educators to discuss, better understand, and improve children's learning.

abstraction—thought processes while performing a task

accommodation—the modification or application of knowledge and skills to a new situation

adaptation—a cognitive, continuous process consisting of assimilation and accommodation

affectivity—behavior that involves feelings, interest, values, attitudes, and maturation

assimilation—the process of incorporating new perceptual stimuli into behavior patterns

associativity—the process of putting together elements in different ways to reach the same results

centration—the tendency of a person to center or focus on one part of a stimuli

cognitive process—mental processes involving reasoning, perceiving, imagining, etc.

concrete operation—a stage of mental development in which a person performs logical operations such as adding, subtracting, seriating, classifying, numbering, and reversing

conservation—the realization that changing an object physically does not change the amount of the object; such as flattening a ball of clay into a "pancake" does not change the amount of clay

egocentricity—the tendency of an individual to perceive others as though they have his or her identical views

epistemology—the branch of philosophy concerned with the nature of knowledge; to Piaget, the investigation of the sequence of mental abilities

equilibration—the regulating process by which the individual continuously changes and develops

formal operations—a stage of mental development in which a person is capable of performing hypothetical, propositional, and reflexive thinking

identity—the operation of comparing, contrasting, or giving an example of a concept

(Continued)

LIST 12–7. (Continued)

intelligence—all the mental processes and coordinations of these that structure the behavior of an individual; to Piaget, not a fixed quantity; it develops

internalization—the process of making symbols, language, memories, and images a part of one's knowledge

intuitive—making judgments without reasoning or problem solving

knowledge—all that has been perceived and grasped by the mind

learning—the process of assimilating or accommodating new information, experiences, knowledge

measurement—the ability to number, order, or perform seriation

memory—using mental images to reconstitute the past through recognition, evocation, etc.; differs from perception by not being dependent upon the present and from intelligence by not being concerned with solving problems

object permanence—the realization that an object continues to exist when not present in the perceptual field

operation—a mental action, e.g., multiplying, combining, classifying, etc. It can be reversible; that is, one can check addition by subtraction and multiplication by division.

ordering or seriating—placing objects in order in a series

perception—the process of being aware of something through the senses

preoperational—the stage of mental development in which a child can learn symbols, names, and language but cannot yet perform operations. For example a child may know the alphabet, but will not be able to write a sentence; may be able to count to ten but will not be able to use the numbers to add, subtract, multiply or divide.

reversibility—the process of transposing or inverting a mental object or process; for example, imaging (in the mind) a stack of different sized rings on a stand in order of largest on the bottom to smallest on the top, then imaging it with the smallest on the bottom to largest on the top.

sensorimotor—the first stage of mental development, during which time the child learns through the senses and muscular responses

stages—a period of development or intelligence characterized by specific general mental structures

structure—mental organization or coordination in systematizing information; may involve the interrelating of parts or schemata

transitivity—the process of being able to perform the following type of mental operation: $A > B$, $B > C$, therefore $A > C$.

transformation—the process of something constantly changing in appearance

LIST 12–8. COLLECTIVE PHRASES

The phrases listed here consist of a collective word (swarm) with the name (bees) of an object such as an animal, plant, earth, substance, or physical force. In the most interesting of these phrases the collective word has a common meaning quite apart from that of the object and provides by analogy a description of the grouping. The phrase does not provide a definite quantity of the object.

Collective Phrases

swarm of bees/other insects

cloud of insects/smoke/dust

school/shoal of fish

kettle/string of fish

gam/pod of whales

route/troop of wolves

pod of dolphins/seals

troop of baboons/kangaroos

hand of bananas

cluster/bunch of fruit/bananas

bucket/can of worms

bed of flowers/moss/oysters

spray of fruit/flowers

clump of grass

bevy of roe/game birds/quail/larks

covey of birds/partridges

flock of birds/sheep

flight of birds/insects

host of angels/sparrows

skein/wedge of geese/ducks (flying)

gaggle of geese (walking)

clutch of eggs/chicks

brood of chicks/hens

harras of horses

string of ponies

drove of cattle/kine/sheep

colony of birds/ants/bacteria

pack of dogs/wolves/grouse

army of ants/caterpillars

gang of elk

pride of lions

congregation of plovers

unkindness of ravens

murder of crows

raft of ducks

rain of thought/mules

shrewdness/troop of apes

pace of asses

cite of badgers

sloth/sleuth of bear

sounder/singular of boars

clowder of cats

rag of colts

yard of deer

badelyne/paddling/flock of ducks

dule of doves/turtledoves

cast of falcons/hawks

herd of cattle/horses/buffalo/cranes/
  curlews/wrens/elephants

range of mountains

chain of lakes/lightning

stretch of water/land/sand/clouds

reach of water

stack of wood/hay

pocket/suite of minerals

shower of meteors

(Continued)

LIST 12–8. (Continued)

vein of rock/ore

book of mica

raft of logs

sheaf of grain/wheat/papers

bundle of sticks/rags/bones

circle/patch/beam/pencil/shaft of light

field of electricity/magnetism

current of electricity/air/water

bolt of cloth/paper/lightning

fleet of ships

charm of finches

skulk of foxes

trembling of goldfish

fall of woodcock

sedge of herons

sounder of hogs/swine

leap of leopards

team/baken of mules

drove/yoke of oxen

muster of peacocks

nye/nide of pheasants

nest of rabbits

down of hares

crash of rhinoceros

dopping of sheldrakes

walk of starlings

doilt of tame swine

rafter of turkeys

litter of whelps

sword/plump of wildfowl

LIST 12–9. SOME FIRSTS AND TECHNOLOGICAL SUPERLATIVES

Firsts

- **First people to separate metal from ore:** early Egyptians, about 4000 B.C.

- **First domesticated animal:** dog

- **First observations of Jupiter, some of its moons, and Saturn** in the early 1600s by Galileo with the telescope that he made.

- **First to conclude and write that Saturn has rings,** Christian Huygens, 1659.

- **First record of the Giant Red Spot on Jupiter** written by Robert Hooke in 1664.

- **First long distance balloon flight:** Charles Green, Robert Holland, and Monck Mason flew 480 miles in a hydrogen balloon from Vauxhall Gardens, London to Nassau, Germany in 1836.

- **First flight in a heavier-than-air craft:** Wilbur Wright flew "Flyer 1" at Kitty Hawk, North Carolina on December 17, 1903; air speed 58 km p.h. (30 m.p.h.). The flight lasted 12 seconds and reached an altitude of 3m (10 ft.).

- **First person to fly the English Channel:** Louis Bleriot, 1909.

- **First flight across the Atlantic Ocean:** A United States crew flew a Curtiss flying boat NC4 from New York City to England in 1919, taking 53 hours and 58 minutes including several stops for refueling.

- **First solo trans-Atlantic flight:** Charles Lindbergh flew from New York to Paris in 1927, in 33 hours, 29 minutes, 30 seconds. See Section 8: Air and Space Section, List 5, Powered Aircraft.

- **First circumnavigational flight:** Two U.S. Navy "amphibians," the Chicago and the New Orleans, began their flight on April 6, 1924 from Seattle, Washington and September 28, 1924.

- **First person to break the sound barrier:** Chuck Yeager in the U.S. Bell XS-1 rocket plane flew 1072 km p.h. (670 m.p.h.), in 1947.

- **First man-made satellite to orbit the Earth:** the Russian-made Sputtnik 1, 1957.

- **First human in space:** Russian cosmonaut, Yuri Gagarin, orbited the earth one time in "Vostok I," taking 89 minutes, 20 seconds on April 12, 1961.

- **First human to set foot on the moon:** Neil Armstrong, command pilot of Apollo 11 on July 21, 1969.

- **First crossing of the Atlantic Ocean by a gas balloon:** Abruzzo, Anderson, and Newman, 3107.62 miles, 1978.

The Science Teacher's Book of Lists, © 1993 by Prentice Hall

(Continued)

LIST 12–9. (Continued)

- **First reusable space shuttle:** Columbia 1, 1981.
- **First American woman in space:** Sally Ride, 1983

Technological Superlatives

- **Fastest airliner*:** British/French supersonic jet *Concorde*, flies from London to New York in 3 hours, 6 minutes.
- **Oldest known writing:** a form of picture writing known as Sumerian, dates back to 3500 B.C. The land of Sumer was located roughly in present-day Iraq.
- **Fastest passenger travel*:** the *Concorde*, an airplane, that travels at 2170 km p.h. (1350 miles per hour), which is faster than the speed of sound.
- **Fastest crossing of the Atlantic Ocean*:** made by *United States*, in 1958 sailed from New York City to France in 3 days, 4 hours, 40 minutes with an average speed of 35.59 knots (65.57 km p.h. or 40.98 m.p.h.).
- **Fastest submerged crossing of the Atlantic Ocean*:** made by *Nautilus* in 1958; 6 days, 11 hours, and 55 minutes.
- **Deepest descent into the ocean:** U.S. Navy bathyscaphe, *Trieste* descended 10.85 km (6.78 miles or 35,820 ft) into the Marianas Trench in the Pacific Ocean.
- **Largest airport*:** Dallas-Fort Worth, in Texas.
- **Busiest airport*:** O'Hare International Airport in Chicago, where a plane takes off or lands every 45 seconds.

---

*Depending on technological developments, records such as busiest, largest, and fastest may be broken in the near future.

LIST 12–10. THE WATER CYCLE

The water cycle consists of water moving through an ecosystem:

- Water in a lake, pond, stream, river or ocean is heated by the sun.
- The heated water at the surface evaporates or changes into water vapor.
- The water vapor rises into the air and cools off.
- The water vapor continues to cool until it changes or condenses from water vapor to water droplets, which eventually form a cloud.
- When the cloud can hold no more water, the water falls to earth as rain, snow, sleet, or hail, determined by the temperature of the air.
- Some of the water that falls to the ground is taken in by the roots of plants.
- Plants use the water during photosynthesis, the process by which they make their own food. They return the extra water to the air through openings on the underside of their leaves.
- Most of the water that falls on the ground seeps through the ground and enters underground aquifers.
- Most of the underground water flows to lakes, ponds, streams, rivers, and oceans.
- The water cycle begins again when the surface water is evaporated by the heat of the sun's rays.

LIST 12–11. THE CARBON-OXYGEN CYCLE

The carbon-oxygen cycle consists of the movement of carbon and oxygen through an ecosystem:

- Plants take in carbon dioxide through openings on the underside of their leaves.
- Plants process the carbon dioxide with water to produce their own food. In doing so, they release extra oxygen into the air.
- Plants and animals take in the oxygen. Through the process of respiration, oxygen chemically combines with the carbon compounds stored in foods, releasing energy and carbon dioxide.
- Animals take in carbon compounds when they eat plants.
- After plants and animals die, decomposers chemically break down the remains releasing carbon dioxide into the air.
- Carbon dioxide in the air is ready to begin the carbon-oxygen cycle again.

LIST 12–12. THE NITROGEN CYCLE

The nitrogen cycle consists of nitrogen moving through an ecosystem.

- Some plants have specific bacteria on their roots which can take nitrogen from the air and convert it to nitrates. Nitrates contain nitrogen and oxygen and are used by plants to make proteins.
- Some bacteria release some nitrates back into the soil ready for use by growing plants.
- After plants and animals die, decomposers release nitrates into the soil.
- Bacteria chemically break down the nitrates releasing nitrogen gas into the air.
- With nitrogen back in the air, the bacteria on the roots of some plants are ready to continue the nitrogen cycle.

LIST 12–13. THE PHOSPHORUS CYCLE

The Aquatic Phosphorus Cycle

- Phosphorus enters water communities when it is absorbed by algae and plants.
- The algae and plants containing phosphorus are eaten by plankton, microorganisms, and large organisms.
- These are in turn eaten by fish and shellfish, which feed upon one another.
- Phosphorus-rich bones, which aren't digested, eventually end up on the ocean floor.
- Sea birds contribute some phosphorus through their droppings.
- The cycle begins again with algae and plants absorbing phosphorus, thus making it available to other organisms in the water and land communities.

Aquatic plant,
Aldrovandiva vesiculosa

The Land Phosphorus Cycle

- Plants take in phosphorus compounds, such as magnesium phosphate, by their roots and store them in their plant tissues.
- Herbivores, animals that live exclusively on plants, obtain phosphorus by eating plants. They store the phosphorus in their tissues, thus, making it available to animals that eat herbivores, to detritus feeders (animals that eat dead organisms), and to decomposers. They also pass some off in their waste products.

(Continued)

The Science Teacher's Book of Lists, © 1993 by Prentice Hall

LIST 12–13. (Continued)

- Carnivores, animals that live exclusively on other animals, obtain phosphorus by eating animals that have phosphorus stored in their tissues. They also store phosphorus in their tissues, thus making it available to animals that eat animals, to detritus feeders, and decomposers. They also pass some off in their waste products, returning phosphorus compounds to the soil.

- Phosphorus compounds in the soil are absorbed by plants, beginning the cycle anew.

Herbivore

Carnivore

Omnivore

LIST 12–14. GENERAL GUIDELINES FOR SCIENCE FAIRS

When guidelines for science fair projects are outlined and taught before any projects are begun, the opportunities for quality investigations and research are enhanced.

1. The individual projects should consist of:
   - a statement of purposes
   - a discussion of the procedures
   - neatly and artistically displayed copies of all tables of data
   - neatly and artistically displayed copies of all charts and or graphs
   - a statement summarizing the findings of the investigation
   - a statement of recommendations based on the findings
   - a first draft and a final copy
2. The project may be presented in written, recorded, or videotaped form.
3. Display any actual equipment or supplies used in the investigation, as well as the written record or videotaped project.
4. Include any photographs taken or sketches drawn during the procedures that would enhance the reader's, listener's, or viewer's understanding of the project.
5. Whenever possible, the final copy of the written work should be word-processed or neatly typed.
6. If animals are used, they must have proper water, food, temperatures, space, and shelter.
7. No animal shall be subjected to cruel, painful, or inhumane treatment.
8. Whenever possible, a booklet including all written work should be displayed along with actual equipment in front of a three-fold display board on which the investigator artistically displays copies of sections of the report including: a title and statements of purpose, procedure, tables of data, graphs and/or charts, summary of findings, and recommendations. Actual upper and lower acceptable dimensions need to be identified by the science teacher or committee in charge of the science fair.

The Science Teacher's Book of Lists, © 1993 by Prentice Hall

LIST 12–15. IDEAS FOR SCIENCE PROJECTS

Science fair projects may take the form of investigations, surveys, or experiments. In each type, the student must demonstrate whatever it was that he or she investigated or learned by presenting a final product that meets the specific guidelines of the science fair and the science teacher.

For primary, elementary, and/or learning disabled science students, simple, well-organized investigations provide valuable experiences in learning and enhancing self-confidence. Investigations in which the student observes, tests, organizes, and classifies findings provides experiences with the basic skills of experimenting as he or she learns about a content area. These investigations are not as demanding as an experiment but move the student beyond drawing posters, building models, and/or displaying pets towards valued research skills. Thus, the following includes ideas for beginning investigations and experiments.

Investigations of Magnetism for Beginning Students

1. Use a magnet to identify and classify which of a given group of objects are magnetic and which are not magnetic. Record findings on a classification chart, for example:

Magnetism

MAGNETIC	*NON-MAGNETIC*

2. Devise an experiment, using paper clips and magnets, to determine which type of a magnet (a horseshoe, bar, or U magnet) is stronger. Record findings on a table of organized data (see example on next page), transfer information to a graph and analyze the results.

(Continued)

The Science Teacher's Book of Lists, © 1993 by Prentice Hall

LIST 12–15. (Continued)

Testing the Strength of Magnets Using Paper Clips
Number of Clips Attracted

TRIAL #	BAR MAGNET	U-MAGNET	HORSESHOE MAGNET

3. Devise an experiment to determine the average number of paper clips a horseshoe, bar, and U magnet will attract. Record information on a chart. Calculate the mode, median, mean, and range. (See List 9–17.)

4. Use a variety of pairs of bar magnets that are marked with *N* and *S*. Observe and record whether they attract or repel each other. Number each pair of magnets. Record results on a table of organized data, such as:

Observations of Magnets

MAGNET #	POLES	ATTRACT	REPEL	CONCLUSIONS
1	N-N		√	Like poles repel;
2	S-S		√	opposite poles attract
3	S-N	√		
4	N-S	√		
5	N-S	√		
6	S-N	√		

Electricity

1. Investigate the invention of the telegraph; build one, provide a video-taped or live demonstration of the workings of the telegraph and explain its use before the invention of telephones and fax machines.

2. Devise circuits which allow multiposition control of lights.

3. Build an electric motor or an electrical generator.

(Continued)

The Science Teacher's Book of Lists, © 1993 by Prentice Hall

LIST 12–15. (Continued)

4. Devise and build an electromagnetic track switch for a model railroad.

5. Build a three-wire tester by connecting one bulb in a holder to one dry cell in a holder using three wires. Open and close the circuit, by touching the ends of two wires to ensure that the bulb lights. Then test and classify items that are conductors and nonconductors of electricity. Record results on a classification chart:

ELECTRICAL CONDUCTORS	*NONCONDUCTORS*

A three-wire tester

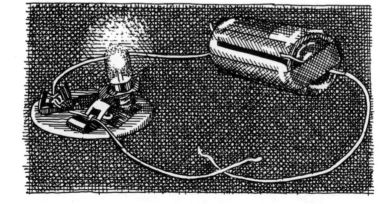

6. Wire three lights in series and another three in parallel. Determine (a) which circuit produces a brighter quality light; (b) what happens to the entire circuit when any one of the bulbs are removed from the circuit; (c) which type of circuit makes more sense for wiring a building.

(Continued)

LIST 12–15. (Continued)

7. Use a 6-volt battery and an electric bell minus its cover to demonstrate how an electromagnet makes a bell ring. Apply this information to explain in diagrams, models, and written explanations how electromagnets are used in our daily lives.

Sound

1. Investigate sound by filling eight or twelve glass bottles of the same size with different amounts of water. Pour a small volume of water in the first bottle, more in the second, etc. Tap each bottle; play sound patterns; compare to notes on a piano or other instrument. Make audio recordings of sound patterns. Formulate generalizations about the height of a column and the quality of the pitch. Write conclusions based on your observations. Diagram the systems. (Can be done with different lengths of string and then plucking the strings.)

2. Measure the speed of sound and determine the effect of weather conditions (can use walkie-talkie, stopwatch, and recorders) to measure time and distance.

3. Demonstrate the effect of pitch on the wavelength of sound.

Light

1. Investigate the nature of light with prisms, separating and recombining colors and using transparent filters.

2. Investigate how light travels by shining the light from a flashlight through different media, such as: transparent glass, frosted glass, clear cellophane, colored cellophane, clear water, muddy water, circular openings in cardboard, slits in cardboard. Diagram equipment used, list observations, record inferences.

3. With a flashlight and variety of objects, investigate how to make a shadow larger and smaller than the object that casts a shadow. Diagram equipment used, list observations, record inferences.

4. Use a water atomizer and a flashlight to investigate the factors that are necessary for a rainbow to occur. Draw and color a rainbow. Diagram equipment used, list observations, record inferences.

(Continued)

The Science Teacher's Book of Lists, © 1993 by Prentice Hall

LIST 12–15. (Continued)

5. Investigate how we see colors by looking through clear and colored cellophane at a variety of green objects, then red objects, then white objects. Make some inferences based on observations, then test them out using objects of a color that haven't been tested. Refine the hypothesis if necessary; test objects of a different color. Consider videotaping objects through clear cellophane, then through colored cellophane. Diagram equipment used, list observations, record inferences and findings. Show a videotape if one was made.

Physics

1. Investigate pendulums and show how the rotation of Earth can be demonstrated.

2. Use different lengths of string and fishing weights to make a variety of pendulums to investigate the effect of length of the string on the behavior of the pendulum. Diagram equipment used, list observations on a table of data, analyze data looking for patterns and generalizations.

3. Determine the viscosity of various liquids and solutions using the falling ball method.

4. Study the wetting properties of various liquids and substrates.

5. Use chromatography to examine the composition of plant colors, synthetic dyes, inks, and so on.

6. Study the fluorescence and phosphorescence of substances using ultraviolet light.

7. Investigate the mechanical advantage of levers, pulleys, inclined planes, gears, screws, cams, etc.

Earth Science

1. Investigate the nature of quicksand and the influence of particle shape. Place various samples of sands, clays, muds, and finger paints in small trays and barely saturate with water. Load each with a similar weight. Wiggle or vibrate load gently. Examine particle size and shape with a microscope.

2. Demonstrate and explain the principles of gold-panning, including observation of the deposition of sands in streambeds and beaches.

3. Use weather equipment; keep weather records for a month including barometric pressure, wind direction and approximate velocity, humidity, etc.; make 24-hour predictions each day, independent of broadcast weather services.

(Continued)

LIST 12–15. (Continued)

4. Make weather equipment including a barometer, rain gauge, wind vane. Record daily weather observations and make predictions based on observations.

Chemistry

1. Investigate and explain the effectiveness of various substances on the freezing point of water (sodium chloride, vinegar, sugars, alcohols, etc.). Diagram equipment used, list observations on a table of data, analyze data, report results.

2. Investigate various materials for the presence of starch, using iodine as a testing tool. (Iodine turns purple-black when in the presence of starch.) Diagram equipment used, list observations on a table of data, analyze data, report results.

3. Investigate the dyeing properties of plants on wool.

4. Grow and characterize crystals formed by sublimation. Some substances to use are menthol, camphor, moth balls (naphthalene), moth flakes (para-dichloro-benzene), sulfur, iodine. *NOTE:* This requires safety procedures in handling and disposing of substances; consequently it is for the mature student only.

5. Investigate solids, liquids, and powders that will form a solution in water.

6. Develop tests for personal-use products such as toothpaste: Does fluoride make a difference with dental check ups? Investigate shampoos and pH.

Life Science

1. Establish a bird feeder and keep records of animals that visit the feeder and types of foods they prefer.

2. With a microscope, examine and then sketch the structure of seashells, feathers, vegetable skin, hair, fur, etc.

3. With a microscope examine samples of diatomaceous earth.

4. Identify and compare pet preferences for pet food.

5. Investigate the possibility of reducing blood pressure and or pulse rate when petting a friendly pet.

6. With permission of nursing home authorities and residents, introduce a pet into a nursing home and determine any positive and negative results.

The Science Teacher's Book of Lists, © 1993 by Prentice Hall

(Continued)

LIST 12–15. (Continued)

7. Investigate ways of reducing the number-one killer of cats and dogs in the United States: euthanaizing unwanted pets.

8. Survey attitudes about having pets neutered.

9. Survey attitudes about smoking, drinking alcohol, using other drugs.

10. Design an experiment to determine if specific preservatives actually do retard the growth of unwanted organisms in baked goods.

History of Science and Technology

1. Summarize the story (in writing and/or video) of a material or technology such as iron, corn, penicillin, or woven fabrics.

2. Summarize the story of an inventor or invention. If possible build a model of the invention.

LIST 12–16. SCIENCE FAIR PROJECT EVALUATION FORM

Student name or number _____

Title of Project _____

_____ **Research:** 30 possible points. May include notecards, journal, computer printouts, research paper, etc.
Excellent: 30–26   Good: 20–10
Very good: 25–21   Poor: 9–0

_____ **Experimental equipment and techniques:** 30 possible points.
Excellent: 30–26   Good: 20–10
Very good: 25–21   Poor: 9–0

_____ **Findings and conclusions:** 10 possible points.
Excellent: 10–9   Good: 6–5
Very good: 8–7   Poor: 4–0

_____ **Clarity of written work:** 10 possible points.
Excellent: 10–9   Good: 6–5
Very good: 8–7   Poor: 4–0

_____ **Communication with graphs, charts, other visuals:** 10 possible points.
Excellent: 10–9   Good: 6–5
Very good: 8–7   Poor: 4–0

_____ **Visual presentation:** 10 possible points.
Excellent: 10–9   Good: 6–5
Very good: 8–7   Poor: 4–0

_____ **Total points** _____ **Recognition**

The Science Teacher's Book of Lists, © 1993 by Prentice Hall

LIST 12–17. BOY SCOUTS OF AMERICA MERIT BADGE PAMPHLETS

The Boy Scouts of America publishes a large number of pamphlets on merit badge subjects, which contain basic information on the topic written by experts. There are almost always references for additional information. These pamphlets are for sale to the general public and are on display and for sale at local Scout Service headquarters and designated retail stores in every community.

Frequently one can find the pamphlets at book sales and flea markets. Older pamphlets may have information not found in later editions.

Below is a list of those which contain material on some aspect of science.

Boy Scouts of America Merit Badge Pamphlets

SUBJECT	YEAR OF LATEST REVISION	SUBJECT	YEAR OF LATEST REVISION
Animal Science	1984	Leatherwork	1983
Astronomy	1983	Machinery	1983
Atomic Energy	1983	Mammal Study	1972
Aviation	1968	Metals Engineering	1984
Beekeeping	1983	Metalwork	1969
Bird Study	1984	Nature	1973
Botany	1983	Oceanography	1983
Chemistry	1973	Orienteering	1974
Computers	1984	Photography	1983
Cooking	1986	Plant Science	1983
Electricity	1974	Printing/Communication	1983
Electronics	1977	Public Health	1985
Energy	1978	Pulp and Paper	1974
Engineering	1978	Radio	1965
Environmental Science	1983	Reptile Study	1972
Fingerprinting	1983	Signaling	1974
Fish and Wildlife Management	1972	Soil and Water Conservation	1983
Fishing	1974	Space Exploration	1983
Forestry	1984	Surveying	1984
Gardening	1982	Textiles	1972
General Science	1972	Veterinary Science	1973
Geology	1985	Weather	1963
Indian Lore	1959	Wilderness Survival	1984
Insect Life	1985	Woodwork	1970

NOTE: There is no set of merit badge pamphlets provided by the Girl Scouts of America. However, they publish a resource booklet: "Contemporary Issues, Leading Girls to Mathematics, Science and Technology in the World of Today and Tomorrow." Inquiries should be directed to: Program, Girl Scouts of the U.S.A., 830 Third Avenue, New York, New York 10022.

LIST 12–18. MORSE CODE

The Morse Code is an alphabet and number code that Samuel F. Morse (1791–1872) devised for use with his telegraph, developed in 1832. It is made up of combinations of short and long signals or of double clicks with short and long spaces between the clicks. Many railroad telegraphs were of the double click kind. Wireless signals are beep-like sounds. The code has several adaptations.

The International Morse Code

A · _	N _ ·	1 · _ _ _ _
B _ · · ·	O _ _ _	2 · · _ _ _
C _ · _ ·	P · _ _ ·	3 · · · _ _
D _ · ·	Q _ _ · _	4 · · · · _
E ·	R · _ ·	5 · · · · ·
F · · _ ·	S · · ·	6 _ · · · ·
G _ _ ·	T _	7 _ _ · · ·
H · · · ·	U · · _	8 _ _ _ · ·
I · ·	V · · · _	9 _ _ _ _ ·
J · _ _ _	W · _ _	0 _ _ _ _ _
K _ · _	X _ · · _	
L · _ · ·	Y _ · _ _	
M _ _	Z _ _ · ·	

In addition to the code itself, there are procedural signals and punctuation marks as well as some abbreviations.

Period . - . - .	Wait . - . . .	Hyphen - . . . . -
Question mark . . - - . .	Error	Parenthesis - . - - . -
End of message . - . - .	Message received . -	
Comma - - . . - -	Apostrophe . - - - - .	

LIST 12–19. SUPERSTITIONS

Superstitions are beliefs in ideas or practices based on the supernatural as opposed to laws of science. People look for answers to their questions, reasons that explain why things happen. Those who understand science, apply known scientific concepts to help explain the natural world. Those who believe in the supernatural use superstitions to explain events.

Some Common Superstitions

- It is unlucky to rock an empty rocker.
- It is bad luck to sleep on a table.
- If you walk under a ladder, you will have bad luck.
- To find a penny heads up, brings good luck.
- An acorn at the window can keep lightning out of the house.
- To kill an albatross is to cause bad luck to the ship and all upon it.
- Animals can talk at midnight on Christmas Eve.
- An apple a day keeps the doctor away.
- You must get out of bed on the same side that you get in on or you'll have bad luck. (Hence the expression, "What's the matter, did you get up on the wrong side of the bed this morning?")
- A bird that comes in your window brings bad luck.
- It is bad luck to chase someone with a broom.
- A rabbit's foot brings good luck.
- If you blow out all of the candles on your birthday cake with the first breath you will get whatever you wished for before blowing out the candles.
- To have a wish come true using a wishbone, two people make a wish, then take hold of each end of the bone and pull and twist until it separates. The person with the longer end gets his or her wish. (The wishbone is the collarbone of a bird.)
- Wearing your birthstone will bring you good luck.
- Wearing an opal when it is not your birthstone will bring you bad luck.
- If a black cat crosses your path you will have bad luck.
- To break a mirror will bring you seven years bad luck.
- To give someone a purse or wallet without some money in it will bring that person bad luck.

(Continued)

LIST 12–19. (Continued)

- To make a happy marriage, the bride needs to wear:
  Something old,
  Something new,
  Something borrowed,
  Something blue.
- The wedding veil protects the bride from the evil eye.
- Washing a car will bring rain.
- A cat will try to take the breath from a baby.
- A cat has nine lives.
- Evil spirits cannot harm you when you are standing inside a circle.
- You can break bad luck by turning seven times in a sunwise circle.
- Clothes worn inside out will bring you good luck.
- Step on a crack, break your mother's back.
- A cricket in the house brings good luck.
- Goldfish in the house bring bad luck.
- Goldfish in the pond bring good luck.
- Crossing your fingers helps to avoid bad luck and helps a wish come true.
- Smell dandelions, wet the bed.
- To drop a dishcloth means bad luck is coming.
- A forked branch, held with a fork in each hand, will dip and point when it passes over water.
- When a dog howls, death is near.
- A person cannot drown before going under three times.
- A drowned woman floats face up, a drowned man floats face down.
- A sailor wearing an earring cannot drown.
- For good luck, wear new clothes on Easter.
- Toads cause warts.
- If the bottom of your feet itch, you will take a trip.
- Eating fish makes one smart.
- After receiving a container of food, the container should never be returned empty.
- To find a four-leaf clover is to find good luck.
- To drop a fork means a woman will visit.
- To drop a knife means a man will visit.
- To drop a spoon means a baby/child will visit.

The Science Teacher's Book of Lists, © 1993 by Prentice Hall

(Continued)

LIST 12–19. (Continued)

- Friday the thirteenth is an unlucky day.
- Garlic protects from evil spirits and vampires.
- If you shiver, someone is casting a shadow on your grave.
- A lock of hair from baby's first haircut should be rolled into a ringlet and saved for good luck.
- Warm hands, cold heart.
- Cold hands, warm heart.
- An itchy palm means money will come your way.
- A beginner will always have good luck: beginner's luck.
- To find a horseshoe brings good luck.
- To refuse a kiss under mistletoe causes bad luck.
- At the end of a rainbow is a pot of gold.
- It is bad luck to sing at the table.
- To cure a sty, rub it with a gold wedding band.
- To open an umbrella in the house is to bring bad luck.
- Our fate is written in the stars.

LIST 12–20. NOTABLE QUOTABLES

Learning without thought is labor lost; thought without learning is perilous.
                                                    Confucius, 551–479 B.C.

There are in fact two things, science and opinion, the former begets knowledge, the latter ignorance.

                                                    Hippocrates, 460–400 B.C.

There is only one good, knowledge, and one evil, ignorance.
                                                    Socrates, 469–399 B.C.

There is superstition in avoiding superstition.
                                                    Francis Bacon, 1561–1626

If I have seen further . . . it is by standing upon the shoulders of giants.
                                                    Sir Isaac Newton, 1642–1727

But in science the credit goes to the man who convinces the world not to the man to whom the idea first occurs.
                                                    Francis Darwin, 1848–1925

Mathematics is the science which draws necessary conclusions.
                                                    Benjamin Pierce, 1809–1880

Science moves, but slowly slowly, creeping on from point to point.
                                                    Alfred, Lord Tennyson, 1809–1892

Science is organized knowledge.

                                                    Herbert Spencer, 1820–1903

The doctor of the future will give no medicine but will interest his patients in the care of the human frame, in diet, and in the cause and prevention of disease.

                                                    Thomas Edison, 1847–1931

Science is the search for truth—it is not a game in which one tries to beat his opponent.

                                                    Linus Pauling, 1901–

He may well win the race that runs by himself.

The body of Benjamin Franklin, Printer (like the cover of an old book, its contents torn out and stripped of its lettering and gilding), lies here, food for worms; but the work shall not be lost, for it will (as he believed) appear once more in a new more elegant edition, revised and corrected by the Author.

                                                    Benjamin Franklin, 1706–1790

In the fields of observation, chance favors only the mind that is prepared.

There are no such things as applied sciences, only applications of science.
                                                    Louis Pasteur, 1822–1895

(Continued)

LIST 12–20. (Continued)

Learn the ABC of science before you try to ascend to its summit.

Learn, compare, collect all of the facts.

Ivan Pavlov, 1849–1936

I shall never believe that God plays dice with the world.

The whole of science is nothing more than a refinement of everyday thinking.

The unleashed power of the atom has changed everything save our modes of thinking, and we thus drift toward unparalleled catastrophes.

Our defense is not in armaments, nor in science, nor in going underground. Our defense is in law and order.

Albert Einstein, 1879–1955

To doubt everything or to believe everything are two equally convenient solutions; both dispense with the necessity of reflection.

Science is built up with facts as a house is with stone. But a collection of facts is no more a science than a heap of stones is a house.

Jules-Henri Poincaré, 1854–1912

True science teaches us to doubt and to abstain from ignorance.

Science increases our power in proportion as it lowers our pride.

Man can learn nothing unless he proceeds from the known to the unknown.

Claude Bernard, 1813–1878

Nature as a whole possesses a store of force which cannot in any way be either increased or diminished . . . I have named (this) general law "The Principle of the Conservation of Force."

Hermann von Helmholtz, 1821–1894

An active field of science is like an immense anthill; the individual almost vanishes into the mass of minds tumbling over each other, carrying information from place to place, passing it around at the speed of light.

The only solid piece of scientific truth about which I feel totally confident is that we are profoundly ignorant about nature. . . . It is the sudden confrontation with the depth and scope of ignorance that represents the most significant contribution of twentieth-century science to the human intellect.

Lewis Thomas, 1913–

All the mathematical sciences are founded on relations between physical laws and of numbers, so that the aim of exact science is to reduce the problems of nature to the determination of quantities by operations with numbers.

James Clerk Maxwell, 1831–1879

(Continued)

LIST 12–20. (Continued)

In our description of nature the purpose is not to disclose the real essence of the phenomena but only to track down, so far as it is possible, relations between the manifold aspects of our experience.

Niels Bohr, 1885–1962

Science is nothing but trained and organized common sense, differing from the latter only as a veteran may differ from a raw recruit: and its methods differ from those of common sense only as far as the guardsman's cut and thrust differ from the manner in which a savage wields his club.

The chess-board is the world; the pieces are the phenomena of the universe; the rules of the game are what we call the laws of Nature.

If a little knowledge is dangerous, where is the man who has so much as to be out of danger?

Irrationally held truths may be more harmful than reasoned errors.

I am too much of a skeptic to deny the possibility of anything.

T. H. Huxley, 1825–1895

The scientists value research by the size of its contribution to that huge, logically articulated structure of ideas which is almost, though not yet half built, the most glorious accomplishment of mankind.

Among scientists are collectors, classifiers, and compulsive tidiers-up; many are detectives by temperament and many explorers; some are artists and others artisans.

Peter Brian Medawar, 1915–

I think that I shall never see
A billboard lovely as a tree.
Indeed, unless the billboards fall
I'll never see a tree at all.

Ogden Nash, 1902–1971

LIST 12–21. RECOMMENDED REFERENCES

Plants

Benyus, J. M., *The Field Guide to Wildlife Habitats of the Eastern United States*, Simon & Schuster, New York, 1989.

Brockman, C. F., *Trees of North America*, Golden Press, Western Publishing Company, Inc., Racine, Wisconsin, 1968.

"Endangered & Threatened Wildlife and Plants," 50 CFR 17.11 & 17.12, Division of Endangered Species and Habitat Conservation, U.S. Fish & Wildlife Service, Washington, D.C., April 15, 1990. Copies are available from the Publication Unit, U.S. Fish and Wildlife Service, 725-ARLSQ, Washington, D.C. 20240.

Grimm, N. C., *The Book of Trees*, Stackpole, Harrisburg, Pennsylvania, 1962.

Harlow, W. M., *Trees of the Eastern and Central United States and Canada*, Dover Press, New York, 1957.

Harrar, E. S., and Harrar, J. G., *Guide to Southern Trees*, Dover Press, New York, 1962.

Johnson, C., *The Nature of Vermont: Introduction and Guide to a New England Environment*, The University Press of New England, Hanover, New Hampshire, 1984.

Little, E. L., Jr., *Important Forest Trees of the United States*, Forest Service Handbook, USDA, Agriculture Handbook No. 519, Washington, D.C., 1979.

Peterson, R. T. and McKenny, M., *A Field Guide to Wildflowers of Northeastern and North-central North America*, Houghton Mifflin Company, Boston, 1968.

Petrides, G. A., *Field Guides to Trees and Shrubs*, Houghton Mifflin, Boston, 1958.

Sargent, C. S., *Manual of the Trees of North America*, Dover Press, New York, 1965.

Slack, A., *Carnivorous Plants*, MIT Press, Cambridge, Massachusetts, 1981.

Animals

Attenborough, D., *Life on Earth*, Little, Brown, and Company, Boston, 1979.

Attenborough, D., Whitfield, P., Moore, P. D., Cox, B., *The Atlas of the Living World*, Houghton Mifflin Company, Boston, 1989.

Burton, R., *Bird Behavior*, Alfred A. Knopf, New York, 1985.

(Continued)

LIST 12–21. (Continued)

Davis, P., Solomon, E. P., Berg, L. R., *The World of Biology*, Fourth Edition, Saunders College Publishing, Philadelphia, 1990.

"Endangered & Threatened Wildlife and Plants," 50 CFR 17.11 & 17.12, Division of Endangered Species and Habitat Conservation, U.S. Fish & Wildlife Service, Washington, D.C. April 15, 1990.

Ehrlich, P. R., Dobkin, D. S., and Wheye, D., *The Birder's Handbook*, Simon & Schuster, New York, 1988.

Fair, J., *The Great American Bear*, North Word Press, Inc., Minocqua, Wisconsin, 1990.

Gorman, J., *The Total Penguin*, Prentice Hall Press, New York, 1990.

Margulis, L., and Schwartz, K., *Five Kingdoms, An Illustrated Guide to the Phyla of Life on Earth*, W. H. Freeman and Company, New York, 1988.

Morris, D., *Animalwatching*, Crown Publishers, Inc., New York, 1990.

Morris, D., *The Animal Contract*, Warner Books, New York, 1991.

Peterson, R. T., *A Field Guide to Birds*, Houghton Mifflin Company, Boston, 1980.

Voous, K. H., *Owls of the Northern Hemisphere*, William Collins Sons and Co., Ltd., London, UK, 1988.

Whitfield, P., edited., *Macmillan Illustrated Animal Encyclopedia*, Macmillan Publishing Company, New York, 1984.

ZOO LIFE Magazine, Spring 1991, Ingle Publishing Company, Los Angeles Publishing Co. Highly recommended for teachers of all levels; inquiries—1-800-777-0733.

Human Body, Foods, and Health

"A Consumer's Guide to Food Labels," FDA Consumer, HHS Publication No. (FDA) 88-2083, Department of Health and Human Services, Rockville, Maryland, 1988.

Brody, J., *Jane Brody's Nutrition Book*, W. W. Norton & Company, New York, 1981.

Clark, N., *Sports Nutrition Guidebook: Eating to Fuel Your Active Lifestyle*, New England Sports Publications, Boston.

Clark, N., "How To Boost Your Iron Intake," Sports Nutrition, Sports Medicine Systems, Inc., Brookline, Massachusetts.

Clark, N., "Carbohydrate Loading: Tips for Endurance Athletes," Sports Nutrition, Sports Medicine Systems, Inc., Brookline, Massachusetts.

Clark, N., "Top Sports Foods: Some Healthful Choices," Sports Nutrition, Sports Medicine Systems, Inc., Brookline, Massachusetts.

(Continued)

LIST 12–21. (Continued)

"Drugs of Abuse," U.S. Department of Justice, Drug Enforcement Administration, 1989.

Marsh, Klippstein and Kaplan, "The Sodium Content of Your Food," U.S. Department of Agriculture, Home and Garden Bulletin Number 233, 1980.

"Nutrition and Your Health: Dietary Guidelines for Americans," Third Edition, 1990, U.S. Department of Agriculture, U.S. Department of Health and Human Services, Home and Garden Bulletin No. 232.

Parmley, M. A., "The Safe Food Book Your Kitchen Guide," United States Department of Agriculture Food and Safety Inspection Service, Home & Garden Bulletin, Number 214, 1985.

Chemistry

Dean, J. A., edited, *Lange's Handbook of Chemistry*, McGraw-Hill, New York, 1973.

Encyclopedia of Science and Technology, 6th edition, McGraw-Hill, New York, 1987.

Grayson, M. edited, *Kirk-Othmer Concise Encyclopedia of Chemical Technology*, Wiley-Interscience, New York, 1985.

Masterson, Slowinski, and Stanitski, *Chemical Principals*, 6th edition, Saunders College Publishing, Pennsylvania, 1985.

Weast, R. C., ed., *Handbook of Chemistry and Physics*, Chemical Rubber Co., Cleveland, 1971.

Physics

Bernstein, Schachter, Winkler, and Wolfe, *Concepts and Challenge in Physical Science*, Cebco Standard Publishing, Fairfield, New Jersey, 1978.

Davies, Paul, Edited, *The New Physics*, Cambridge University Press, New York, 1990.

Fox, E., *Simple Machines*, Teacher's Guide, Delta Education Inc., Nashua, NH, 1988.

Fritzsch, H., *The Stuff of Matter*, Basic Books, Inc., Publishers, New York, 1983.

Hawking, S. W., *A Brief History of Time*, Bantam Books, New York, 1988.

McGraw-Hill Encyclopedia, Science and Technology, Vols. 2, 6, and 10, McGraw-Hill, New York, 1987.

(Continued)

LIST 12–21. (Continued)

Time, *The Ultimate Quest*, Reported by Philip Elmer-DeWitt/New York, J. Madeleine Nash/Chicago and Christopher Redman/Geneva, April 16, 1990, pp. 50–56.

Earth Science

Arduini, P., Teruzzi, G., and Morenstein, S., *Simon and Schuster's Guide to Fossils*, Simon & Schuster, New York, 1986.

Benton, M., *The Dinosaur Encyclopedia*, Simon & Schuster, New York, 1984.

Charig, A., *A New Look at the Dinosaurs*, The British Museum (Natural History), London, Mayflower Books, New York, 1979.

Colbert, E. H., *Dinosaurs: An Illustrated History*, Hammond Incorporated, New Jersey, 1983.

Desautels, P., *The Gem Collection: Treasures in the Smithsonian*, Smithsonian Press, Washington, D.C., 1979.

Desautels, P., *The Mineral Kingdom*, Grosset and Dunlap, New York, 1968.

Dott, Jr., R. H., Batten, R. L., *Evolution of the Earth*, Fourth edition, McGraw-Hill Book Company, New York, 1988.

Encyclopedia Americana, Vol. 12, Grolier Inc., Danbury, Connecticut, 1990.

Encyclopedia of Science and Technology, McGraw-Hill, New York, Vol. 14, 1987.

Fenton, C. L. and Fenton, M. A., *The Fossil Book*, Doubleday, Garden City, New York, 1989.

Fenton, C. L. and Fenton, M. A., *The Rock Book*, Doubleday, Garden City, New York, 1940.

Foster, R. J., *General Geology*, 4th edition, Charles E. Merrill, Columbus, Ohio, 1983.

Hoehn, R. G., *Earth Science Curriculum Activities Kit*, The Center for Applied Research in Education, West Nyack, New York, 1991.

Horner, J. R., and Gorman, J., *Digging Dinosaurs*, Harper & Row, Publishers, New York, 1988.

Pellant, C., and Phillips, R., *Rocks, Minerals & Fossils of the World*, Little, Brown and Company, Boston, 1990.

Pough, F. H., *A Field Guide to Rocks and Minerals*, Houghton-Mifflin, Boston, 1981.

Prinz, M., Harlow, G., and Peters, J., *Guide to Rocks and Minerals*, Simon & Schuster, New York, 1977.

McBiles, J. L., *Rock Guide*, Delta Education, Inc., Nashua, New Hampshire, 1985.

(Continued)

LIST 12–21. (Continued)

Mineral Digest, Vol. 4, 1972, Mineral Digest Ltd., New York.

Simkin, T., Tilling, R., Taggert, J., Jones, W., and Spall, H., compiled, "This Dynamic Planet: World Map of Volcanoes, Earthquakes, and Plate Tectonics," Smithsonian Institution and the U.S. Geological Survey, 1998. (Map with data.)

Stanley, S. M., *Earth and Life Through Time*, W. H. Freeman and Company, New York, 1986.

Thrush, P. W., ed., *A Dictionary of Mining, Mineral, and Related Terms*, U.S. Department of Interior, Washington, D.C., 1968. (Printed by the U.S. Government Printing Office.)

Toksoz, M., "The Subduction of the Lithosphere," *Scientific American*, Vol. 233 (5), 88–89 (1975).

Werner, B., *Rocks and Minerals*, Delta Education, Inc., Nashua, New Hampshire, 1988.

Zim, H. and Shaffer, P., *Rocks and Minerals: A Golden Guide*, Western Publishing Company, Inc., Racine, Wisconsin, 1957.

"World Water Balance and Water Resources of the Earth," UNESCO, Paris, 1978.

Meteorology

"Aviation Weather Services," A C 0 0 - 45 C, U.S. Department of Transportation, Federal Aviation Administration, Office of Flight Operations and U.S. Department of Commerce, National Oceanic & Atmospheric Administration, National Weather Service, Washington, D.C., Revised 1985. Available from Superintendent of Documents, U.S. Government Printing Office, Washington, D.C., 20402.

Dappen, A., "Weather Rhymes and Reasons," 33 E. Minor St., Emmaus, PA 18096, Reader's Digest, July 1990, p. 60.

"Decoding Surface Weather Observations," U.S. Department of Commerce, National Oceanic and Atmospheric Administration, National Weather Service, WS Form T A B - 0-1 (Revised 8-82).

"Guide to National Weather Service Office and Products in Southern New England," prepared by the Weather Service Forecast Office, Boston, Massachusetts, revised 1991.

Lee, A., *Weather Wisdom*, Congdon & Weed, Inc., New York, 1990.

Lehr, P., Burnett, R., and Zim, H., *Weather: A Golden Guide*, Western Publishing Company, Inc., 1965.

(Continued)

LIST 12–21. (Continued)

Air and Space

Astronomy, Space Science, Mathematics, Vol. 1, *The New Book of Popular Science*, Grolier, Danbury, Connecticut, 1988.

Crouch, T. C., *The Bishop's Boys; A Life of Wilbur and Orville Wright*, W. W. Norton, New York, New York, 1989.

Frazier, K., and the Editors of Time-Life Books, *Planet Earth, Solar System*, Time-Life Books, Alexandria, Virginia, 1985.

Grosser, M., *Gossamer Odyssey*, Houghton Mifflin, Boston, 1981.

Miller, R., and Hartmann, William, K., *The Grand Tour: A Traveler's Guide to the Solar System*, Workman Publishing, New York, 1981.

Mondey, D. and Taylor, M. J. H., *The Guiness Book of Aircraft*, 5th ed; Guiness Publishing Co., Enfield, England, 1988.

Taylor, M. J. H., *Jane's Aviation Review*, Jane Publishing, London, 1987.

Josephy, Jr., A. M., ed., *The American History of Flight*, American Heritage Publishing, W. W. Norton, New York, New York, 1962.

Washburn, M., *Distant Encounters: The Explorations of Jupiter and Saturn*, Harcourt Brace Jovanovich, New York, 1983.

Zim, H., Baker, R., *Stars: A Golden Guide*, Western Publishing Company, Inc., New York, Racine, Wisconsin, 1985.

Measurements and Number Systems

Chemical & Engineering News, April 29, Washington, D.C., 1991.

Hogben, L., *The Wonderful World of Mathematics*, Doubleday & Company, Inc., New York, 1955.

West, B. H., Griesbach, E. N., Taylor, J. D., Taylor, L. T., The Prentice Hall Encyclopedia of Mathematics, Prentice Hall, Englewood Cliffs, New Jersey, 1982.

Scientists and Their Contributions

Abbott, David, general editor, *The Biographical Dictionary of Scientists; Chemists*, Peter Bedrick Books, New York, 1984.

Asimov, I., *Frontiers*, Truman Tally Books, E. P. Dutton, New York, 1989.

Hellemans, A. and Bunch, B., *The Timetables of Science*, Simon & Schuster, New York, 1988.

(Continued)

The Science Teacher's Book of Lists, © 1993 by Prentice Hall

LIST 12–21. (Continued)

Herzenberg, Caroline L., *Women Scientists From Antiquity to the Present: An Index*, Locust Hill Press, West Cornwall, Connecticut, 1986.

Ogilvie, Marilyn Bailey, *Women in Science*, The MIT Press, Cambridge, Massachusetts, 1986.

Pelletier, Paul A., *Prominent Scientists: An Index to Collective Biographies*, Neal-Schuman Publishers, Inc. 1980.

Siegman, Gita, editor, and Spomer, Cynthia R., contributing editor, *World of Winners, A Current and Historical Perspective on Awards and Their Winners*, Gale Research Inc., Book Tower, Detroit, Michigan, 1989.

Science and Science Education Resources

A Teachers' Resource Guide: Alternatives to Animal Dissection, ALDF Dissection Hotline, Pat Graham, Director, The Animal Defense Fund, 1363 Lincoln Ave., # 7, San Rafael, CA 94901.

Barhydt, F., *Science Discovery Activities Kit*, The Center for Applied Research in Education, West Nyack, New York, 1989.

Barhydt, F. and Wier, E., *BUZ Lesson Plans and Activities*, Delmarva Power, Wilmington, Delaware, 1990.

Carin, A. and Sund, R., *Teaching Science Through Discovery*, Merrill Publishing Company, Columbus, Ohio, 1985.

Collette, A. T. and Chiappetta, *Science Instruction in the Middle and Secondary Schools*, Merrill Publishing Company, Columbus, Ohio, 1989.

Cousteau, J., *The Cousteau Almanac*, Dolphin Books, Doubleday & Company, New York, 1981.

Gega, P. C., *Science in Elementary Education*, Macmillan Publishing Company, New York, 1986.

National Wildlife, National Wildlife Federation, Virginia, December–January 1992.

"Objecting to Dissection: A College Student's Handbook," ALDF Dissection Hotline, Pat Graham, Director, The Animal Defense Fund, 1363 Lincoln Ave., # 7, San Rafael, California 94901.

Roget, P., *Everyman's Thesaurus of English Words and Phrases*, J. M. Dent, London, 1952.

Science and Children, National Science Teacher Association, Washington, D.C.

Scope, National Science Teachers Association, Washington, D.C.

(Continued)

LIST 12–21. (Continued)

Trowbridge, L. and Bybee, R. W., *Becoming a Secondary Science Teacher*, Merrill Publishing Company, Columbus, Ohio, 1986.

General References

Bartlett, J., *Familiar Quotations*, Fifteenth Edition, Little, Brown and Co., Boston, 1980.

The American Heritage Dictionary of the English Language, William Morris, Editor, Houghton Mifflin Company, Boston, 1980.

The American Heritage Dictionary of the English Language, Third Edition, Anne H. Soukhanov, Executive Editor, Houghton Mifflin Company, Boston, 1992.

The Oxford Dictionary of Quotations, Third Edition, Oxford University Press, Oxford, 1980.

DATE DUE

Demco, Inc. 38-293